DEUTSCH AKTUELL 1

SIXTH EDITION

Wolfgang S. Kraft

CHIEF CONSULTANTS

Rudolf Elstner
Materé Gymnasium
Meerbusch, Germany

Hans J. König
The Blake School
Hopkins, Minnesota

Isolde Mueller
St. Cloud State University
St. Cloud, Minnesota

CONSULTANTS

Stephen Brock
Omaha Public Schools
Omaha, Nebraska

Diane Dunk
Eisenhower High School
New Berlin, Wisconsin

Claudia Fischer
Haverford High School
Havertown, Pennsylvania

Deborah Edwards Ford
William R. Boone High School
Orlando, Florida

Ronald W. Harvey
Pickerington High School
Pickerington, Ohio

Joan G. Jensen
School District of the Chathams
Chatham, New Jersey

Johanna Keil
Hanau Middle/High School
Hanau, Germany

Christopher H. Nelson
Norfolk Academy
Norfolk, Virginia

Jennifer Robinson
Loudoun County Public Schools
Sterling, Virginia

Eric Wegner
Mannheim Middle School
Mannheim, Germany

EMC
Publishing

ST. PAUL • LOS ANGELES • INDIANAPOLIS

Editorial Director
Alejandro Vargas

Product Manager
Charisse Litteken

Production Editor
Donna Mears

Associate Editor
Hannah da Veiga

Cover and Text Designer
Leslie Anderson

Production Specialists
Leslie Anderson, Jaana Bykonich,
Ryan Hamner, Petrina Nyhan

Illustrator
Rolin Graphics Inc.

Cartoon Illustrator
Raul Ferran, Jive Studios

Cover Photographer
Wolfgang S. Kraft

About the Cover

Berlin, the capital of Germany, has always been an important metropolis connecting eastern and western Europe. Because of its historical importance, Berlin serves as the focus on the cover of *Deutsch Aktuell 1*, welcoming students to the German-speaking world.

The photo shows one of the landmarks in Berlin, the *Alexanderplatz*. At the beginning of the 19th century, the *Alexanderplatz* was one of the busiest squares in the city. Originally, the square was called the *Ochsenmarkt* or "ox market," but after a visit by Czar Alexander I it was renamed to *Alexanderplatz*. The locals simply call this large square *Alex*.

In the center of the square is the *Fernsehturm*, the TV tower built in 1969. With a height of 365 meters (1,197 ft.) it is one of the largest structures in Europe. The top of the TV tower contains a revolving restaurant and a viewing platform just below. The same year, the *Weltzeituhr* (World Time Clock) seen on the book cover was added. Here you can view the different time zones of major cities around the world.

Care has been taken to verify the accuracy of information presented in this book. However, the authors, editors, and publisher cannot accept responsibility for Web, e-mail, newsgroup, or chat room subject matter or content, or for consequences from application of the information in this book, and make no warranty, expressed or implied, with respect to its content.

Photo Credits: See back of the textbook.

Acknowledgments: See back of the textbook.

We have made every effort to trace the ownership of all copyrighted material and to secure permission from copyright holders. In the event of any question arising as to the use of any material, we will be pleased to make the necessary corrections in future printings. Thanks are due to the aforementioned authors, publishers, and agents for permission to use the materials indicated.

ISBN 978-0-82195-205-4

© 2010 by EMC Publishing, LLC
875 Montreal Way
St. Paul, MN 55102
E-mail: educate@emcp.com
Web site: www.emcp.com

Printed in the United States of America

18 17 16 15 14 13 12 11 10 09   1 2 3 4 5 6 7 8 9 10

Willkommen!

Welcome to an exciting new language and culture! As the title *Deutsch Aktuell* suggests, you will become familiar with a language that mirrors teenagers' everyday lives in German-speaking countries. By being exposed to numerous real-life situations, you will be able to better relate to your own surroundings and make comparisons between the cultures of German-speaking countries and your own.

"Why should I study German? What do I need it for?" you may ask yourself. Did you know these facts?

- German is the most widely spoken language in Europe.
- Germany is the economic powerhouse in Europe.
- Germans form the largest single heritage group in the United States.
- German is the second most widely used language on the Internet.
- Germans are the biggest spenders of tourist dollars in the world.
- One in ten books in the world is published in German.
- Germany is the world's second largest exporter.
- German is the second most commonly used scientific language.
- Most surveyed companies would choose someone with German literacy over an equally qualified candidate who does not know German.

You will learn skills that will help you to communicate about many topics. As you begin learning German, you will initially listen, then gradually learn to speak about topics that interest you. Don't be afraid to express yourself. It's natural to make mistakes, but your language skills and cultural understanding will gradually become stronger each time you use German. In a short time, your confidence will increase as you experience success communicating in German.

Much success and lots of fun!

Viel Erfolg und viel Spaß!

Contents

Kapitel 7
Wie gefällt dir das?.. 191

Kapitel 8
Geburtstag............. 221

EUROPA

ISLAND
Reykjavik

NORWEGEN
Oslo
Stockholm
SCHWEDEN

ATLANTISCHER OZEAN

Schottland

VEREINIGTES

Nordirland

IRLAND
Dublin
KÖNIGREICH

England
Wales
Thames
London

DÄNEMARK
Kopenhagen

Elbe

Amsterdam
NIEDERLANDE
Weser
Berlin
P O

Brüssel
DEUTSCHLAND
Oder

BELGIEN
Seine
Luxemburg
TSCHECHISCHE

Paris
LUXEMBURG
Prag
REPUBLIK

LIECHTENSTEIN
Preßburg

Loire
Donau
Wien

FRANKREICH
Rhein

Bern
ÖSTERREICH

SCHWEIZ
Vaduz

Rhône
U N G

Po
Laibach
Zagreb

PORTUGAL
Andorra
la Vella
MONACO
SLOWENIEN
KROATIEN

Monaco
San Marino
BOSNIEN -

Lissabon
Tajo
Madrid
ANDORRA
SAN
Sarajevo

Elbro
MARINO
HERZEGOWINA

SPANIEN
MONTENEGR

Guadalquivir
Rom

ITALIEN

M I T T E L L Ä N D I S C H E S

Rabat

Algier

Tunis

MAROKKO
A L G E R I E N
Valletta

TUNESIEN
MALTA

FINNLAND

Helsinki

RUSSLAND

Wolga

Tallinn

ESTLAND

Riga

LETTLAND

Moskau

Ural

LITAUEN

Wilna

RUSSLAND

Minsk

WEISSRUSSLAND

KASACHSTAN

L E N

Warschau

Weichsel

Kiew

Don

UKRAINE

Dnjepr

Don

Wolga

SLOWAKISCHE
REPUBLIK

Dnjestr

Budapest

MOLDAWIEN

Kischinew

A R N

RUMÄNIEN

Belgrad

Bukarest

GEORGIEN

Tbilisi

ASERBAID-
SCHAN

SERBIEN

Donau

ARMENIEN

KOSOVO

BULGARIEN

Jerewan

Pristina

Sofia

Tirana

Skopje

I R A N

MAKEDONIEN

ALBANIEN

Ankara

GRIECHENLAND

T Ü R K E I

Athen

Euphrat

Bagdad

M E E R

Nikosia

S Y R I E N

I R A K

ZYPERN

LIBANON

Damaskus

Beirut

© edigol

DEUTSCHLAND

DÄNEMARK

OSTSEE

NORDSEE

Sylt

Flensburg

Nordfriesische Inseln

Fehmarn

Rügen

Usedom

Kiel

Schleswig-Holstein

Rostock

Mecklenburg-Vorpommern

Lübeck

Schwerin

Neubrandenburg

Ostfriesische Inseln

Cuxhaven

Hamburg

Hamburg

Wilhelmshaven

Bremerhaven

Elbe

Oldenburg

Bremen

Bremen

POLEN

NIEDERLANDE

Niedersachsen

Weser

Hannover

Wolfsburg

Brandenburg

Berlin

Berlin

Oder

Spree

Frankfurt

Osnabrück

Braunschweig

Potsdam

Hildesheim

Magdeburg

Brandenburg

Münster

Bielefeld

Salzgitter

Sachsen-Anhalt

Elbe

Cottbus

Neiße

Nordrhein-Westfalen

Weser

Göttingen

Dessau

Recklinghausen

Halle

Leipzig

Görlitz

Duisburg

Essen

Dortmund

Mönchen-gladbach

Düsseldorf

Leverkusen

Kassel

Weimar

Jena

Sachsen

Dresden

Aachen

Köln

Siegen

Eisenach

Erfurt

Gera

Chemnitz

Bonn

Rhein

Hessen

Thüringen

Zwickau

BEL-GIEN

Koblenz

Main

Main

TSCHECHISCHE REPUBLIK

Wiesbaden

Frankfurt

Bamberg

LUXEM-BURG

Rheinland-Pfalz

Mainz

Offenbach

Würzburg

Bayreuth

Mosel

Darmstadt

Erlangen

Ludwigshafen

Fürth

Nürnberg

Saarland

Mannheim

Kaiserslautern

Heidelberg

Rothenburg ob der Tauber

Saarbrücken

Heilbronn

Regensburg

Karlsruhe

Bayern

Pforzheim

Stuttgart

Ingolstadt

Donau

Tübingen

Donau

Passau

FRANKREICH

Ulm

Augsburg

Baden-Württemberg

München

ÖSTERREICH

Freiburg

Rhein

Berchtesgaden

Garmisch-Partenkirchen

Watzmann 2713

Bodensee

Rhein

▲ 2963 Zugspitze

SCHWEIZ

LIECHTENSTEIN

© edigol

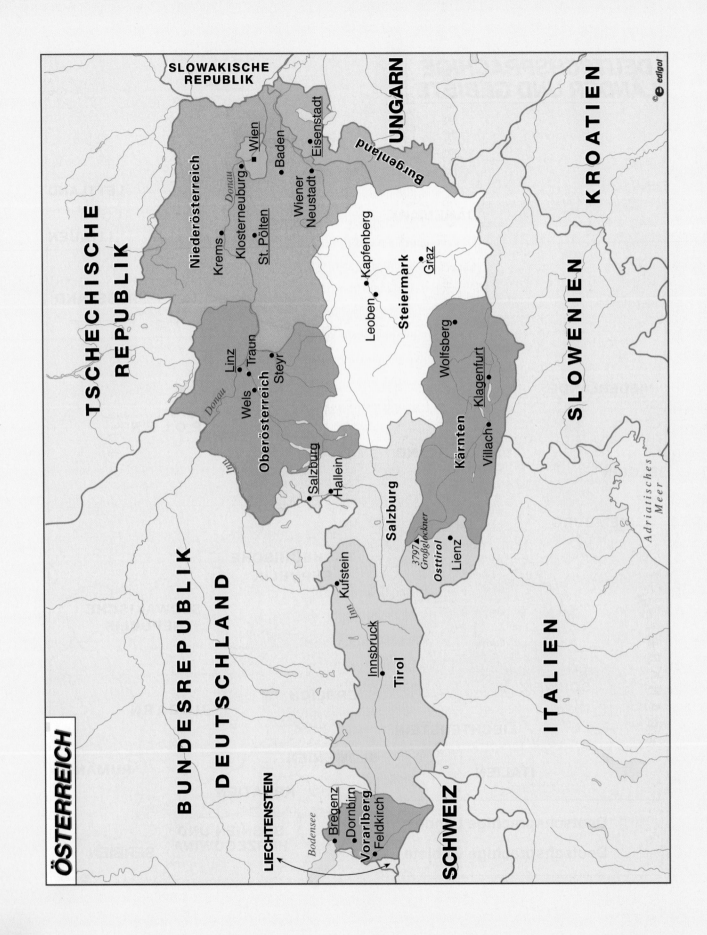

ÖSTERREICH

SLOWAKISCHE REPUBLIK

UNGARN

KROATIEN

TSCHECHISCHE REPUBLIK

SLOWENIEN

BUNDESREPUBLIK DEUTSCHLAND

ITALIEN

LIECHTENSTEIN

SCHWEIZ

Eisenstadt

Wien

Baden

Niederösterreich

Burgenland

Krems

Klosterneuburg

St. Pölten

Wiener Neustadt

Donau

Kapfenberg

Graz

Steiermark

Leoben

Wolfsberg

Linz

Traun

Steyr

Klagenfurt

Wels

Oberösterreich

Kärnten

Villach

Donau

Salzburg

Hallein

Salzburg

3797 Großglockner

Osttirol

Lienz

Kufstein

Inn

Innsbruck

Tirol

Bregenz

Dornbirn

Vorarlberg

Feldkirch

Bodensee

Adriatisches Meer

© edigol

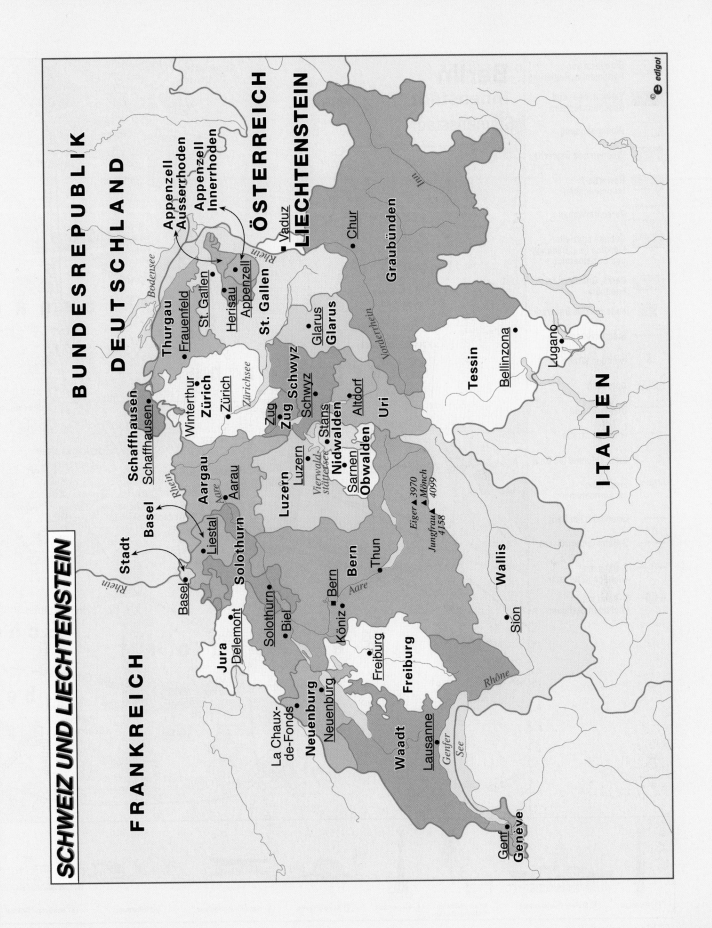

SCHWEIZ UND LIECHTENSTEIN

FRANKREICH

BUNDESREPUBLIK DEUTSCHLAND

ÖSTERREICH

LIECHTENSTEIN

ITALIEN

Appenzell Ausserrhoden
Appenzell Innerrhoden
Vaduz

Bodensee

Rhein

Thurgau
Frauenfeld
St. Gallen
Herisau
Appenzell
St. Gallen

Chur

Graubünden

Inn

Schaffhausen
Schaffhausen

Winterthur
Zürich
Zürich
Zürichsee

Glarus
Glarus

Vorderrhein

Tessin
Bellinzona

Lugano

Basel
Stadt
Basel

Rhein

Aargau
Aarau
Aare

Zug
Zug
Schwyz
Schwyz
Stans
Nidwalden
Sarnen
Obwalden

Altdorf
Uri

Liestal

Luzern
Luzern
Vierwald-
stättersee

Eiger ▲ 3970
Mönch ▲ 4099
Jungfrau ▲ 4158

Rhein

Basel

Jura
Delémont

Solothurn
Solothurn
Biel

Bern
Bern
Thun

Aare

Wallis

Sion

Köniz

Neuenburg
Neuenburg

La Chaux-
de-Fonds

Freiburg
Freiburg

Waadt
Lausanne

Genfer See

Rhône

Genf
Genève

© edigol

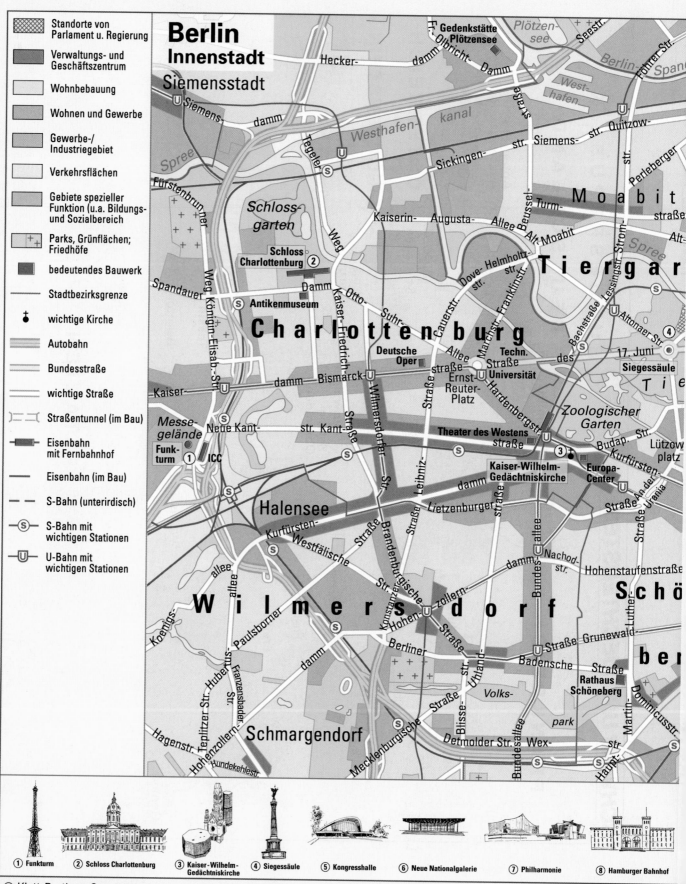

Berlin
Innenstadt

Legend:

- Standorte von Parlament u. Regierung
- Verwaltungs- und Geschäftszentrum
- Wohnbebauung
- Wohnen und Gewerbe
- Gewerbe-/Industriegebiet
- Verkehrsflächen
- Gebiete spezieller Funktion (u.a. Bildungs- und Sozialbereich)
- Parks, Grünflächen; Friedhöfe
- bedeutendes Bauwerk
- Stadtbezirksgrenze
- ♱ wichtige Kirche
- Autobahn
- Bundesstraße
- wichtige Straße
- Straßentunnel (im Bau)
- Eisenbahn mit Fernbahnhof
- Eisenbahn (im Bau)
- S-Bahn (unterirdisch)
- Ⓢ S-Bahn mit wichtigen Stationen
- Ⓤ U-Bahn mit wichtigen Stationen

① Funkturm ② Schloss Charlottenburg ③ Kaiser-Wilhelm-Gedächtniskirche ④ Siegessäule ⑤ Kongresshalle ⑥ Neue Nationalgalerie ⑦ Philharmonie ⑧ Hamburger Bahnhof

© Klett-Perthes, Germany

W e d d i n g

Müllerstr.-Chaussee

Fr.-Ludwig Jahn-Sport-park

Mauer-park

str.

Danziger Staße

Kastanien-allee

Allee

Grellstr. Straße

Storkower

Straße

P r e n z l a u e r   B e r g

Gedenkstätte Berliner Mauer

Bernauer-

straße

Schönhauser

Greifswalder

Danziger Straße Petersburger

Volkspark Anton Saefkow

Straße

Heide-Jahnstkana

Poststadion

Fritz-Schloss-Park

Hamburger Bahnhof ⑧

Lehrter Stadtbahnhof

Charité

straße Tor-

Oranienburger

Am Friedrichshain

Frieden-

Volkspark Friedrichs-hain

Platz der Vereinten Nationen

Kniprode-

Landsberger

Allee

Mitte

Alexander-platz

Fernseh-turm ⑮ Ⓢ

K.-Marx-Allee

Straußberger

Friedrich-

Invaliden-

Moabit

Reinhardtstr.

Friedrich-

Sitz der Bundes-regierung

str. ②

Museums-insel ⑫ Ⓤ

Berliner Dom ⑬

Humboldt-Universität

Unter den Linden

Liebknecht-

Karl-

Spandauer

str.-Moll-

straße

Rotes Rathaus ⑭

Platz

Karl- Marx- Allee Ⓤ

Friedrichshain

n

Kongress-halle ⑤ ⑨

Reichstagsgebäude

⑩

Wilhelm-

Straße

Ⓤ

Deutsche Staatsoper ⑪

Stralauer Str.

Holz-marktstr.

Ostbahnhof

Schloss-ellevue-straße

des 17. Juni

Branden-burger Tor

Französ. Dom

Schauspielhaus

Deutscher Dom

Fischer-insel

Köpenicker

Str. Brückenstr.

Mühlen-

str.

Warschauer

r g a r t e n

Philharmonie str. ⑦

Neue Nationalgalerie ⑥

ergarten-

Leipziger Straße

Potsdamer Platz

Stresemannstraße

Kochstraße Oranien-

H.-Heine-

Marianen-platz

Straße

Schiesische Str.

Spree

Reichpietsch-

Schöneberger

ufer

Uter

Tempelhofer

Ⓢ

K r e u z b e r g

Mehring-platz

Gitschiner

Straße

Skalitzer Ⓤ

straße

Stralauer Allee Ⓤ

Landwehrkanal

Bülow-

straße

Pallas-str.

Potsdamer Goebenstr.

Straße

Yorck-

Ⓤ

Ⓢ

Hallesches Ufer

Ufer

Haupt

Urban-

Prinzen-

str.

Kottbusser Damm

str. Sonnen-

Treptow

-ne-

straße

Kolonnen-

straße Duden-

Monumentenstr.

Kreuzberg-

str.

Viktoria-park

straße Gneisenau-

Bergmann-

Mehring-

straße Süd-

Hasen-

stern

heide Sonnen-

Karl-

g

Platz der Luftbrücke

Columbia-

Volkspark Hasenheide

Hermann-

damm

Tempelhof

Neukölln

Flughafen-

straße

Richthofen-Str.

Boelcke-

Tempelhofer Damm

Sachsen-damm

✈ **Flughafen Berlin-Tempelhof**

sur Marx-

allee

---

⑨ **Reichstagsgebäude, Sitz des Deutschen Bundestages**   ⑩ **Brandenburger Tor**   ⑪ **Deutsche Staatsoper**   ⑫ **Museumsinsel**   ⑬ **Berliner Dom**   ⑭ **Rotes Rathaus**   ⑮ **Fernsehturm**

Berlin Innenstadt

Deutschland

HELGOLAND - meine Insel

Deutschland

1 *background:* Brandenburger Tor
2 Frankfurt
3 Deutsche Bahn
4 Fest in Stuttgart
5 Karlsruhe
6 Fähre an der Nordsee
7 Ballonfahren
8 Fußball

1

2

3

Deutschland

1 *background:* Rathaus in Leipzig
2 die Alpen
3 Fest in Oberammergau
4 Fußballspiel
5 moderne Gebäude in Berlin
6 Schwimmbad in den Bergen
7 Krapfen
8 Thüringer Klöße

Österreich

Österreich

Schweiz

Schweiz

1 *background:* Bern, die Hauptstadt der Schweiz

2 Herrgottsgrenadiere

3 Gletscherbahn

4 Grossmünster in Zürich

5 Rodelbahn

6 Mit der Seilbahn geht's hoch auf den Berg.

7 Der Rhein fließt durch Basel.

8 Hunde ziehen einen Schlitten.

Kapitel 1
Hallo!

Objectives

In this chapter you will learn how to:

► greet and say farewell to someone
► ask and tell someone's name
► introduce someone else
► ask and tell someone's age
► give telephone numbers
► ask and tell how things are going
► inquire where someone is from

Auf Wiedersehen!

Lektion A

1 Wer ist das?

With a partner, look at the photos below and identify each person by answering your partner's question *Wer ist das?* Be sure to take turns and point to the various people out of sequence.

BEISPIEL Wer ist das?
Das ist Christian.

1. Florian

2. Bettina

3. Simone

4. Ali

5. Andreas

6. Nadine

7. Silke

8. Jan

Für dich

Hallo!, *Tag!* and *Grüß dich!* all mean "Hello" or "Hi." Although *Hallo!* is commonly heard throughout Germany, *Grüß dich!* is more often heard in southern Germany and *Tag!* in the rest of the country. All three are informal greetings and are used among young people, friends and relatives. Additional greetings that often can be heard for "Hello" are *Grüß Gott!* in southern Germany and *Guten Tag!* in other parts of the country.

Tschüs! or *Tschau!* is a casual form of *Auf Wiedersehen!*, meaning "good-bye." *Tschüs!* is derived from the French farewell "adieu" and *Tschau!* comes from the Italian greeting or farewell "ciao."

2 Wie heißt er? Wie heißt sie?

It's your first day in school. Ask the person next to you about different students in your class and then introduce yourself to that person. Use either *Tag* or *Grüß dich*.

BEISPIELE Wie heißt sie? (Sophia)
Sie heißt Sophia.
Tag, Sophia!

Wie heißt er? (Marco)
Er heißt Marco.
Grüß dich, Marco!

> Sie heißt Daniela.

> Er heißt Boris.

ein Junge　　　　　**ein Mädchen**

Die populärsten Vornamen
von deutschen Teenagern

Jungen

Ich heiße Florian.

Jan	Dominic
Lucas	Kevin
Niclas	Florian
Tim	Tom
Jannik	Luca
Leon	Nico
Philipp	Tobias
Daniel	Moritz
Felix	Nils
Maximilian	Paul
Alexander	Dennis
Jonas	Max
Julian	Patrick
Lennard	David
Fabian	Frederik
Finn	Sebastian
Marvin	Timo
Marcel	Simon

Namen

Mädchen

Ich heiße Julia.

Anna	Carolin
Sarah	Jennifer
Laura	Lara
Vanessa	Johanna
Julia	Nele
Lena	Antonia
Katharina	Leonie
Lisa	Marie
Lea	Melina
Michelle	Isabel
Annika	Kim
Nina	Nadine
Jana	Natalie
Jasmin	Pia
Alina	Paula
Sofie	Sophia
Hanna	Jacqueline
Luisa	Christina

3 Wer kommt?

Manfred wants to invite eight of his friends to his birthday party. His friends are eager to find out who will be there. Manfred challenges them by writing all the syllables of the guests' names on pieces of paper. Can you help Manfred's friends figure out who will be at his party? If you figure out who is coming, the beginning letters of the eight names when put in the right sequence will spell a girl's name shown in the illustration on page 2.

zwei Freundinnen

Dennis und Uli

Bettina und Stefanie

Dialog

Hallo!

Hallo, Tina!

Tag, Anne!

Wie heißt der
Junge da?

ANNE:	Hallo, Tina!
TINA:	Tag, Anne!
ANNE:	Wie heißt der Junge da?
TINA:	Michael. Er ist neu hier.
ANNE:	Wirklich? Kennst du Michael?
TINA:	Ja, er ist sehr nett.

4 Wer ist diese Person?

Identify the person. You may need to know these two verb forms: *sagt* (says) and *fragt* (asks). *Diese Person...*

1. sagt: „Tag!"
2. ist sehr nett.
3. fragt: „Kennst du Michael?"
4. ist ein Junge.
5. ist neu hier.

5 Auf Deutsch, bitte! (In German, please.)

What do you say in German when you...

1. greet someone?
2. ask someone what a boy's or a girl's name is?
3. ask someone if he or she knows a person?
4. tell someone that he or she is new here?

Wir kennen Thomas sehr gut.

Das Mädchen heißt Daniela.

Wie geht's?

Wie geht's, Michael?

Ganz gut. Ist das deine Freundin?

Ja, das ist meine Freundin Anne.

TINA:	Wie geht's, Michael?
MICHAEL:	Ganz gut. Ist das deine Freundin?
TINA:	Ja, das ist meine Freundin Anne.
MICHAEL:	Grüß dich, Anne!
ANNE:	Woher kommst du?
MICHAEL:	Aus Regensburg.
ANNE:	Wie interessant!

6 Auf Deutsch, bitte!

1. Give another expression for *Tag!*
2. Ask how someone is doing.
3. Say that you're quite well.
4. Ask where your classmate is from.

7 Stimmt das? Stimmt das nicht?

If the statement is correct indicate it with „*Das stimmt.*"
If it is incorrect, indicate it with „*Das stimmt nicht*" and
then give the correct statement in German.

1. Tina sagt: „Wie geht's?"
2. Anne ist Michaels Freundin.
3. Michael geht's ganz gut.
4. Michael kommt aus Hamburg.

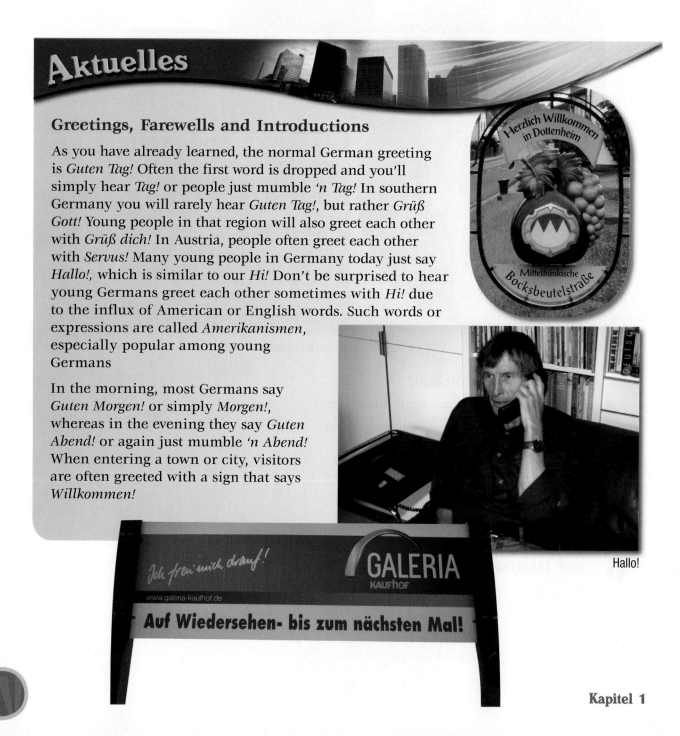

Aktuelles

Greetings, Farewells and Introductions

As you have already learned, the normal German greeting
is *Guten Tag!* Often the first word is dropped and you'll
simply hear *Tag!* or people just mumble *'n Tag!* In southern
Germany you will rarely hear *Guten Tag!*, but rather *Grüß
Gott!* Young people in that region will also greet each other
with *Grüß dich!* In Austria, people often greet each other
with *Servus!* Many young people in Germany today just say
Hallo!, which is similar to our *Hi!* Don't be surprised to hear
young Germans greet each other sometimes with *Hi!* due
to the influx of American or English words. Such words or
expressions are called *Amerikanismen*,
especially popular among young
Germans

In the morning, most Germans say
Guten Morgen! or simply *Morgen!*,
whereas in the evening they say *Guten
Abend!* or again just mumble *'n Abend!*
When entering a town or city, visitors
are often greeted with a sign that says
Willkommen!

Hallo!

Auf Wiedersehen! (literally, "Until I see again") or simply *Wiedersehen!* means "good-bye." *Tschüs!* or *Tschau!* are very casual forms of "good-bye." It comes closest to the American "See you!" or "So long!"

Germans do a lot more handshaking than Americans. Germans not only shake hands when being introduced, but many still consider a handshake as part of the everyday greeting. To a German, it means little more than saying "Hello." A nod of the head usually accompanies the handshake. When meeting acquaintances in the street, in shops or elsewhere in public, Germans usually shake hands only if they intend to chat.

Guten Tag!

8 **Was weißt du?** (What do you know?)

Complete each statement with the appropriate German phrase or expression based on the *Aktuelles* section.

1. ___! is a more formal form of "good-bye" than ___! or ___!
2. The standard greeting in the morning is ___!
3. In southern Germany, people in the street will greet each other with ___!; however, young people in that region will say ___!
4. The normal German greeting during the day is ___!
5. ___! is the typical good-bye phrase.
6. Austrians will often greet one another with ___!

Wie alt bist du?

0 null	**1** eins	**2** zwei	**3** drei	**4** vier
5 fünf	**6** sechs	**7** sieben	**8** acht	**9** neun
10 zehn	**11** elf	**12** zwölf	**13** dreizehn	**14** vierzehn
15 fünfzehn	**16** sechzehn	**17** siebzehn	**18** achtzehn	**19** neunzehn
20 zwanzig				

9 Wie alt ist er? Wie alt ist sie?

Imagine a German student is staying with you for a while. You introduce him or her to several people in your neighborhood. Your German guest asks you about the ages of the various people he or she is meeting. Respond accordingly.

BEISPIEL Tina, 13
Das ist Tina.
Wie alt ist Tina?
Sie ist dreizehn.

1. Susanne, 16 3. Ali, 12 5. Bärbel, 8
2. Heidi, 18 4. Robert, 19 6. Christine, 15

Schreiben

Ask five classmates their names and phone numbers. Write this information on a piece of paper. Your classmates will collect the same information from others. Taking turns with a partner, say each name and phone number one at a time, and write them down. After each of you has written down all five names and phone numbers, compare your sheets to make sure the information is correct. (Note: *die Telefonnummer* is the expression for "phone number.")

BEISPIEL

– Wie heißt du?

– Ich heiße... *(name of classmate)*

– Deine Telefonnummer?

– 730-8124 (sieben, drei, null, acht, eins, zwei, vier)

Was ist Uwes Telefonnummer?

sein (to be)

As you have already seen, *sein* (to be) is a frequently used verb in German. The following are the subject pronouns (*ich*/I, *du*/you, *er*/he, *sie*/she, *es*/it) with their corresponding forms of *sein*:

ich bin	I am
du bist	you are
er ist	he is
sie ist	she is
es ist	it is

Wie alt bist du?   How old are you?
Ich bin sechzehn.   I'm 16.

Note: You will learn the plural forms of *sein* in a later chapter.

10   Wie viel ist...?

State each problem and then answer it in German.

> **BEISPIELE**   1 + 3 = ?
> Wie viel ist eins plus drei?
> Eins plus drei ist vier.
>
> 10 – 1 = ?
> Wie viel ist zehn minus eins?
> Zehn minus eins ist neun.

1. 8 + 11 = ?
2. 13 – 1 = ?
3. 5 + 2 = ?
4. 20 – 6 = ?
5. 16 – 5 = ?
6. 7 + 9 = ?

11 Was fehlt hier? (What's missing here?)

Complete each sentence using the proper forms of *sein*.

1. Woher ___ Dieter?
2. ___ du vierzehn oder fünfzehn?
3. Ich ___ fünfzehn.
4. ___ Petra neu hier?
5. Wie alt ___ Ali?
6. Er ___ nett.
7. ___ du Heike?
8. Nein, ich ___ Angelika.

12 Du weißt das. (You know that.)

You are trying to demonstrate to your friend that you know some German. Your friend starts to say something, and you finish the sentence.

BEISPIEL Wie alt bist ___?
Wie alt bist du?

1. Guten ___!
2. Woher kommst ___?
3. Auf ___!
4. Grüß ___!
5. Wie heißt ___?
6. Martina ist ein ___.
7. Vier plus sieben ist ___.
8. Wer ist ___?

Persönliches

You are talking to another student. What are the logical statements to complete this short conversation? You may want to use some of the cues listed below for possible answers.

> **Ich bin... / Ich heiße... / Tschüs... / Tag / Sie ist...**

A: Tag!
B: (1)

A: Wie heißt du?
B: (2)

A: Wer ist das?
B: (3)

A: Wie alt ist sie?
B: (4)

A: Tschüs!
B: (5)

Ich heiße Rafael.

Rollenspiel

Carry on a brief conversation with the person next to you asking such questions as: *Wie heißt du? Wie alt bist du?* (Point to others in your class.) *Wer ist das? Wie heißt er? Wie heißt sie? Wie alt ist er? Wie alt ist sie?*

> **BEISPIEL**
>
> **KARSTEN:** Hallo! Wie heißt du?
>
> **MONIKA:** Monika. Und du?
>
> **KARSTEN:** Ich heiße Karsten.
>
> **MONIKA:** Wie heißt er?
>
> **KARSTEN:** Er heißt Dieter.
>
> **MONIKA:** Wie alt ist er?
>
> **KARSTEN:** Vierzehn.

Sie heißen Melissa und Sofia.

Er heißt Fabio.

Sie heißt Frau Kröger.

Wörter und Ausdrücke

Asking for Someone's Name

Wie heißt du? What is your name?
Ich heiße... / Ich bin... My name is... /
 I am...
Wie heißt er (sie)? What is his (her) name?
Das ist... That is...

Greetings

Hallo!/Tag!/Grüß dich! Hello!
Guten Tag, Herr Schulz! Hello, Mr. Schulz!
Tschüs!/Tschau! Bye!
Auf Wiedersehen, Frau Meier! Good-bye,
 Mrs. Meier!
Wie geht's? How are you?
Ganz gut. Quite well.

Other Expressions

Wer ist der Junge? Who is the boy?
Er ist neu hier. He is new here.
Wirklich? Really?
Kennst du...? Do you know...?
Sie ist nett. She is nice.
Woher kommst du? Where are you from?
Aus... From...
Wie interessant! How interesting!
Wie alt bist du? How old are you?
Ich bin... I am...
Wie viel ist...? How much is...?

Zungenbrecher

Tag, Karl!
Wie geht's, Karl?
Gut, Karl.
Kahl, Karl.
Ja, Karl, ganz kahl.

-Hello, Karl. -How are you, Karl? -Fine, Karl. -Bald, Karl? -Yes, Karl, completely bald.

Lektion B

13 Kennt sie Tanja?

Petra is talking to her friend Maria. Select the appropriate words from the list to complete the conversation.

hier	Wie	sehr	Hallo	du	Gut	Ecke	ist	Guten

PETRA: (1), Maria!

MARIA: (2) Tag, Petra!

PETRA: (3) geht's?

MARIA: (4).

PETRA: Wohnst du um die (5)?

MARIA: Nein, gleich (6).

PETRA: Wer (7) das?

MARIA: Kennst (8) Tanja?

PETRA: Nicht (9) gut.

Für dich

There are many German words that look the same or are similar to English words. Examples are *Butter, Doktor, Milch, Park* and *Rekord*. These words are called *cognates*. The word "**cogn**ate" comes from "re**cogn**ize." If you recognize a word in German because there is a similar word in English, it may be a cognate. You won't have any problems identifying the cognates that are shown in the photos on the right. Unfortunately, there are words in German that are *false cognates*. A false cognate is a German word that looks like an English word but means something quite different. For example, if you would like to send a gift to someone in Germany, don't mark your package with the word "gift." The word **Gift** in German means "poison."

Aktuelles

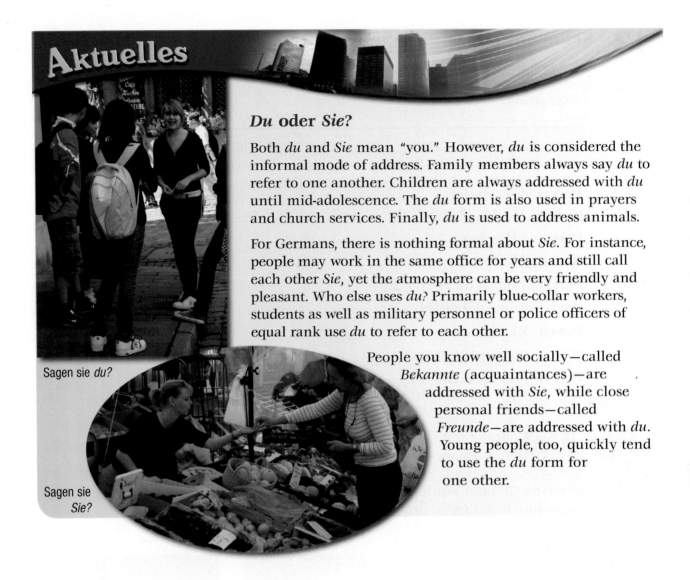

Sagen sie *du?*

Sagen sie *Sie?*

Du oder *Sie?*

Both *du* and *Sie* mean "you." However, *du* is considered the informal mode of address. Family members always say *du* to refer to one another. Children are always addressed with *du* until mid-adolescence. The *du* form is also used in prayers and church services. Finally, *du* is used to address animals.

For Germans, there is nothing formal about *Sie*. For instance, people may work in the same office for years and still call each other *Sie*, yet the atmosphere can be very friendly and pleasant. Who else uses *du?* Primarily blue-collar workers, students as well as military personnel or police officers of equal rank use *du* to refer to each other.

People you know well socially—called *Bekannte* (acquaintances)—are addressed with *Sie*, while close personal friends—called *Freunde*—are addressed with *du*. Young people, too, quickly tend to use the *du* form for one other.

14 *Du* oder *Sie?*

Indicate which form you, as a student in Germany, would use if you were to talk to these people or animals.

1. a fifteen-year-old exchange student
2. your doctor
3. a police officer
4. your friend
5. your father or mother
6. a teacher
7. a six-year-old child
8. your cat
9. your aunt
10. your friend's uncle

Sagt er *du* oder *Sie?*

The Familiar Form: *du* and *ihr*

The familiar forms *du* and *ihr*, both meaning "you," are used when speaking to relatives, close friends, children and animals.

(Mrs. Schmidt is speaking to a child)

Wo wohnst du?   Where do you live?

(Andreas is talking to his new classmates)

Woher kommt ihr?   Where do you come from?

Note that *du* is used to address one person and *ihr* is used for two or more people.

(Kerstin asks Andreas and Petra)

Wohnt ihr hier?   Do you live here?

The Formal Form: *Sie*

The formal form *Sie*, meaning "you," is used when speaking to adults and to those not addressed by their first name.

(Thomas is talking to his teacher)

Wo wohnen Sie, Herr Schulz?   Where do you live, Mr. Schulz?

(Mrs. Müller is talking to her new neighbors)

Kennen Sie die Hoffmanns,   Do you know the Hoffmanns,
Herr und Frau Meier?   Mr. and Mrs. Meier?

The formal form *Sie*, in both singular and plural, is always capitalized.

15 Du, ihr, Sie?

Which of these forms would you use in the following situations? You are talking to your...

1. cousin
2. parents
3. coach
4. dog
5. dentist
6. brother
7. girlfriend
8. pet rabbits
9. relatives
10. school principal

Personal Pronouns

SINGULAR		PLURAL	
ich	I	**wir**	we
du	you (familiar)	**ihr**	you (familiar)
er, sie, es	he, she, it	**sie**	they
Sie	you (formal)	**Sie**	you (formal)

Present Tense Verb Forms

In the present tense in English, there are basically two different verb forms for all persons. For example, "live" is used for all persons, except after "he," "she" or "it" where it is "live**s**." In German, however, the verb has more forms, as can be seen in the chart.

To use the proper form, you need to know the infinitive of the particular verb. The infinitive of the English verb forms "came" or "comes" is "to come." The infinitive of a German verb ends with *-en* as in *gehen, kommen* or *wohnen* (in a few cases just *-n*). The infinitive is a combination of the stem of the verb and the ending (infinitive = stem + ending).

When the stem of a verb is known, you need to know the appropriate ending for the particular singular or plural form.

The present tense of regular verbs requires the endings as indicated in the verb *gehen* (to go) below.

		STEM + ENDING	MEANING
SINGULAR	ich	geh + *e*	I go, I am going, I do go
	du	geh + *st*	you go, you are going, you do go
	er		he goes, he is going, he does go
	sie	geh + *t*	she goes, she is going, she does go
	es		it goes, it is going, it does go

		STEM + ENDING	MEANING
PLURAL	wir	geh + *en*	we go, we are going, we do go
	ihr	geh + *t*	you go, you are going, you do go
	sie	geh + *en*	they go, they are going, they do go
	Sie	geh + *en*	you go, you are going, you do go

Note: If the stem of the verb for *du* ends in *s* or *ß*, then the *s* in the ending is dropped.

Heißt du Martina?   Is your name Martina?

16 Wo wohnst du?

Assume that you are being asked if you live in a certain location. How might you answer the following questions?

BEISPIEL Wohnst du hier? (da)
Nein, ich wohne da.

1. Wohnst du da? (hier)
2. Wohnst du hier? (gleich um die Ecke)
3. Wohnst du weit von hier? (nicht weit von hier)
4. Wohnst du fünf Minuten von hier? (zehn Minuten)

17 Wie heißt sie? Wie heißt er?

Your friend is interested in getting to know some students in your school. Tell your friend their names.

BEISPIELE Wie heißt sie? (Natascha)
Sie heißt Natascha.

Wie heißt er? (Boris)
Er heißt Boris.

1. Tina

2. Britta

3. Ingo

4. Manfred

5. Michael

6. Julia

18 Tag!

Pretend that one of your classmates (*Klassenkamerad* or *Klassenkameradin*) is meeting you for the first time. Respond in German.

Klassenkamerad(in):	Tag!
Du:	(1)
Klassenkamerad(in):	Wie heißt du?
Du:	(2)
Klassenkamerad(in):	Wo wohnst du?
Du:	(3)
Klassenkamerad(in):	Ist das deine Freundin?
Du:	(4)
Klassenkamerad(in):	Wie heißt sie?
Du:	(5)

Persönliches

1. Wie heißt du?
2. Wie alt bist du?
3. Wie geht's?
4. Wohnst du weit von hier?
5. Wie heißt dein Freund? Deine Freundin?
6. Wo wohnt er? Wo wohnt sie?
7. Wer ist neu hier?

Michael ist neu hier.

Ich heiße Luis. Ich bin fünfzehn.

Praktisches

With the class divided into pairs, ask your partner his or her name, age and where he or she lives. Then get together with another pair of students and share with them what you have learned about your partner.

BEISPIEL   A: *Wie heißt du?*
B: *Ich heiße Heidi.*

A: *Wie alt bist du?*
B: *Ich bin 16.*

A: *Wo wohnst du?*
B: *Ich wohne in Chicago.*

After Student B has asked the same questions, the following sample conversation might take place:

Student A talks to Students C and D: *Sie heißt Heidi. Heidi ist 16. Sie wohnt in Chicago.*

Students B, C and D also present their partner to the others.

Finally, your teacher may select one of you to present the other three to the entire class.

Das Alphabet

A ah	**G** geh	**M** emm	**S** ess	**Y** üpsilon
B beh	**H** hah	**N** enn	**T** teh	**Z** tset
C tseh	**I** ih	**O** oh	**U** uh	**ä** äh
D deh	**J** jott	**P** peh	**V** fau	**ö** öh
E eh	**K** kah	**Q** kuh	**W** weh	**ü** üh
F eff	**L** ell	**R** err	**X** iks	**ß** ess-tset

Für dich

You probably noticed that there are four additional letters in the German language: ß, ä, ö, ü.

The letter ß is equivalent to ss but cannot necessarily be substituted. The ß is used after a long vowel *(Straße)* or vowel combination *(heißen)*.

The ß is never used when all the letters in a word are capitalized *(Straße*, but *STRASSE)*.

19 **Wie buchstabiert man...?** (How do you spell...?)

Spell the following words out loud.

1. alt
2. Katja
3. fünf
4. Tag
5. Mädchen
6. Frau
7. sie
8. plus

20 **Im Telefonbuch**

Look at a section from a German telephone book. Pick eight different entries and read them aloud, including their first and last names as well as their telephone numbers; then spell each first and last name.

Gonzalez Maria	62 28 16
Grabe Andreas	19 02 43
Grabowski Ute	81 14 91
Griese Marco	63 24 07
Gröger Rosemarie	52 05 96
Grommitsch Hildegard	28 90 49
Groning Klaus	33 42 78
Großmann Anke	27 32 69
Grotenick Helga	31 72 40
Groth Grete	21 30 47
Grube Bodo	58 00 13
Grubert Wilfried	41 58 27

Schreiben

Ask a classmate at least three personal questions such as:

Wie heißt du?
Wie alt bist du?
Wo wohnst du?

Then write down the answers to your questions. For example:

Er heißt Robert.
Er ist fünfzehn.
Er wohnt in Denver.

After you have written the answers, ask a classmate to check them for accuracy. Reverse roles.

Wörter und Ausdrücke

Additional Greetings

Wie geht es Ihnen, Herr Dörner? How are you, Mr. Dörner?
Nicht schlecht. Not bad.
Sehr gut. Very well.

Asking Where a Person Lives

Wo wohnen Sie, Frau Dobler? Where do you live, Mrs. Dobler?
Nicht weit. Not far.
Nur zehn Minuten von hier. Only ten minutes from here.
Wohnst du hier? Do you live here?
Nein, da drüben. No, over there.

Sie wohnen nur zehn Minuten von hier.

Wie geht's?

21 Das stimmt.

You are agreeing with everything you are asked.

BEISPIEL Wohnst du hier?
Ja, ich wohne hier.

1. Wohnst du um die Ecke?
2. Kennst du Gisela?
3. Ist das Dieter?
4. Ist er neu hier?
5. Ist Boris vierzehn?
6. Ist vier plus neun dreizehn?
7. Heißt sie Frau Lehmann?
8. Wohnt Heike in Hamburg?

22 Wie viel ist...?

Follow the example.

BEISPIEL zwei plus vier
Zwei plus vier ist sechs.

1. sieben plus drei
2. zwölf minus fünf
3. acht minus vier
4. zehn plus neun
5. zwanzig minus vierzehn
6. sechs plus elf

23 Auf Deutsch, bitte!

State each problem and then answer it in German.

BEISPIEL 4 + 1 = ___
Vier plus eins ist fünf.

1. 5 + 8 = ___
2. 1 + 6 = ___
3. 12 – 3 = ___
4. 20 – 11 = ___
5. 4 + 10 = ___
6. 17 – 15 = ___

24 Was fehlt hier?

Select one of the words from the list to complete the dialog.

gut Tschüs Tag ist kommt Wie du Ecke alt neu

Heidi: __(1)__ , Christine!

Christine: __(2)__ geht's, Heidi?

Heidi: Ganz __(3)__ .

Christine: Ist Jens __(4)__ hier?

Heidi: Ja, er __(5)__ aus Hamburg.

Christine: Kennst __(6)__ Jens?

Heidi: Ja, er wohnt gleich um die __(7)__ .

Christine: Wie __(8)__ ist er?

Heidi: Er __(9)__ sechzehn.

Christine: __(10)__ , Heidi.

25 Kombiniere... (Combine...)

How many sentences can you make using the following words in various combinations? Choose one word or phrase from each column.

Ich	ist	ein Mädchen
Ali	bin	mein Freund
Tina	wohnst	fünf Minuten von hier
Du	kennt	Gisela
		da drüben
		hier

Die Jungen wohnen
fünf Minuten von hier.

26 Richtig oder falsch? (Correct or incorrect?)

Decide whether or not the response to each question or statement is appropriate. If it is inappropriate, give a response in German that makes sense.

1. Wie geht's?
   Nein.

2. Wo wohnst du?
   Da drüben.

3. Wie heißt er?
   Sie heißt Maria.

4. Guten Tag, Frau Meier!
   Gut.

5. Wohnen Sie hier?
   Ja.

6. Kennst du Rainer?
   Ja, er ist mein Freund.

7. Wie viel ist fünf plus vier? Nein.

8. Wo ist deine Freundin?
   Da drüben.

9. Wie geht es Ihnen, Herr Schmidt?
   Nicht schlecht.

10. Heißt du Uwe?
    Ja, gut.

Was weißt du?

This section is intended to check your general understanding of this chapter. Unless *Auf Englisch* (in English) is indicated, all your responses should be in German.

1. Say hello and good-bye to your classmates and teacher.

2. Ask a classmate these questions and listen to the answers. Then reverse roles.

   a. What is your name?

   b. How old are you?

   c. Where do you live?

   d. Do you live far from here?

   e. Who is that?

   f. Do you know (name of classmate)?

3. Count from 0 to 20 and spell each number in writing.

4. What are the answers to these questions?

   a. Explain the difference between *du* and *Sie*. (*Auf Englisch.*)

   b. How do young people greet each other in southern Germany?

   c. What are the casual and more formal forms of saying good-bye?

   d. What do Austrians often say when they greet each other informally?

Vokabeln

alt old *1A*
aus from, out of *1A*
da there; *da drüben* over there *1A*
das that *1A*
dein(e) your (familiar singular) *1A*
du you (familiar singular) *1A*
die **Ecke,-n** corner *1B*
ein(e) a, an *1A*
er he *1A*
es it *1A*
die **Frau,-en** Mrs., woman *1A*
der **Freund,-e** boyfriend *1A*
die **Freundin,-nen** girlfriend *1A*
ganz quite; *ganz gut* quite well, pretty good *1A*
gehen to go; *Wie geht's? 1A, Wie geht es Ihnen?* How are you? *1B*
gleich immediately, right; *gleich um die Ecke* right around the corner *1B*
Grüß dich! Hi! Hello! *1A*
gut good; *ganz gut* quite well *1A*
Hallo! Hi! Hello! *1A*
heißen to be called; *Wie heißt du?, Wie heißen Sie?* What's your name? *1A*
der **Herr,-en** Mr., gentleman *1A*
hier here *1B*
ich I *1A*
ihr you (familiar plural) *1B*
interessant interesting *1A*
ja yes *1A*
der **Junge,-n** boy *1A*
kennen to know (person, place) *1A*
kommen to come *1A*
das **Mädchen,-** girl *1A*
mein(e) my *1A*

minus minus *1A*
die **Minute,-n** minute *1B*
nein no *1B*
nett nice *1A*
neu new *1A*
nicht not *1B*
nur only *1B*
plus plus *1A*
schlecht bad *1B*
sehr very *1A*
sein to be *1A*
sie she, they *1A*
Sie you (formal) *1A*
der **Tag,-e** day; *Tag!* Hello! *Guten Tag!* Hello! *1A*
Tschau! See you! Bye! *1A*
Tschüs! See you! Bye! *1A*
um around; *um die Ecke* around the corner *1B*
und and *1A*
viel much; *wie viel* how much *1A*
von from *1B*
weit far *1B*
wer who *1A*
wie how, what; *Wie heißt du?, Wie heißen Sie?* What's your name? *Wie geht's?, Wie geht es Ihnen?* How are you?; *wie viel* how much *1A*
Wiedersehen! Bye! *Auf Wiedersehen!* Good-bye! *1A*
wir we *1A*
wirklich really *1A*
wo where *1B*
woher where from *1A*
wohnen to live *1B*

Ich heiße Daniela.
Wie heißt du?

zwei Mädchen und zwei Jungen

Hallo!

Kapitel 2
Zu Hause

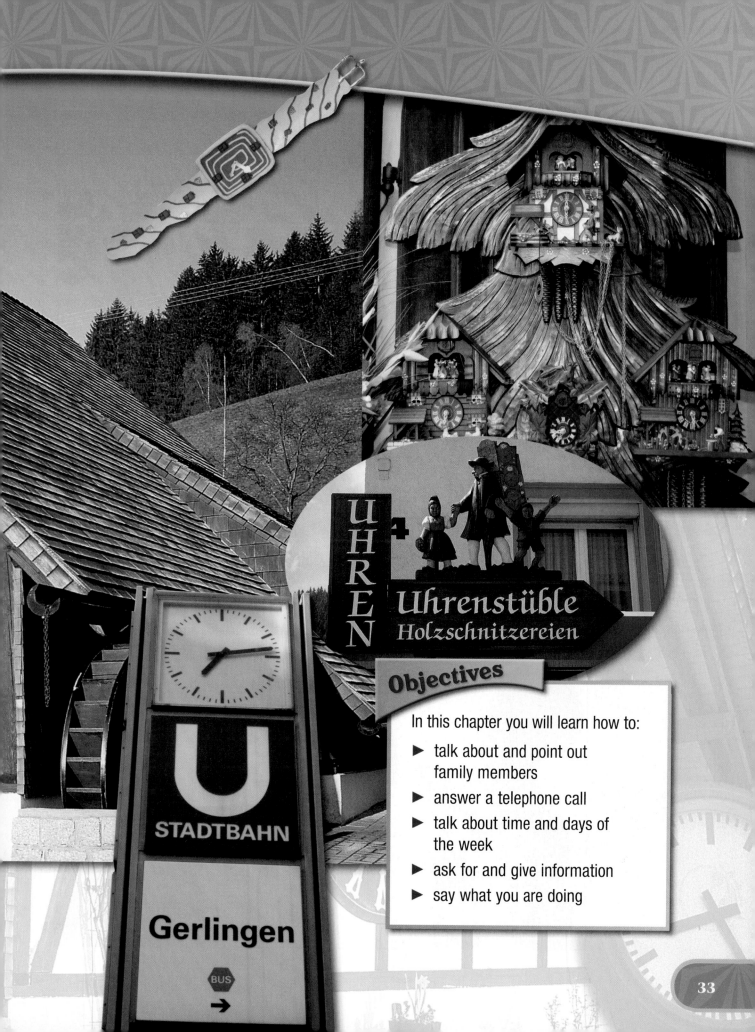

UHREN

Uhrenstüble
Holzschnitzereien

Objectives

In this chapter you will learn how to:

▶ talk about and point out family members

▶ answer a telephone call

▶ talk about time and days of the week

▶ ask for and give information

▶ say what you are doing

STADTBAHN

Gerlingen

BUS

Lektion A

Vokabeln

Die Familie

Manfred Müller
der Großvater (Opa)

Renate Müller
die Großmutter (Oma)

Sabine Schmidt
die Tante

Peter Schmidt
der Onkel

Hans Schmidt
der Vater (Vati)

Andrea Schmidt
die Mutter (Mutti)

Felix Schmidt
der Cousin

Lisa Schmidt
die Cousine

Oliver Schmidt
der Sohn

Anne Schmidt
die Tochter

Wer ist Hans Schmidt?

Er ist Annes Vater.

Sie ist Olivers Cousine.

Und Lisa?

1 Fragen

Beantworte diese Fragen! (Answer these questions!)

1. Wer ist Olivers Schwester?
2. Wie heißt Annes Tante?
3. Wie heißt Andrea Schmidts Vater?
4. Wer ist Annes Cousine?
5. Wer ist Olivers Großmutter?
6. Wer ist Peter Schmidts Bruder?
7. Wie heißt Hans Schmidts Sohn?
8. Wie heißt Olivers Cousin?

2 Deine Familie

Talk with a classmate about his or her family members. Then reverse roles and talk about your own family.

BEISPIEL Wie heißt deine Schwester (dein Bruder, deine Tante, dein Onkel)?
Wie alt ist er (sie)?
Wo wohnt er (sie)?

In welcher Straße wohnt Katrin?

Monika ist Katrins Freundin.

Monika wohnt in der Bahnhofstraße.

Ist sie zu Hause?

Thomas ist Alexanders Freund.

Wie alt ist sie denn?

Sechzehn.

THOMAS: Ich kenne deine Schwester nicht.

ALEXANDER: Schwester? Das ist meine Cousine Julia.

THOMAS: Echt? Wie alt ist sie denn?

ALEXANDER: Sechzehn.

THOMAS: Toll! Ist sie zu Hause?

ALEXANDER: Ja. Komm mit! Da ist ein Telefon.

3 Falsch!

The following statements are incorrect. Provide the correct statements in German.

1. Thomas kennt Alexanders Schwester gut.
2. Julia ist Alexanders Schwester.
3. Julia ist fünfzehn.
4. Julia ist nicht zu Hause.

4 Auf Deutsch, bitte!

Tell your classmate that...

1. you know a certain person.
2. you think (name a person) is terrific.
3. your friend is 14.
4. (name a person) is your friend.

Für dich

German families are slightly smaller than American families. Almost half of married couples in Germany have no children living in the household. Families with three or more children are becoming increasingly rare, while the percentage of families with one or two children is growing.

Germans use the word *denn* frequently in conversations. In this context (for example, *Wie alt ist sie denn?*) the word *denn* itself has no meaning and is used strictly for emphasis to make the question sound less formal or direct.

Mutter und Sohn

Eine deutsche Familie ist meistens nicht groß.

Woher? Where from?

Woher kommst du?
(Where from come you?)
Where do you come
from?

Was? What?

Was magst du?
What do you like?

Was bist du?
What are you?

Formation of Questions

To form a question you must use the inverted word order. The sequence of the subject and the verb in the sentence is reversed.

Statement: *Du kommst spät.*	You are coming late.
Question: *Kommst du spät?*	Are you coming late?
Wohnt Herr Riebe in Hamburg?	Does Mr. Riebe live in Hamburg?
Ist Jürgen zu Hause?	Is Jürgen at home?
Kennst du Tina?	Do you know Tina?

The formation of questions in German is simpler than in English where most questions use a form of "to do" (do you?, does he?, etc.).

The inverted word order is also used with such question words as those listed below:

Wie? How? What?	*Wie spät ist es?* How late is it? What time is it?
Wo? Where?	*Wo wohnst du?* Where do you live?
Wer? Who?	*Wer ist das?* Who is that?
Wie viel? How much?	*Wie viel ist drei plus vier?* How much is three plus four?

5 Das stimmt.

Hartmut is very inquisitive. He asks you lots of questions. Answer affirmatively.

1. Ist Monika vierzehn?
2. Kommst du mit?
3. Kennst du Rainer?
4. Ist Petra zu Hause?
5. Wohnst du weit von hier?
6. Ist es zehn Uhr?

Ist Petra zu Hause?

6 Wie? Wo? Wer?

Complete each sentence using the appropriate question word.

1. ___ alt bist du?
2. ___ wohnt dein Freund?
3. ___ geht um die Ecke?
4. ___ ist Regensburg?
5. ___ heißen Sie?
6. ___ viel ist achtzehn minus neun?
7. ___ ist Ivanas Bruder? Das ist Sven.
8. ___ kennt deine Freundin?

7 Fragen

Ask questions about the italicized words or phrases.

BEISPIEL Sie heißt *Beate*.
Wie heißt sie?

1. *Dieter* kennt Ali sehr gut.
2. Das ist *Anne*.
3. Herr Tielmann wohnt *in München*.
4. Vier plus neun ist *dreizehn*.
5. Tina ist *zu Hause*.
6. Rainer kommt *aus Berlin*.
7. *Björn* wohnt um die Ecke.
8. Katja ist *15 Jahre* alt.

Rainer kommt aus Berlin.

Herr Tielmann wohnt in München.

The Telephone

The official word for telephone is *Fernsprecher*, but everyone says *Telefon*. Today, cell phones *(Handys)* are widely used inside and outside of people's homes. However, some Germans still use public phones. The word for phone booth is *die Telefonzelle*. These public phone booths are easily recognized by their bright yellow color. The newer phone booths of *Telekom* are no longer yellow but gray with a bit of lilac. There are always public phones located in local post offices, railroad stations, hotels, public buildings and even in trains and planes. The *Telefonzelle* has been replaced in many places with the more maintenance-free *Telefonsäule* (phone post) where the weatherproof telephone is mounted to a post.

Er hat ein Handy.

Public phones found in phone booths require a *Telefonkarte* (phone card) which can be purchased at post offices, railroad stations, newspaper stands and telephone stores for 10 or 25 euro *(Euro)*. The phone card is inserted into a slot with the magnetic tape side down. The digital display informs the caller how much credit is left on the card before, during and after the call is made.

Telefonzellen

Telefonsäulen

There are still some public phones that accept coins when making local or long-distance calls. However, the number of these coin-operated public phones is rapidly decreasing. The dialing instructions are usually posted. In calling, you should follow these steps:

1. Lift the receiver.
2. Insert your phone card or coins.
3. Wait for the dial tone.
4. Dial the number *(Telefonnummer)*.

Long-distance calls to other German cities or foreign countries can be made from any phone booth, at a post office or hotel or from any private phone. If you place a *Ferngespräch* (long-distance call), you should know the *Vorwahl* or *Vorwahlnummer* (area code). In case you don't know this number, you can either look it up in a telephone directory, on the Internet or call *Auskunft* or *Information*. The number for *Auskunft* is 11833 (national) or 11834 (international).

Hier braucht man eine Telefonkarte oder Münzen *(coins)*.

When making calls from the United States to Germany, Austria or Switzerland, you must dial first the international code 011, followed by the country code (Germany = 49, Austria = 43, Switzerland = 41), the city or town area code and then the local number. For example, if you want to call Frankfurt, you would dial the international code (011), the country code for Germany (49) and then the city code for Frankfurt (69) followed by the local phone number.

Sie ist am Telefon.

8 Was weißt du?

Identify the German words described.

1. The German word for "long distance call" is ___.
2. The ___ for Germany is "49."
3. Another word for *Telefon* is ___.
4. A cell phone is called a ___.
5. If the public phone won't accept coins, you'll need a ___.
6. When a phone number is not known, the caller can either look it up in a phone book or call ___.
7. The official currency in Germany is the ___.
8. A ___, located outside of buildings, is where many people make their calls.

Persönliches

1. Wie alt bist du?
2. Wie heißen sie? *(Answer question by naming at least five family members and/or relatives.)*
3. Wo wohnen sie? *(Answer question relating it to Question 2.)*
4. Kennst du *(name of person)*?
5. Wer ist zu Hause?

Rollenspiel

You are curious about a classmate's friends. Ask your classmate some questions about his or her friends. Then reverse roles.

BEISPIEL

- *Wer ist* (person's name) *Schwester?*
- *Kennst du* (person's name)?
- *Wo wohnt* (person's name)?
- *Wie alt ist* (person's name)?
- *Ist* (person's name) *dein Freund/deine Freundin?*

Sie wohnt hier.

Wörter und Ausdrücke

Family Members

der Bruder,∵ brother
der Cousin,-s cousin (male)
die Cousine,-n cousin (female)
die Eltern (pl.) parents
die Familie,-n family
die Großeltern (pl.) grandparents
die Großmutter,∵ (Oma,-s) grandmother (grandma)
der Großvater,∵ (Opa,-s) grandfather (grandpa)
die Mutter,∵ (Mutti,-s) mother (mom)
der Onkel,- uncle
die Schwester,-n sister
der Sohn,∵e son
die Tante,-n aunt
die Tochter,∵ daughter
der Vater,∵ (Vati,-s) father (dad)

Some other Words/Expressions

echt real(ly)
toll great, terrific
zu Hause at home
Komm mit! Come along!

Sie ist zu Hause.

Weißt du das, dass das „das" das meistgebrauchte Wort im Satz ist?

Do you know that "that" is the most used word in the sentence?

Lektion B

Wie viel Uhr ist es?

Es ist eins.
Es ist ein Uhr.

Es ist acht.
Es ist acht Uhr.

Es ist elf. Es ist elf Uhr.

Wie viel Uhr ist es?
Wie spät ist es?

Es ist halb drei.

Es ist halb zehn.

10 zehn **20** zwanzig **30** dreißig **40** vierzig **50** fünfzig

60 sechzig **70** siebzig **80** achtzig **90** neunzig **100** hundert einhundert

1000 tausend eintausend

21 einundzwanzig **22** zweiundzwanzig

Days of the Week

9 ## Wie viel Uhr ist es?

Look at the different clocks and indicate in words what time it is.

10 Wie ist die Telefonnummer von...?

You have been asked to look up several phone numbers.
Read aloud each name and corresponding phone number
as listed.

BEISPIEL You see: *Hannelore
Schuster 12 34 60*
You say: *Hannelore
Schuster, zwölf -
vierunddreißig - sechzig*

1. Toni Schreiber
2. Maria Schiller
3. Andrea Siebert
4. Rita Skaboski
5. Barbara Schlosser
6. Naomi Saber
7. Veronika Sollner
8. Markus Schenker

Naomi Saber	87 02 18
Josef Sähler	22 71 39
Petra Sawatski	93 24 20
Elfriede Schelle	75 10 54
Markus Schenker	37 19 03
Harald Schiermann	83 60 47
Maria Schiller	68 21 49
Claudia Schlafer	31 02 48
Barbara Schlosser	58 84 01
Arthur Schlotrich	95 26 75
Marianne Schnorre	80 39 63
Iwan Schölkl	61 94 08
Rosa Scholtes	29 77 53
Toni Schreiber	48 39 81
Hannelore Schuster	12 34 60
Andrea Siebert	73 88 93
Hanno Sieger	13 87 59
Konstantin Siewanus	52 06 69
Rita Skaboski	97 49 33
Andrea Sölke	26 09 27
Veronika Sollner	48 53 67

11 Um wie viel Uhr...?

Imagine you are in charge of a club event. Various
members of the club ask you questions pertaining to
time. Answer with the appropriate time.

BEISPIEL Um wie viel Uhr kommt Tanja? (sieben Uhr)
Sie kommt um sieben Uhr.

1. Um wie viel Uhr kommt Günter mit? (halb vier)
2. Um wie viel Uhr ist Gabi da? (drei Uhr)
3. Um wie viel Uhr ist deine Freundin zu Hause? (halb zwei)
4. Um wie viel Uhr kommen Gisela und Tina? (halb neun)
5. Um wie viel Uhr ist dein Freund hier? (sechs Uhr)

12 Welcher Tag ist morgen?

BEISPIEL Heute ist Freitag. Und morgen?
Morgen ist Sonnabend.

1. Heute ist Donnerstag. Und morgen?
2. Heute ist Dienstag. Und morgen?
3. Heute ist Samstag. Und morgen?
4. Heute ist Mittwoch. Und morgen?
5. Heute ist Sonntag. Und morgen?

Wie viel Uhr ist es?

Wir kommen rüber

Hast du
heute Zeit?

Wer ist *wir?*

Wir kommen rüber.

(am Telefon)

JULIA:	Julia Strunk.
ALEXANDER:	Hallo, Julia! Hast du heute Zeit?
JULIA:	Um wie viel Uhr?
ALEXANDER:	So gegen sieben. Wir kommen rüber.
JULIA:	Wer ist *wir?*
ALEXANDER:	Thomas und ich. Thomas ist mein Freund.
JULIA:	Na gut. Bis später!

13 Fragen

Beantworte diese Fragen!

1. Wie heißt Alexanders Cousine?
2. Wie alt ist sie?
3. Ist Julia zu Hause?
4. Ist da ein Telefon?
5. Um wie viel Uhr kommen Alexander und Thomas rüber?

14 Wer ist das?

Identify each person. *Diese Person...*

1. ist zu Hause.
2. ist am Telefon.
3. ist Alexanders Freund.
4. kommt mit Thomas zu Julia rüber.
5. ist sechzehn.

Für dich

Hier Weber!

When answering the phone, whether at home or at the office, it is customary in Germany to give one's family name (*Weber!* or *Hier Weber!*). Young people usually answer the phone with their first and last name. For safety reasons, some people tend to answer the phone simply with *Hallo* or with their phone number.

When calling someone you know, you would say *Hier ist...* If you don't know the person, you should start out with *Mein Name ist...*

Germans do not use the A.M./P.M. system for time of day. The traveler will have to become familiar with the 24-hour system in a hurry, particularly when dealing with the official language used on radio and TV or at train stations and airports. The 24-hour system is used primarily to avoid misunderstandings. Numbers 1 to 12 designate the A.M. period of time. Numbers 13 to 24 indicate the P.M. hours. A train leaving at 2:21 P.M., for instance, would be announced as *14.21 (vierzehn Uhr einundzwanzig)*.

In everyday conversation, Germans often use the time expressions *morgens, nachmittags* and *abends* to avoid misunderstanding. For example, Germans might tell their friends that they are coming over at 8 P.M. by saying, *Wir kommen um acht Uhr abends rüber.*

Um wie viel Uhr ist dieses Geschäft am Montag geschlossen? *(closed)*

Um wie viel Uhr kommt die Post?

Sprache

The Definite Article (Nominative Singular): *der, die, das* (the)

In German there are three variations of the definite article "the" in the nominative singular, *der, die* and *das*. The nominative is used to identify the subject.

Der Junge ist siebzehn.	The boy is seventeen.
Die Frau wohnt nicht sehr weit von hier.	The woman doesn't live very far from here.
Das Telefon ist da drüben.	The telephone is over there.

Note that all nouns in German (including names and places) are capitalized. It is extremely important to learn the articles that accompany the individual nouns. We refer to these as masculine *(der)*, feminine *(die)* and neuter *(das)*. Be aware, however, that the nouns associated with either of the three articles are not necessarily "masculine" or "feminine" or "neuter" by context—the article for a man's tie *(die Krawatte)* is feminine, while a woman's scarf *(der Schal)* is masculine.

SINGULAR		
	masculine	feminine	neuter
nominative	der	die	das

15 *der, die* oder *das?*

Indicate the definite article for each noun.

BEISPIEL Uhr
die Uhr

1. Mädchen
2. Junge
3. Frau
4. Ecke
5. Tag
6. Telefon

7. Freund
8. Schwester
9. Tante
10. Cousin
11. Zeit
12. Freundin

Tolle CDs!

Jana wohnt mit ihrer Familie[1] in Cuxhaven. Cuxhaven ist eine Stadt im Norden von Deutschland[2]. Jana hat[3] heute[4] viel Zeit. Was macht sie[5] heute? Vielleicht[6] kommt Carmen, Janas Freundin, mit in die Stadt. Jana ist am Telefon.

Wo wohnt Jana?

Jana: Was machst du denn heute?

Carmen: Ich höre[7] Musik. Und du?

Jana: Ich gehe in die Stadt. Kommst du mit?

Carmen: Es ist schon so spät[8].

Jana: Steffen kommt auch[9] mit.

Carmen: Wohin[10] geht ihr denn?

Jana: Zum Kaufhaus[11]. Wir sind[12] um halb fünf[13] da.

Carmen: Na gut. Ich komme auch zum Kaufhaus.

Jana: Tschüs!

Jana

Carmen

Jana und ihr Stiefbruder[14] Steffen gehen so gegen vier Uhr zum Kaufhaus in die Stadt.

Die Auswahl hier ist sehr groß.

Steffen: Die Auswahl[15] hier ist sehr groß[16].

Jana: Kennst du diese[17] CD?

Steffen: Ja, sie ist ganz neu. Ich habe[18] diese CD schon zu Hause.

Jana: Und die hier?

Steffen: Die ist von der Pastell-Rockgruppe[19]. Wirklich super! Ah, da kommt Carmen!

Und die hier?

[1]*mit ihrer Familie* with her family; [2]*eine Stadt im Norden von Deutschland* a city in the north of Germany; [3]*hat* has; [4]*heute* today; [5]*Was macht sie?* What is she doing?; [6]*vielleicht* perhaps; [7]*hören* to listen to; [8]*schon so spät* already so late; [9]*auch* also; [10]*wohin* where (to); [11]*das Kaufhaus* department store; [12]*wir sind* we are; [13]*um halb fünf* at 4:30; [14]*der Stiefbruder* stepbrother; [15]*die Auswahl* selection; [16]*groß* big, large; [17]*diese* this; [18]*ich habe* I have; [19]*die Rockgruppe* rock group

Für dich

In informal conversations in which a person or an object has been identified and is immediately referred to again, Germans often use the article *der, die* or *das* (Example: *Und die CD hier? Die ist wirklich super!*)

16 Was passt hier? (What matches?)

Complete these sentences by using the appropriate words or phrases listed. Make sure that the completed sentence reflects the content of the *Lesestück*.

1. Jana und Steffen gehen	A. eine Stadt
2. Die Auswahl ist	B. um halb fünf da
3. Cuxhaven ist	C. zum Kaufhaus
4. Carmen hört	D. heute viel Zeit
5. Jana und Steffen sind	E. ganz neu
6. Jana ist	F. Musik
7. Die CD ist	G. groß
8. Jana hat	H. am Telefon

17 Fragen

Beantworte diese Fragen!

1. Wo wohnt Jana?
2. Wer ist Carmen?
3. Was macht Carmen zu Hause?
4. Wohin gehen Carmen und Steffen?
5. Um wie viel Uhr sind sie da?
6. Geht Carmen auch zum Kaufhaus?
7. Wie ist die Auswahl?
8. Kennt Steffen die Pastell-Rockgruppe?

Persönliches

1. Was machst du heute?
2. Um wie viel Uhr machst du das?
3. Wie spät ist es?
4. Wo ist ein Telefon?
5. Wo ist ein Kaufhaus?
6. Welche Musik hörst du gern?

Rollenspiel

Pretend you are calling your friend. Ask if your friend has any CDs. Your friend tells you that he or she has some from a well-known rock group. Your friend asks if you know this rock group. You answer the question and tell your friend that you'll be over at a certain time.

BEISPIEL

Du: Hast du CDs?

Freund: Ja, ich habe CDs von *(name of group)*. Kennst du diese Rockgruppe?

Du: Ja, sehr gut. Ich komme um fünf Uhr rüber.

Freund: Tschau! Bis später!

Kennst du diese Rockgruppe?

Praktisches

Um wie viel Uhr kommt...? Your teacher is organizing an all-day field trip to an amusement park nearby. Not everyone can go at the same time. Form groups of three to five. Write your name and the time that you can go on a piece of paper. Then pass your paper to another student in the group. One student in each group is the recorder and asks each group member, *Um wie viel Uhr kommt (name of person)?* The person holding the paper with that name responds, *(name of person) kommt um...Uhr.* The recorder makes a complete list of names and times and reports the information to the class spokesperson, who writes all the names and times in chronological order on the board or on a transparency.

Schreiben

Meine Familie. Develop your own family tree using the vocabulary from the chapter. Some additional names for relatives you may wish to use are: *der Urgroßvater* (great-grandfather), *die Urgroßmutter* (great-grandmother), *der Neffe* (nephew), *die Nichte* (niece), *der Stiefvater* (stepfather), *die Stiefmutter* (stepmother), *der Stiefbruder* (stepbrother), *die Stiefschwester* (stepsister), *der Halbbruder* (half brother), *die Halbschwester* (half sister).

Wörter und Ausdrücke

Time Expressions

Wie viel Uhr ist es? (Wie spät ist es?)
　What time is it?
Es ist zwei (Uhr). It is two (o'clock).
Es ist halb drei. It is 2:30.
Um wie viel Uhr kommst du rüber?
　At what time are you coming over?
Hast du Zeit? Do you have time?
So gegen sieben. Around seven.
Bis später! See you later!

Days of the Week

Welcher Tag ist heute? Which day is today?
Heute ist... Today is...
Und morgen? And tomorrow?

der Montag Monday
der Dienstag Tuesday
der Mittwoch Wednesday
der Donnerstag Thursday
der Freitag Friday
der Sonnabend (Samstag) Saturday
der Sonntag Sunday

18   Kombiniere...

Kennt	Roland	deine Freundin
Ist	Frau Riebe	sechzehn
Bist	Heidi	toll
Kommt	dein Freund	gegen sieben
	du	zu Hause
		rüber

19   Deine Telefonnummer?

You are meeting several young people from Germany and would like to have their phone numbers. They give you their numbers. Say them in German.

1. 7 13 05
2. 60 24 19
3. 9 03 31 82
4. 12 52 77
5. 3 22 38
6. 5 09 83 11

20   Was fehlt hier?

1. elf, ___, dreizehn, vierzehn, ___ , sechzehn, ___, achtzehn, neunzehn, ___

2. Montag, ___, Mittwoch, ___, Freitag, Sonnabend, ___

3. vier, ___, zwölf, sechzehn, ___, ___ achtundzwanzig, zweiunddreißig, ___, vierzig

Hast du meine Telefonnummer?

21 Wie viel Uhr ist es?

A number of people don't have a watch. They are asking you for the time. Respond to them by using the cues given.

BEISPIEL Wie viel Uhr ist es? (10)
Es ist zehn.

1. Wie viel Uhr ist es? (8)
2. Wie viel Uhr ist es? (12)
3. Wie viel Uhr ist es? (5)

4. Wie viel Uhr ist es? (2)
5. Wie viel Uhr ist es? (9)

22 Grüß dich!

You are meeting Maria, an acquaintance of yours, in the cafeteria after school. Respond to Maria based on the information given.

Maria: Grüß dich!

Du: (1)

Maria: Was machst du hier?

Du: (2)

Maria: Wie spät ist es?

Du: (3)

Maria: Kommst du später rüber?

Du: (4)

Maria: So gegen acht.

Du: (5)

in der Cafeteria

23 Was fehlt hier?

Use one of the words from the list below to complete each sentence of the conversation. Use each word only once.

macht	Zeit	kommt	Wo	Freundin
Ecke	weit	sechzehn	ist	wohnt

1. Wo ___ Rainer?
2. Gleich um die ___.
3. Was ___ er heute?
4. Er ___ zu Hause.
5. Hat Rainer eine ___?

6. Ja, Bianca. Sie ist ___.
7. ___ wohnt Bianca?
8. Nicht ___ von Rainer.
9. Hat Rainer heute ___?
10. Ja. Bianca ___ rüber.

24 Falsch

Your cousin's younger brother has difficulty with simple addition and subtraction problems. You help him solve each problem.

BEISPIEL Drei plus vier ist sechs.
Falsch. Drei plus vier ist sieben.

1. Neun plus drei ist fünf.
2. Zehn minus acht ist null.
3. Zwanzig minus neun ist zehn.
4. Vierzehn plus drei ist dreizehn.
5. Elf plus zwei ist fünfzehn.

Was weißt du?

1. Tell your classmates about four family members or relatives and indicate their names, their ages and where they live.

2. Write down four times of the day and tell what happens at that time. Working in pairs, take turns pointing to each activity on one another's list and identify the time. Sample activities could be: getting up (6:30), breakfast (7:00), beginning of school (8:00), etc. Use only full or half-hours on your list.

3. Write down several names and their respective phone numbers. The names and phone numbers can be your own, your relatives', your friends', etc. Exchange your list with a classmate. Ask each other questions such as: *Wer ist das? Was ist Onkel Herberts Telefonnummer?* Respond accordingly.

4. Describe where you live, who else lives there and what times you are usually at home.

5. Describe some of the differences in making phone calls on a public telephone in this country and in Germany. *(Auf Englisch.)*

6. Count in fives from 0 to 100.

7. Say in German
   A. how old your friend is.
   B. where he or she lives.
   C. that your friend's brother or sister is terrific.
   D. that you will come over at a certain time.

Vokabeln

an (am) at, on; *am Telefon* on the telephone 2B
auch also, too 2B
die **Auswahl** selection, choice 2B
bis until; *Bis später!* See you later! 2B
der **Bruder,** ̈ brother 2A
die **CD,-s** CD 2B
der **Cousin,-s** cousin (male) 2B
die **Cousine,-n** cousin (female) 2A
das the 2B
dein(e) your 2A
denn (used for emphasis) 2A
der the 2B
Deutschland Germany 2B
die the 2B
der **Dienstag,-e** Tuesday 2B
dies,- this 2B
der **Donnerstag,-e** Thursday 2B
echt real(ly) 2A
die **Eltern** (pl.) parents 2A
die **Familie,-n** family 2A
der **Freitag,-e** Friday 2B
gegen about, around; *so gegen sieben* around seven (o'clock) 2B
groß large, big 2B
die **Großeltern** (pl.) grandparents 2A
die **Großmutter,** ̈ grandmother 2A
der **Großvater,** ̈ grandfather 2A
haben: ich habe I have 2B
halb half; *um halb fünf* at 4:30 2B
hast: Hast du...? Do you have...? 2B
hat: sie hat she has 2B
Hause: zu Hause at home 2A
heute today 2B
hören to hear, listen to 2B
ihr her; *mit ihrer Familie* with her family 2B
in in; *im Norden* in the north 2B
das **Kaufhaus,** ̈**er** department store 2B
machen to do, make; *Was machst du?* What are you doing? 2B
mit with 2B
mitkommen to come along; *Komm mit!* Come along! 2A

der **Mittwoch,-e** Wednesday 2B
der **Montag,-e** Monday 2B
morgen tomorrow 2B
die **Musik** music 2B
die **Mutter,** ̈ mother 2A
die **Mutti,-s** mom 2A
na well; *na gut* oh well 2B
der **Norden** north; *im Norden* in the north 2B
die **Oma,-s** grandma 2A
der **Onkel,-** uncle 2A
Opa,-s grandpa 2A
die **Rockgruppe,-n** rock group 2B
rüberkommen to come over 2B
der **Samstag,-e** Saturday 2B
schon already 2B
die **Schwester,-n** sister 2A
sind: wir sind we are 2A
so so; *so spät* so late 2B
der **Sohn,** ̈**e** son 2A
der **Sonnabend,-e** Saturday 2B
der **Sonntag,-e** Sunday 2B
spät late; *Bis später!* See you later! 2B

die **Stadt,** ̈**e** city; *in die Stadt gehen* to go downtown 2B
der **Stiefbruder,** ̈ stepbrother 2B
super super 2B
die **Tante,-n** aunt 2A
das **Telefon,-e** telephone 2A
die **Tochter,** ̈ daughter 2A
toll great, terrific 2A
die **Uhr,-en** clock, watch; *Um wie viel Uhr?* At what time?; *Es ist zwei Uhr.* It's two o'clock. 2B
um at; *Um wie viel Uhr?* At what time?
der **Vater,** ̈ father 2A
der **Vati,-s** dad 2A
vielleicht perhaps 2B
was what 2B
welch,- which 2B
wohin where (to) 2B
die **Zeit,-en** time 2B
zu at, to; *zu Hause* at home 2A; *zum Kaufhaus gehen* to go to the department store 2B

in der Stadt
(Berlin)

Die Auswahl
ist gut.

Kapitel 3
Was machst du?

Fußweg zur Burg Rheinstein

500 m

Objectives

In this chapter you will learn how to:

► ask and tell what someone is doing
► talk about what interests you
► express likes and dislikes
► inquire about times of specific events
► report information

Lektion A

Vokabeln

Was machst du gern?

1 Was machen diese Personen gern?

1. Bianca   **2.** Rolf und Jürgen   **3.** meine Freundin und ich

4. Dieter   **5.** Herr und Frau Köhler   **6.** Herr Schulz

2 Was machst du diese Woche? (What are you doing this week?)

Your friend wants to get together with you this week. Unfortunately, you are busy with various activities. Tell your friend what you are doing each day.

BEISPIEL   Ich spiele am Montag Fußball.

Montag	Dienstag	Mittwoch	Donnerstag	Freitag	Samstag	Sonntag
11	12	13	14	15	16	17

3 Was machst du gern?

You and your classmate make a list of various activities. Then ask each other whether or not you like to do each activity. Write *ja* if your response is positive and *nein* if it is negative.

BEISPIEL A: Spielst du gern Tennis?
B: Ich spiele nicht gern Tennis, aber ich spiele gern Fußball.

Dialog

Holen wir ein Video!

Was machen Sarah und Tobias in der Videothek?

Kennt Sarah *Die Blechtrommel?*

Sarah und Tobias gehen zur Videothek. Dort ist die Auswahl an Videos sehr groß.

SARAH: Was für ein Video holst du denn?

TOBIAS: In Deutsch lesen wir Günter Grass. Kennst du *Die Blechtrommel?*

SARAH: Ja, das Buch ist sehr bekannt und interessant.

TOBIAS: Es gibt auch ein Video.

SARAH: Oh ja. Hier ist es. Ich möchte es gern sehen.

TOBIAS: Komm doch mit mir nach Hause!

SARAH: Nicht jetzt. Ich komme etwas später.

TOBIAS: Aber nicht zu spät. Der Film dauert zwei Stunden.

4 Falsch

The following statements are incorrect. Provide the correct statements in German.

1. Sarah und Tobias gehen nach Hause.
2. Tobias holt ein Buch.
3. Sarah möchte *Die Blechtrommel* lesen.
4. Sarah geht jetzt mit Tobias nach Hause.
5. Das Video dauert drei Stunden.

5 Wie fragt man? (How do you ask?)

Read the following questions in English. Then ask the same questions in German. Your classmate will respond in German.

1. Where are you going?
2. How is the video selection there?
3. What kind of video are you getting?
4. Do you know *(name of video)*?
5. Is your book interesting?
6. Does the film take three hours?
7. How long is it?

Für dich

Günter Grass wrote the bestseller novel *Die Blechtrommel (The Tin Drum)* for which he received the Nobel Prize in literature. In 1979, Volker Schlöndorff, producer of the film, received a major award at the Cannes Film Festival for his adaptation of Grass' book. In 1980, *The Tin Drum* won an Oscar for the best foreign film.

Present Tense of *haben*

You have already seen a few forms of *haben* (to have) in the context of a dialog and a reading selection. The following are all the forms of the present tense of *haben* that you will need to learn. Note that these forms are irregular and do not follow the pattern of regular verb forms such as *gehen* and *kommen* that you have learned.

SINGULAR		
ich habe		I have
du hast		you have
er		he has
sie	**hat**	she has
es		it has

PLURAL	
wir haben	we have
ihr habt	you have
sie haben	they have
Sie haben	you have
(sg. & pl.)	

Hast du Zeit?	Do you have time?
Ja, ich habe Zeit.	Yes, I have time.
Habt ihr einen Computer zu Hause?	Do you have a computer at home?
Ja, wir haben einen Computer.	Yes, we have a computer.

6 Ich auch.

You are agreeing with your friend on several issues.

BEISPIEL Ich habe einen Computer? Und du?
Ich habe auch einen Computer.

1. Ich habe Zeit. Und du?
2. Ich habe CDs. Und du?
3. Ich habe eine Freundin. Und du?
4. Ich habe ein Computerspiel. Und du?
5. Ich habe ein Buch. Und du?
6. Ich habe ein Video. Und du?

7 Wer hat heute Zeit?

You are inquiring who has some time today. Luckily, everyone does.

> **BEISPIEL** Hat Natascha heute Zeit?
> Ja, sie hat heute Zeit.

1. Hast du heute Zeit?
2. Habt ihr heute Zeit?
3. Haben Herr und Frau Bilski heute Zeit?
4. Hat Frau Wiedemann heute Zeit?
5. Haben Sabine und Udo heute Zeit?
6. Hat Bruno heute Zeit?

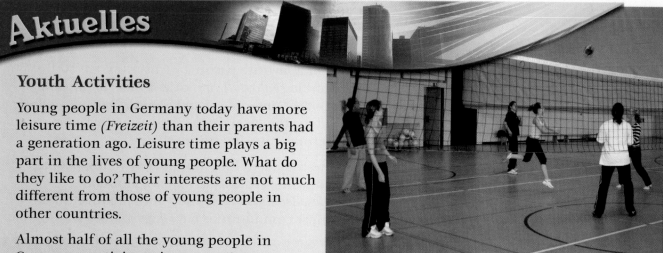

Aktuelles

Youth Activities

Young people in Germany today have more leisure time *(Freizeit)* than their parents had a generation ago. Leisure time plays a big part in the lives of young people. What do they like to do? Their interests are not much different from those of young people in other countries.

Almost half of all the young people in Germany participate in sports *(Sport)*, ranging from organized sports sponsored by local clubs to neighborhood get-togethers. Soccer clubs *(Fußballklubs)* are the most popular.

Sie spielen gern Volleyball.

Was machen sie gern?

Was ist so interessant?

Jugendliche sehen gern fern.

Many young people enjoy hanging around and talking to friends about such things as which fashion designers are "in" and all the things they can't afford on a monthly allowance *(Taschengeld)* which most of them receive from their parents.

Television *(Fernsehen)* occupies a tremendous amount of their time as do the Internet, DVD players *(DVD-Spieler)*, CD players *(CD-Spieler)* as well as other electronic devices such as iPods and MP3 players. Most Germans have a computer *(Computer)* at home which is used not only for family business transactions, but also for playing the many computer games *(Computerspiele)* now available for young and old alike.

Going to the movies is still a favorite pastime *(Zeitvertreib)* as well as cruising around by bicycle *(Fahrrad)*, motorized bicycle *(Mofa* or *Motorfahrrad)*, motor scooter *(Motorroller)* and *Moped*. On weekends, many young people head for the local discos *(Diskos* or *Diskotheken)* that can be found in every German city and town.

There is no lack of leisure-time activities available to young people, offered by the local communities *(Gemeinschaften)*, churches *(Kirchen)*, social clubs *(Gesellschaftsklubs)* and youth organizations *(Jugendorganisationen)*. Most communities have *Jugendklubs* where

Sie spielen gern Computerspiele.

young people go, meet their friends and hang around. The numerous sports facilities, hobby centers, libraries, continuing education courses, trips and youth exchange programs offer young people in Germany many choices on how to spend their free time.

German teenagers have hobbies (Hobbys) too. Besides sports, the most popular hobbies are photography (Fotografie), music (Musik) and travel (Reisen). When young people travel, they sometimes share a ride in a car or use youth discounts on public transportation. Others travel by bicycle or hike. They may camp or stay overnight in one of the approximately 700 youth hostels located throughout Germany.

Sie gehen gern auf Reisen.

Er fotografiert gern.

Sie fahren oft mit dem Fahrrad.

8 Was passt hier?

Complete the sentences using the words listed.

1. Many young people like to join ___.
2. When showing a video, you'll need a ___.
3. The most popular clubs are the ___.
4. The word ___ suggests a German's favorite activity in visiting other parts of the country.
5. More than 50 percent of all Germans own a ___.
6. A bike with an attached motor is called a ___.
7. Just as in this country, many Germans like to watch ___.
8. Similar to American teenagers, German teenagers have ___, like photography and sports.
9. Young Germans enjoy more ___ than their parents.
10. Young Germans like to go to their local ___ on weekends.
11. A two-wheel vehicle without a motor is called a ___.
12. Most parents give their children ___ for spending money.

A. *Fernsehen*

B. *Hobbys*

C. *Diskos*

D. *Mofa*

E. *Taschengeld*

F. *Freizeit*

G. *DVD-Spieler*

H. *Jugendorganisationen*

I. *Reisen*

J. *Fahrrad*

K. *Computer*

L. *Fußballklubs*

Er spielt bei einem Fußballklub.

Was für ein Hobby haben sie?

Word Order

As you have seen so far, you can form a sentence in German by starting with the subject followed by the verb and then adding more information.

Wir lesen ein Buch von Günter Grass.	We're reading a book by Günter Grass.
Ich mache meine Hausaufgaben später.	I'll do my homework later.

As discussed in the previous chapter, you must use the inverted word order to form questions.

Gehst du nach Hause?	Are you going home?
Was machst du heute?	What are you doing today?

The inverted word order is also used when you start a sentence with words other than the subject of the sentence.

Heute sehe ich fern.	Today I'll watch TV.
Um halb vier spielen wir Fußball.	At half past three we'll play soccer.

9 Was machen sie?

Tell what everyone is doing at the time indicated. Start your sentence with the time and use the inverted word order.

 wir
Um zehn Minuten nach sechs lesen wir ein Buch.

1. Barbara

2. Herr und Frau Taube

3. Viktor

4. Rainer und Maria

5. Petra und Julia

Persönliches

1. Was möchtest du morgen machen?
2. Was ist so interessant?
3. Was für ein Video möchtest du sehen?
4. Hast du einen Computer zu Hause?
5. Um wie viel Uhr möchtest du fernsehen?
6. Kommt dein Freund oder deine Freundin rüber?

Rollenspiel

You and your friend discuss what you would like to do today. In your conversation include such items as (1) what activity it is, (2) where it will take place and (3) what time you'll get together.

BEISPIEL

Du:	Was machst du heute?
Freund/Freundin:	Vielleicht sehe ich fern.
Du:	Zu Hause?
Freund/Freundin:	Nein, ich gehe zu *(name of person)*.
Du:	Um wie viel Uhr?
Freund/Freundin:	So gegen sieben. Kommst du?
Du:	Ja, ich komme rüber.

Was ist so interessant?

Was macht sie gern?

What one Likes to Do

Ich spiele gern... I like to play...
  Tennis tennis
  Fußball soccer
  Basketball basketball
  Gitarre guitar
  Klavier piano
  Karten cards

Ich sehe gern fern. I like to watch TV.
Ich lese gern. I like to read.
Ich höre gern Musik. I like to listen to music.
Ich schwimme gern. I like to swim.
Ich tanze gern. I like to dance.
Ich spiele gern Computerspiele. I like to play computer games.
Ich gehe gern in die Disko. I like to go to the disco.

Other Expressions

Was für ein Video holst du? What kind of video are you getting?
Wie ist das Buch? How is the book?
Es ist bekannt und interessant. It is well known and interesting.
Es gibt... There is (are)...
Komm doch mit mir nach Hause! Why don't you come home with me.
Jetzt nicht. Not now.
Der Film dauert zwei Stunden. The film lasts two hours.

Sie spielen Karten.

Zungenbrecher

Vier fünfmal vervierfacht macht mehr als fünf viermal verfünffacht.

Four multiplied by four five times is more than five multiplied by five four times.

Lektion B

Wie viel Uhr ist es?

vor   nach

Wie viel Uhr ist es?
(Wie spät ist es?)

Es ist Viertel nach eins.

Es ist Viertel vor zehn.

Es ist fünf Minuten nach zwölf.

Es ist acht Minuten vor vier.

Was gibt's heute im Fernsehen?

Um 15.10 Uhr (Um fünfzehn Uhr zehn) gibt es einen Krimi. Um 17.00 Uhr gibt es eine Sportschau. Um 20.00 Uhr kommen die Nachrichten.

Wann beginnt das Fernsehprogramm?

Es beginnt um 19 Uhr 35 (neunzehn Uhr fünfunddreißig).

heute Morgen   heute Mittag   heute Nachmittag   heute Abend

10 Was gibt's im Fernsehen?

Look at the TV schedule and tell what is being shown at the time indicated. (Note: *In der ARD... Im ZDF...*)

BEISPIEL 17.30
In der ARD gibt es um siebzehn Uhr dreißig ein Fernsehprogramm. Sie heißt „Sportschau".

1. 8.55
2. 20.00
3. 22.35
4. 14.45
5. 9.30
6. 19.50
7. 11.45
8. 23.10

ARD

6.00 Kinderprogramm 8.30 ☺ Die Pfefferkörner (1/13) 9.03 Tom, Jerry & Co. 9.30 ★ ☺ Nikolaus geht durch die Stadt. Jugendfilm (Tschechien 1992) 11.30 Isnogud 11.45 ☺ Schloss Einstein 12.10 ☺ fabrixx 12.35 ☺ Tigerenten-Club. Kindermagazin 14.03 höchstpersönlich. Maria Ketikidou, Schauspielerin 14.30 ☺ Kinderquatsch mit Michael. Show

15.00 Tagesschau 15.05 ★ Immer Ärger mit Hochwürden. Komödie (D 1972). Mit Georg Thomalla 16.35 Europamagazin. U.a.: wie sich Schweden BSE-frei hält 17.03 Ratgeber: Reise 17.30 ○ Sportschau

18.00 Tagesschau
18.10 ▧ Brisant
Boulevard-Magazin
18.45 ☺▧ Dr. Sommerfeld –
Neues vom Bülowbogen
Arztserie
19.50 ☺ Lottozahlen
20.00 ▧ Tagesschau
20.15 ☺ Die Lotto-Show
Unterhaltung
Mit Ulla Kock am Brink
Im Showteil: André Rieu,
Hape Kerkeling
22.15 Tagesthemen
22.35 ▧ Wort zum Sonntag
Mit Oda-Gebbine
Holze-Stäblein, Burgdorf
22.40 ★ Das dreckige Dutzend
Kriegsfilm (USA/Spanien/
Großbritannien 1966)
Mit Lee Marvin

ZDF

6.00 Kinderprogramm 8.55 Die Biene Maja 9.20 Löwenzahn 9.45 Tabaluga-Tivi 10.50 ○ Sport extra. Biathlon: 4 x 7,5-km-Staffel Damen, Antholz; Rodeln: Einsitzer Damen, Oberhof; Ski: Nordische Kombination, Kuopio; Zweierbob Weltcup, Altenberg 13.30 heute 13.35 Top 7. Magazin 14.00 Weißblaue Wintergeschichten. Serie 14.45 Ich heirate eine Familie. Serie

15.35 mach mit. Aktion „Mensch aktuell" und Gewinner der Aktion-Mensch-Lotterie 15.45 ○ Skispringen. Weltcup: Großschanze, Kuopio (Finnland) 18.00 Freunde fürs Leben. Arztserie

19.00 heute
19.25 ☺ V.I.P. Star-Magazin
Mit Nina Ruge
Beiträge über Werner
Baldessarini, Til Schweiger,
Sasha, Virginie Taittinger
20.15 ☺ Lachen tut gut
Comedy-Gala für Unicef
Mitwirkende: Anke Engelke,
Erkan und Stefan, Michael
Mittermeier, Sissi Perlinger,
Dieter Hallervorden, Atze
Schröder, Esther Schweins,
Helge Schneider u.a.
22.00 heute-journal
22.15 ○ Sportstudio
Fußball: Auslosung
DFB-Pokal, Viertelfinale
23.10 ★ Planet der Affen
Science-Fiction-Film
(USA 1967)

11 Wann?

Indicate when these various activities take place. Do they take place *heute Morgen, heute Mittag, heute Nachmittag* or *heute Abend?* The times are given using the 24-hour system.

BEISPIEL Der Krimi beginnt um 21.30 Uhr.
Heute Abend.

1. Die Sportschau kommt um 19.30 Uhr.
2. Ich bin um 7.30 zu Hause.
3. Meine Tante kommt um 12.00 Uhr.
4. Um 9.00 Uhr spielen wir Tennis.
5. Wir gehen um 20.00 Uhr zur Disko.
6. Die Nachrichten beginnen um 18.00 Uhr.
7. Der Film beginnt um 14.10 Uhr.

Dialog

Wohin gehst du?

Wohin geht Dirk?

Zuerst mache ich die Hausaufgaben.

Und was machst du?

JAN: Wohin gehst du so schnell?

DIRK: Nach Hause. Ich habe einen Computer. Der ist ganz neu.

JAN: Na und?

DIRK: Ich spiele mit Ilona Computerspiele. Und was machst du?

JAN: Zuerst mache ich die Hausaufgaben. Dann spielen Peter und ich Tennis. Am Abend sehen wir fern.

DIRK: Viel Spaß!

12 Fragen

Beantworte diese Fragen!

1. Wohin geht Dirk?
2. Wie geht Dirk?
3. Was hat Dirk jetzt zu Hause?
4. Wer spielt mit Dirk Computerspiele?
5. Was macht Jan zuerst?
6. Und was machen Jan und Peter später?

13 Was passt hier?

Select one of the words from the list to complete the dialog.

kommt	du	später	Videos	Buch
nicht	Film	es	wir	lest

A: Was (1) ihr?

B: Ein (2).

A: Ist (3) interessant?

B: Nein, (4) sehr.

A: Warum (5) ihr nicht rüber?

B: Was machen (6) denn da?

A: Wir sehen einen (7).

B: Hast (8) denn ein Video?

A: Ich habe zwei (9).

B: Gut, bis (10)!

Holen sie ein Video?

Für dich

In informal conversation in which a person or object has been identified and is immediately referred to again, Germans often use the article *der, die* or *das* without the respective name or object. (Example: *Ich habe einen Computer. Der ist ganz neu.*)

The German television system is considerably different from the American system. The two major networks (*ARD* and *ZDF*) carry a high proportion of documentaries, news magazines, talk shows, cultural programs and commentaries. On the other hand, the new private channels allow a relatively broad latitude in programming compared with *ARD* and *ZDF*, although the television market is more restricted by regulations in comparison to American television. The two state-owned channels *ARD* and *ZDF* are not allowed to show commercials after 8 p.m.

Even though there is some advertising on German TV, generally packed into several short broadcasts at the beginning of the evening programs, the main source of income is the monthly operating license fee which each radio and television set owner pays. In recent years, several commercial TV channels (cable and satellite) have been introduced in Germany to offer viewers more diverse programming. The commercial stations do not share in the license fee and, therefore, show more commercials than public stations. It is also noteworthy that TV programs do not necessarily start at half past the hour or on the hour.

Sprache

zu Hause and *nach Hause*

There is a distinct difference in using these two phrases. *Zu Hause* means "at home" (location), whereas *nach Hause* implies "(going) home" (motion).

Wo ist Heidi?	Where is Heidi?
Sie ist zu Hause.	She is at home.
Wohin geht Uwe?	Where is Uwe going?
Er geht nach Hause.	He is going home.

14 *zu Hause* oder *nach Hause?*

State whether the various people are at home *(zu Hause)* or are going home *(nach Hause)*.

1. Um wie viel Uhr gehen Tanja und Silke___?
2. Werner ist nicht ___.
3. Hast du Videos ___?
4. Maria kommt spät ___.
5. Herr Braun ist am Abend ___.
6. Ich möchte jetzt ___ gehen.

Wer geht zum Rockkonzert?

Sonja und Claudia wohnen in Wilhelmshaven. Wilhelmshaven ist eine Stadt in Norddeutschland. Beide[1] Mädchen kommen aus dem Kaufhaus. Da sehen sie Heiko und Marco. Sie kennen die zwei Jungen aus der Schule[2].

Karstadt ist ein großes Kaufhaus.

Heiko:	Hallo! Was macht ihr denn hier?
Sonja:	Heute Nachmittag haben wir viel Zeit. Jetzt gehen wir aber nach Hause.
Claudia:	Wie gefällt dir[3] diese CD?
Heiko:	Toll! Ich kenne diese Hits sehr gut.
Marco:	Ja, am Sonnabend und am Sonntag spielt die Band hier in Wilhelmshaven. Für[4] das Rockkonzert gibt es aber keine Karten mehr[5].
Claudia:	So? Wir haben schon zwei Karten. Hier!
Marco:	Wir haben auch Karten.
Sonja:	Warum[6] gehen wir nicht zusammen[7]?
Heiko:	Das ist ein Problem. Diese Karten sind[8] für Sonntag. Wir gehen aber am Sonnabend.

Sonja und Claudia kommen aus dem Kaufhaus.

Hallo! Was macht ihr denn hier?

Heiko kennt diese Hits sehr gut.

Was für eine Idee hat Sonja?

Claudia: Und wohin geht ihr jetzt?

Marco: Zum Bahnhof[9]. Mein Cousin kommt aus Dresden. Er bleibt zwei Wochen bei uns[10]. Sonja, du kennst doch Tilo. Er ist immer[11] im Sommer hier.

Sonja: Ach ja! Er ist sehr nett und charmant[12].

Heiko: Das sagt er auch von dir[13].

Sonja: Ich habe eine Idee. Warum gehe ich nicht mit Tilo am Sonntag zum Rockkonzert. Und du, Claudia, gehst mit Heiko und Marco am Sonnabend.

Claudia: Moment mal![14] Das geht nicht.[15] Am Sonnabend habe ich keine Zeit. Ich muss meiner Schwester bei den Hausaufgaben helfen[16].

Sonja: Kein Problem! Ich mache mit deiner Schwester die Hausaufgaben.

Claudia: Du bist aber ein Schlauberger[17]!

---

[1]*beide* both; [2]*aus der Schule* from school; [3]*Wie gefällt dir...?* How do you like...?; [4]*für* for; [5]*es gibt keine Karten mehr* there are no tickets available any more; [6]*warum* why; [7]*zusammen* together; [8]*sind* are; [9]*der Bahnhof* (train) station; [10]*Er bleibt zwei Wochen bei uns.* He is staying two weeks with us.; [11]*immer* always; [12]*charmant* charming; [13]*sagt...von dir* says about you; [14]*Moment mal!* Just a moment!; [15]*Das geht nicht.* That's not possible; [16]*muss...bei den Hausaufgaben helfen* have to help...with homework; [17]*der Schlauberger* smartie

15 Was fehlt hier?

1. Wilhelmshaven ist eine ___ in Norddeutschland.
2. Claudia und Sonja kommen ___ dem Kaufhaus.
3. Die zwei Mädchen kennen Heiko und Marco aus der ___.
4. Sonja und Claudia gehen ___ Hause.
5. Es gibt keine ___ mehr für das Rockkonzert.
6. Claudia und Sonja haben ___ zwei Karten.
7. Heikos Karten sind für ___.
8. Marco und Heiko gehen jetzt zum ___.
9. Tilo kommt immer im ___ nach Wilhelmshaven.
10. Sonja hat eine ___.
11. Claudia hat ___ Sonnabend keine Zeit.
12. Sonja ist ein ___.

16 Fragen

Beantworte diese Fragen!

1. Wo wohnen Claudia und Sonja?
2. Woher kommen die zwei Mädchen?
3. Wohin gehen Sonja und Claudia jetzt?
4. Wer spielt am Sonnabend und am Sonntag?
5. Gibt es für das Rockkonzert Karten?
6. Sind Sonjas Karten für Sonnabend?
7. Wer kommt heute aus Dresden?
8. Wann kommt er immer?
9. Wie ist Tilo?
10. Wann macht Sonja die Hausaufgaben mit Claudias Schwester?

Sind Sonjas Karten für Sonnabend?

Persönliches

1. Welches Fernsehprogramm hast du gern? Warum?
2. An welchem Tag und um wie viel Uhr ist dieses Fernsehprogramm?
3. Was machst du gern am Nachmittag? Was machst du nicht gern?
4. Spielst du gern Computerspiele?
5. Um wie viel Uhr kommst du in der Woche nach Hause?
6. Hast du oft Hausaufgaben? Wann machst du sie?

Rollenspiel

Um wie viel Uhr...? Write down three to five questions dealing with the time of day and pass them to another classmate who will answer them. Your questions could include topics such as asking the time for going home, meeting with other friends, participating in activities, watching TV, reading a book, listening to music, etc.

> **BEISPIEL** *Um wie viel Uhr machst du deine Hausaufgaben?*
>
> *Um wie viel Uhr spielst du Fußball?*
>
> *Um wie viel Uhr gehst du nach Hause?*

Praktisches

Was machst du gern? Was machst du nicht gern? Form groups of three to find out what each of you likes or doesn't like to do.

Student 1 makes a list under the heading *Was ich gern mache.*

Student 2 makes a list under the heading *Was ich nicht gern mache.*

Student 3 makes two lists: one under the heading *Was ich gern mache;* the other under the heading *Was ich nicht gern mache.*

Student 3 also serves as the group's recorder. To begin, Student 3 asks Student 1 what activities he or she likes. If Student 1 likes the same activity as Student 3, Student 3 makes a check mark beside the name of that activity on the appropriate sheet. Then Student 3 asks Student 2 the same questions. If Student 3 finds that Student 2 dislikes the same activity, Student 3 makes a check mark beside the name of that activity on the appropriate sheet. After Students 1 and 2 have reported all their likes and dislikes to Student 3, Student 3 may tell the entire class what likes and dislikes all group members share.

Schreiben

You and your classmate each list the activities you are planning for the next week. Make one weekly calendar including the days and times. Then write down all the activities you each listed, with your names next to the activity. Discuss the upcoming activities, asking and answering questions.

Er macht die Hausaufgaben.

Wörter und Ausdrücke

Additional Time Expressions

Es ist Viertel nach eins. It's a quarter after one.
Es ist Viertel vor zehn. It's a quarter to ten.
Was gibt's im Fernsehen? What is there on TV?
Um 15.30 Uhr gibt es... At 3:30 P.M. there is...
    einen Krimi a detective story
    eine Sportschau a sports show
    die Nachrichten the news

Wann beginnt das Fernsehprogramm? When does the TV program begin?
    Um 19 Uhr 35. At 7:35 P.M.
    heute Morgen this morning
    heute Mittag today at noon
    heute Nachmittag this afternoon
    heute Abend this evening
    am Abend in the evening

Other Expressions

Wohin gehst du so schnell? Where are you going so fast?
Nach Hause. Home.
Ich mache die Hausaufgaben. I'm doing homework.
Viel Spaß! Have fun!

17 Kombiniere...

Daniel	haben	drei Karten
Katarina	spiele	CDs
Claudia und Renate	hört	Zeit
Ich	hat	einen Computer
	holen	Tennis

18 Was fehlt hier?

From the list below, select the appropriate words to complete the various conversational exchanges.

meine	viel	aus	ganz	ist	zwei	sechzehn	nach

1. Woher kommst du?

   Ich komme ___ Düsseldorf.

2. Wie alt bist du?

   Ich bin ___.

3. Kennst du Uwe?

   Ja, er ___ Petras Freund.

4. Kommst du am Mittwoch rüber?

   Nein, am Mittwoch habe ich nicht ___ Zeit.

5. Was machst du jetzt?

   Ich gehe ___ Hause. Und du?

6. Ich hole Julia ___ Videos.

   Wer ist denn Julia?

7. Das ist ___ Freundin. Kennst du sie?

   Nein.

8. Sie ist ___ toll.

   Na dann, bis später.

19 Was passt hier?

Choose the most logical response to each question.

1. Wie viel Uhr ist es denn?
2. Hast du Videos?
3. Habt ihr Karten für das Rockkonzert?
4. Was gibt's heute Abend im Fernsehen?
5. Spielst du Computerspiele?
6. Wohnst du im Norden?
7. Hat dein Bruder einen Computer?
8. Warum gehst du jetzt schon nach Hause?
9. Woher kommt Tilo?
10. Wann beginnt das Fernsehprogramm?

A. Ja, in Hamburg.
B. Einen Krimi.
C. Aus Dresden.
D. Nein, es gibt keine Karten mehr.
E. Um 20 Uhr 15.
F. Mein Onkel aus Köln ist da.
G. Es ist jetzt Viertel vor drei.
H. Nein, heute nicht.
I. Ja, ich habe zehn.
J. Nein, aber meine Schwester.

20 Was fehlt hier?

Complete the paragraph choosing the appropriate forms from these verbs: *kommen, haben, heißen, wohnen, tanzen, spielen, hören, sein.*

Susanne __(1)__ in Flensburg. Flensburg __(2)__ im Norden von Deutschland. Susanne __(3)__ einen Bruder. Er __(4)__ Rainer. Rainer und Susanne __(5)__ gern Klavier. Heute __(6)__ Susannes Freundin Monika rüber. Susanne und Monika __(7)__ gern CDs. Am Freitag, so gegen 21 Uhr, __(8)__ sie gern in einer Disko.

21 Wann? Was? Wie? Wo? Woher? Wohin?

Complete each sentence using the appropriate question word.

1. ___ kommt Dieter? Aus Heidelberg.
2. ___ machst du jetzt?
3. ___ geht ihr denn? Nach Hause.
4. ___ alt ist Katarina? Schon siebzehn.
5. ___ spielen wir Fußball? Um halb drei.
6. ___ liegt Bremen?

22 Wer ist...?

Look at the family tree and determine who is described.

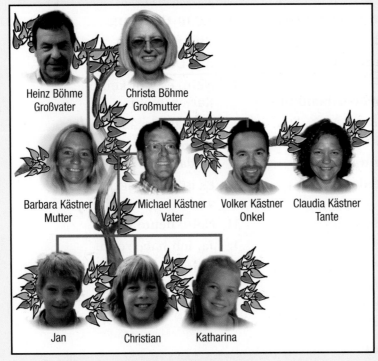

Heinz Böhme
Großvater

Christa Böhme
Großmutter

Barbara Kästner
Mutter

Michael Kästner
Vater

Volker Kästner
Onkel

Claudia Kästner
Tante

Jan

Christian

Katharina

1. Er ist Jans Bruder.
2. Sie sind Christians Eltern.
3. Sie ist Heinz Böhmes Tochter.
4. Sie ist Christians Schwester.
5. Sie sind Katharinas Großeltern.
6. Er ist Michaels Bruder.
7. Sie ist Katharinas Tante.
8. Er ist Barbaras Vater.

23 Wie viel Uhr ist es?

Tell the time of each clock.

1.

2.

3.

4.

5.

6.

24 Kennst du das Mädchen?

You are talking to your friend and are trying to find out more about a girl in your class. Complete the following dialog using the correct forms of the verbs provided.

Du: Wie (heißen) (1) sie?

Freund: Karin. Sie (wohnen) (2) gleich um die Ecke.

Du: (Kennen) (3) du sie?

Freund: Nicht sehr gut. Sie (haben) (4) einen Bruder und eine Schwester.

Du: Wie (heißen) (5) sie?

Freund: Uwe und Maria. Uwe (spielen) (6) Tennis und Maria (tanzen) (7) gern. Hallo, Karin!

Karin: Hallo! Was (machen) (8) du jetzt?

Freund: Wir (gehen) (9) nach Hause. Oh, das ist mein Freund.

Karin: Tag! Ich (haben) (10) heute viel Zeit. Ich (möchten) (11) in die Stadt gehen. (Kommen) (12) du mit?

Freund: Nein.

Du: Ich (gehen) (13) auch in die Stadt, zum Kaufhaus. Ich (lesen) (14) ein Buch.

Karin: Dann (gehen) (15) wir zwei.

Du: Gut.

25 Gisela in Augsburg

Gisela has moved from Lübeck to Augsburg. Read her letter to her friend Natascha and answer the questions on page 86.

Grüß Gott, Natascha!

Das sagen sie hier und nicht „Tag!" Die Stadt Augsburg ist super. Meine Eltern, mein Bruder Peter und ich wohnen hier in der Stadt nicht weit vom Bahnhof. Zur Schule gehe ich fünfzehn Minuten. Meine Freundin Sarah wohnt gleich um die Ecke. Heute am Samstag (hier sagen sie nicht „Sonnabend") kommt Sarah rüber. Dann hören wir CDs, spielen Karten und gehen um acht zur Disko. Und wie geht's dir? Wie geht's deinem Freund Michael? Spielt er jetzt nicht Gitarre in einer Rockgruppe? Es ist jetzt halb elf. Ich gehe gleich zum Kaufhaus. Da kaufe ich ein Computerspiel. Tschüs!

Deine Gisela

Beantworte diese Fragen!

1. Sagen sie „Tag!" in Augsburg?
2. Wie ist Augsburg?
3. Wo wohnt Gisela in Augsburg?
4. Wie weit ist es zur Schule?
5. Wer ist Giselas Freundin?
6. Was machen Gisela und ihre Freundin am Samstag?
7. Wie heißt Nataschas Freund?
8. Wohin geht Gisela?

Was weißt du?

1. *Am Sonnabend gehen wir zum Rockkonzert.* Develop a conversation with a classmate in which you discuss a rock concert that both of you would like to attend. Your conversation may include such items as the time and place of the concert, where you can buy tickets, the names of others who might come along and at what time you have to be home.

2. *Was gibt's im Fernsehen?* Everyone in your class writes down the names of five TV programs (including the days and times) they would like to watch during the week. Ask one of your classmates at least two questions about each TV program and then reverse roles. You might ask such questions as: *Was gibt's am Sonntag im Fernsehen? Um wie viel Uhr beginnt das Fernsehprogramm? Wie ist es?*

3. Describe what you like to do after school or on the weekend.

4. Point out three activities that you do that Germans your age do not. *Auf Englisch!*

5. Make a calendar for the week indicating at least four different activities you will be doing.

6. Identify and describe the following words *(auf Englisch)*: *Freizeit, Taschengeld, Mofa, Reisen.*

Vokabeln

der **Abend,-e** evening; *heute Abend* this evening; *am Abend* in the evening *3B*
aber but *3A*
ach ja oh yes *3B*
der **Bahnhof,-̈e** train station *3B*
der **Basketball,-̈e** basketball *3A*
beginnen to begin *3B*
bei at, near, with; *bei uns bleiben* to stay with us *3B*
beide both *3B*
bekannt well known *3A*
bleiben to stay *3B*
das **Buch,-̈er** book *3A*
charmant charming *3B*
der **Computer,-** computer *3A*
das **Computerspiel,-e** computer game *3A*
dann then *3B*
dauern to take, last *3B*
Deutsch German (subject) *3A*
dir: von dir about you *3B*
die **Disko,-s** disco *3A*
doch used for emphasis; *Komm doch mit!* Why don't you come along! *3A*
dort there *3A*
etwas some, a little *3A*
fernsehen to watch television *3A*; *im Fernsehen* on television *3B*
das **Fernsehprogramm,-e** television program *3B*
der **Film,-e** film, movie *3A*
für for *3B*
der **Fußball,-̈e** soccer, soccer ball *3A*
gefallen to like; *Wie gefällt dir...?* How do you like...? *3B*
gehen to go *3A*; *Das geht nicht.* That's not possible. *3B*
gern gladly, with pleasure; *gern spielen* like to play *3A*
gibt: es gibt there is (are); *Was gibt's im Fernsehen?* What is there on TV? *3B*
die **Gitarre,-n** guitar *3A*
haben to have *3A*

die **Hausaufgabe,-n** homework; *Hausaufgaben machen* to do homework *3B*
helfen to help *3B*
der **Hit,-s** hit (song) *3B*
holen to get, fetch *3A*
die **Idee,-n** idea *3B*
immer always *3B*
jetzt now *3A*
die **Karte,-n** ticket, card *3A*
kein(e) no *3B*
das **Klavier,-e** piano *3A*
der **Krimi,-s** detective story, thriller *3B*
lesen to read *3A*
mir: mit mir with me *3A*
mehr more; *es gibt keine Karten mehr* there are no more tickets available *3B*
der **Mittag,-e** noon; *heute Mittag* today at noon *3B*
möchten would like to *3A*
der **Moment,-e** moment; *Moment mal!* Just a moment! *3A*
der **Morgen,-** morning; *heute Morgen* this morning *3B*
muss: ich muss...helfen. I have to help. *3B*
na und so what *3B*
nach after, to; *nach Hause gehen* to go home *3A*; *Es ist Viertel nach eins.* It's a quarter after one. *3B*
der **Nachmittag,-e** afternoon; *heute Nachmittag* this afternoon *3B*

die **Nachricht,-en** news *3B*
das **Problem,-e** problem *3B*
das **Rockkonzert,-e** rock concert *3B*
sagen to say, tell *3B*
der **Schlauberger** smartie *3B*
schnell fast *3B*
die **Schule,-n** school *3B*
schwimmen to swim *3A*
sehen to see; *ein Fernsehprogramm sehen* to watch a television program *3A*
der **Sommer,-** summer *3B*
der **Spaß** fun; *Viel Spaß!* Have fun! *3B*
spielen to play *3A*
die **Sportschau** sports show (news) *3B*
die **Stunde,-n** hour *3A*
tanzen to dance *3A*
das **Tennis** tennis *3A*
das **Video,-s** video *3A*
die **Videothek** name of video rental store *3A*
das **Viertel,-** quarter *3B*
vor before; in front of *3B*
wann when *3B*
warum why *3B*
was what; *Was für ein...?* What kind of a...? *3A*
die **Woche,-n** week *3B*
zu too *3A*
zuerst first *3B*
zusammen together *3B*

Wo ist der Bahnhof?

Schule

KAISERIN-FRIEDRICH-GYMNASIUM

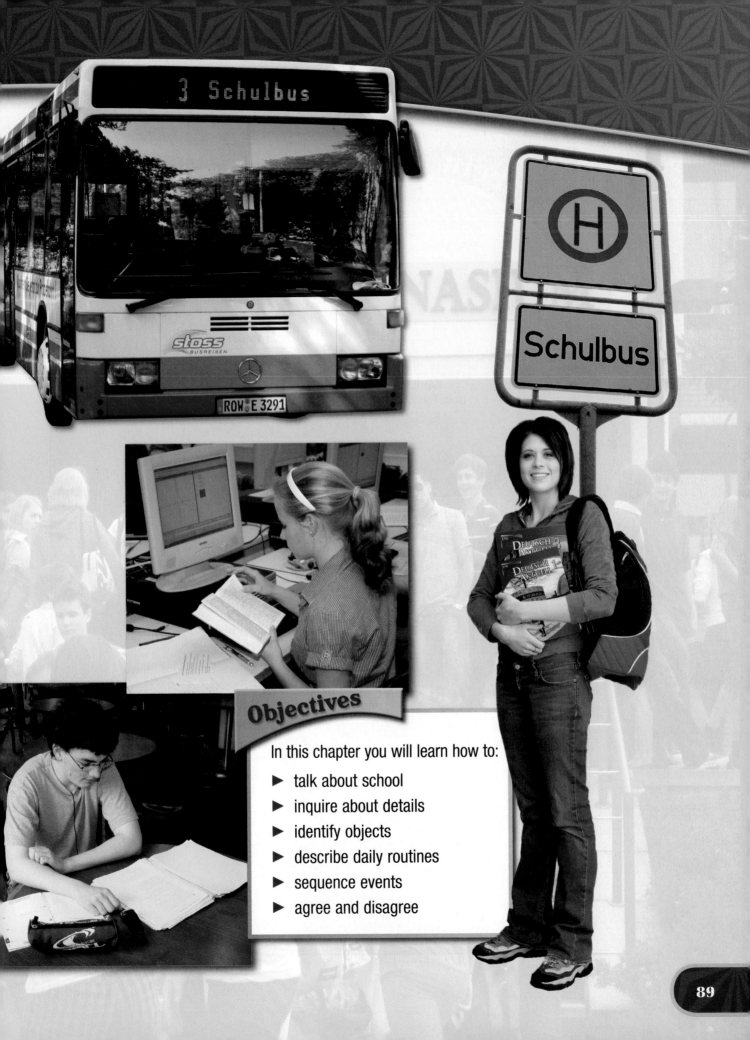

3 Schulbus

Schulbus

Objectives

In this chapter you will learn how to:

► talk about school
► inquire about details
► identify objects
► describe daily routines
► sequence events
► agree and disagree

Lektion A

Die Klasse

1 Rate mal! (Guess!)

Guess the name of each object in German, including its article. This object is used to...

1. erase a word that was incorrectly penciled in.
2. point out the location of a city.
3. learn some information as you page through it.
4. write the answers on several pages that are bound together.
5. write some information on the board.
6. indicate that the class period is over.
7. retrieve electronic information.
8. sit on.
9. write with and use as an eraser.
10. measure line length and draw straight lines.

2 Wer oder was ist das?

Identify the missing words. The beginning letters of each word, when read in sequence, will spell out the topic of this chapter. Although you haven't learned the words *sitzen* and *Geometrie*, can you guess what they mean?

1. Silke sitzt auf einem ___.
2. Petra und Elisabeth spielen Computerspiele auf dem ___.
3. Wir machen die Hausaufgaben im ___.
4. Wie viel ___ ist es? Es ist halb drei.
5. Für Geometrie brauchen wir ein ___.
6. Herr ___ ist der Deutschlehrer.

Wer ist dein Deutschlehrer?

Wo machen sie die Hausaufgaben?

Wie klug du bist!

Daniel

Matthias

Sebastian

DANIEL: Warum bist du so nervös?

MATTHIAS: Wir haben heute Mathe. Die Probleme sind ganz schwer.

SEBASTIAN: Meinst du? Sie sind doch leicht.

MATTHIAS: Für dich.

SEBASTIAN: Wo ist denn dein Rechner?

MATTHIAS: Zu Hause.

DANIEL: Ohne Rechner geht's auch nicht.

MATTHIAS: Wie klug du bist!

3 Was fehlt hier?

1. Wo ist der ___ von Matthias? Er ist zu ___.
2. Ist Matthias heute ___? Ja, er hat ___.
3. Sind die Probleme für Mathe ___? Nein, sie ___ schwer.
4. Geht es in Mathe ___ Rechner? Nein, das geht ___.

4 Auf Deutsch, bitte!

A German exchange student in your school insists on speaking English as he wants to learn the language. You have the opposite goal: you want to learn German. Answer all his questions in German.

1. Do you have math today?
2. Is math easy?
3. Is math at 9:30?
4. Are you a little nervous?
5. Are you going home later?

Für dich

Sie sind in der Grundschule.

After attending the elementary school *(Grundschule)* for four years, most students continue either at the junior secondary school *(Hauptschule)* or at the intermediate secondary school *(Realschule)*. The rest of the students, slightly more than one-fourth, will continue from grades 5 through 12 or 13 at the senior secondary school *(Gymnasium)*, depending on where they live in Germany as the 16 federal states *(Bundesländer)* have different laws. Upon successfully passing oral and written examinations during their last year, students receive the final certificate *(Abitur)* which is a prerequisite for attending a university *(Universität)*. During the last few decades, the *Gesamtschule* (comprehensive school) has become more popular as this school combines the *Gymnasium, Realschule* and the *Hauptschule*. At the comprehensive school students can switch between different tracks without changing buildings. Students attending the *Gymnasium* have a very concentrated curriculum. It is not uncommon for these students to take at least ten or more different subjects a week. A typical schedule readily shows the emphasis on academic subjects.

Grundschule am Mäuseturm

The Definite Article (Accusative Singular)

In the sentence *Andrea kauft die Karte* (Andrea buys the ticket), *Andrea* is called the subject (nominative), *kauft* the verb and die *Karte* the direct object (accusative) of the sentence.

Kennst du den Onkel?	Do you know the uncle?
Ich höre die Musik.	I am listening to the music.
Wir lesen das Buch.	We are reading the book.

	SINGULAR		
	masculine	feminine	neuter
nominative	der	die	das
accusative	den	die	das

From the chart, you can see that the *die* and *das* articles do not change in the accusative and that *der* changes to *den*. In informal conversations, names are often preceded by a form of *der* or *die*.

Kennst du den Peter?	Do you know Peter?

Sie lesen das Buch.

5 Wo ist...?

You always seem to misplace things. Ask where each one is.

BEISPIEL Wo ist das Buch?

1.
2.
3.
4.
5.
6.

6 Möchtest du das?

Your father or mother is asking what you would like for your birthday. As he or she points to certain items, you indicate that you would like each one.

BEISPIEL Ja, ich möchte die Schultasche.

1.
2.
3.
4.
5.
6.

7 Was kaufst du?

You and your friends are going shopping. Everyone seems to be buying something different. Your friends tell you what they are buying, but they also want to know what you plan to purchase.

BEISPIEL   Ich kaufe die CD. Und du?
Ich kaufe das Buch hier.

1.   2.   3.

4.   5.   6.

1. Ich kaufe den Fußball. Und du?
2. Ich kaufe die Karte. Und du?
3. Ich kaufe den Rechner. Und du?
4. Ich kaufe das Lineal. Und du?
5. Ich kaufe die Uhr. Und du?
6. Ich kaufe den Krimi. Und du?

8 *der, die, das* oder *den?*

Complete each sentence using the appropriate form of the article.

1. Kennst du ___ Lehrer?
2. Kaufen Sie ___ Klavier?
3. Wir lesen ___ Buch.
4. Wo hast du ___ Schultasche?
5. Wann beginnt ___ Schule?
6. Ich brauche ___ Kuli.
7. Habt ihr ___ Bleistift?
8. Renate spielt ___ Computerspiel.

Hohenzollern-Gymnasium in Sigmaringen

A visitor to a German *Gymnasium* may assume that the curriculum and academic activities are the same in all secondary high schools in Germany. Such an assumption will most likely prove to be incorrect. Although local and regional differences from one *Gymnasium* to another become quite apparent, there are nevertheless many similarities.

The *Hohenzollern-Gymnasium* is located in Sigmaringen, a small town in southern Germany, about 30 miles north of Switzerland and 70 miles northwest of Austria. The school was founded in 1818, at which time most of the students were taught by the clergy. Since 1975, when a new school was built, the *Hohenzollern-Gymnasium* has been a public secondary school under the jurisdiction of the City of Sigmaringen.

Die Stadt Sigmaringen

The school is attended by 680 students (grades 5-13) in 28 classes. Less than half of these students come directly from Sigmaringen, with the rest commuting from 26 other towns or communities. Most students come by bus or train. During the warmer months, many students ride their bikes or walk to school. Since German teenagers cannot get a driver's license before they are 18, only very few students come by

Wie kommen sie in die Schule?

car or motorcycle. About 4 percent of the students in this school are foreigners from such countries as Turkey, Afghanistan, Italy, Hungary and Yugoslavia.

School starts Monday through Friday at 7:45 A.M. Each class period is 45 minutes long. After the first two periods, there is a 15-minute recess (*Große Pause*) followed by two more periods with a second 10-minute recess. After another two periods, students are dismissed three of five days at 12:55 P.M. On the other two days, students have a lunch break (*Mittagspause*) until 2:20 p.m. and get out of school after 3:55 P.M. Most students bring sandwiches or snacks to school which they eat during their recess or lunch break. They also can purchase food in a cafeteria around the block from the school or at a fast-food restaurant nearby. Beverages can be bought from a vending machine located in the cafeteria.

Students have a choice of the three following curriculum tracks, called *Profil: Sprachliches Profil* (Language Profile) with students taking English, Latin and French; *Naturwissentschaftliches Profil* (Natural Science Profile) with students taking English and French with an emphasis on mathematics, physics, chemistry, biology and technology. Finally, the *Musikprofil* (Music Profile) offers students an opportunity in taking English, Latin or French and music with emphasis on music from fifth through seventh grade. Eighth graders can choose to take music rather than a third foreign language. Depending on the students' ability and interest, each class schedule may look considerably different. The following is a possible class schedule for a tenth grade student:

Was lernen sie?

MEIN STUNDENPLAN

Zeit	Montag	Dienstag	Mittwoch	Donnerstag	Freitag
7.45-8.30	Englisch	Sport	Gemeinschaftskunde	Biologie	Mathematik
8.35-9.20	Mathematik	Sport	Religion	Französisch	Englisch
9.20-9.35	Große Pause	Große Pause	Große Pause	Große Pause	Große Pause
9.35-10.20	Französisch	Geschichte	Französisch	Mathematik	Gemeinschaftskunde
10.25-11.10	Chemie	Mathematik	Englisch	Englisch	Geschichte
11.10-11.20	Pause	Pause	Pause	Pause	Pause
11.20-12.05	Physik	Latein	Latein	Deutsch	Religion
12.10-12.55	Deutsch	Deutsch	Chor	Chemie	Latein
14.20-15.05		Biologie	Kunst		
15.10-15.55		Französisch	Musik		

You will notice that this student as well as many of his classmates have 15 subjects scattered throughout the weekly school schedule. Particularly noteworthy is the fact that students in several grades must take either religion or ethics. Religion is offered as Protestant or Catholic instruction and exposes students primarily to the history and philosophy of Protestantism and Catholicism as well as other world religions. Students who don't want to attend these classes must take ethics instead.

At the end of their final year at this *Gymnasium*, students receive their *Abitur* certification after passing two oral and three written examinations. The final grade is a combination of the scores on these examinations, as well as a calculated average of various basic and selected courses.

The *Hohenzollern-Gymnasium* sponsors student exchange programs (*Austauschprogramme*) with schools in France and with Overland High School in Aurora, Colorado. Throughout the year, students have several recreational opportunities. They go on at least two field trips (*Klassenausflüge*) and can also participate during the *Wintersporttag* in various winter activities such as skiing, skating, etc. Finally, students can participate in some school-sponsored sports tournaments, in several choirs and in theater performances.

Er ist Englischlehrer in der 12. Klasse.

Die deutsche Klasse besucht eine High School in Colorado.

9 Was weißt du?

At what age can Germans go to the *Fahrschule* and get their driver's license?

1. How many subjects a week do many tenth graders have?

2. What do students receive after passing their final written and oral examinations?

3. What is the ancient language offered?

4. How long is the *Große Pause*?

5. Why don't most 17-year-old Germans drive a car?

6. How often does this tenth grade student have English during the week?

7. What class can students take instead of *Religion*?

In dieser Schule lernen sie vier Fremdsprachen.

8. How do most students get to school?

9. When can students eat a snack on Tuesdays?

10. To which countries does this school have some ties?

Persönliches

1. Wer ist dein Deutschlehrer oder deine Deutschlehrerin?
2. Was ist für dich schwer?
3. Hast du einen Rechner? Wo ist er?
4. Wo ist dein Deutschbuch?
5. Was brauchst du für die Schule?
6. Was gibt es alles in deiner Deutschklasse? (*Name at least eight items including articles.*)

Rollenspiel

Working with a partner, take turns telling one another to point at an object in the classroom. Use a question such as *Wo ist die Landkarte?* The answer may be *Die Landkarte ist da (hier, dort, da drüben)*. Make sure to include the article when identifying various classroom objects.

Wörter und Ausdrücke

Describing a Classroom

der Lehrer,- teacher (male)
die Lehrerin,-nen teacher (female)
der Bleistift,-e pencil
der Computer,- computer
das Heft,-e notebook
die Kreide chalk
der Kuli,-s (ballpoint) pen
die Landkarte,-n map
das Lineal,-e ruler
das Papier paper
der Radiergummi,-s eraser
die Schultasche,-n schoolbag
der Stuhl,¨e chair
die Tafel,-n (chalk) board
der Tafellappen,- rag (to wipe off board)
der Tisch,- table
die Uhr,-en clock

About School

Wer ist dein Deutschlehrer? Who is your German teacher?
Was brauchst du? What do you need?
Meinst du? Do you think so?
Ohne Rechner geht's nicht. It won't work without a calculator.
nervös nervous
schwer difficult, hard
leicht easy

Ohne Rechner geht's nicht.

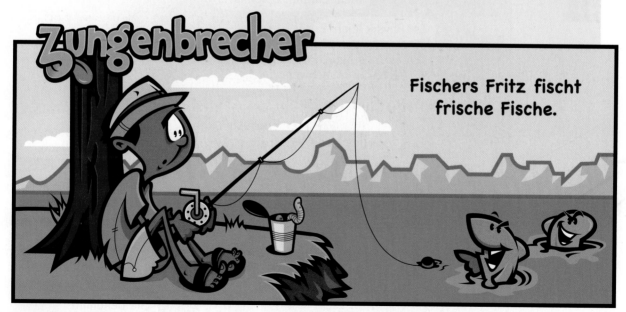

Fritz Fischer is fishing for fresh fish.

Lektion B

Daniels Stundenplan

Zeit	Montag	Dienstag	Mittwoch	Donnerstag	Freitag
7.55-8.40	Deutsch	Englisch	Deutsch	Mathematik	Englisch
8.45-9.30	Biologie	Geschichte	Biologie	Musik	Französisch
9.30-9.50	Große Pause				
9.50-10.35	Chemie	Erdkunde	Mathematik	Deutsch	Naturwissenschaften
10.40-11.25	Mathematik	Französisch	Chemie	Englisch	Physik
11.25-11.45	Große Pause				
11.45-12.30	Physik	Religion	Sport	Religion	Musik
12.35-1.20	Französisch	Mathematik	Sport	Geschichte	Mathematik
1.25-2.10		Informatik			

10 Was für Fächer hat Bettina am Mittwoch?

Can you figure out the seven subjects that Bettina has
every Wednesday? To find the answers, combine the
appropriate syllables.

11 Eine Umfrage (A Survey)

Imagine that you are enrolled in a German *Gymnasium*.
Your host family inquires about your new schedule.
You have the same schedule that is presented above.
Beantworte die Fragen!

1. Um wie viel Uhr beginnt die Erdkundeklasse?
2. Was hast du um viertel vor zwölf am Montag?
3. Wie viele Französischstunden hast du in der Woche?
4. Um wie viel Uhr ist Große Pause?
5. Wann hast du Biologie?
6. Wann kommst du am Freitag aus der Schule?
7. Um wie viel Uhr beginnt die Schule?
8. Was hast du um zwanzig vor elf am Donnerstag?

Dialog

Am Computer

Der Computer ist gut genug.

Ich mache noch schnell meine Arbeit.

Wir spielen zuerst Karten.

GABRIELE:	Dieser Computer ist aber sehr langsam.
LEHRER:	Na ja, für die Informatikaufgaben ist er gut genug.
GABRIELE:	Oh, es klingelt schon. Jetzt geht's nach Hause.
DIANA:	Noch nicht ganz. Ich mache noch schnell meine Arbeit.
GABRIELE:	Warum denn? Komm her! Wir spielen zuerst Karten.
DIANA:	Du hast Recht. Die Arbeit kommt später.

12 Fragen

Beantworte diese Fragen!

1. Wie ist der Computer?
2. Was meint der Lehrer?
3. Geht Diana gleich nach Hause?
4. Was spielen beide Mädchen?
5. Wann macht Diana ihre Arbeit?

13 Was passt zusammen?

1. Ist er klug?
2. Es klingelt.
3. Sind die Probleme leicht?
4. Machst du jetzt deine Arbeit?
5. Wo spielst du Karten?
6. Ist dieser Computer alt?
7. Ich bin ganz nervös.
8. Ohne Rechner sind die Matheaufgaben zu schwer.

A. Warum denn? Wir haben doch heute keine Mathe.
B. Nein, schwer.
C. Du hast Recht.
D. Oh, es ist schon halb zwei. Dann geht's gleich nach Hause.
E. Ja, ein Schlauberger.
F. Am Computer.
G. Ja, und auch sehr langsam.
H. Vielleicht später.

Sind die Hausaufgaben leicht?

Für dich

Grades in German schools are assigned by numbers (1-6) rather than letters (A, B, C, D, F) as we know them. The following grading system is commonly used:

1 = *sehr gut/ausgezeichnet* (very good/excellent)

2 = *gut* (good)

3 = *befriedigend* (satisfactory)

4 = *ausreichend* (adequate)

5 = *mangelhaft* (inadequate)

6 = *ungenügend* (unsatisfactory)

Baden-Württemberg
Hohenzollern - Gymnasium Sigmaringen
Zeugnis des Gymnasiums

Klasse 8a
Vor- und Zuname   ***Anne Bauer***
Leistungen in den einzelnen Fächern

Religionslehre	gut
Deutsch	gut
Englisch	sehr gut
Latein	befriedigend
Französisch	sehr gut
Mathematik	befriedigend
Gemeinschaftskunde	gut
Geschichte	gut
Physik	befriedigend
Chemie	gut
Bildende Kunst	gut
Musik	gut
Sport	befriedigend

It is difficult to receive a 1 *(eine Eins)* in a German high school *(Gymnasium)*. Getting a 1 is similar to receiving an A+ in our high schools. Both 5 and 6 are considered failing grades. Generally, tests and quizzes in German schools are more subjective *(essay)* and contain fewer objective-type answers (multiple choice, true or false). In general, teaching in the upper levels of a *Gymnasium* focuses on more logical thinking rather than just the learning of mere facts.

Sprache

Question Words: *Wer? Wen? Was?*

Both question words *wer* (who) and *wen* (whom) ask about a person. *Wer* inquires about the subject of the sentence, whereas *wen* asks about the direct object of the sentence. You can use either word, regardless of the gender and number of the noun. To inquire about objects, you must use the question word *was* (what).

***Heike** wohnt in Dresden.*   Heike lives in Dresden.
***Wer** wohnt in Dresden?*   Who lives in Dresden?

*Ich kenne **die Lehrerin**.*   I know the teacher.
***Wen** kennst du?*   Whom do you know?

*Wir kaufen **die Gitarre**.*   We are buying the guitar.
***Was** kauft ihr?*   What are you buying?

14 Wer wohnt dort?

Pretend it's noisy and you can't hear what is being said about where various people live. So you ask whom they are talking about.

BEISPIEL Frau Schiller wohnt in der Stadt.
Wer wohnt in der Stadt?

1. Susanne wohnt gleich um die Ecke.
2. Der Lehrer wohnt hier.
3. Petra wohnt beim Kaufhaus.
4. Karin und Petra wohnen in Hamburg.
5. Frau Tobler wohnt in Deutschland.
6. Wir wohnen da.

15 Was/Wen kennst du?

Imagine you haven't visited your uncle for years. He doesn't know how much you still remember from the time you saw him last.

BEISPIELE Was kennst du? (Kaufhaus)
Ich kenne das Kaufhaus.

Wen kennst du? (Christine)
Ich kenne die Christine.

1. Was kennst du ? (Stadt)
2. Wen kennst du? (Dieter)
3. Wen kennst du? (Heidi)
4. Was kennst du? (Film)
5. Wen kennst du? (Onkel)
6. Was kennst du? (Schule)

ein Kaufhaus in Heidelberg

16 *Wer? Wen? oder Was?*

Complete each sentence using the appropriate question word.

1. ____ ist das? Das ist Herr Schmidt.
2. ____ hast du in Deutsch? Frau Krüger.
3. ____ lesen Sie? Einen Krimi.
4. ____ macht ihr heute? Wir spielen Tennis.
5. ____ kommt um sieben? Peter und Angelika.
6. ____ kennt er? Frau Meier.
7. ____ hörst du? Rockmusik.
8. ____ hat Hausaufgaben? Monika und Dieter.

Schon früh in die Schule

Vanessa und Manuela sind gute Freundinnen. Beide wohnen in Ingolstadt. Diese Stadt liegt im Bundesland Bayern[1], in Süddeutschland. Jeden Morgen[2], Montag bis Freitag, kommt Manuela schon früh[3], so gegen Viertel vor sieben Uhr, zu Vanessa. Vanessas Mutter macht immer das Frühstück[4] für beide.

Vanessas Mutter macht immer das Frühstück.

Manuela: Warum bist du heute so froh[5]?

Vanessa: Heute ist doch Donnerstag.

Manuela: Na und?

Vanessa: Ich habe gleich in der ersten Stunde[6] mein Lieblingsfach.

Manuela: Stimmt![7] Dein Lieblingsfach Erdkunde hast du ja sehr gern[8]. Da bekommst du immer eine Eins.

Vanessa: Und dann haben wir Biologie, dein Lieblingsfach.

Manuela: Haha! Biologie finde ich sehr langweilig[9].

Vanessa: In der Klasse haben wir aber fast nie[10] Hausaufgaben.

Manuela: Da hast du Recht. Komm, schnell! Der Bus ist in zehn Minuten da.

Manuela und Vanessa warten auf den Bus.

Manuela und Vanessa gehen schnell aus
dem Haus. Um diese Zeit im Herbst[11] ist es
immer noch dunkel[12]. Sie warten nicht lange[13]
bis der Bus kommt. Zur Schule dauert es nur eine viertel
Stunde. Dann sind sie auch schon da. Vor der ersten Stunde treffen sie
Schulfreunde[14]. Sie warten bis Herr Schröder, ihr Lehrer, kommt. Die
erste Klasse beginnt um 7 Uhr 50. Heute haben Vanessa und Manuela
sechs Klassen. Um viertel nach eins kommen sie aus der Schule. Jeden
Donnerstag gehen beide Mädchen zuerst zu Manuelas Haus. Dort
machen sie immer die Hausaufgaben. Manchmal[15] kommt Manuela
später zu Vanessa rüber. Sie spielen gern Klavier zusammen, hören CDs
oder sehen fern.

Beide treffen
Schulfreunde.

[1]*das Bundesland Bayern* federal state of Bavaria; [2]*jeden Morgen* every morning; [3]*früh*
early; [4]*das Frühstück* breakfast; [5]*froh* happy; [6]*in der ersten Stunde* in the first hour;
[7]*Stimmt!* That's right!; [8]*Das hast du ja sehr gern.* You like it very well.; [9]*langweilig finden*
to find boring; [10]*fast nie* almost never; [11]*im Herbst* in the fall; [12]*dunkel* dark; [13]*lange
warten* to wait for a long time; [14]*Schulfreunde treffen* to meet schoolmates; [15]*manchmal*
sometimes

Vanessa hat jetzt Erdkunde.

17 Die richtige Reihenfolge (The correct sequence)

Place the following sentences in the proper sequence according to what happened in the *Lesestück*.

1. Der Bus kommt.
2. Manuela spielt bei Vanessa Klavier.
3. Herr Schröder kommt.
4. Vanessas Mutter macht das Frühstück.
5. Manuela und Vanessa kommen aus der Schule.
6. Manuela kommt am Morgen zu Vanessa.
7. Beide sind in fünfzehn Minuten in der Schule.
8. Manuela und Vanessa treffen Schulfreunde.
9. Die Mädchen warten bis der Bus kommt.
10. Vanessa macht die Hausaufgaben bei Manuela.
11. Die erste Klasse beginnt zehn Minuten vor acht.
12. Beide Mädchen gehen aus dem Haus zum Bus.

18 Fragen

Beantworte diese Fragen!

1. Wo wohnen Manuela und Vanessa?
2. Wo liegt diese Stadt?
3. Um wie viel Uhr kommt Manuela am Morgen zu Vanessa?
4. Was macht Vanessas Mutter?
5. Was für ein Fach hat Vanessa in der ersten Stunde?
6. Hat sie dieses Fach gern?
7. Findet Manuela Biologie interessant?
8. Wie lange dauert es, bis sie in der Schule sind?
9. Was machen sie vor der Klasse?
10. Wie viele Klassen haben beide Mädchen heute?
11. Um wie viel Uhr kommen sie aus der Schule?
12. Was machen sie manchmal bei Vanessa?

Wo ist Vanessa?

Kapitel 4

Present Tense of *sein*

You have already learned the singular forms of *sein* in Chapter 1 and have seen some plural forms in context. The following is a listing of all the present tense forms including those that you have already learned.

SINGULAR	ich	bin	I am
	du	bist	you are
	er		he is
	sie	} ist	she is
	es		it is
PLURAL	wir	sind	we are
	ihr	seid	you are
	sie	sind	they are
	Sie	sind	you are
	(*sg. & pl.*)		

Wie alt bist du?   How old are you?

Wolf und Frank sind schon da.   Wolf and Frank are already there.

19   Wie sind sie?

Pretend you are interested in finding out about several people at a party. Ask some questions using the cues.

BEISPIEL   Rudi und Peter / neu hier
Sind Rudi und Peter neu hier?

1. Andrea und Willi / klug
2. Uwe / ein Schlauberger
3. du / Katharinas Freundin
4. ihr / in Mathe gut
5. Anne / langweilig
6. Herr Schröders Klasse / interessant

Diese Klasse ist interessant.

20 Wo sind alle?

Your classmates are meeting in front of your school to go on a field trip. A few minutes before departure, your teacher asks where several of your classmates are. Using the cues, tell your teacher where the missing students are.

Sie sind alle in der Schule.

BEISPIEL   Uwe / zu Hause
Uwe ist zu Hause.

1. Rudi und Toni / da
2. Heidi / an der Ecke
3. Sven / in der Schule
4. Dieter und Ralf / hier
5. Bettina / am Telefon
6. Kerstin und Doris / vor dem Kaufhaus

21 Weißt du das?

Supply the correct forms of *sein*.

1. Wie viel Uhr ___ es jetzt?
2. Melanie und Sonja ___ in der Stadt.
3. ___ du um acht Uhr zu Hause?
4. Ihr ___ immer so spät.
5. Ich ___ schon früh da.
6. Deutschland ___ weit von hier.
7. ___ Sie Herr Krüger?
8. ___ ihr um sieben hier?
9. Wer ___ das Mädchen?
10. Die Informatikaufgaben ___ leicht.

Welches Fach haben sie?

1. Wie viele Fächer hast du?
2. Um wie viel Uhr hast du Deutsch?
3. Ist Deutsch leicht?
4. Wie heißt dein Deutschlehrer (deine Deutschlehrerin)?
5. Wie viele Jungen und Mädchen sind in deiner Klasse?
6. Um wie viel Uhr beginnt deine Schule?
7. Was ist dein Lieblingsfach? Warum?

Rollenspiel

Imagine that you have been invited to Germany for a few months. During that time you are going to a *Gymnasium*. It is your first day and you are curious about what school will be like. You discuss it with your host family's son or daughter (your classmate), who will provide all the answers. Your conversation should cover at least the following items: the time school starts, if he or she has English class, what grades he or she gets, if the class is difficult, who the teacher is and the time you will leave for school.

BEISPIEL

– *Um wie viel Uhr beginnt die Schule?*
– *Hast du Englisch?*
– *Was für eine Note hast du in Deutsch, Mathe...?*
– *Wer ist dein Lehrer/deine Lehrerin?*
– *Um wie viel Uhr gehst du in die Schule?*

Was braucht Sebastian für Mathe?

Er hat heute viele Hausaufgaben.

Praktisches

Wann hast du (haben Sie) Zeit? Form groups of three. One student plays the role of a teacher; the other two play the roles of students. The two students must agree on a time when they are both free to see the teacher for additional help. (The teacher must be free at the same time.) Each group member (students and teacher) begins by creating a weekly school schedule. It includes what class meets at what time each day. Be sure to include 7 to 10 free periods during the week.

First, the two students must find at least one mutual free period. For example:

Student 1: *Hast du am Montag um acht Uhr Zeit?*

Student 2: *Nein, dann habe ich Mathe. Hast du am Freitag um neun Uhr Zeit?*

Student 1: *Ja.*

Then, after two students have agreed on a time, they need to ask if the teacher is available also. For example:

Student 1: *Haben Sie am Mittwoch um elf Uhr Zeit?*

Teacher: *Nein, aber ich habe um ein Uhr Zeit.*

Student 1: *Das geht nicht.*

Student 2: *Haben Sie heute um elf Uhr Zeit?*

Teacher: *Ja, das geht.*

Note: You may or may not find a mutually convenient hour to meet.

Schreiben

1. Make a weekly class schedule including days, subjects and class periods. Exchange your schedule with another person and then ask each other such questions as: *Um wie viel Uhr hast du am Montag Mathe? Was für ein Fach hast du um acht Uhr am Dienstag? Um wie viel Uhr kommst du aus der Schule?*

2. Compare a German class schedule with yours by making a list with the headings "Similarities" and "Differences." *Auf Deutsch, bitte!* Here are some samples of similarities: *Wir haben auch Englisch und Deutsch. Die Schule ist von Montag bis Freitag. Meine Deutschklasse ist auch 45 Minuten. Ich habe nicht Latein. Ich habe am Dienstag sechs Fächer. Eine Große Pause haben wir nicht. Religion gibt es nicht.*

Deutschland

Deutschland passt 22 mal[1] in die USA (Vereinigten Staaten von Amerika), ohne Alaska und Hawaii. Das Land ist ungefähr halb so groß[2] wie der Staat Texas. Die weiteste Entfernung[3] von Norden nach Süden ist 830 Kilometer, von Osten nach Westen 630 Kilometer. Es gibt 16 Bundesländer. Ungefähr 82 Millionen Einwohner[4] wohnen in Deutschland. Mehr als 7 Millionen sind Ausländer[5].

Berlin ist die Hauptstadt[6] von Deutschland. Berlin liegt[7] im Osten. Berlin ist auch die größte[8] Stadt. Andere[9] große Städte sind Hamburg, München, Köln, Frankfurt, Essen, Dortmund, Stuttgart, Düsseldorf, Bremen, Duisburg, Hannover, Nürnberg, Leipzig und Dresden. Wo liegen die Städte? Im Norden, Süden, Osten oder Westen[10]?

Hamburg

Berlin

[1]*passt 22 mal* fits 22 times; [2]*ungefähr halb so groß* approximately half as big; [3]*die weiteste Entfernung* the farthest distance; [4]*der Einwohner* inhabitant; [5]*der Ausländer* foreigner; [6]*die Hauptstadt* capital; [7]*liegen* to be located; [8]*größte* biggest; [9]*andere* other; [10]*im Norden, Süden, Osten oder Westen* in the north, south, east or west

Leipzig

22 Was passt hier?

Complete each statement by matching it with the appropriate answer from the list below. You will not need all the answers listed.

1. Berlin ist
2. Deutschland ist
3. In Deutschland wohnen
4. Deutschland passt 22 mal in die
5. Die weiteste Entfernung von Norden nach Süden ist
6. Berlin liegt
7. Die weiteste Entfernung von Westen nach Osten ist
8. Ungefähr 7 Millionen sind

A. Ausländer
B. eine alte Stadt
C. 82 Millionen Einwohner
D. im Osten
E. 830 Kilometer
F. halb so groß wie Texas
G. 630 Kilometer
H. USA (ohne Alaska und Hawaii)
I. im Westen
J. die Hauptstadt von Deutschland

23 Wo liegt...?

Look at the German map at the front of this textbook and locate the following cities. Then tell whether each city is located in the north, south, east or west of Germany.

BEISPIEL   Hamburg
Hamburg liegt im Norden.

Welche Stadt ist das?

1. Stuttgart
2. Kiel
3. Dresden
4. Leipzig
5. Düsseldorf
6. Bremen
7. Rostock
8. Augsburg

Wörter und Ausdrücke

School-related Expressions

Was für Fächer hat er? What (kind of) subjects does he have?

Was lernt sie? What is she learning?

Was ist dein Lieblingsfach? What is your favorite subject?

Was für eine Note bekommst du? What (kind of) grade are you getting?

Der Computer ist gut genug. The computer is good enough.

Es klingelt. The bell is ringing.

Warum denn? Why is that?

Du hast Recht. You're right.

School Day and Class Schedule

der Stundenplan, ̈e class schedule

die Große Pause long recess, break

Biologie biology

Chemie chemistry

Deutsch German

Englisch English

Erdkunde geography

Französisch French

Geschichte history

Mathematik, Mathe mathematics, math

Musik music

Naturwissenschaften natural sciences

Physik physics

Religion religion

Sport sports

Was ist dein Lieblingsfach?

Welches Fach haben sie heute in der Schule?

Warum ist der Computer so langsam?

24 Kombiniere...

Wir	kommt	immer	den Rechner
Britta und Tina	haben	heute	Zeit
Herr Schuber	brauchen	jetzt	Recht
			Probleme
			spät

25 In der ersten Woche

You run into your friend in the hallway during the first week of school. Respond to your friend appropriately.

Du: (1) _____

Freund(in): Na, wie geht's?

Du: (2) _____

Freund(in): Was für Fächer hast du heute?

Du: (3) _____

Freund(in): Was machst du nach der Schule?

Du: (4) _____

Freund(in): Nach Hause? Warum?

Du: (5) _____

Freund(in): Ich habe auch Hausaufgaben. Wir machen sie später zusammen.

Du: (6) _____

Freund(in): Ich gehe in die Stadt.

Du: (7) _____

Na, wie geht's?

Was machen wir nach der Schule?

26 Auf Deutsch, bitte!

Imagine your German is fluent enough that you can help others who are having difficulties. They start a statement or question, but don't know the German words to finish it. Help them out.

1. Um wie viel Uhr *(begins)* ___ die Schule?
2. Um *(half)* ___ acht.
3. Haben wir am Mittwoch *(chemistry)* ___?
4. Nein, am *(Thursday)* ___.
5. Ich *(have)* ___ heute viele Hausaufgaben.
6. Für *(German)* ___?
7. Ja, und auch für *(history)* ___.
8. Dann hast du heute *(afternoon)* ___ keine Zeit?
9. Nein, aber *(tomorrow)* ___.
10. Gut. Ich *(come)* ___ morgen rüber.

27 Meine Klasse

Complete Julia's observations about her class by using the words provided. You will not need all the words listed.

schwer	beginnt	braucht	Klasse	bekomme
Herr	Uhr	dauert	Jungen	immer

1. Frau Novak ist um 7 Uhr 15 in der ___.
2. Die Mädchen und ___ kommen um fünf vor acht.
3. Die Matheklasse ___ pünktlich.
4. Die Klasse ___ von 7 Uhr 55 bis 8 Uhr 35.
5. Nach der Matheklasse kommt ___ Kowalski.
6. Die Klasse ist nicht ___.
7. Es gibt aber ___ viele Hausaufgaben.
8. Ich ___ in Mathe gute Noten.

Heute Nachmittag haben wir doch viel Zeit.

28 Wir gehen zur Schule.

Describe (in narrative and/or dialog style) the following sequence, using the cues merely as a guideline.

You are walking to school...picking up your friend on the way...waiting several minutes before he or she comes out of the house...greeting him or her...talking about several items concerning school...arriving at school...hurrying because the first class begins soon.

Was weißt du?

1. *Zur Schule.* On your way to school with your friend, you ask about several things. Write five questions that you would like to have answered.

2. Discuss in English some of the differences between your school and a German school.

3. Point to at least seven classroom objects and identify them, including the articles (*der, die, das*).

4. Prepare a class schedule of the subjects that you are taking and include days of the week and times.

5. *Ein Interview.* Talk to a classmate, asking questions and using the question words *wer, wen* and *was*.

6. Describe your daily school routine, starting with the time you leave home until you return home.

Sie bekommt eine gute Note.

Sie haben heute Geschichte.

Vokabeln

die **Arbeit,-en** work *4B*
auf on, on top of *4A*
Bayern Bavaria *4B*
bekommen to get, receive *4A*
die **Biologie** biology *4B*
der **Bleistift,-e** pencil *4A*
brauchen to need *4A*
das **Bundesland,-̈er** federal state (Germany) *4B*
der **Bus,-se** bus *4B*
die **Chemie** chemistry *4B*
dunkel dark *4B*
das **Englisch** English (subject) *4A*
die **Erdkunde** geography *4B*
erst- first *4B*
das **Fach,-̈er** (school) subject *4B*
fast almost *4B*
finden to find; *Ich finde es langweilig. I think it's boring. 4B*
das **Französisch** French *4B*
froh glad, happy *4B*
früh early *4B*
das **Frühstück** breakfast *4B*
genug enough *4B*
gern haben to like; *Das hast du ja sehr gern. You like it very well. 4B*
die **Geschichte** history *4B*
das **Haus,-̈er** house *4B*
das **Heft,-e** notebook *4A*
der **Herbst,-e** fall, autumn *4B*
herkommen to come here; *Komm her! Come here! 4B*

die **Informatik** computer science *4B*
die **Informatikaufgabe,-n** computer science assignment *4A*
jed- every, each *4B*
kaufen to buy *4A*
die **Klasse,-n** class *4B*
klingeln to ring (bell); *Es klingelt. The bell is ringing. 4B*
klug smart, intelligent *4A*
die **Kreide** chalk *4A*
der **Kuli,-s** (ballpoint) pen *4A*
die **Landkarte,-n** map *4A*
lang(e) long *4B*
langsam slow *4A*
langweilig boring *4B*
das **Latein** Latin *4B*
der **Lehrer,-** teacher (male) *4A*
die **Lehrerin,-nen** teacher (female) *4A*
leicht easy *4A*
lernen to learn *4A*
das **Lieblingsfach,-̈er** favorite (school) subject *4A*
das **Lineal,-e** ruler *4A*
manchmal sometimes *4B*
die **Mathematik (Mathe)** mathematics (math) *4A; die Mathestunde/Matheklasse* math class *4B*
meinen to mean; *Meinst du?* Do you think so? *4A*

die **Naturwissenschaften** (pl.) natural sciences *4B*
nervös nervous *4A*
nie never *4B*
noch still, yet; *noch nicht ganz* not quite yet *4B*
die **Note,-n** grade *4A*
ohne without *4A*
das **Papier** paper *4A*
die **Pause,-n** recess, break; *Große Pause* long recess *4B*
die **Physik** physics *4A*
der **Radiergummi,-s** eraser *4A*
der **Rechner,-** calculator *4A*
das **Recht** right; *Recht haben* to be right *4B*
die **Religion,-en** religion *4B*
der **Schulfreund,-e** schoolmate *4B*
die **Schultasche,-n** schoolbag *4A*
schwer hard, difficult *4A*
der **Sport** sports *4B*
stimmen to be correct; *Das stimmt. That's right. 4B*
der **Stuhl,-̈e** chair *4A*
der **Stundenplan,-̈e** class schedule *4B*
die **Tafel,-n** (chalk) board *4A*
der **Tafellappen,-** rag (to wipe off [chalk] board) *4A*
der **Tisch,-e** table *4A*
treffen to meet *4B*
warten to wait *4B*
wie viele how many *4A*

der Lehrer

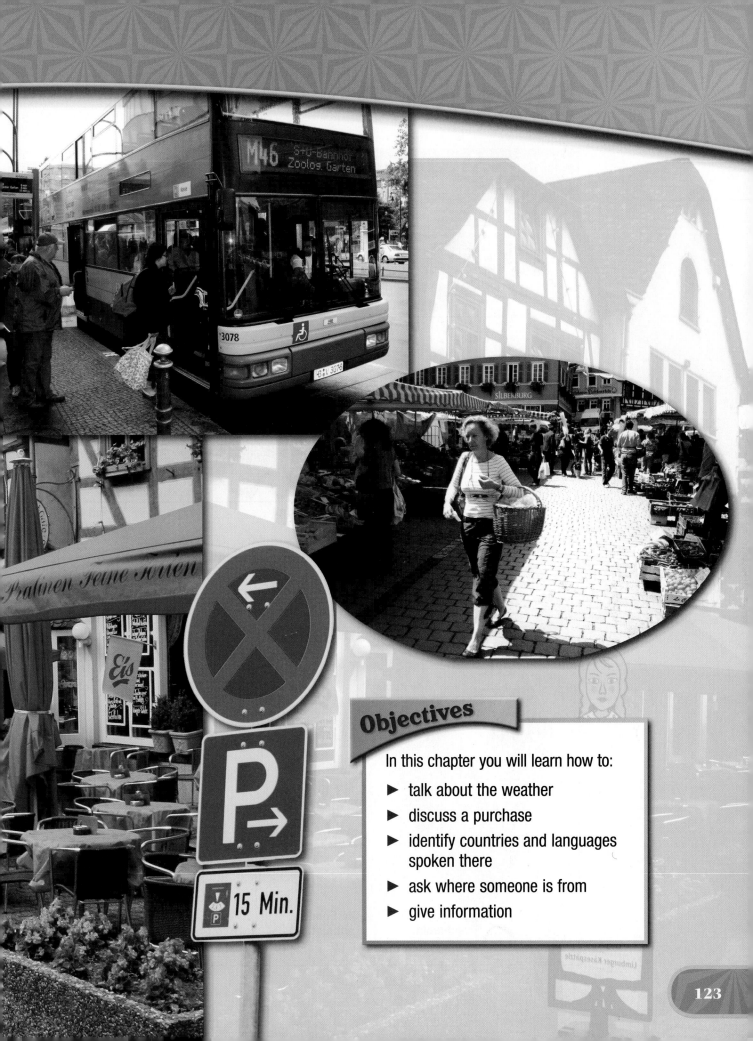

Objectives

In this chapter you will learn how to:

► talk about the weather
► discuss a purchase
► identify countries and languages spoken there
► ask where someone is from
► give information

Lektion A

Die Monate und Jahreszeiten

Herbst	September	Oktober	November
Winter	Dezember	Januar	Februar
Frühling	März	April	Mai
Sommer	Juni	Juli	August

Wie ist das Wetter im Sommer und im Winter?

Es ist kalt.

Es ist kühl.

Es ist warm.

Es ist heiß.

Es ist schön.

Es ist schlecht.

Die Sonne scheint.

Es ist regnet.

Es schneit.

1 Welche Jahreszeit?

Im Frühling, Sommer, Herbst oder Winter? During which season does each month occur?

BEISPIEL Januar
Januar ist im Winter.

1. Juli
2. März
3. Dezember

4. September
5. Mai
6. August

2 Wie ist das Wetter?

Look at the photos and determine what the weather is like. Use a different expression for each photo.

1.

2.

3.

4.

5.

6.

3 Welcher Monat ist das?

During which month does each holiday or event take place?

1. Thanksgiving
2. Valentine's Day
3. Independence Day
4. Halloween

5. Memorial Day
6. New Year's Day
7. first day of school
8. your birthday

4 Wie ist das Wetter da?

Look at the European weather report and give an answer to this question for the various cities listed.

BEISPIELE   Budapest
In Budapest ist es wolkig.

Amsterdam
In Amsterdam gibt es Regen (regnet es).

1. Frankfurt
2. Warschau

3. London
4. Lissabon

5. Prag
6. Rom

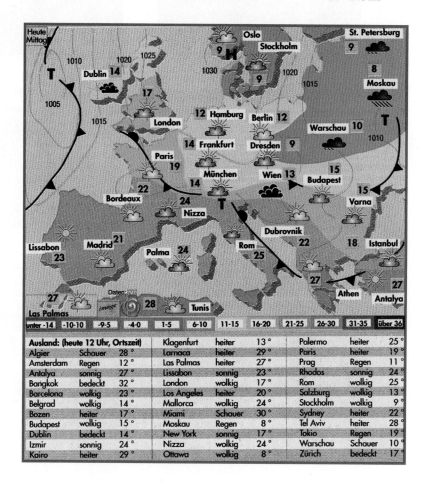

Ausland: (heute 12 Uhr, Ortszeit)			Klagenfurt	heiter	13 °	Palermo	heiter	25 °
Algier	Schauer	28 °	Larnaca	heiter	29 °	Paris	heiter	19 °
Amsterdam	Regen	12 °	Las Palmas	heiter	27 °	Prag	Regen	11 °
Antalya	sonnig	27 °	Lissabon	sonnig	23 °	Rhodos	sonnig	24 °
Bangkok	bedeckt	32 °	London	wolkig	17 °	Rom	wolkig	25 °
Barcelona	wolkig	23 °	Los Angeles	heiter	20 °	Salzburg	wolkig	13 °
Belgrad	wolkig	14 °	Mallorca	wolkig	24 °	Stockholm	wolkig	9 °
Bozen	heiter	17 °	Miami	Schauer	30 °	Sydney	heiter	22 °
Budapest	wolkig	15 °	Moskau	Regen	8 °	Tel Aviv	heiter	28 °
Dublin	bedeckt	14 °	New York	sonnig	17 °	Tokio	Regen	19 °
Izmir	sonnig	24 °	Nizza	wolkig	24 °	Warschau	Schauer	10 °
Kairo	heiter	29 °	Ottawa	wolkig	8 °	Zürich	bedeckt	17 °

Dialog

Kommt der Bus bald?

Für März ist es nicht so kalt.

Da steht es: Stadt, Linie 6.

Hier ist der Fahrplan.

Immer mit der Ruhe!

JENS: Für März ist es nicht so kalt.

WOLF: Die Sonne scheint ja auch.

JENS: Kommt der Bus nicht bald?

WOLF: Immer mit der Ruhe! Wir haben doch Zeit.

JENS: Hier ist der Fahrplan. Da steht es: Stadt, Linie 6.
Die Busse kommen alle zwölf Minuten.

WOLF: Da ist er ja schon.

5 Was fehlt hier?

Complete the following narrative based on the information provided in the dialog. There are a few words that you may not be familiar with. However, you should be able to figure them out within the context.

Heute (1) die Sonne. Im (2) ist es oft noch (3) . (4) ist es aber warm. Wolf (5) Jens warten auf den (6) . Jens fragt, wann der Bus (7) . Wolf meint, sie (8) viel (9) . Die (10) sehen einen (11) . Da steht, wann (12) Bus kommt. Sie (13) nicht lange. (14) kommt schon der Bus.

6 Fragen

Beantworte diese Fragen!

1. Ist es heute kalt?
2. Was scheint?
3. Was kommt bald?
4. Haben die Jungen Zeit?
5. Was steht auf dem Fahrplan?

Für dich

Geographically, Germany lies approximately at the same latitude as southern Canada. Summer days in Germany are longer than in the United States, winter days are shorter. In winter, the average daily temperature is between 35°F in central and northern Germany and 21°F in southern Germany. In July, the warmest month of the year, average temperatures in these regions vary between 64° and 68°F. Exceptions are the Upper Rhine Valley in the southwest with its extremely mild climate, Bavaria with its warm alpine wind *(Föhn)* from the south, and the Harz Mountains, a climate zone of its own with cold winds, cool summers and heavy snow in winter.

Wie ist das Wetter heute?

German thermometers use the centigrade (Celsius) scale. To convert Fahrenheit to centigrade, subtract 32, then multiply by 5 and divide by 9. To convert centigrade to Fahrenheit, multiply by 9, divide by 5 and add 32. The chart below gives some sample readings with the conversions.

Examples:

48°F = 9°C (48 – 32 × 5 ÷ 9 = 8.89)

20°C = 68°F (20 × 9 ÷ 5 + 32 = 68)

A simplified (less accurate) method you can use without a calculator is to subtract 30 from the Fahrenheit degrees and take half to get centigrade; or double the centigrade and add 30 to get degrees in Fahrenheit.

Example: 60°F = 60 – 30 x ½ = 15°C

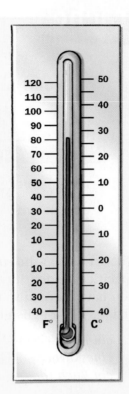

Persönliches

1. Wie ist das Wetter, wo du wohnst? Im Sommer, Herbst, Winter und Frühling?

2. Wie kalt ist es da im Januar und im Juli?

3. Was machst du gern im Sommer?

4. Welche Jahreszeit hast du besonders gern? Warum?

Wie ist das Wetter in Berlin?

Heute ist es in Rothenburg schön.

Indefinite Article
(Nominative and Accusative Singular)

SINGULAR			
	masculine	feminine	neuter
nominative	ein	eine	ein
accusative	einen	eine	ein

The articles in the *ein*-group are called indefinite because they do not specifically identify the noun they are associated with. All articles you have learned so far, e.g., *der, die, das*, are *der*-words (definite articles). In English the indefinite article is either "a" or "an."

ein Junge (der)
eine Karte (die)
ein Buch (das)

You can see that only the accusative of the masculine article differs from the nominative *(ein, einen)*. You will remember that this is also true of the definite article *(der, den)*.

Ich lese den Fahrplan.	I am reading the schedule.
Ich lese einen Fahrplan.	I am reading a schedule.

The forms of *mein* (my) and *dein* (your) are similar to *ein*-words as they take the same endings. You have already seen some examples in the various dialogs and reading selections.

Ein Heft ist in der Schultasche?	A notebook is in the school bag?
Wo ist mein Englischbuch?	Where is my English book?
Hast du einen Bleistift?	Do you have a pencil?
Ich finde deinen Freund toll.	I think your friend is great.

Sie hat einen Kuli und einen Computer.

7 Was ist das?

Your friends want to learn some German words. As they point to different items, help them identify each.

BEISPIEL Das ist eine CD.

1.
2.
3.
4.
5.
6.
7.
8.

8 Wo ist...?

Several people are asking for your help in locating specific objects, places or people. Can you help them?

BEISPIEL Bahnhof / in Bremen
Ein Bahnhof ist in Bremen.

1. Lehrer / am Telefon
2. Stuhl / da
3. Klavier / zu Hause
4. Stadt / im Norden
5. CD / hier
6. Tisch / da drüben

Wo ist der Kiosk?

9 Was brauchst du?

Tell your classmates that various people need the following items. Use the cues provided.

BEISPIEL ich
Ich brauche einen Bleistift.

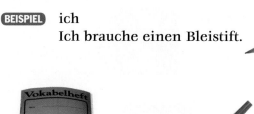

1. Christa

2. wir

3. mein Bruder

4. Herr Schmidt

5. meine Mutter

6. der Mathelehrer

Aktuelles

Berlin, die Hauptstadt

No other city reflects German history as graphically as Berlin. In the period of the Cold War *(der Kalte Krieg)*, the confrontation between East and West, the divided city with its Four-Power Agreement *(Viermächteabkommen)* could only dream about reunification *(Wiedervereinigung)* of Germany. The German question remained open as long as the Brandenburg Gate *(Brandenburger Tor)* was closed, dividing East from West Berlin.

The new Berlin presents itself to visitors as an open city once again. The Brandenburg Gate—once a symbol of the divided Germany—has again become the emblem

Was gibt's alles in Berlin?

of the united German capital. Around it, the new center of Berlin is still in the process of being completed. It's a unique urban setting in which the old joins with the new, and the future of the city becomes visible. In 1989, as soon as the Wall *(die Mauer)* began to come down, the other obstacles started to be cleared away to erase the ugly and hated division and to make room for future progress.

Das Brandenburger Tor

Berlin is both a federal state *(Bundesland)* and a city. It has a population of more than 3.4 million. Not only do Germans from all over the country live here, but there are more than 470,000 foreigners *(Ausländer)* from 184 different countries inhabiting Berlin. In an area as large as the cities of *München, Stuttgart* and *Frankfurt* combined, Berlin unites a large number of urban districts, centers and boroughs that are vastly different in character. In the inner part of the city, the buildings of the *Kulturforum* on the southern edge of the *Tiergarten* and the modern office and shopping complex on the *Potsdamer Platz* link the western city around *Kurfürstendamm* with the eastern city in the historical center of Berlin between the *Brandenburger Tor* and *Alexanderplatz*. To the north of the *Tiergarten*, the government and parliament buildings are situated along the winding Spree River.

Kaiser-Wilhelm-Gedächtnis-Kirche
am Kurfürstendamm

Berlin heute

The ring of the *S-Bahn*, the city train, encloses the most densely populated area of the city. Outside the ring of the *S-Bahn*, the density of urban development is significantly lower. The outlying boroughs are characterized by large areas of new development, established villa districts, lakes, rivers and even forests. These areas form a gentle transition to the less populated surrounding area with its idyllic woodland, its lake scenery and wide open agricultural spaces. For Berlin, which is surrounded by the federal state of *Brandenburg*, the newly regained open space is a unique recreation spot "outside the front door" that offers sports, leisure and recreational facilities and major tourist attractions.

The Berlin cultural scene with its volume, variety, liveliness and attractiveness contributes significantly to the unmistakable profile of the city. The 17 state museums of the Prussian Cultural Foundation *(Stiftung Preußischer Kulturbesitz)* form the largest museum complex of the whole European continent. Berlin is unquestionably Germany's most important cultural center with its 3 opera houses, over 150 theaters and stage companies, 800 choirs, more than 175 museums and collections, about 300 communal and private galleries, over 250 public libraries, 130 cinemas and numerous other cultural institutions.

Viele Ausländer wohnen in Berlin.

Die Mauer, 1989

Sie warten auf eine S-Bahn.

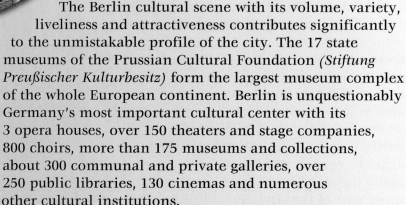

10 Was weißt du?

Auf Deutsch, bitte!

1. It was a symbol of Germany's division.
2. It is the German equivalent of "federal state."
3. This structure was dismantled to reconnect all parts of the city.
4. Berlin is surrounded by this federal state.
5. It is the same size as three other major German cities combined.
6. This agreement was reached between the United States, England, France and the Soviet Union.
7. It is the name for "cultural foundation."
8. A major shopping center is found there.
9. It serves as a major means of transportation for people who don't want to drive.
10. It flows through the city of Berlin.
11. They are people from other countries.
12. It is a historical name that suggests friction between the Soviet Union and the Western Allied Forces after the Second World War.

11 Wo ist das?

Look at the Berlin map at the front of your textbook and then answer these questions. *Auf Deutsch, bitte!*

> **BEISPIEL** Wo ist die Hohenstaufenstraße.
> Die Hohenstaufenstraße ist im Süden.

1. Wo ist Charlottenburg?
2. Wo ist die Köpenicker Straße?
3. Wo ist die Gedenkstätte Berliner Mauer?
4. Wo ist die Kaiser-Wilhelm-Gedächtnis-Kirche?
5. Wo ist der Flughafen Berlin-Tempelhof?
6. Wo ist die Technische Universität?
7. Wo liegt Friedrichshain?
8. Wo ist das Antikenmuseum?
9. Wo ist Wedding?
10. Wo ist die Kolonnenstraße?

Rollenspiel

You are asked to list various sights, streets and/or other items indicated on the Berlin map (in the front section of this textbook). Your partner will list the other specific geographic locations of the various sights, streets, etc. such as *Norden, Osten, Süden, Westen (Nordosten, Nordwesten, Südosten, Südwesten)*. When your lists are complete, ask your partner such questions as: *Wo ist...?, Wo liegt...?* or *Wo steht...?* to which he or she will give you the location. After you are finished, reverse roles.

Fernsehturm am Alexanderplatz

Kreuzberg, ein Stadtteil Berlins

Oper im Zentrum Berlins

Potsdamer Platz

Wörter und Ausdrücke

Seasons and Months

im Herbst in the fall
im Winter in the winter
im Frühling in the spring
im Sommer in the summer

Januar January
Februar February
März March
April April
Mai May
Juni June
Juli July
August August
September September
Oktober October
November November
Dezember December

Weather-related Expressions

Wie ist das Wetter im Sommer? How is the weather in the summer?
Es ist...
    warm warm
    heiß hot
    kalt cold
    schön beautiful
    schlecht bad

Die Sonne scheint. The sun is shining.
Es regnet. It is raining.
Es schneit. It is snowing.

Other Expressions

Immer mit der Ruhe! Take it easy!
Da steht es. There it is.
Die Busse kommen alle zwölf Minuten. The buses come every twelve minutes.
Da ist er ja schon. There it is.

Zungenbrecher

Ich stehe im Regen und
warte auf dich.
Ich warte im Regen und
steh' auf dich.

I'm standing in the rain and waiting for you. I'm waiting in the rain and like you.

Lektion B

Vokabeln

Länder und Sprachen

Er kommt aus Italien.
Er spricht
italienisch.

Sie kommt aus Frankreich.
Sie spricht französisch.

Er kommt aus Österreich.
Er spricht deutsch.

Er kommt aus Amerika.
Er spricht englisch.

Sie kommt aus Spanien.
Sie spricht spanisch.

Wie heißen die Nachbarländer von Deutschland?

Dänemark

die Niederlande
(Holland)

Belgien

Polen

Deutschland

Luxemburg

Frankreich

die Tschechische
Republik

die Schweiz

Österreich

12 Wo liegt...?

Answer this question by locating cities within Germany.
You may want to use the map in the front of this book.

BEISPIEL Hamburg
Hamburg liegt im Norden.

Wo liegt Heidelberg?

1. Dresden
2. Halle
3. Köln
4. München
5. Bremen
6. Bonn
7. Chemnitz
8. Regensburg

13 Welche Sprache spricht man da?

Tell what language is spoken in each of these
international cities or countries. You haven't seen the
German names for some of the cities and countries
indicated, but you should be able to recognize them.

BEISPIEL Boston
In Boston spricht man englisch.

1. Madrid
2. Berlin
3. Costa Rica
4. Paris
5. Rom
6. München
7. Mexiko
8. London
9. Florenz
10. Kolumbien
11. Chicago
12. Quebec

Welche Sprache spricht man in Paris?

Dialog

Ist das Fahrrad teuer?

Ist es denn teuer?

Nein, ganz preiswert.

Lisa hat genug Geld.

WOLF: Brauchst du denn ein Fahrrad?

JENS: Nein, ich nicht. Es ist für meine Schwester. Wir fahren in den Ferien nach Österreich. Dort besuchen wir unseren Vater in Bregenz.

WOLF: Wie gefällt dir denn dieses Fahrrad?

JENS: Nicht schlecht. Ist es denn teuer?

WOLF: Nein, ganz preiswert.

JENS: Gut. Ich sage das Lisa. Sie hat ja genug Geld für dieses Fahrrad.

14 Richtig oder falsch?

Determine whether the following statements are correct or incorrect. If they are incorrect, provide a correct statement in German.

1. Jens braucht ein Fahrrad.
2. Jens und Lisa fahren nach Österreich.
3. Bregenz liegt in der Schweiz.
4. Wolf kauft vielleicht das Fahrrad.
5. Wolf meint, das Fahrrad ist nicht teuer.
6. Lisa hat kein Geld für ein Fahrrad.

15 Was passt hier?

Complete the sentences in the dialog using the words listed.

| bin | besuchen | hast | fahre |
| kommst | macht | bleibst | beginnt |

Yvonne: Am Donnerstag __(1)__ ich mit meinen Eltern nach München.

Elke: Was __(2)__ ihr da?

Yvonne: Wir __(3)__ meinen Onkel und meine Tante.

Elke: Wie viele Tage __(4)__ du denn in München?

Yvonne: Nur drei Tage. Ich __(5)__ am Sonntag schon zu Hause.

Elke: Warum __(6)__ du so früh nach Hause?

Yvonne: Die Schule __(7)__ doch am Montag.

Elke: Ja, du __(8)__ Recht.

Was macht Yvonne in München?

Für dich

Although school vacation varies slightly among the 16 federal states *(Bundesländer)*, it's common for students to have two or three weeks of vacation around Easter *(Osterferien)* which is either in March or April. In most federal states, students get one day and up to one week off during Pentecost *(Pfingstferien)* in the month of May or June. To avoid congestion on the German highways and freeways during the summer, the federal states stagger the six-week summer vacation period *(Sommerferien)* from the end of June through the early part of September. Students have another one to two weeks of school vacation during October *(Herbstferien)*. Finally, students have two weeks off at Christmas time *(Weihnachtsferien)*.

Segeln macht Spaß.

Die Sommerferien

Baden-Württemberg	26.7.–8.9.
Bayern	26.7.–10.9.
Berlin	19.7.–1.9.
Brandenburg	19.7.–1.9.
Bremen	28.6.–11.8.
Hamburg	19.7.–29.8.
Hessen	21.6.–3.8.
Mecklenburg-Vorpommern	19.7.–29.8.
Niedersachsen	28.6.–8.8.
Nordrhein-Westfalen	5.7.–18.8.
Rheinland-Pfalz	28.6.–10.8.
Saarland	21.6.–1.8.
Sachsen	28.6.–8.8.
Sachsen-Anhalt	28.6.–8.8.
Schleswig-Holstein	19.7.–1.9.
Thüringen	28.6.–8.8.

Viele schwimmen gern im Sommer.

Winterferien in den Bergen

Plural Forms of Nouns

For singular nouns, you must know the gender; that is, you must know whether the noun is a *der-, die-* or *das*-word. You will have to learn these, of course. In the plural, however, all nouns take the article *die* in the nominative and accusative, regardless of their gender.

	SINGULAR			PLURAL
	masculine	**feminine**	**neuter**	
nominative	der	die	das	die
accusative	den	die	das	die

When you look up nouns at the end of each chapter and in the vocabulary section at the back of this textbook, you will notice that each noun is followed by a comma and an indication of its plural form. Here are some examples of how nouns are listed in this book and in most German dictionaries and reference books.

die **Klasse,-n** class
Singular = *die Klasse*; Plural = *die Klassen* (*n* is added)

der **Lehrer,-** teacher
Singular = *der Lehrer*; Plural = *die Lehrer* (no change)

das **Buch,-̈er** book
Singular = *das Buch*; Plural = *die Bücher* (*u* changes to *ü* and *er* is added)

There is no definite rule for the formation of plural nouns. You must learn the plural form when you learn a new noun.

Wie viel? or *Wie viele?*

Generally speaking, *wie viel?* (how much?) is used when expressing a mass or a sum.

Wie viel Uhr ist es?	What time is it?
Wie viel Deutsch hast du für morgen?	How much German (homework) do you have for tomorrow?

On the other hand, *wie viele?* (how many?) is used when referring to items that can be counted.

Wie viele Karten kaufen wir?	How many tickets do we buy?
Wie viele Freunde hat Tina?	How many friends does Tina have?

16 Wie viele holen sie?

You and your friends are planning a fun party and need to get more than just one of each item for some of the games planned.

Wie viele Fußbälle sind da?

> **BEISPIEL** Klaus / viele / Bleistift
> Klaus holt viele Bleistifte.

1. Renate / acht / Kuli
2. Rolf und Sabine / zwei / Video
3. Petra / zehn / Buch
4. Aki / fünf / Karte
5. Ralf / vier / Computerspiel
6. Heike und Monika / acht / CD
7. Günter / drei / Stuhl

17 Markos Familie

Marko's parents are planning a family reunion with their relatives who live in different parts of Germany. Marko asks his father about various relatives.

> **BEISPIEL** Hat Tante Anna eine Schwester? (vier)
> Sie hat vier Schwestern.

1. Hat Onkel Bruno einen Bruder? (zwei)
2. Hat Mutti eine Cousine? (fünf)
3. Hat deine Schwester eine Tochter? (drei)
4. Hat Tante Elisabeth einen Sohn? (zwei)
5. Hat Opa einen Cousin? (vier)
6. Hat Muttis Bruder eine Tante? (drei)

18 *Wie viel?* oder *Wie viele?*

Complete each sentence using the appropriate question words.

1. ___ Zeit hast du morgen?
2. ___ Wochen bleibt ihr in Deutschland?
3. ___ CDs hast du zu Hause?
4. ___ Geld brauchst du?
5. ___ Arbeit hast du heute?
6. ___ Städte besuchen sie?
7. ___ Tage besucht ihr Onkel Walter?

19 Wie bitte? (What did you say?)

The music at a party is quite loud and you can't hear everything that is being said. Ask the appropriate questions using *wie viel* and *wie viele*.

BEISPIEL Morgen kaufen wir *vier* Karten zum Rockkonzert.
Wie viele Karten kauft ihr morgen?

1. Die Matheklasse beginnt heute um *elf* Uhr.
2. Wir kaufen *vier* Computerspiele im Kaufhaus.
3. Familie Rückert wohnt erst *zwei* Monate hier.
4. Vierzig minus zwölf ist *achtundzwanzig*.
5. Mein Onkel hat *drei* Söhne.
6. Ich habe am Sonntag *keine* Zeit.
7. Rainer bringt *sieben* Bücher zur Schule.
8. Dieter hat *zwei* Freundinnen.

Im Kaufhaus

Steffen und Carsten möchten im Juli eine Radtour machen[1]. Carstens Fahrrad ist schon sehr alt. Steffen braucht auch noch ein paar Sachen[2] für die Radtour. Deshalb[3] fahren beide in die Stadt. Heute sind die Fahrräder im Kaufhaus besonders[4] preiswert.

Steffen: Wie gefällt dir dieses Fahrrad?

Carsten: Klasse![5] Wo ist denn der Verkäufer[6]? Ah, da kommt er schon.

Verkäufer: Dieses Rad[7] verkaufen[8] wir viel. Ist es für Sie?

Carsten: Ja, mein Freund und ich fahren in den Ferien zum Rhein[9]. Da bleiben wir zwei Wochen.

Verkäufer: Für eine Reise[10] ist dieses Rad besonders gut. Es ist ganz stabil[11] und nicht sehr teuer. Nur 250 Euro[12]

Steffen: Ich finde das Fahrrad sehr gut.

Carsten: Der Preis ist auch nicht schlecht. Hast du Geld? Ich brauche noch etwas.

Für eine Reise ist dieses Rad besonders gut.

Steffen: Bis morgen geht es.

Carsten: Danke![13] Morgen bekommst du es dann.

Von Steffen bekommt Carsten noch etwas Geld. Dann kauft er das Fahrrad. Steffen braucht einen Helm[14] und einen Reifen[15].

Steffen: Da sind die Helme. Ist dieser Helm nicht zu groß?

Carsten: Nicht der Helm, dein Kopf[16].

Verkäufer: Der Helm hier passt gut.

Carsten: Und einen Reifen brauchst du auch?

Steffen: Ja, ein Reifen ist kaputt[17].

Carsten: Wie ist dieser?

Steffen: Der ist nicht schlecht. Na gut, ich kaufe den Reifen.

Verkäufer: Sonst noch etwas?[18]

Steffen: Nein, das ist alles.

Verkäufer: Gehen Sie bitte zur Kasse![19]

Ist der Helm zu groß?

Carsten und Steffen gehen zur Kasse und bezahlen[20] dort. Beide gehen dann nach Hause. Carstens Vater kommt später mit dem Auto und holt das Fahrrad. Jetzt haben Carsten und Steffen alles, was sie für die Radtour im Sommer brauchen.

---

[1]*möchten...eine Radtour machen* would like to go on a bike trip; [2]*ein paar Sachen* a few things; [3]*deshalb* that's why; [4]*besonders* especially; [5]*Klasse!* Great!; [6]*der Verkäufer* salesperson; [7]*das Rad* bike; [8]*verkaufen* to sell; [9]*der Rhein* Rhine River; [10]*die Reise* trip; [11]*stabil* solid; [12]*der Euro* euro; [13]*Danke!* Thank you!; [14]*der Helm* helmet; [15]*der Reifen* tire; [16]*der Kopf* head; [17]*kaputt* broken; [18]*Sonst noch etwas?* Anything else?; [19]*Gehen Sie bitte zur Kasse!* Please go to the cash register!; [20]*bezahlen* to pay

Was kauft Steffen?

20 Was fehlt hier?

Complete each sentence by selecting the appropriate verb and changing it to the correct verb form where necessary. Use each verb only once.

machen	gehen	bekommen	finden	holen	passen
kommen	bleiben	brauchen	fahren	sein	haben

1. Carsten und Steffen ___ im Sommer eine Radtour.
2. Carsten ___ ein Fahrrad, aber es ist sehr alt.
3. Die beiden Jungen ___ in die Stadt.
4. Die Fahrräder im Kaufhaus ___ heute nicht teuer.
5. Der Verkäufer ___ und spricht mit Steffen und Carsten.
6. Carsten und Steffen ___ zwei Wochen am Rhein.
7. Steffen ___ das Rad sehr gut.
8. Carsten ___ noch etwas Geld.
9. Steffen ___ das Geld morgen zurück.
10. Der Helm ___ Steffen gut.
11. Steffen und Carsten ___ zur Kasse.
12. Carstens Vater ___ das Fahrrad später.

21 Fragen

Beantworte diese Fragen!

1. Wie ist Carstens Fahrrad?
2. Was braucht Steffen für die Radtour?
3. Wohin fahren beide?
4. Für wen ist das Fahrrad?
5. Wohin fahren Steffen und Carsten im Sommer?
6. Wie lange bleiben sie da?
7. Wie findet Steffen das Fahrrad?
8. Hat Carsten genug Geld für das Fahrrad?
9. Welche beiden Sachen kauft Steffen?
10. Was macht Carstens Vater später?

Persönliches

Write a short letter to a friend, inviting him or her to visit you during your summer vacation. Start your letter with either *Liebe...* (name of girl) or *Lieber...* (name of boy) which means "Dear..." and finish your letter with *Dein...* (if you are a boy) or *Deine...* (if you are a girl) which means "Yours..."

Rollenspiel

You are asking your classmate what he or she will be doing during the next vacation. For example, you could ask such questions as: "What are you doing during school vacation?" *(Was machst du in den Ferien?)*, "Whom will you visit?" *(Wen besuchst du?)*, "Will you need a bike?" *(Brauchst du ein Fahrrad?)*, "Who will come along?" *(Wer kommt mit?)*, etc. After you have asked various questions, reverse roles and have your classmate ask similar questions, with you answering them.

Praktisches

You and your partner each select a European country, city or area of Germany that you would like to visit. Then, taking turns, ask and answer questions about why you selected the place you would like to visit, what time of year you would go there and what the weather would be like during your visit.

> **BEISPIEL** Student 1: *Ich möchte nach Österreich fahren.*
>
> Student 2: *Warum nach Österreich?*
>
> Student 1: *Es ist nicht so weit von hier.*
>
> Student 2: *Wann möchtest du nach Österreich fahren?*
>
> Student 1: *Im Frühling.*
>
> Student 2: *Wie ist das Wetter da im Frühling?*
>
> Student 1: *Es ist etwas kühl.*

Schreiben

1. You are planning to buy a bicycle or other item. Write a dialog or paragraph in which you discuss the following details with a salesperson *(Verkäufer/Verkäuferin):* what you are

looking for, how much money you have to spend, when you need this item and for what purpose, etc. Here is a sample that you may want to follow:

Verkäufer: Wie gefällt dir dieses Fahrrad?

Du: Nicht schlecht. Ist es teuer? Ich habe nur 150 Euro.

Verkäufer: Das Fahrrad ist sehr preiswert, heute nur 120 Euro.

Du: Gut, ich hole mein Geld. Ich brauche das Fahrrad für die Schule.

Verkäufer: Bis später!

2. You don't want one of your relatives (cousin, aunt, uncle, etc.) to come and visit you during a certain time of the year. Write a short letter in which you give at least three reasons why he or she should not come at that time and why it is better to come at a different time. For example, your reasons may include: *das Wetter ist schlecht, ich habe zu viel Arbeit, ich bin nicht zu Hause,* etc. Begin your letter with *Lieber* or *Liebe* and end it with *Dein* or *Deine.* To get you started, you may want to use the following information:

Lieber Rolf,
Kommst du im Winter? Im Sommer ist es besser. Dann ist das Wetter warm und wir haben mehr Spaß. Besonders im Juli habe ich viel Zeit. Dann gibt es keine Schule und ich habe keine Arbeit zu Hause. Im Winter habe ich viele Hausaufgaben und keine Zeit für dich. Meine Oma kommt auch im Januar und Februar.
Dein

Wörter und Ausdrücke

Countries and Languages

Er/Sie kommt aus... He/She comes from...
  Amerika America
  Frankreich France
  Italien Italy
  Österreich Austria
  Spanien Spain
Er/Sie spricht... He/She speaks...
  englisch English
  französisch French
  italienisch Italian
  deutsch German
  spanisch Spanish

Wie heißen die Nachbarländer von Deutschland? What are the names of the neighboring countries of Germany?
  Dänemark Denmark
  die Niederlande Netherlands
  Belgien Belgium
  Luxemburg Luxembourg
  Frankreich France
  die Schweiz Switzerland
  Österreich Austria
  die Tschechische Republik Czech Republic
  Polen Poland

22 Was passt hier?

Find each word that has something in common with the one provided in the list.

Fußball	Lehrerin	Musik	Uhr	Wetter	Reise
Reifen	Mittwoch	Juni	Zwei	Physik	Herbst

1. das Rockkonzert
2. der Tag
3. die Zeit
4. der Monat
5. die Radtour
6. die Schule
7. die Note
8. das Fach
9. die Sonne
10. der Sport
11. das Fahrrad
12. die Jahreszeit

Sie machen eine Reise.

23 Was fehlt hier?

Complete each word by adding another noun. Make sure that the given article is the same as that of the added noun.

BEISPIEL die Haus___
die Hausaufgabe

1. das Computer___
2. das Fernseh___
3. das Kauf___
4. die Land___
5. das Lieblings___
6. der Bahn___
7. die Rock___
8. die Schul___
9. der Stunden___
10. die Rad___

24 Kombiniere...

Brauchst	wir	ein Fahrrad
Kaufen	Rudi und Dieter	nach Österreich
Besucht	du	eine Karte
Fahren	ihr	den Deutschlehrer
		in die Stadt
		Renate

25 Was machst du jetzt?

On the way to your aunt's house you meet a friend and talk about various things. Complete the conversation based on what your friend is saying.

Freund(in): Wohin gehst du denn?
Du: (1)

Freund(in): Wo wohnt deine Tante denn?
Du: (2)

Freund(in): Kommst du später rüber?
Du: (3)

Freund(in): Und morgen?
Du: (4)

Freund(in): Um wie viel Uhr kommst du morgen?
Du: (5)

Freund(in): Gut, bis morgen.
Du: (6)

Gut, bis morgen.

Was weißt du?

1. Indicate that you would like to buy a bicycle and give three reasons why.

2. Describe the weather in your area throughout the year. Say something about each season.

3. Give three reasons why you would like to go to Berlin and what you would like to see there. *(Auf Englisch, bitte!)*

4. Name the nine countries that border Germany.

5. Select eight international cities and indicate the language spoken in each one.

6. Tell your classmate that you have more than one of each of these: book, (school) subject, friend, computer game, teacher, notebook, video, detective story, telephone. Start your sentence with *Ich habe...*

Warum kommen viele Touristen nach Berlin?

Scheint die Sonne heute in Salzburg?

Vokabeln

alle all; *alle zwölf Minuten* every twelve minutes *5A*

alles everything; *Das ist alles.* That's all. *5B*

Amerika America *5B*

der **April** April *5A*

der **August** August *5A*

das **Auto,-s** car *5B*

bald soon *5A*

Belgien Belgium *5B*

besonders especially *5B*

besuchen to visit *5B*

bezahlen to pay *5B*

bitte please *5B*

Dänemark Denmark *5B*

Danke! Thank you! *5B*

deshalb therefore, that's why *5B*

deutsch German; *Er spricht deutsch.* He speaks German. *5B*

der **Dezember** December *5A*

englisch *Er spricht englisch.* He speaks English. *5B*

fahren to drive, go *5B*

der **Fahrplan,-e** schedule *5A*

das **Fahrrad,-er** bicycle *5B*

der **Februar** February *5A*

die **Ferien** (pl.) vacation; *in den Ferien* on vacation; *in die Ferien fahren* to go on vacation *5B*

Frankreich France *5B*

französisch French; *Er spricht französisch.* He speaks French. *5B*

der **Frühling,-e** spring *5A*

das **Geld** money *5B*

heiß hot *5A*

der **Helm,-e** helmet *5B*

Holland Holland *5B*

Italien Italy *5B*

italienisch Italian; *Er spricht italienisch.* He speaks Italian. *5B*

die **Jahreszeit,-en** season *5A*

der **Januar** January *5A*

der **Juli** July *5A*

der **Juni** June *5A*

kalt cold *5A*

kaputt broken *5B*

die **Kasse,-n** cash register *5B*

Klasse! Great! Terrific! *5B*

der **Kopf,-e** head *5B*

kühl cool *5A*

die **Linie,-n** line *5A*

Luxemburg Luxembourg *5B*

der **Mai** May *5A*

der **März** March *5A*

der **Monat,-e** month *5A*

das **Nachbarland,-er** neighboring country *5B*

die **Niederlande** Netherlands *5B*

der **November** November *5A*

der **Oktober** October *5A*

Österreich Austria *5B*

paar: ein paar a few *5B*

Polen Poland *5B*

der **Preis,-e** price *5B*

preiswert reasonable *5B*

das **Rad,-er** bike *5B*

die **Radtour,-en** bike tour; *eine Radtour machen* to go on a bike tour *5B*

regnen to rain *5A*

der **Reifen,-** tire *5B*

die **Reise,-n** trip *5B*

der **Rhein** Rhine River *5B*

die **Ruhe** peace, quiet; *Immer mit der Ruhe!* Take it easy! *5A*

die **Sache,-n** thing, item *5B*

scheinen to shine *5A*

schneien to snow *5A*

schön beautiful *5A*

die **Schweiz** Switzerland *5B*

der **September** September *5A*

die **Sonne** sun *5A*

sonst besides, otherwise; *Sonst noch etwas?* Anything else? *5B*

Spanien Spain *5B*

spanisch Spanish; *Er spricht spanisch.* He speaks Spanish. *5B*

sprechen to speak, talk; *er/sie spricht* he/she speaks *5B*

stabil solid, sturdy *5B*

stehen to stand, be; *Da steht es.* There it is. *5A*

teuer expensive *5B*

die **Tschechische Republik** Czech Republic *5B*

unser our *5B*

verkaufen to sell *5B*

der **Verkäufer,-** salesperson *5B*

warm warm *5A*

das **Wetter** weather *5A*

der **Winter,-** winter *5A*

Sie bezahlt.

Viele Touristen besuchen Leipzig.

Kapitel 6
Wie schmeckt's?

Objectives

In this chapter you will learn how to:

- ▶ choose from a menu and order at a café
- ▶ offer something to eat and drink
- ▶ express likes and dislikes
- ▶ make requests
- ▶ give advice
- ▶ talk about what to do today

Lektion A

1 Was essen wir diese Woche?

Your mother or father is planning the menu for the week and would like your advice.

BEISPIEL Sonntag / Sauerbraten
Am Sonntag möchte ich Sauerbraten.

1. Montag / eine Pizza
2. Dienstag / Fisch mit Kartoffeln
3. Mittwoch / einen Hamburger mit Pommes frites
4. Donnerstag / Kalte Platte
5. Freitag / Bratwurst mit Brötchen
6. Sonnabend / Wiener Schnitzel mit Gemüse

2 Ich esse gern...

Tell one of your classmates what you usually eat for breakfast, lunch and dinner. Reverse roles by asking your classmate what he or she likes to eat. *Was isst du gern zum Frühstück, Mittagessen und Abendessen?*

beim Mittagessen

Was schmeckt?

belegte Brötchen

Lektion A

157

Wir wollen etwas essen

Wohin gehen alle drei?

Wie weit ist der Imbiss?

MONIKA: Möchtest du mitkommen?

SVEN: Wohin geht's denn?

EMINE: Wir wollen etwas essen. Beim Imbiss.

MONIKA: Komm doch mit!

SVEN: Ich kann leider nicht. Ich muss nach Hause.

MONIKA: Die Pommes schmecken dort besonders gut.

EMINE: Die Hamburger sind auch nicht schlecht.

MONIKA: Wir treffen dort noch andere.

SVEN: Na gut. Ich habe ja auch Hunger.

3 Was fehlt hier?

Complete the dialog using the appropriate forms of the verbs listed. You will not need all the verbs listed.

haben	sein	gehen	essen
kommen	können	fahren	treffen

A: Wohin (1) ihr denn?

B: Wir (2) mit den Rädern zum Imbiss.

A: Wer (3) mit?

B: Ich (4) leider nicht, aber andere kommen mit.

A: (5) du Hunger?

B: Ja, ich möchte einen Hamburger (6).

A: Beim Imbiss (7) wir noch andere Schulfreunde.

B: Ja, da (8) immer viele da.

Für dich

A *Schnellimbiss, Schnellgaststätte, Imbissstube* or simply an *Imbiss* is a snack bar where you can get sausages with bread or a roll and mustard *(Würstchen mit Brot oder Semmel mit Senf)* and a soft drink at a reasonable price. You usually eat standing at a counter or at a small round table.

Most of these snack bars offer a variety of sausages. The *Bratwurst* is fat, white and spicy; the *Currywurst* is similar, but served with a curry sauce; *Bockwurst* is longer and reddish, something like a thick American hot dog. The *Frankfurter* is thinner and usually sold in pairs. At an *Imbiss* sausages are eaten using the fingers. You don't get a bun, but often a slice of bread *(eine Scheibe Brot)* or a small roll *(Brötchen* or *Semmel)* comes with the sausages.

Other fast-food places sell pizza and American-style hamburgers and hot dogs as well as grilled chicken *(Brathähnchen)*. Many restaurants and snack bars also offer the very popular *Döner Kebap,* a Turkish dish made of meat cooked on a vertical spit and sliced off to order.

der Imbiss

Döner

The Modal Auxiliaries:
mögen (möchten), müssen, wollen

Modal auxiliaries (sometimes called helping verbs) help to set the mood of the particular sentence in which they occur. Look at the English sentence and see how each modal auxiliary changes the meaning.

Anne **likes** to read a book.	*Anne **mag** ein Buch lesen.*
Rainer **would like** to read a book.	*Rainer **möchte** ein Buch lesen.*
Boris **must (has to)** read a book.	*Boris **muss** ein Buch lesen.*
Julia **wants to** read a book.	*Julia **will** ein Buch lesen.*

As you can see, the meaning or "mood" in each of these sentences is different. The same is true in German. You will notice, however, that the word order remains constant in these sentences.

Mögen is most commonly used to express a liking or preference in the sense of *gern haben* (like to have), *gern essen* or *trinken* (like to eat or drink). Today it is frequently used in the negative, often without the main verb: *Er mag das Buch nicht.* (He doesn't like the book.). A more common form derived from *mögen* is *möchten* (would like to). *Sie möchte nach Deutschland fahren.* (She would like to go to Germany.) You have already learned some of the *möchte*-forms in earlier chapters.

When using a modal auxiliary, it is very important to remember that the infinitive of the main verb is placed at the end of the sentence. The modal auxiliary appears in the position normally held by the verb.

	MODAL	AUXILIARY	INFINITE	
statement	Tina	will	in die Stadt	gehen.
question	Will	Tina	in die Stadt	gehen?

Sometimes the main verb can be eliminated, provided that the meaning is clear by using only the modal auxiliary.

Ich muss um sieben Uhr in die Schule.	I have to go to school at seven o'clock.
Möchtest du ein Glas Milch?	Would you like (to have) a glass of milk?

	mögen	möchten	müssen	wollen
	to like	*would like (to do)*	*must, to have to*	*to want to*
ich	mag	möchte	muss	will
du	magst	möchtest	musst	willst
er } sie } es }	mag	möchte	muss	will
wir	mögen	möchten	müssen	wollen
ihr	mögt	möchtet	müsst	wollt
sie	mögen	möchten	müssen	wollen
Sie	mögen	möchten	müssen	wollen

4 Was möchten alle nach der Schule machen?

Tell what everyone would like to do after school.

BEISPIEL   Christa / nach Hause gehen
Christa möchte nach Hause gehen.

1. Uli und Stefan / Frau Riedel besuchen
2. Heidi / zu Petra rüberkommen
3. wir / Fußball spielen
4. Rudi / einen Krimi lesen
5. mein Freund / Rockmusik hören
6. deine Schwester / zum Imbiss gehen

Was möchten alle nach der Schule machen?

5 Sie wollen das.

Everyone wants to do the things suggested.

BEISPIEL Willst du deinen Onkel besuchen?
Ja, ich will meinen Onkel besuchen.

1. Wollt ihr nach Hause fahren?
2. Will Gisela jetzt essen?
3. Wollen Ralf und Ali Karten spielen?
4. Willst du mit Anne sprechen?
5. Will Gabriele fernsehen?
6. Wollt ihr in die Stadt gehen?
7. Will Frau Schulz heute schon früh das Abendessen machen?

6 Was musst du heute Nachmittag machen?

Before going to a party, you have to take care of several things.

BEISPIEL meine Hausaufgaben machen
Ich muss meine Hausaufgaben machen.

1. ein Buch lesen
2. etwas Deutsch lernen
3. eine halbe Stunde Gitarre spielen
4. zum Kaufhaus gehen
5. einen Rechner kaufen
6. etwas essen

7 Warum mögen sie das nicht?

You've heard that several people you know don't like certain things. You are asking them why not.

BEISPIEL Dieter / Krimi
Warum mag Dieter den Krimi nicht?

1. Ursula und Sabine / Musik
2. Frau Lehmann / Buch
3. Rainer / Fach
4. Elisabeth / Fernsehprogramm
5. ihr / Kaufhaus
6. du / Sport

The Modal Auxiliaries: *dürfen, können, sollen*

You have already learned the forms of these modal auxiliaries: *mögen (möchten), müssen* and *wollen*. The three new modal auxiliaries *(dürfen, können, sollen)* follow the same word order as the others. Notice that the forms of *dürfen* and *können* have a stem vowel change when using *ich, du, er, sie* and *es*, whereas the forms of *sollen* follow a regular pattern.

Darfst du in die Stadt gehen?	Are you allowed to go downtown?
Wir können die Arbeit machen.	We can do the work.
Meine Schwester soll ein Buch lesen.	My sister is supposed to read a book.

	dürfen	können	sollen
	may, to be allowed to	*can, to be able to*	*should, to be supposed to*
ich	darf	kann	soll
du	darfst	kannst	sollst
er **sie** **es** }	darf	kann	soll
wir	dürfen	können	sollen
ihr	dürft	könnt	sollt
sie	dürfen	können	sollen

Er soll noch schnell seine Hausaufgaben machen.

8 Was könnt ihr alles?

Tell what the various people can do.

BEISPIEL Gisela / deutsch sprechen
Gisela kann deutsch sprechen.

1. Paul / Gitarre spielen
2. Christine und Karin / französisch lesen
3. meine Freundin / die Hausaufgaben machen
4. Dieters Schulfreunde / im Juli in die Schweiz fahren
5. dein Bruder / schon früh nach Hause kommen
6. wir / morgen Onkel Walter besuchen

9 Das dürfen sie.

Mr. and Mrs. Gerlach often limit the leisure-time activities of their three children, Julia, Angelika and Jochen. They are describing to their visiting relatives what their children are allowed to do during the week.

BEISPIEL Julia / nach vier Uhr zu ihren Freundinnen gehen
Julia darf nach vier Uhr zu ihren Freundinnen gehen.

1. Jochen / nach der Schule zum Imbiss gehen
2. Angelika und Julia / am Sonntag Rockmusik hören
3. Jochen / heute Abend fernsehen
4. Angelika / nur zehn Minuten am Telefon sprechen
5. alle drei / nach der Arbeit Basketball spielen
6. Julia und Angelika / am Sonnabend ihre Freundinnen besuchen

Vati, darf ich heute Abend meine Freundin besuchen?

10 Was sollen sie bis morgen machen?

Your German teacher is telling students what their responsibilities are. Indicate what everyone is supposed to do.

BEISPIEL ein Buch lesen (Maria)
Maria soll ein Buch lesen.

1. nach der Klasse die CD hören (Tina und Peter)
2. die Hausaufgaben machen (ich)
3. deutsch sprechen (wir)
4. bis drei Uhr in der Schule bleiben (Roland)
5. zehn Minuten vor acht Uhr kommen (Susi und Anke)
6. jeden Tag Klavier spielen (Wolf und Günter)

Aktuelles

Eating Out

Almost all German restaurants display their menu *(Speisekarte)* outside, next to the entrance. When entering a German restaurant, men generally precede women. This is clearly a remainder from earlier times when the man was the one to decide whether the locality was fit for the woman to enter. In entering first, he could screen her from curious stares and relieve her of the task of choosing a table.

Contrary to American custom, there are no hosts in typical German restaurants to greet and seat you. Normally, you look for a table yourself. If you can't find an empty table, it's customary to join people you don't know if there is room at their table. When joining others at a table, you should ask *Ist hier noch frei?* The usual response will be *Ja, bitte* or *Bitte sehr*. In above-average

Die Speisekarte ist direkt vor dem Restaurant.

Was gibt's heute zum Mittagessen?

restaurants, a food server will approach you and suggest a table, or lead you to the table that has been reserved for you.

When asking for the menu, just say *Die Speisekarte, bitte*. Never ask for *das Menü*, unless you want to order a complete meal with several courses. Many restaurants offer a complete dinner with soup *(die Suppe)* and dessert *(der Nachtisch)* called *das Gedeck* or *das Menü*. The male server *(der Kellner)* is addressed as *Herr Ober*, the female server *(die Kellnerin)* as *Fräulein*. In recent years, the more commonly used address for both the male and the female server is simply *Bedienung*. In small towns and villages, the local restaurant is often a family enterprise, where the proprietor and spouse wait on their guests. In such a place, you would call the proprietor *Herr Wirt* and his wife *Frau Wirtin*.

German table manners are somewhat different from ours. Whenever Germans eat something that requires cutting, they hold the fork in the left hand and the knife in the right, keeping them this way throughout the meal. The knife is also used to push the food onto the fork. If a knife is not needed, the left hand is placed on the table beside the plate, not in the lap.

Most Germans do not cut potatoes with a knife, but use a fork instead. This dates back to the times when blades were not yet made of stainless

Was kann man hier essen?

steel. Fish is not cut with a regular knife either; instead, a special fish knife or a second fork is used. Rarely will you see a German drink plain water with the meal; mostly beer, wine, fruit juice or soft drinks are ordered. If you would like to drink regular water, you need to ask for *Leitungswasser* (tap water); otherwise, the server may bring you a bottle of mineral water *(Mineralwasser)*.

How do you ask for the check? *Bedienung, ich möchte zahlen!* or *Die Rechnung, bitte!* or for short, *Zahlen, bitte!* Normally you pay the server at your table; rarely do you pay at the counter or cash register. A 10 to 15 percent service charge *(Bedienungsgeld)* and a 19 percent value-added tax *(Mehrwertsteuer)* are included in the total amount shown on the menu. Since a tip is already part of the bill, an extra tip is not necessary. However, most people do round off the bill to the nearest euro or more, according to the amount to be paid and the service rendered. For instance, if the check amounts to 8,60 you may say *Neun Euro, bitte!* to the server, indicating that you expect change for only 9 euro and that the rest can be kept. The small additional tip *(Trinkgeld)* is given to the food server upon paying and is not left on the table when leaving the restaurant.

Many Germans prefer to pay cash, especially in smaller local establishments. However, major credit cards are widely accepted.

Sonst noch etwas?

Hier ist die Rechnung, bitte!

11 Was passt hier?

1. The ___ is an added service charge.
2. The ___ is usually served before the main course.
3. The menu is called the ___.
4. After eating the main meal, you might order a ___.
5. The female server is called ___.
6. The value-added tax is called the ___.
7. A male server is called ___ when you want to get his attention.
8. When you are ready to pay your bill, you will ask the server for the ___.
9. A ___ is a complete meal.
10. The ___ is the owner of a small restaurant in a town.

A. *Kellnerin*
B. *Speisekarte*
C. *Gedeck*
D. *Herr Ober*
E. *Wirt/Wirtin*
F. *Nachtisch*
G. *Suppe*
H. *Rechnung*
I. *Bedienungsgeld*
J. *Mehrwertsteuer*

Persönliches

1. Was isst du gern? Was isst du nicht gern?
2. Gibt es einen Imbiss, nicht weit von deiner Schule?
3. Was kann man da essen?
4. Hast du manchmal Hunger in der Schule? Was machst du dann?
5. Wohin gehst du nach der Schule?

Rollenspiel

Working with a partner, take turns asking and answering at least four questions about what and when you eat certain meals.

BEISPIEL

Was isst du zum Abendessen?
Ich esse Kalte Platte.

Was essen sie zum Abendessen?

Wörter und Ausdrücke

Talking about Food

Was isst du zum Frühstück? What are you eating for breakfast?
Ich esse... I'm eating...
  ein Brötchen a roll
  eine Scheibe Brot a slice of bread
  ein Wurstbrot a sausage sandwich
  ein Käsebrot a cheese sandwich
  Kalte Platte cold-cut platter
  eine Pizza a pizza
  einen Hamburger a hamburger
  eine Bratwurst a bratwurst
  Sauerbraten sauerbraten (marinated beef roast)
  Wiener Schnitzel breaded veal cutlet

Schmeckt dir...? Do you like...?
  das Mittagessen lunch
  das Abendessen dinner
  die Wurst sausage
  der Käse cheese

ein paar Brötchen und eine Scheibe Brot

Other Expressions

Wohin geht's denn? Where are you going?
Zum Imbiss. To the snack bar.
Ich kann leider nicht. Unfortunately, I can't (go).
Ich muss nach Hause. I have to go home.
Ich habe Hunger. I'm hungry.

Zungenbrecher

Selten ess' ich Essig;
ess' ich Essig,
ess' ich Essig mit Salat.

Seldom I eat vinegar; when I eat vinegar I eat vinegar with salad.

Lektion B

Eis und Eiscafé

12 Wir sind in einem Imbiss.

You are joining several friends for lunch. You tell the food server what everyone wants to have.

BEISPIEL Tobias
Tobias möchte Vanilleeis.

1. Sandra

2. Michael

3. Silke und Angelika

4. Katrin

5. Bruno

6. Holger und Karsten

13 Möchtest du ins Café gehen?

You and your friend want to eat or drink something. One of you gives reasons why you don't want to go to a particular café, while the other gives reasons why you *do* want to go there. Come up with at least four reasons either for or against going to the café. Here are some reasons that you may wish to use.

Ich möchte ins Café gehen.
Ich habe Hunger.
Martina und Renate kommen auch.
Sie haben da Erdbeereis mit Schlagsahne.
Ich kenne das Café sehr gut.
Da spielen sie oft Musik.
Im Café haben wir immer Spaß.

Ich möchte nicht ins Café gehen.
Ich habe keine Zeit.
Rolf geht doch auch nicht.
Das Café ist zu weit.
Es kostet zu viel.
Es schmeckt mir da nicht.
Im Café ist es nicht preiswert.

Dialog

Es schmeckt gut!

Wo sind Sabrina und Alexander?

Was für ein Eis isst Sabrina?

Wie schmeckt das Nusseis?

SABRINA:	Wie schmeckt das Nusseis?
ALEXANDER:	Es schmeckt gut. Willst du nicht auch eins?
SABRINA:	Ich möchte lieber ein Vanilleeis.
ALEXANDER:	Etwas zu trinken?
SABRINA:	Nein, danke. Ich habe keinen Durst. Und du?
ALEXANDER:	Ich trinke gern eine Cola.
SABRINA:	Wo sind denn Karin und Jürgen?
ALEXANDER:	Sie gehen in die Pizzeria. Wir treffen sie später.

14 Was fehlt hier?

Complete the dialog using appropriate words.

A: Was möchtest du (1) ?

B: (2) Zitroneneis, bitte.

A: Das (3) mir nicht. Ich möchte (4) ein Erdbeereis.

B: (5) du auch etwas?

A: Nein, ich (6) keinen Durst. Und (7) ?

B: Ja, ich trinke ein (8) Apfelsaft.

15 Fragen

Beantworte diese Fragen!

1. Wie schmeckt Alexander das Nusseis?

2. Was für ein Eis möchte Sabrina?

3. Möchte Sabrina etwas trinken?

4. Was will Alexander trinken?

5. Wohin gehen Karin und Jürgen?

6. Was machen Alexander und Sabrina später?

Für dich

The café *(Café* or *Konditorei)* is a German institution that dates back centuries. It's quite common for Germans to sit in a café with friends for an hour or two, order a cup of coffee *(Tasse Kaffee)* and a piece of delicious cake *(Kuchen)* or torte *(Torte)* or just some ice cream *(Eis).* Depending on the weather, people can be seen sitting outdoors in sidewalk cafés from early May through September.

Wo sitzen die Leute?

Future Tense

In expressing events that will take place at any time after the present, you may use the future tense.

> *Ich werde eine Gitarre kaufen.*   I will buy a guitar.
> *Wirst du dein Buch holen?*   Will you get your book?

Similar to the modal auxiliaries, *werden* acts as a helping (auxiliary) verb and requires a second verb in the infinitive form. This verb is found at the end of a clause or sentence. Note: There is a vowel change from *e* to *i* in the *du, er, sie* and *es* forms.

werden		
ich	werde	I will
du	wirst	you will
er		he will
sie }	wird	she will
es		it will
wir	werden	we will
ihr	werdet	you will
sie	werden	they will
Sie	werden	you will

Should the content of the conversation or description imply future events, the present tense often is used with an adverb of time *(morgen, heute)*.

> *Wir spielen morgen Fußball.*   We'll play soccer tomorrow.
> *Im Herbst fahren wir*   In the fall we'll be going
> *nach Frankreich.*   to France.

Was werden sie vielleicht kaufen?

16 Was wird Sabine nach der Schule machen?

Describe what Sabine will be doing after school.

BEISPIEL Gitarre spielen
Sabine wird Gitarre spielen.

1. Rockmusik hören
2. Hausaufgaben machen
3. mit Petra Tennis spielen
4. ein Fernsehprogramm sehen
5. ihre Freunde treffen
6. ein Buch lesen

17 Wann wird das sein?

Indicate when the various events take place. Use the
future tense.

BEISPIEL Wir gehen zum Imbiss. (heute Nachmittag)
Wir werden heute Nachmittag zum Imbiss gehen.

1. Anke besucht ihre Freundin. (am Sonntag)
2. Eine Rockgruppe spielt in der Stadt. (in zwei Tagen)
3. Wir gehen zum Kaufhaus. (heute Morgen)
4. Jürgen und Tina fahren nach Österreich. (im Winter)
5. Mein Lehrer kommt eine Stunde später. (morgen)
6. Ich kaufe Bücher. (am Dienstag)

Sie werden langsam
nach Hause gehen.

Negation

The word *kein* means "no" or "not any" and negates nouns.

Ich habe kein Buch.	I have no book.
Tanja hat keine Zeit.	Tanja doesn't have time. (Tanja has no time.)

The endings of *kein* are identical to those of *ein*-words.

Peter kauft eine Gitarre.	Peter is buying a guitar.
Angelika kauft keine Gitarre.	Angelika doesn't buy a guitar. (Angelika buys no guitar.)
Hast du einen Bleistift?	Do you have a pencil?
Nein, ich habe keinen Bleistift.	No, I don't have a pencil. (No, I have no pencil.)

The word *nicht* means "not" and negates verbs, adjectives and adverbs.

David schreibt nicht.	David is not writing.
Carola will die Arbeit nicht machen.	Carola doesn't want to do the work.

Although there is no specific rule as to the position of *nicht* within a sentence—its position depends upon what is being negated in the sentence—*nicht* always appears after the subject and verb and usually after the object.

Wir essen nicht.	We aren't eating.
Wir essen die Pizza nicht.	We aren't eating the pizza.
Wir essen die Pizza jetzt nicht.	We aren't eating the pizza now.

Sie haben heute keine Hausaufgaben. Sie machen sie in der Klasse.

18 Was bringst du nicht mit?

Your friends want to know what you are bringing
to a party this weekend. Tell them that you are *not*
bringing the following things.

BEISPIEL Ich bringe kein Video mit.

1.   2.   3.

4.   5.   6.

19 Etwas stimmt nicht.

There is a mix-up in the school cafeteria. Many students
are missing part of their lunch. Tell what each person
does *not* have.

BEISPIEL Christa
Christa hat kein Wurstbrot.

1. Susanne	5. Tobias
2. Ralf	6. Karsten
3. Bettina	7. Tanja
4. Melanie	8. Sven

1.   2.   3.   4.

5.   6.   7.   8.

20 Nein,...

Beantworte diese Fragen mit „nein"!

BEISPIEL Macht Tina die Arbeit?
Nein, sie macht keine Arbeit.

1. Haben Renate und Ingrid Zeit?
2. Bekommt Hans in Englisch eine Zwei?
3. Besucht Gabriele einen Onkel?
4. Trinkst du Cola?
5. Isst er einen Hamburger?
6. Kauft ihr ein Buch?
7. Lernst du jetzt Englisch?

21 Ihr habt nicht Recht.

You don't seem to be in a good mood today and you contradict everything your friend tells you.

BEISPIEL Herr Gerlach sagt das.
Nein, Herr Gerlach sagt das nicht.

1. Die Musik ist toll.
2. Das Fernsehprogramm beginnt um halb sieben.
3. Die Pommes frites schmecken gut.
4. Günter geht in die Stadt.
5. Es ist sehr kalt.
6. Heiko kennt den Lehrer gut.
7. Der Zug kommt bald.
8. Das Mittagessen schmeckt gut.

Ist das Eis teuer?

22 Nein, ich...

Your classmates ask you some questions, all of which you answer negatively.

BEISPIELE Hast du heute Zeit?
Nein, ich habe heute keine Zeit.

Kommst du um vier?
Nein, ich komme nicht um vier.

1. Lernst du viel?
2. Bist du um eins zu Hause?
3. Hast du einen Bruder?
4. Möchtest du ein Wurstbrot?
5. Willst du zum Kaufhaus gehen?
6. Trinkst du eine Cola?
7. Kommst du um drei nach Hause?
8. Isst du eine Pizza?

Lesestück Lesestück Lesestück Lesestück Lesestück

Wohin fahren sie?

Im Eiscafé

Nach der Schule wollen Tobias, Sarah, Gülten und Karin zum Eiscafé fahren. Mit den Fahrrädern dauert es nur fünf Minuten. Die vier Schulfreunde kommen hier oft zusammen. Heute ist es nicht so kalt. Deshalb können sie draußen sitzen[1]. Die Auswahl an Eis und anderen Leckerbissen[2] ist hier immer sehr gut.

Kellner: Bitte schön?[3]

Karin: Einen Schokoshake[4] für mich.

Sarah: Eisschokolade[5], bitte.

Gülten: Schokolade mag ich nicht. Bringen Sie[6] mir bitte einen Erdbeershake.

Tobias: Ich möchte Spaghetti Eis[7]. Das ist alles.

Kellner: Danke schön[8]. Alles kommt gleich.

22 SPAGHETTI EIS
Sahne, Vanilleeis, Kokosraspel, Erdbeersoße

Spaghetti Eis

Der Kellner kommt auch schon bald und bringt die Leckerbissen.

Was trinkt Karin?

Kellner: Guten Appetit![9]

Karin: Wie lecker[10] das schmeckt!

Tobias: Mir auch. Das ist mein Lieblingseis.

Sarah: Nur noch zwei Monate, dann gibt's Ferien.

Gülten: Was wirst du denn dann machen?

Sarah: Wir fahren im Juli zur Insel Rügen[11].

Karin: Dort soll es sehr schön sein. Mein Bruder ist jeden Sommer zwei oder drei Wochen dort.

Tobias: Und du, Gülten?

Gülten: Wir bleiben vielleicht zu Hause. Ich schreibe noch diese Woche einen Brief an[12] meinen Cousin. Er besucht uns fast jedes Jahr aus der Türkei[13].

Sarah: Du schreibst einen Brief? Das dauert doch viel zu lange, bis er da ist. Warum schickst du nicht eine E-Mail[14]?

Gülten: Da hast du Recht.

Karin: Wir werden auch nichts[15] in den Ferien machen.

Tobias: Unsere Familie will im August nach Italien.

Sie sprechen noch viel über[16] die Ferien und die Schule. Dann bezahlen sie für alles. In diesem Eiscafé kosten[17] die Leckerbissen nicht sehr viel. Es ist schon spät. Sie müssen jetzt schnell nach Hause fahren.

Tobias isst Spaghetti Eis.

[1]*draußen sitzen* to sit outside; [2]*der Leckerbissen* treat; [3]*Bitte schön?* May I help you?; [4]*der Schokoshake* chocolate shake; [5]*die Eisschokolade* chocolate sundae; [6]*Bringen Sie mir...* Bring me...; [7]*das Spaghetti Eis* strawberry sundae; [8]*Danke schön.* Thank you very much.; [9]*Guten Appetit!* Enjoy your meal!; [10]*lecker* delicious; [11]*Insel Rügen* Island of Rügen; [12]*einen Brief schreiben an* to write a letter to; [13]*die Türkei* Turkey; [14]*eine E-Mail schicken* to send an e-mail; [15]*nichts* nothing; [16]*sprechen über* to talk about; [17]*kosten* to cost

Sie sprechen über die Ferien und die Schule.

23 Wer ist das?

1. ___ und ihre Familie fahren zu einer Insel.
2. ___ schreibt an ihren Cousin.
3. ___ wird nach Italien fahren.
4. ___ möchte einen Schokoshake.
5. ___ bringt die Leckerbissen.
6. ___ hat einen Bruder.
7. ___ isst Spaghetti Eis.
8. ___ kommt aus der Türkei.
9. ___ sprechen über die Schule.
10. ___ möchte Eisschokolade.

24 Fragen

Beantworte diese Fragen!

1. Wohin fahren die vier Schulfreunde nach der Schule?
2. Wie ist das Wetter?
3. Wo sitzen sie?
4. Warum isst Gülten keine Eisschokolade?
5. Dauert es lange, bis der Kellner alles bringt?
6. Was ist Tobias' Lieblingseis?
7. Was haben die Schulfreunde in zwei Monaten?
8. Wohin fahren Sarah und ihre Familie?
9. Was will Gülten schreiben, aber was wird sie schicken?
10. Wohin wollen Tobias und seine Familie im Sommer fahren?
11. Ist es in diesem Eiscafé teuer?

Wo sitzen Tobias, Sarah, Gülten und Karin?

Persönliches

1. Gehst du manchmal in ein Eiscafé oder in eine Pizzeria?
2. Was gibt es da zu essen und zu trinken?
3. Was ist dein Lieblingseis?
4. Was trinkst du gern?
5. Schreibst du manchmal einen Brief oder eine E-Mail?
   An wen?

Rollenspiel

You and a classmate decide to go to a café and order something to eat and drink. While waiting for the food server (a third classmate), you talk about what you would like to have. The server takes your order. Be as creative as possible.

Praktisches

Was gibt es zum Frühstück, Mittagessen und Abendessen? To find out what your partner likes to eat and drink for each meal, begin by making three columns on a piece of paper with the headings *Frühstück, Mittagessen* and *Abendessen*. In each column write down your favorite foods and beverages. Then with your partner, take turns asking and answering questions about what you like to eat and drink for each meal.

BEISPIEL Student 1: *Was möchtest du zum Frühstück?*

Student 2: *Zum Frühstück möchte ich eine Scheibe Brot, Butter und Marmelade.*

Student 2: *Was möchtest du trinken?*

Student 1: *Zum Frühstück möchte ich ein Glas Milch trinken.*

Write your partner's responses next to yours. After you have finished asking and answering questions, each of you writes a summary stating what foods and beverages you both like (if any) for each meal.

Was möchte Manuela zum Frühstück essen und trinken?

Schreiben

Was gibt's heute? Imagine that you and one of your classmates own an *Imbiss*. Make a daily menu that lists various beverages, meals and prices. While making your menu, ask such questions as *Was gibt's zu essen/trinken? (Was haben wir zu essen/trinken?)* and *Wie viel soll das kosten?*

Wörter und Ausdrücke

Talking about Desserts and Beverages

Was für Eis möchtest du? What kind of ice cream would you like?
Ich möchte... I would like...
    Schokoeis mit Schlagsahne chocolate ice cream with whipped cream
    Zitroneneis lemon ice cream
    Vanilleeis vanilla ice cream
    Erdbeereis strawberry ice cream
Ich möchte lieber... I would prefer...

Hast du Durst? Are you thirsty?
Etwas zu trinken? Something to drink?
Ich trinke gern... I like to drink...
    Apfelsaft apple juice
    eine Cola a cola
    ein Glas Milch a glass of milk
    ein Glas Eistee a glass of iced tea
    eine Tasse Kaffee a cup of coffee
    eine Tasse Kakao a cup of hot chocolate

Wohin gehst du? Where are you going?
    Ins Eiscafé. To the ice cream parlor.
    In die Pizzeria. To the pizza restaurant.

Was für Eis kann man hier kaufen?

Das Eis schmeckt gut.

25 Was passt hier?

Select the most appropriate answer to each question.

1. Wie schmeckt es?
2. Was möchten Sie essen?
3. Etwas zu trinken?
4. Wann musst du zu Hause sein?
5. Schickst du eine E-Mail?
6. Was machst du in den Ferien?
7. Willst du später rüberkommen?
8. Was wollen wir heute Nachmittag machen?
9. Was gibt's heute Abend im Fernsehen?
10. Geht ihr ins Eiscafé?

A. Wir fahren in die Schweiz.
B. Einen tollen Krimi.
C. Ja, ein Glas Milch, bitte.
D. Nein, in die Pizzeria.
E. So gegen halb neun.
F. Nein, ich habe heute keine Zeit.
G. Gut, danke.
H. Ein Wiener Schnitzel mit Kartoffeln, bitte.
I. Nein, ich habe keinen Computer.
J. Gehen wir doch ins Eiscafé!

26 Was fehlt hier?

Complete the sentences in the dialog. Make sure each sentence makes sense.

A: Hast du (1)?

B: Ja, ich (2) etwas essen.

A: Möchtest (3) einen Hamburger?

B: Ja, bitte, mit (4).

A: Willst du auch etwas (5)?

B: Nein, danke. Ich habe keinen (6).

A: Da drüben (7) ein Eiscafé.

B: (8) kenne es.

A: Was für (9) schmeckt da besonders gut?

B: Das Schokoeis (10) mir immer.

A: Na gut. (11) wir zum Eiscafé!

27 Kombiniere...

Meine Freundin	wollt	morgen	in die Stadt fahren
Herr Tobler	müssen	heute Abend	deine Arbeit machen
Ihr	möchte	am Sonntag	Klavier spielen
Björn und Christian	musst		einen Hamburger essen
Du	will		

28 Bitte schön?

Pretend that you are in a German restaurant. When the food server comes, discuss the menu, meals and beverages.

Kellner: Bitte schön?

   Du: (1)

Kellner: Möchtest du Cola oder Apfelsaft?

   Du: (2)

Kellner: Gut, das bringe ich gleich. Etwas zu essen?

   Du: (3)

Kellner: Bratwurst, Hamburger oder Schnitzel.

   Du: (4)

Kellner: Oh ja. Die Bratwurst schmeckt sehr gut.

   Du: (5)

Kellner: Möchtest du den Hamburger mit Pommes frites?

   Du: (6)

Was gibt's zu essen?

29 Wer? Was? Wo? Wohin? Wie viel? Wie viele?

Complete each sentence using the appropriate question word or words.

1. ___ möchte zum Imbiss mitkommen? Dieter und Anne.
2. ___ spielt die Rockgruppe? In München.
3. ___ Schwestern hast du? Nur die eine.
4. ___ ist das? Sie heißt Erika.
5. ___ fahren wir alle? Nach Deutschland.
6. ___ Uhr ist es jetzt? Viertel vor acht.
7. ___ wird deine Eltern besuchen? Meine Tante aus Dortmund.
8. ___ ist Jürgen? Zu Hause.
9. ___ machst du am Sonntag? Wir besuchen meinen Opa in Halle.
10. ___ Zeit hast du heute? Ein paar Stunden.

30 Christine hat viel Zeit.

Complete the following paragraph by providing the proper verb forms from the list below.

schmecken	dauern	bringen	sein
müssen	kennen	gehen	möchten
kommen	essen	heißen	haben

Christine (1) heute Nachmittag zu Hause. Es ist langweilig. Sie (2) mit ihrer Freundin Karin zur Pizzeria in die Stadt fahren. Karin (3) aber heute keine Zeit. Sie (4) ihre Hausaufgaben machen. Christine (5) zum Eiscafé Rialto, gleich um die Ecke. Sind Schulfreunde da? Es (6) nicht lange, bis zwei Schulfreundinnen kommen. Christines Schulfreundinnen (7) Carmen und Julia. Christine (8) Carmen und Julia schon viele Jahre. Alle drei (9) Eis. Das Erdbeereis (10) besonders gut. Später (11) Ctarmen und Julia zu Christine rüber. Julia (12) ein paar CDs. Sie haben alle viel Spaß.

31 Was brauchen wir?

You and your classmates are planning a party. Indicate
what you need or don't need.

BEISPIELE   kein / Kalte Platte
Wir brauchen keine Kalte Platte.

                drei / Bleistift
Wir brauchen drei Bleistifte.

1. ein paar / Tasse
2. viele / Glas
3. zwanzig / Kuli
4. kein / Tisch
5. kein / Eistee
6. zwölf / Brötchen
7. kein / Wurst
8. zwei / Video

32 Nein, das stimmt nicht.

You don't agree with what is being said.

BEISPIELE   Tobias hat eine Freundin.
Tobias hat keine Freundin.

                Wir schreiben das.
Wir schreiben das nicht.

1. Wir trinken gern Cola.
2. Das Wiener Schnitzel schmeckt gut.
3. Der Kellner bringt eine Tasse Kaffee.
4. Tina möchte mit Frau Tucholski sprechen.
5. Wir haben Zeit.
6. Peter geht oft ins Eiscafé.
7. Christa schreibt eine E-Mail.
8. Herr Werner kauft einen Computer.

Nein, ich kann nicht
rüberkommen.

Was weißt du?

1. *Was isst und trinkst du zum Frühstück, Mittagessen und Abendessen?* Name at least one item that you eat and drink at breakfast, lunch and dinner.

2. *Was möchtest du oder musst du machen?* Indicate three activities that you would **like to do** and three activities that you **have to do** during the week. Start the sentences with either *Ich möchte...* or with *Ich muss...*

3. Respond to each of these questions:
   A. *Was trinkst du gern?*
   B. *Was für Eis möchtest du essen?*
   C. *Was willst du am Sonnabend oder am Sonntag machen?*
   D. *Gehst du gern in eine Pizzeria oder in ein Eiscafé? Warum?*
   E. *Warum nicht?*
   F. *Was isst du gern?*

4. Describe some differences you might experience when going to a German restaurant versus an American restaurant (types of restaurants, service, eating, foods, etc.). *Auf Englisch, bitte!*

5. Pretend that you are a food server in a German restaurant. How would you say the following:
   A. May I help you?
   B. Are you hungry?
   C. Would you like a bratwurst with french fries?
   D. How does it taste?
   E. Would you like a cola?
   F. Enjoy your meal!

6. Complete each of the following sentences:
   A. *Heute Nachmittag möchte ich...*
   B. *Ich will...*
   C. *Wir sitzen....*
   D. *Morgen muss ich...*
   E. *Ich esse gern...*
   F. *Zum Abendessen trinke ich...*

7. *Was wirst du machen?* Discuss at least three activities that you will do in the near future. Use *werden*.

Vokabeln

das **Abendessen** supper, dinner *6A*
der **Apfelsaft** apple juice *6B*
der **Appetit** appetite; *Guten Appetit!* Enjoy your meal! *6B*
Bitte schön? May I help you? *6B*
die **Bratwurst,-̈e** bratwurst *6A*
der **Brief,-e** letter *6B*
bringen to bring *6B*
das **Brot,-e** bread *6A*
das **Brötchen,-** hard roll *6A*
die **Butter** butter *6A*
die **Cola,-s** cola *6B*
Danke schön. Thank you very much. *6B*
draußen outside *6B*
dürfen may, to be permitted to *6A*
der **Durst** thirst; *Durst haben* to be thirsty *6B*
die **E-Mail,-s** e-mail; *eine E-Mail schicken* to send an e-mail *6B*
das **Eis** ice cream *6B*
das **Eiscafé,-s** ice cream parlor, café *6B*
die **Eisschokolade** chocolate sundae *6B*
der **Eistee** iced tea *6B*
das **Erdbeereis** strawberry ice cream *6B*
der **Erdbeershake,-s** strawberry shake *6B*
essen to eat *6A*
der **Fisch,-e** fish *6A*
das **Gemüse** vegetable(s) *6A*
das **Glas,-̈er** glass *6B*
der **Hamburger,-** hamburger *6A*
der **Hunger** hunger; *Hunger haben* to be hungry *6A*
der **Imbiss,-e** snack bar (stand) *6A*
die **Insel,-n** island; *Insel Rügen* name of island in the *Ostsee* (Baltic Sea) *6B*
der **Kaffee** coffee *6B*
der **Kakao** hot chocolate, cocoa *6B*
die **Kalte Platte** cold-cut platter *6A*
die **Kartoffel,-n** potato *6A*
der **Käse** cheese *6A*
das **Käsebrot,-e** cheese sandwich *6A*

der **Kellner,-** waiter, food server *6B*
können can, to be able to *6A*
kosten to cost *6B*
lecker delicious *6B*
der **Leckerbissen,-** treat *6B*
leider unfortunately *6A*
lieber rather; *Ich möchte lieber...essen.* I would rather eat... *6B*
das **Lieblingseis** favorite ice cream *6B*
die **Marmelade,-n** jam, marmalade *6A*
die **Milch** milk *6B*
das **Mittagessen** lunch *6A*
mögen to like *6A*
müssen to have to, must *6A*
nichts nothing *6B*
das **Nusseis** nut-flavored ice cream *6B*
oft often *6B*
die **Pizza,-s** pizza *6A*
die **Pizzeria,-s** pizza restaurant *6B*
die **Platte,-n** plate; *Kalte Platte* cold-cut platter *6A*
die **Pommes frites** (pl.) french fries; *die Pommes* colloquial for "french fries" *6A*
der **Salat,-e** salad *6A*
der **Sauerbraten** sauerbraten (marinated beef roast) *6A*
die **Scheibe,-n** slice; *eine Scheibe Brot* a slice of bread *6A*
schicken to send *6B*
die **Schlagsahne** whipped cream *6B*
schmecken to taste; *Schmeckt dir...?* Do you like (to eat)...? *6A*
das **Schokoeis** chocolate ice cream *6B*
die **Schokolade** chocolate *6B*
der **Schokoshake,-s** chocolate shake *6B*
schreiben to write; *schreiben an* to write to *6B*
sitzen to sit *6B*
sollen should, to be supposed to *6A*
das **Spaghetti Eis** strawberry sundae *6B*
die **Spätzle** spaetzle (kind of homemade pasta) *6A*

sprechen über to talk about *6B*
die **Tasse,-n** cup *6B*
trinken to drink *6B*
die **Türkei** Turkey *6B*
das **Vanilleeis** vanilla ice cream *6B*
werden will, shall *6B*
das **Wiener Schnitzel** breaded veal cutlet *6A*
wollen to want to *6A*
die **Wurst,-̈e** sausage *6A*
das **Wurstbrot,-e** sausage sandwich *6A*
das **Zitroneneis** lemon ice cream *6B*

Das Essen ist hier ganz lecker.

Kapitel 7
Wie gefällt dir das?

Bücher
ab
2,50€

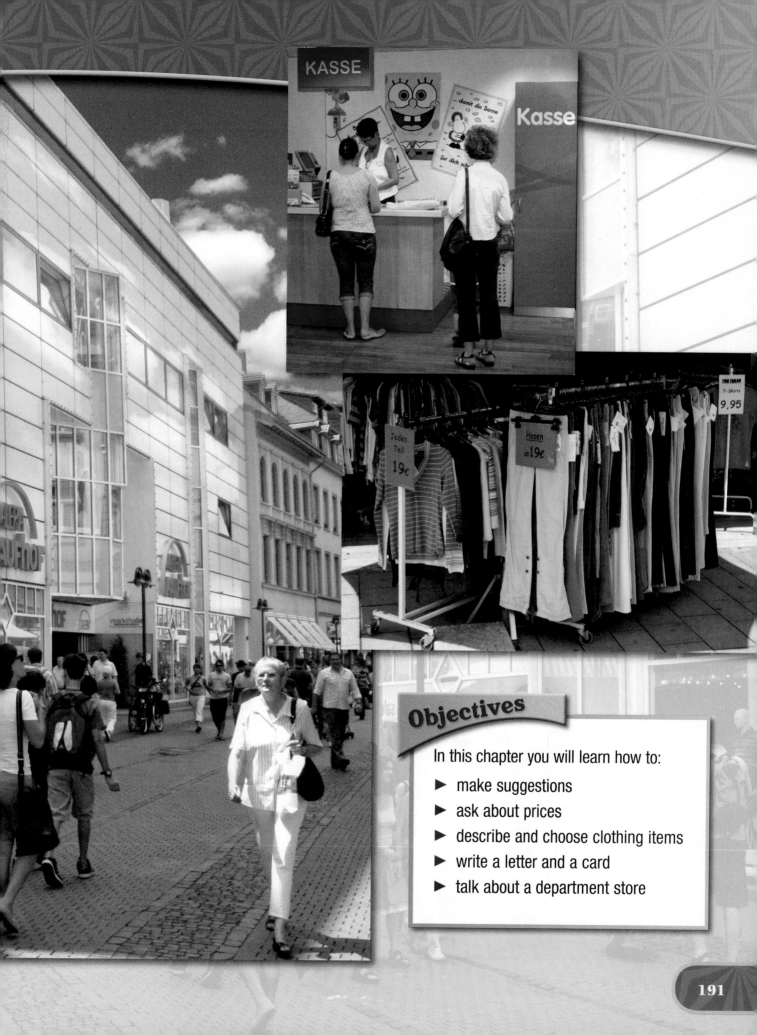

Objectives

In this chapter you will learn how to:

► make suggestions
► ask about prices
► describe and choose clothing items
► write a letter and a card
► talk about a department store

Lektion A

Kleidungsstücke

1 Was haben sie an?

Describe what everyone is wearing.

BEISPIEL Gisela
Gisela hat ein T-Shirt an.

1. Herr Holzke

2. Andreas

3. Tanja

4. Heike

5. meine Lehrerin

6. Holger

2 Wie gefällt dir...?

With a classmate, discuss what others in the class are wearing. Your conversation should include such questions as: *Wie gefällt dir...? Was hat...an?*

3 Was passt oder was passt nicht? Und warum?

Describe the clothing items worn by the people in the illustration and indicate what does or doesn't fit.

So preiswert!

Carmen und Nadja gehen zur Boutique.

Wie gefällt dir dieses Shirt?

Ich finde es zu groß für dich.

JANA: Sieh mal! Hier gibt's heute ein Sonderangebot.

CARMEN: Ja, hier draußen ist alles billiger.

JANA: Wie gefällt dir dieses Shirt? Es ist so preiswert.

NADJA: Nimmst du es, Jana?

CARMEN: Ich finde es zu groß für dich. Die Qualität ist auch nicht so gut.

NADJA: Na ja, der Preis ist nicht alles.

JANA: Ich möchte lieber eine Jacke. Ich glaube, in der Boutique ist die Auswahl besser.

CARMEN: Komm, wir sehen, was es drinnen gibt!

4 Fragen

Beantworte diese Fragen!

1. Was gibt es heute in dieser Boutique?
2. Ist das Shirt teuer?
3. Wie findet Carmen das Shirt?
4. Wie ist die Qualität?
5. Sind die Mädchen in der Boutique drinnen?
6. Was wollen sie machen?

Für dich

Running sales throughout the year, which is quite common in this country, is not as common in Germany. Although stores offer reduced items as they see fit, there are two major sales during the year, each lasting two weeks. One is called *Sommerschlussverkauf* (end-of-summer sale) and the other *Winterschlussverkauf* (end-of-winter sale). Each sale starts officially on the last Monday in July and the last Monday in January, respectively. Many shops have started to run an *Ausverkauf* (seasonal, bargain sale) much earlier than on the fixed dates, offering certain items at reduced prices as *Sonderangebote* (special offers).

During the warmer season, major department stores as well as smaller shops display some of their reduced merchandise outside on the sidewalk in front of the store to entice shoppers to stop and shop.

For many years, English words have made an impact on the German language. For example, *das Shirt* is usually a woman's shirt, whereas *das Hemd* is considered to be a man's shirt.

Was ist das Sonderangebot hier?

Wie viel kosten die Socken?

Verbs with Stem Vowel Change

A number of verbs in German do not follow the regular pattern of conjugation, but undergo a change in the *du* and *er, sie* and *es* forms. You will become familiar with two such groups of verbs, one changing from *a* to *ä*, the other from *e* to *i* (or *ie*). However, the verb endings still follow the pattern of regular verbs.

Stem vowel change *a* to *ä*

Here are the verbs with vowel changes that you already know.

	du	er, sie, es
fahren	fährst	fährt
gefallen	gefällst	gefällt

Ralf fährt mit dem Fahrrad zu seiner Freundin.	Ralf rides his bike to his girlfriend's.
Gefällt dir diese Krawatte?	Do you like this tie?

Stem vowel change *e* to *i* and *e* to *ie*

Here are the verbs with vowel changes that you already know.

	du	er, sie, es
essen	isst	isst
geben	gibst	gibt
lesen	liest	liest
nehmen	nimmst	nimmt
sehen	siehst	sieht
sprechen	sprichst	spricht

Um wie viel Uhr isst du Mittagessen?	At what time do you eat lunch?
Frau Meier spricht englisch.	Mrs. Meier speaks English.

Was liest sie?

5 Wohin fahren alle?

Tell where everyone is going.

BEISPIEL Frau Tobler / Stuttgart
Frau Tobler fährt nach Stuttgart.

1. Tobias und Robert / Deutschland
2. Herr Krüger / Hamburg
3. Petra und Maria / Südösterreich
4. Rudis Freundin / München
5. Meine Schulfreunde / Norddeutschland
6. Anne / Köln

6 Was machen Angelika und Tanja heute Nachmittag?

Complete the short narrative and the dialog using the appropriate forms of the verbs listed below. Use each verb only once.

gefallen	sehen	machen	haben
geben	nehmen	lesen	sprechen
fahren	rüberkommen	sein	

Angelika (1) mit ihrer Freundin Tanja am Telefon. Sie will heute Nachmittag mit dem Bus in die Stadt (2) .

ANGELIKA: (3) du jetzt Zeit? Kannst du um drei (4) ?

TANJA: Nein. Vielleicht in zwei Stunden. Wann (5) du dein Buch für die Deutschklasse?

ANGELIKA: Das kann ich heute Abend (6).

TANJA: (7) du dann nicht fern? Um 19 Uhr 30 (8) im Fernsehen ein toller Krimi.

ANGELIKA: Das Fernsehprogramm (9) mir nicht. Kommst du mit in die Stadt?

TANJA: Klar, bis später. Du musst mir aber bis morgen etwas Geld (10).

ANGELIKA: Warum (11) du nicht dein Geld?

TANJA: Ich habe leider nicht genug.

7 Kombiniere...

Andrea	sehen	morgen	am Telefon
wir	isst	heute Nachmittag	im Fernsehen
Günter und Helmut	sprechen	jetzt	einen Krimi
du	liest	nichts	ein Käsebrot

Aktuelles

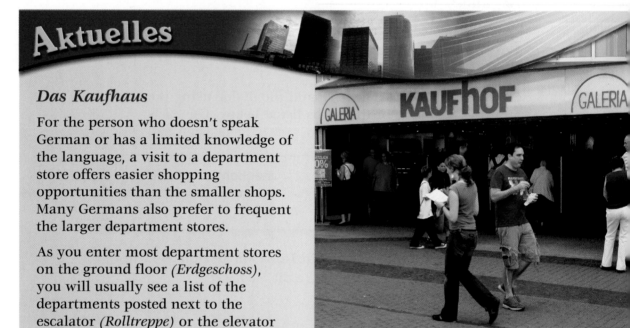

Das Kaufhaus

For the person who doesn't speak German or has a limited knowledge of the language, a visit to a department store offers easier shopping opportunities than the smaller shops. Many Germans also prefer to frequent the larger department stores.

As you enter most department stores on the ground floor *(Erdgeschoss)*, you will usually see a list of the departments posted next to the escalator *(Rolltreppe)* or the elevator *(Fahrstuhl)*. Let's take a tour through a department store, starting downstairs *(Untergeschoss)*. What will you find there?

In almost all major department stores, you'll find a supermarket *(Supermarkt)*. As in this country, Germans take a shopping cart *(Einkaufswagen)* and then select their groceries. Few shoppers will pass by the bread and pastry counter without stopping; Germans are great bread and pastry eaters. The selection there is overwhelming.

In diesem Kaufhaus gibt's eine große Auswahl.

Neben der Rolltreppe ist eine Liste von allen Abteilungen.

Don't be surprised if you find a line of people waiting patiently at a counter to order from the wide assortment of sausages and cold cuts *(Wurst)* or cheeses *(Käse)*. You can order chunks or slices that are weighed according to your request. If you prefer to buy prepackaged cold cuts and meats, you can go directly to the packaged meat display and help yourself.

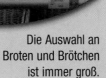

Die Auswahl an Broten und Brötchen ist immer groß.

The fresh fruits and vegetables are found in the *Obst und Gemüse* section. The fruit display closely resembles that found in American supermarkets; however, the unit of measurement is different. The metric pound *(Pfund)* used in Germany weighs about 10 percent more than the U.S. pound. It's easy to weigh the different kinds of fruit. Just place them on a scale that has all the various items graphically displayed on buttons. Push the button that displays the selected fruit or vegetable and the scale will print out the exact weight and price.

Man bezahlt an der Kasse.

Although some Germans still believe that frozen foods are *ungesund* (unhealthy), you will nevertheless find a large selection in the frozen food section. If you need assistance, look for sales personnel dressed in white smocks.

After you have finished your grocery shopping, you can proceed directly to any of the cash registers *(Kasse)*. If you haven't brought your own shopping bag *(Einkaufstasche)*, the clerk will sell you a plastic bag and expect you to bag your own groceries while he or she is ringing up the various items. There is usually a small charge for each bag. However, many department stores and some shops give you a plastic bag for free.

You'll find the greatest selection of goods on the ground floor. Shoppers usually will spend more time here than on any other floor, thus most of the specials *(Sonderangebote)* are located on that floor for the shopper who doesn't want to spend a lot of time roaming around the entire store. All of the specials are clearly marked and arranged on various tables. Other items you may find on this floor are jewelry *(Schmuck)*, leather goods *(Lederwaren)*, books and stationery *(Bücher und Schreibwarenartikel)*, greeting cards *(Glückwunschkarten)* and even a travel agency *(Reisebüro)*.

Was kann man hier kaufen?

Hier gibt's viele Bücher.

Standing in the music department *(Musikabteilung)*, you may have the feeling you're back in the United States. Much of the music on CDs *(CDs)* comes from here. You'll find hits by American artists along with recordings by German rock groups that have become popular in Germany and beyond its borders.

Although small clothing items, such as stockings, ties, scarfs and other special accessories, are found on the ground floor, major items of clothing for children, women and men are normally located on the second floor *(Erstes Obergeschoss)*. Remember that all sizes are in metric measurements. On the third floor *(Zweites Obergeschoss)*, you'll find a beauty shop *(Friseursalon)* and a photography studio *(Fotostudio)* that specializes in family portraits.

Continuing your tour through the department store, you'll come to the fourth floor *(Drittes Obergeschoss)*. Here you'll find household articles *(Haushaltsartikel)*, such as electric coffeepots and cooking utensils. If you want to buy a gift, look for the department called *Geschenkartikel*.

in der Musikabteilung

Spielzeug für Kinder

Eventually, you'll get to the fifth floor *(Viertes Obergeschoss)*. Here you'll come across a popular department, the *Computer-Center*, which displays the most technologically advanced computers and software.

If you are ready to sit down and have a beverage and a snack or meal, you'll also find a *Restaurant* on the top floor of the department store. Most major department stores also have a sports department *(Sportabteilung)* and a toy department *(Spielwarenabteilung)*.

das Computer-Center

8 Was passt hier?

1. place where you pay for your purchases
2. measurement for weighing fruits and vegetables
3. department where you can buy earrings
4. movable device when buying groceries
5. sign that announces reduced prices or special offers
6. means of transportation that will take several people at a time from one floor to the next
7. word that refers to an upper floor of a building
8. department where you would buy pots and pans
9. card that you would like to send to your friend for his or her birthday
10. place where you would go to find out about vacation specials
11. item for carrying groceries
12. word that categorizes items such as apples and oranges

A. *Haushaltsartikel*
B. *Einkaufswagen*
C. *Fahrstuhl*
D. *Reisebüro*
E. *Obst*
F. *Pfund*
G. *Einkaufstasche*
H. *Glückwunschkarte*
I. *Obergeschoss*
J. *Schmuck*
K. *Kasse*
L. *Sonderangebote*

Write a paragraph in which you discuss what you are planning to do this weekend, including the purchase of a certain clothing item that you need due to the changing seasons. Be as creative as possible.

Rollenspiel

You and one of your classmates play the roles of the shopper and the salesperson in a department store *(Kaufhaus)*. In your conversation you should cover such details as: what clothing item you are looking for, how much you want to spend and whether or not you consider the item expensive. Ask the salesperson's opinion and express what you like and dislike about the item. Then reverse roles. You may want to use the expressions of the photo captions (see below) in your conversation.

Wo kann ich Hemden bekommen?

Warum warten sie an der Kasse?

Was kann man in dieser Abteilung kaufen?

Was ist sehr preiswert?

Describing and Commenting on Clothing Items

Was für Kleidungsstücke hat er an? What kind of clothing items does he have on?
Er hat...an. He has...on.
    einen Pulli (Pullover) a sweater
    ein Hemd a shirt
    eine Krawatte a tie
    einen Anzug a suit
    ein Sweatshirt a sweatshirt
    ein Paar Handschuhe a pair of gloves
    ein T-Shirt a T-shirt
    Jeans jeans

Was hat sie an? What does she have on?

Sie hat...an. She has...on.
    ein Kleid a dress
    einen Rock a skirt
    eine Jacke a jacket
    eine Bluse a blouse
    ein Shirt a shirt
    ein Paar Schuhe a pair of shoes
    ein Paar Socken a pair of socks
    ein Paar Strümpfe a pair of stockings
    einen Mantel a coat

Passt die Bluse? Does the blouse fit?
Wie ist die Hose? How are the pants?
Sie ist... It is...
    zu lang too long
    zu kurz too short
    zu eng too tight

Zungenbrecher

Hinter Hermann Hannes Haus hängen
hundert Hemden raus.
Hundert Hemden hängen raus, hinter
Hermann Hannes Haus.

Behind Hermann Hanne's house a hundred shirts are hanging out.
A hundred shirts are hanging out behind Hermann Hanne's house.

Lektion B

Die Farben

grün
braun
gelb
weiß
grau
rosa
rot
beige
schwarz
orange
blau

hell   dunkel   bunt

Welche Farbe hat der Pulli?

Und das T-Shirt?

Er ist rot.

Es ist bunt.

9 Welche Farbe hat...?

Describe the various items shown.

BEISPIEL Jeans
Die Jeans sind blau.

1.

2.

3.

4.

5.

6.

10 Beschreibe dein Klassenzimmer! (Describe your classroom.)

Look around your classroom and identify at least five objects, including their colors.

BEISPIEL Da drüben ist ein Tisch. Er ist braun.
Hier ist ein Heft. Es ist blau.

Welche Farben siehst du auf diesem Foto?

Das steht dir sehr gut!

Ich weiß nicht. Die Farbe ist zu hell.

Dunkel gefällt mir besser.

Ich nehme diese Jacke.

CARMEN: Diese Wolljacke ist wirklich schick.

JANA: Ich weiß nicht. Die Farbe ist zu hell.

NADJA: Möchtest du lieber diese hier?

CARMEN: Ja, die Jacke steht dir sehr gut.

NADJA: Willst du vielleicht eine andere Farbe? Weiß oder schwarz?

JANA: Dunkel gefällt mir besser. Besonders grau.

NADJA: Na, kauf sie doch!

JANA: Ja, ich nehme diese Jacke.

NADJA: Komm, da ist die Kasse!

11 Richtig oder falsch?

Determine whether the following statements are correct. If they are incorrect, provide a correct statement in German.

1. Carmen findet die Wolljacke schlecht.
2. Jana meint, die Wolljacke ist zu dunkel.
3. Carmen glaubt, die Jacke passt Jana gut.
4. Jana gefällt eine Jacke mit dunkler Farbe besser.
5. Jana kauft keine Jacke.
6. Jana bezahlt an der Kasse.

12 Was passt hier?

Complete the dialog by providing the correct forms of the verbs listed.

bezahlen	gehen	glauben	stehen	kosten
sein	haben	möchten	machen	

UWE: Der Pullover __(1)__ dir gut.

HEIKO: __(2)__ die Farbe nicht zu dunkel?

UWE: Nein, das __(3)__ ich nicht.

HEIKO: Ich __(4)__ lieber diesen hier.

UWE: Aber der __(5)__ doch so viel Geld.

HEIKO: Nein, 35 Euro kann ich für diesen Pulli __(6)__.

UWE: Na gut. Du __(7)__ ja auch genug Geld.

HEIKO: Du __(8)__ wirklich Spaß.

UWE: Ich __(9)__ gleich zur Kasse.

Wo bezahlt Jana für die Wolljacke?

Für dich

When shopping in Germany, you should become familiar with the monetary system: the euro *(der Euro)*. The written symbol for the euro is €. There are eight coins: 1, 2, 5, 10, 20, 50 cent and 1 and 2 euro. There are seven euro bills: 5, 10, 20, 50, 100, 200 and 500.

ein paar Münzen *(coins)* und Geldscheine *(bills)*

German shops are not open as many hours as American stores. Although stores, according to the law, may open from 6 A.M. to 8 P.M. Monday through Friday and on Saturday from 6 A.M. to 4:00 P.M., most stores open around 9 A.M.

You should always try on footwear *(anprobieren)* and clothing because not only do the sizes vary, but also the cuts. There are many variations among products from various countries as well—France, Italy, Greece, Spain, eastern Europe or the Far East. When trying on a clothing item, look for the dressing room *(Umkleidekabine)*. Exchanging an item is called *Umtausch*. You'll always need the receipt to exchange or return merchandise.

In comparison to Americans, many Germans still pay for almost everything in cash, although credit cards are used more and more today. When you see a price tag in a German store you can be sure that it shows the total price, including the value-added tax *(Mehrwertsteuer)*. Most Germans have a credit card called *Kreditkarte*. They are able to pay with these in all EU (European Union) countries.

Wie viele Stunden ist dieses Geschäft am Dienstag geöffnet?

Wann kann man hier Information bekommen?

wissen

The verb *wissen* (to know) has irregular forms when it is used with *ich*, *du* and *er*, *sie* and *es*. The plural forms are regular.

ich	weiß	wir	wissen
du	weißt	ihr	wisst
er		sie	wissen
sie }	weiß	Sie	wissen
es			

Note that both words, *kennen* and *wissen*, mean "to know." However, *kennen* means "to know a person, a place or a thing," whereas *wissen* means "to know something" (as a fact).

Kennst du Sabine?	Do you know Sabine?
Weißt du, wer Sabine ist?	Do you know who Sabine is?
Wir kennen Hamburg.	We know Hamburg.
Wir wissen, wo Hamburg liegt.	We know where Hamburg is located.
Kennen Sie dieses Buch?	Do you know this book?
Wissen Sie, wo dieses Buch ist?	Do you know where this book is?

13 Wer weiß die Antwort?

Your teacher is asking several questions, to which your classmates have the answers.

BEISPIEL Gloria
Gloria weiß die Antwort.

1. Robert und Doris
2. Ich
3. Uwe
4. Alex und David
5. Sonja und Peter
6. Heidi

Er weiß die Antwort.

14 *Kennen* oder *wissen?*

Provide the correct form of the appropriate verb.

1. ___ Sie, um wie viel Uhr Ali kommt?
2. Ich ___ Tina. Sie ist sehr klug.
3. ___ du Frau Kowalski?
4. ___ ihr, was Günter und Ralf heute Nachmittag machen?
5. ___ Christine, wann ihr Onkel und ihre Tante sie besuchen werden?
6. Wir ___, wo Herr Böhme wohnt.
7. ___ ihr Frau Thielmanns Tochter?
8. Beate ___ Susanne gut.

Sprache

Words Used for Emphasis

A number of German words are used strictly for emphasis. Such words are *aber, denn, doch* and *ja*. These words cannot be translated literally, but are particularly important in conversational usage. They make the expression sound less direct and friendlier.

Du bist klug.	You're smart.
*Du bist **aber** klug!*	**Aren't** you smart!
Was machst du hier?	What are you doing here?
*Was machst du **denn** hier?*	What are **you** doing here? or: Tell me, what are you doing here?
Bring deine neue CD mit.	Bring along the new CD.
*Bring **doch** deine neue CD mit.*	Why **don't** you bring along your new CD?
Du weißt, wir wohnen in der Stadt.	You know, we live in the city.
*Du weißt **ja**, wir wohnen in der Stadt.*	As you know **very well**, we live in the city.

Ist es denn
so schwer?

15 Was ist der Unterschied? (What's the difference?)

Read the dialog between Katja and Lars. Then read it again, including the words used for emphasis. Do you notice a difference in meaning and in mood?

KATJA: Tag, Lars! Wohin gehst du (denn)?

LARS: Ins Kaufhaus. Ich will die neue CD von der Pastell-Rockgruppe kaufen.

KATJA: Du hast (doch) schon eine.

LARS: Na klar. Ich höre (aber) immer nur die eine CD. Willst du mitkommen? Du hast (doch) bestimmt Zeit?

KATJA: Wann bist du (denn) wieder zu Hause? Um fünf?

LARS: Du weißt (ja), ich habe nicht viel Zeit. In einer Stunde kommt mein Klavierlehrer. Dann muss ich wieder zu Hause sein.

KATJA: Wie viel kostet (denn) die CD?

LARS: Zehn Euro. Warum fragst du (denn)?

KATJA: Ich möchte (doch) auch eine kaufen.

Wer die Wahl hat, hat die Qual!¹

Wolf und Jens fahren mit dem Bus in die Stadt. Wolf braucht Jeans. Seine² Jeans sind schon sehr alt und er kann sie nicht mehr tragen³. Jens weiß nicht, ob⁴ er auch noch ein anderes Paar kaufen soll. Beide gehen in ein Geschäft⁵. Dort ist die Auswahl an Jeans besonders groß.

Wolf: Siehst du? Die Jeans sind stark reduziert⁶.

Jens: Meinst du, die passen dir?

Wolf: Na klar⁷. Die Größe⁸ ist richtig⁹ und der Preis ist auch nicht schlecht.

Jens: Aber die Qualität ist doch nicht ganz so gut. Da drüben gibt's¹⁰ noch mehr Jeans.

Wolf: Wie findest du diese hier?

Die Jeans sind stark reduziert.

Wann geht's denn los?

Jens: Die sind sehr praktisch¹¹, besonders für deine Campingreise¹².

Wolf: Deshalb brauche ich auch ein Paar.

Jens: Wann geht's denn los¹³?

Wolf: In den Sommerferien.¹⁴

Jens: Fahrt ihr wieder¹⁵ in den Schwarzwald¹⁶?

Wolf: Ja, zum Schluchsee¹⁷. Da ist immer viel los¹⁸. Viele Jugendliche¹⁹ fahren dorthin²⁰. Wir haben immer viel Spaß.

Jens: Was kosten die Jeans denn?

Wolf: Nur 38,40 Euro.

Jens: Nicht schlecht. Nimmst du sie?

Wolf: Ja, die Größe, der Preis und die Qualität sind sehr gut.

In den Sommerferien.

Wolf und Jens gehen an die Kasse. Eine Verkäuferin21 bedient22 sie dort. Wolf bezahlt und bekommt auch eine Quittung23. Dann gehen beide aus dem Geschäft. Jens will im Musikgeschäft24 noch ein paar CDs kaufen.

---

¹*Wer die Wahl hat, hat die Qual!* The more choices, the more problems!; ²*sein(e)* his; ³*tragen* to wear; ¹⁴*ob* if; ⁵*das Geschäft* store; ⁶*stark reduziert* greatly reduced; ⁷*na klar* of course; ⁸*die Größe* size; ⁹*richtig* right, correct; ¹⁰*da drüben gibt's* over there they have; ¹¹*praktisch* practical; ¹²*die Campingreise* camping trip; ¹³*Wann geht's denn los?* When will you take off?; ¹⁴*die Sommerferien* summer vacation; ¹⁵*wieder* again; ¹⁶*der Schwarzwald* Black Forest; ¹⁷*der Schluchsee* name of lake; ¹⁸*Da ist immer viel los.* There is always a lot going on; ¹⁹*der Jugendliche* teenager, young person; ²⁰*dorthin* there; ²¹*die Verkäuferin* salesperson (female); ²²*bedienen* to wait on, assist; ²³*die Quittung* receipt; ²⁴*das Musikgeschäft* music store

Wolf und Jens gehen an die Kasse.

16 Was fehlt hier?

Provide the correct words from the list to complete the narrative.

los	heute	Qualität	praktisch
kosten	Stadt	findet	Schwarzwald
neu	will	fahren	Paar

Warum (1) Wolf und Jens in die (2)? Wolf (3) Jeans kaufen. Seine Jeans sind nicht mehr (4). Vielleicht wird Jens auch ein (5) kaufen. Die Jeans sind (6) sehr preiswert. Jens (7) die Jeans für die Campingreise ganz (8). In den Ferien wird Wolf in den (9) fahren. Dort ist im Sommer viel (10). Die Jeans (11) mehr als 30 Euro. Die Größe und die (12) sind sehr gut.

17 Fragen

Beantworte diese Fragen!

1. Fahren Jens und Wolf mit dem Auto in die Stadt?
2. Warum will Wolf Jeans kaufen?
3. Wohin gehen sie?
4. Gibt es dort viele Jeans?
5. Sind die Jeans teuer?
6. Wann macht Wolf eine Campingreise?
7. Wohin wird er dann fahren?
8. Wie viel kosten die Jeans?
9. Kauft Wolf die Jeans?

Wohin gehen sie?

Gibt es dort viele Jeans?

Was haben sie heute an? Select three of your classmates and describe what they are wearing, including the colors.

Rollenspiel

Pretend you are standing in front of a counter in a big department store and the salesperson (a classmate) is ready to help you. You are looking for a specific clothing item. Ask him or her about the cost, the color you want and any suggestions for purchasing your desired item. Be as creative as possible. Some useful expressions might be: *Wie viel kostet...?, Welche Farbe?, Möchten Sie...?* Reverse roles.

Praktisches

In groups of three, play the roles of a department store manager *(Manager)* with a 6,000 euro budget, a salesperson in the men's department *(Verkäufer/Verkäuferin)* and a salesperson in the women's department. The salespeople are going to inventory their present stock and then submit to the manager a list of clothing items needed in each department. First, the two salespeople present the manager with a list of items they have in stock and the prices for their respective departments. Then they present the manager with a second list of items they would like to add to their inventory, and their prices. The manager and salespeople, working together, must agree on the items to be purchased, making sure that they stay within the budget. The manager should write the final list and submit it to the corporate purchasing department (your teacher). Some useful words and expressions that you have learned are: *Was für/Wie viele Kleidungsstücke brauchen wir (nicht)? Wir haben 3000 Euro. Wir müssen (sollen, können)...kaufen. Wie viel kostet...? Das ist zu teuer/preiswert.*

Wie viel kosten die Jeans?

Schreiben

Write a short narrative of what you should take along when visiting a friend or relative during the summer. Indicate the items, their colors and how appropriate they will be for normal weather in the area you are visiting. Here is a sample narrative:

Im Sommer besuche ich meine Freundin Susanne in... Am Tag ist es da sehr warm und am Abend ist es kühl. Was für Kleidungsstücke brauche ich dann? Ich glaube, ich bringe diese Kleidungsstücke mit: Jeans, einen Pullover (rot), ein Sweatshirt, eine Jacke (dunkel), zwei T-Shirts, ein Paar Tennisschuhe und Socken.

Wörter und Ausdrücke

Talking about Colors and Making Additional Comments about Clothing Items

Welche Farbe ist...? What color is...?
Es ist... It is...
  grün green
  braun brown
  gelb yellow
  weiß white
  grau gray
  rosa pink

rot red
beige beige
schwarz black
orange orange
blau blue
hell light
bunt colorful
Das steht dir gut. It looks good on you.
Wie ist die Wolljacke? How is the cardigan?
Sie ist schick. It is chic (smart looking).
Ich weiß nicht. I don't know.
Ich nehme diese Jacke. I'll take this jacket.

Welche Farbe ist die Wolljacke?

18 Bitte schön?

Imagine you are employed in a department store and have to assist customers *(Kunde/Kundin)*. Complete the following two dialogs, making sure the sentences make sense.

Du: <u>(1)</u>

Kunde: Ich möchte ein Hemd.

Du: <u>(2)</u>

Kunde: Blau oder grau. Finden Sie dieses Hemd zu lang?

Du: <u>(3)</u>

Kunde: Wie viel kostet es?

Du: <u>(4)</u>

Kunde: Das ist preiswert. Ich kaufe es.

Kundin: Wo sind die Blusen?

Du: <u>(5)</u>

Kundin: Oh, die Auswahl ist groß.

Du: <u>(6)</u>

Kundin: Diese Bluse ist etwas zu kurz.

Du: <u>(7)</u>

Kundin: Prima. Die passt. Ist die Bluse teuer?

Du: <u>(8)</u>

19 Was ist logisch? (What is logical?)

From the list below, find the verbs that best complete the phrases.

trinken	gehen	haben	bleiben
schreiben	essen	kosten	anhaben

1. eine Bratwurst
2. einen Mantel
3. etwas Geld
4. zwei Wochen

5. ein Glas Milch
6. nach Hause
7. viel Spaß
8. einen Brief

20 Etwas Persönliches.

1. Du hast 200 Euro. Was möchtest du kaufen?

2. Was hast du heute an? Welche Farben haben deine Kleidungsstücke?

3. Wo kannst du in deiner Stadt Kleidungsstücke kaufen?

4. Wohin fährst du im Sommer? Wen besuchst du dann?

21 Kannst du den Brief nicht lesen?

You received a letter from a pen pal in Germany but, unfortunately, you have difficulty reading it as the letter was dropped and got dirty. Rewrite the letter including the missing details.

25. Februar

Lieber Robert!

Wie (1) es dir? Mir geht es ganz (2). Mein Vater, meine (3) und ich werden im August nach (4) fahren. Wie du weißt, kann ich italienisch sprechen. Wir werden viel Spaß (5). Von Stuttgart (6) wir zuerst nach Österreich fahren. Von dort fahren (7) direkt nach Italien. Wir (8) eine Woche in Rom und eine (9) in Florenz bleiben. Im September beginnt die (10). Wir müssen schon um (11) acht da sein. Das (12) sehr früh.

Viele (13), auch an deine Eltern!

22 Im Sommer komme ich mit.

Your classmate has invited you to come along on a camping trip *(eine Campingreise)* during the summer. With your classmate, develop a conversation discussing what you should bring along, expected weather conditions, when you'll leave, how long you'll stay, who is coming along, and so on.

Was weißt du?

1. *Kleidungsstücke.* Identify three clothing items and indicate their colors, whether or not you like them, and why.

2. Describe some of the differences in shopping in an American versus a German department store. *Auf Englisch.*

3. *Ich habe...an.* Tell your classmate what you are wearing today. Give as many details as possible.

4. Identify five items in your classroom, including their colors.

5. Write a short letter or e-mail to a friend or relative in which you inform him or her that you would like to come for a visit during the summer. Ask several questions concerning clothing items, weather, the best time to come and so forth.

Hier gibt's viele Geschäfte.

Vokabeln

anhaben to have on, wear *7A*
der **Anzug,-̈e** suit *7A*
bedienen to wait on *7B*
beige beige *7B*
besser better *7A*
billig cheap *7A*
blau blue *7B*
die **Bluse,-n** blouse *7A*
die **Boutique,-n** boutique *7A*
braun brown *7B*
bunt colorful *7B*
die **Campingreise,-n** camping trip *7B*
dorthin (to) there *7B*
drinnen inside *7A*
eng tight *7A*
die **Farbe,-n** color; *Welche Farbe hat...?* What color is...? *7B*
geben to give; *es gibt* there is (are) *7A*
gelb yellow *7B*
das **Geschäft,-e** store, shop *7B*
glauben to believe *7A*
grau gray *7B*
die **Größe,-n** size *7B*
grün green *7B*
der **Handschuh,-e** glove *7A*
hell light *7B*
das **Hemd,-en** shirt *7A*
die **Hose,-n** pants, slacks *7A*
die **Jacke,-n** jacket *7A*
die **Jeans** (pl.) jeans *7A*
der **Jugendliche,-n** teenager, young person *7B*
klar clear; *na klar* of course *7B*

das **Kleid,-er** dress *7A*
das **Kleidungsstück,-e** clothing item *7A*
die **Krawatte,-n** tie *7A*
kurz short *7A*
lang long *7A*
los: Da ist viel los. There is a lot going on. *7B*
losgehen to start; *Wann geht's denn los?* When will it start? *7B*
der **Mantel,-̈** coat *7A*
das **Musikgeschäft,-e** music store *7B*
nehmen to take *7A*
ob if *7B*
orange orange *7B*
das **Paar,-e** pair *7A*
passen to fit *7A*
praktisch practical *7B*
der **Pulli,-s** sweater, pullover *7A*
der **Pullover,-** sweater, pullover *7A*
die **Qualität,-en** quality *7A*
die **Quittung,-en** receipt *7B*
reduziert reduced *7B*
richtig right, correct *7B*
der **Rock,-̈e** skirt *7A*
rosa pink *7B*
rot red *7B*
schick chic, smart (looking) *7B*
Schluchsee name of lake (located in the Black Forest) *7B*
der **Schuh,-e** shoe *7A*
schwarz black *7B*

der **Schwarzwald** Black Forest *7B*
sehen to see; *Sieh mal!* Just look! *7A*
sein(e) his *7B*
das **Shirt,-s** shirt *7A*
die **Socke,-n** sock *7A*
die **Sommerferien** (pl.) summer vacation *7B*
das **Sonderangebot,-e** special (sale) *7A*
stark strong; *stark reduziert* greatly reduced *7*
stehen to stand, be; *Das steht dir gut.* It looks good on you. *7B*
der **Strumpf,-̈e** stocking *7A*
das **Sweatshirt,-s** sweatshirt *7A*
das **T-Shirt,-s** T-shirt *7A*
tragen to wear *7B*
die **Verkäuferin,-nen** salesperson (female) *7B*
die **Wahl** choice; *Wer die Wahl hat, hat die Qual!* The more choices, the more problems! *7B*
weiß white *7B*
wieder again *7B*
wissen to know *7B*
die **Wolljacke,-n** cardigan *7B*

Was kann man hier kaufen?

Reduziert

Jedes Teil
REDUZIERT
12,- bis 14,- €

Die Kleidungsstücke sind stark reduziert.

Kaffee

Kuchen

Eigene Konditorei

Eis

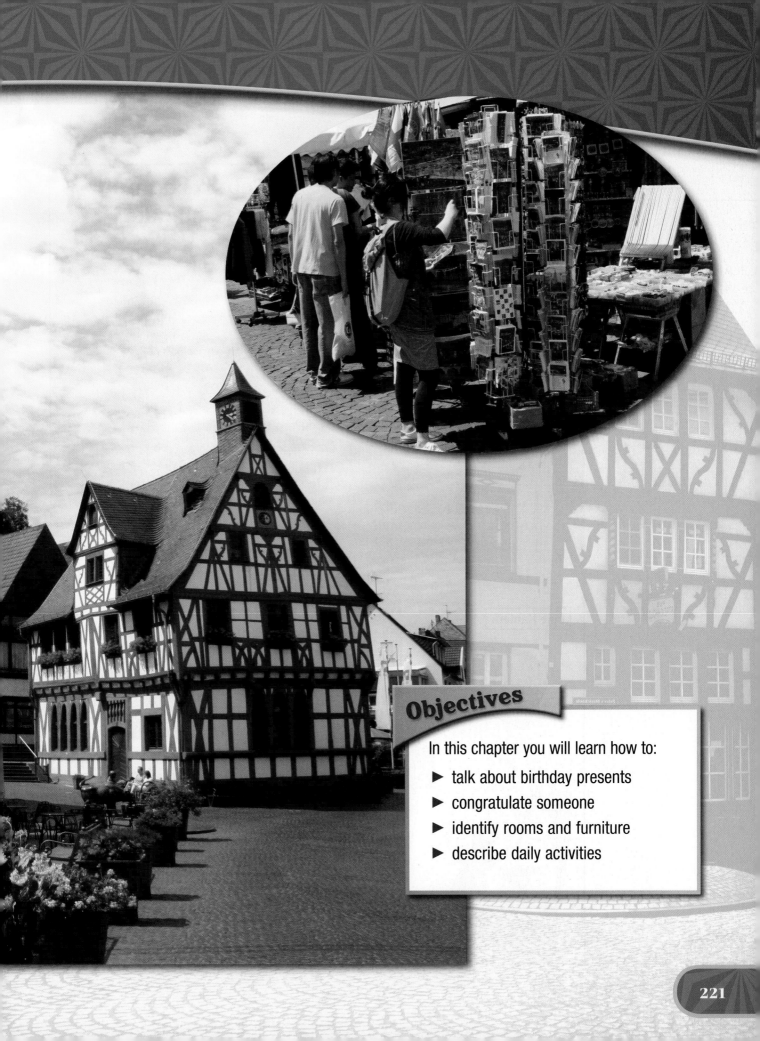

Objectives

In this chapter you will learn how to:

► talk about birthday presents
► congratulate someone
► identify rooms and furniture
► describe daily activities

221

Lektion A

Geburtstag und Geschenke

Wann hast du Geburtstag?

Am vierzehnten April. Und du?

Am dritten August.

Ich habe am ersten Oktober Geburtstag.

Was für ein Geschenk bekommst du?

Schmuck.

ein Fernseher

eine Kamera

eine Uhr

ein Radio

Ohrringe

ein Radiowecker

Kleidung

1 Wann haben sie Geburtstag?

You and your classmate each select six people (friends, relatives or famous people). Then alternate telling your partner the name and birthday of each person. Each of you records this information on a sheet of paper. When you are finished, compare one another's list to make sure you both have recorded the information correctly.

> *Du:* Martin Luther Kings Geburtstag ist am sechzehnten Januar.
>
> *Schulfreund:* Meine Mutter hat am fünften Mai Geburtstag.

2 Was für ein Geschenk wirst du kaufen?

Several birthdays are coming up and you want to buy some presents. Select three people you know, then indicate when their birthdays are, what you will buy and how much each item costs.

BEISPIELE Jürgen hat am achtundzwanzigsten Juli Geburtstag. Ich werde Jürgen ein Buch kaufen. Es kostet zwölf Euro.

Angelika hat am Mittwoch Geburtstag. Ich kaufe Angelika eine Uhr. Sie kostet achtzehn Euro.

Timo hat von seinem Großvater ein Geschenk bekommen.

Von seiner Freundin Karla bekommt er auch ein Geschenk.

Wer hat Geburtstag?

– Hast du eine Idee? – Ich glaube schon.

Also, was ist sein Geschenk?

Ein Radiowecker?

MELANIE:	Ich kaufe ein Paar Ohrringe.
BIRGIT:	Für dich?
MELANIE:	Nein, meine Mutter hat am Montag Geburtstag.
BIRGIT:	Du, ich komme mit. Ich will Matthias auch ein Geschenk kaufen.
MELANIE:	Hast du eine Idee?
BIRGIT:	Ich glaube schon. Matthias hört gern Musik und kommt oft zu spät zur Schule. Also, was ist sein Geschenk?
MELANIE:	Ein Radiowecker?
BIRGIT:	Du bist wirklich ein Genie!

3 Das stimmt nicht.

The following statements are incorrect. Provide the correct statements. *Auf Deutsch, bitte!*

1. Melanie will ein Paar Schuhe kaufen.
2. Melanies Bruder hat Geburtstag.
3. Birgit weiß nicht, was sie Matthias kaufen will.
4. Matthias sieht gern fern.
5. Matthias kommt oft zu früh zur Schule.
6. Birgit wird Matthias eine Uhr kaufen.

Für dich

As is customary here, Germans attach a greeting card *(Glückwunschkarte)* to a gift. *Herzlichen Glückwunsch zum Geburtstag!* is the most accepted and popular form of wishing someone a happy birthday. The first two words, *Herzlichen Glückwunsch,* or the plural, *Herzliche Glückwünsche,* will fit almost any occasion if you wish to congratulate someone in German, be it a birthday *(Geburtstag),* a name day or Saint's Day *(Namenstag),* a wedding *(Hochzeit)* or an anniversary *(Jubiläum).*

Geburtstagskarten

Herzlichen Glückwunsch zum Geburtstag!

eine Hochzeit

Possessive Adjectives

A possessive adjective is a pronoun that is used as an adjective to indicate who owns the noun that follows it. It replaces the article in front of the noun and takes on the same endings as those of the indefinite article (*ein*-words). You are already familiar with some possessive adjectives such as *mein, dein* and *sein*. These as well as the new possessive adjectives for the nominative and accusative cases are summarized below.

NOMINATIVE

	SINGULAR			PLURAL
	masculine	feminine	neuter	
ich	mein *(my)*	meine	mein	meine
du	dein *(your)*	deine	dein	deine
er	sein *(his)*	seine	sein	seine
sie	ihr *(her)*	ihre	ihr	ihre
es	sein *(its)*	seine	sein	seine
wir	unser *(our)*	uns(e)re*	unser	uns(e)re*
ihr	euer (your)	eu(e)re*	euer	eu(e)re*
sie	ihr (their)	ihre	ihr	ihre
Sie	Ihr (your)	Ihre	Ihr	Ihre

Meine Freundin heißt Angelika.　　My friend's name is Angelika.
Wo ist unser Fußball?　　Where is our soccer ball?

ACCUSATIVE

	SINGULAR			PLURAL
	masculine	feminine	neuter	
ich	meinen	meine	mein	meine
du	deinen	deine	dein	deine
er	seinen	seine	sein	seine
sie	ihren	ihre	ihr	ihre
es	seinen	seine	sein	seine
wir	uns(e)ren*	uns(e)re*	unser	uns(e)re*
ihr	eu(e)ren*	eu(e)re*	euer	eu(e)re*
sie	ihren	ihre	ihr	ihre
Sie	Ihren	Ihre	Ihr	Ihre

Kennst du seinen Bruder?　　Do you know his brother?
Ich kaufe ihr Buch.　　I'm buying her book.

*The *e* in front of the *r* in *unser* and *euer* is often omitted if the ending begins with a vowel.

4 Habt ihr...?

Imagine you're organizing a club function. You will need a number of items before your meeting. Ask the assembled club members if they have these items.

> **BEISPIEL** Habt ihr euere Gitarre?

1.
2.
3.
4.
5.
6.
7.
8.

5 Wer kann das mitbringen?

Your class is planning a short camping trip. Your teacher is asking your class who has specific things that will be needed. Several students are responding.

> **BEISPIEL** Wer hat einen Radiowecker? (Uwe)
> Uwe kann seinen Radiowecker mitbringen.

1. Wer hat ein Computerspiel? (Axel)
2. Wer hat einen Fußball? (Lars)
3. Wer hat eine Kamera? (Christine)
4. Wer hat ein Paar Tennisschuhe? (Cornelia)
5. Wer hat eine Landkarte? (Boris)
6. Wer hat einen Pulli? (Angela)

6 Wen besuchen wir noch?

Tell whom else we are visiting.

BEISPIEL Schwester / sein
Wir besuchen seine Schwester.

1. Oma / unser
2. Bruder / dein
3. Mutter / euer
4. Onkel / mein
5. Lehrerin / ihr
6. Cousin / sein

Seine Großeltern besuchen ihn.

7 Was brauchst du für deine Ferien?

Several people ask you what items you need to take along on your vacation trip. Use the cues in your response.

BEISPIEL Handschuhe / mein
Ich brauche meine Handschuhe.

1. Kamera / unser
2. Bücher / dein
3. Fußbälle / euer
4. Rad / ihr
5. Gitarre / sein
6. Jeans / mein
7. Schmuck / unser

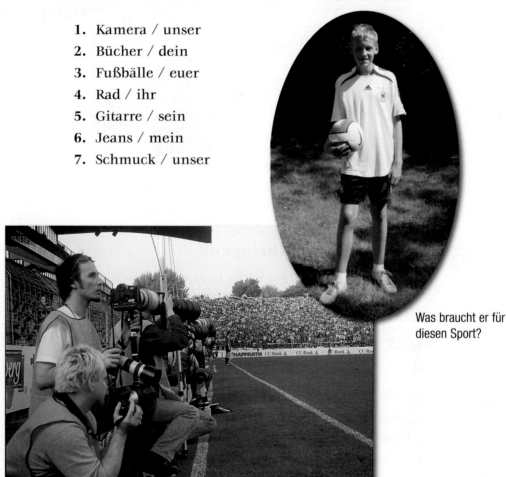

Was braucht er für diesen Sport?

Sie brauchen ihre Kameras.

Sprache

Personal Pronouns

Nominative *(er, sie, es)*

In German, as you have learned in previous chapters, there are three personal pronouns *er, sie* and *es*, which can replace *der, die* and *das* respectively.

Der Sommer *ist heiß.*	The summer is hot.
Er *ist heiß.*	It is hot.
Die Lehrerin *steht an der Tafel.*	The teacher is standing at the board.
Sie *steht an der Tafel.*	She is standing at the board.
Das Land *ist groß.*	The country is big.
Es *ist groß.*	It is big.

Accusative *(ihn, sie, es)*

The accusative case for the personal pronouns *er, sie* and *es* is *ihn, sie* and *es.* Notice that only the masculine pronoun *er* changes to *ihn.* The other pronouns *sie* and *es* have the same forms in the nominative and in the accusative case.

*Dieter kauft **einen Kuli**.*	Dieter is buying a pen.
*Dieter kauft **ihn**.*	Dieter is buying it.
*Kennst du **Frau Kuhlmann**?*	Do you know Mrs. Kuhlmann?
*Ja, ich kenne **sie**.*	Yes, I know her.
*Gabi sieht **das Fernsehprogramm** gern.*	Gabi likes to watch the TV program.
*Sieht ihre Freundin **es** auch gern?*	Does her girlfriend like to watch it too?

The following table shows these as well as other personal pronouns.

SINGULAR		PLURAL	
nominative	accusative	nominative	accusative
ich	mich *(me)*	wir	uns *(us)*
du	dich *(you)*	ihr	euch *(you)*
er	ihn *(him, it)*	sie	sie *(them)*
sie	sie *(her, it)*	Sie *(sg. & pl.)*	Sie *(you)*
es	es *(it)*		

8 Wie finden sie die Kleidungsstücke?

Tina is going shopping with several of her friends. Tell what everyone thinks about the various clothing items.

BEISPIEL Findet Andrea den Pulli schön? Nein,...
Nein, sie findet ihn nicht schön.

1. Findet Thomas die Jeans zu lang? Ja,...
2. Finden Ursula und Renate die Bluse zu bunt? Nein,...
3. Findet Julia den Mantel teuer? Ja,...
4. Findet Hans das Paar Schuhe zu groß? Ja,...
5. Finden Peter und Rainer die Jacken preiswert? Nein,...
6. Findet Angelika den Rock zu kurz? Nein,...

9 Sie macht es nicht.

Alexandra does not want to do what her sister does, and tells her so.

BEISPIEL Ich mache meine Arbeit.
Ich mache sie nicht.

1. Ich kaufe eine Geburtstagskarte.
2. Ich werde meine Jacke anhaben.
3. Ich trinke den Eistee.
4. Ich höre das Rockkonzert gern.
5. Ich will ein Geschenk kaufen.
6. Ich brauche deinen Stuhl.
7. Ich schicke eine Karte.
8. Ich kann die Hausaufgaben schreiben.

Er kann die Hausaufgaben schreiben.

10 Was fehlt in den Dialogen?

Complete the short dialogs using appropriate personal pronouns.

BEISPIEL Ich gehe in die Stadt.
Kann ich *dich* in die Stadt fahren?

1. Karin kennt Frau Albers sehr gut.
   Ich kenne ___ auch gut.

2. Es ist so dunkel.
   Das stimmt. Wir können ___ gar nicht sehen, Jens und Johann.

3. Guten Tag!
   Kenne ich ___? Heißen Sie Frau Köhler?

4. Kommst du am Samstag mit Rudi zur Party?
   Klar, ich bringe ___ mit.

5. Steffie hat um halb elf Deutsch.
   Hat sie ___ denn gern?

6. Ich lese das Buch für die Englischklasse am Montag.
   Musst du ___ bis dann schon lesen?

7. Warum könnt ihr ___ nicht besuchen?
   Du hast doch keine Zeit.

8. Schreibst du Christine eine E-Mail?
   Ja, ich schicke ___ heute Nachmittag.

Aktuelles

Special Occasions

There are many special occasions that can mark a family calendar throughout the years. Birthdays in Germany are celebrated not unlike ours. Generally, children's birthdays are celebrated among the immediate family. Teenagers often invite their friends to a birthday party.

Although the presence of many foreign workers and their families has greatly increased the importance of religious communities, which decades ago were hardly represented in Germany, most Germans belong to a Christian church—Protestant or Roman Catholic.

About half are Protestant (mostly in northern Germany), the other half Catholic (mostly in southern and western Germany). A special occasion in the Christian church that usually takes place within the first three months of a child's birth is baptism *(Taufe)*, to which the closest relatives are invited.

Even though a birthday *(Geburtstag)* is the most common celebration, in southern Germany the saint's day or name day *(Namenstag)* is still observed. Children here are often named after a saint whose birthday is observed on that day. Similar to a birthday, gifts are also given on *Namenstag*. At the age of 13 or 14, many Germans go through a religious instruction process that culminates in confirmation *(Konfirmation)*, when these young adults become full members of the church.

As you have already learned in an earlier chapter, there are three different schools after the *Grundschule* that students can attend. Upon graduating from the Hauptschule, students receive a certificate called *Abschlusszeugnis*. When they graduate from the *Realschule*, they get a certificate called *Mittlere Reifezeugnis*. Finally, students graduating from the *Gymnasium* receive their *Abitur*, which they will need if they want to continue their education.

The road to marriage usually starts with the engagement *(Verlobung)*. When the engagement becomes official, couples send out written announcements to their friends and relatives who will respond with cards of congratulations. Many will also send flowers or a gift. Bridal showers, a common practice in the United States, are not customary in Germany. Engagement presents are given on the day of the engagement. Most engaged couples exchange matching wedding rings which are worn on the left hand.

The engagement eventually leads to the wedding *(Hochzeit)*. Some American customs, such as the big wedding cake,

ein Hochzeitspaar

the throwing of confetti or rice and the wedding march are not part of the German tradition. However, the custom of *Polterabend* (*poltern* = to make a loud noise) is still popular in many parts of Germany. The evening before the wedding, friends of the couple go to the bride's house and smash piles of old pottery (no glass is allowed) at the door or under the window. It's an old superstition that the loud noise helps to avert bad luck. To ensure future married bliss, both bride and groom are expected to sweep up the broken pieces together at the beginning of their marriage.

In Germany, the civil marriage is obligatory. It takes place at the local registrar's office (*Standesamt*) in the presence of two witnesses. A church wedding usually follows the civil ceremony. The clergy cannot marry a couple without the civil wedding certificate.

Wedding presents often are delivered at the house while the family is attending the church ceremony or—if you are invited to the *Polterabend*—on the eve of the wedding. At the wedding ceremony, the wedding rings are changed from the left to the right ring finger.

die Hochzeitsgäste vor dem Standesamt

Similar to our country, an anniversary (*Jubiläum*) is considered a special occasion. A silver wedding anniversary (*silberne Hochzeit* or *Silberhochzeit*) means that a couple has been married for 25 years. After 50 years of marriage it is a golden anniversary (*goldene Hochzeit*).

Mother's Day (*Muttertag*), which falls on the second Sunday in May, was introduced in the United States in 1914 and in Germany in 1923. Contrary to the United States, however, in Germany, Father's Day (*Vatertag*) is not celebrated on a Sunday but on Ascension Day (*Himmelfahrtstag*), which is on a Thursday, 40 days after Easter (*Ostern*).

When someone dies in Germany, it is customary for the family members of the deceased to place an obituary (*Todesanzeige*) in the local paper that often includes personal and emotional comments from the immediate family. In most cases a black-rimmed announcement is mailed out to relatives and friends of the deceased.

Perhaps one of the quickest ways to learn about special occasions in Germany is by going to a department store or bookstore and browsing through the numerous greeting cards.

11 Wovon spricht man hier?

Identify the special occasions or events that are described in German. You may not understand every word, but you should be able to figure out what is being referred to. These are words that you may need to know: *viel Lärm machen* to make lots of noise; *die Geburt* birth; *das Ereignis* event; *ist gestorben* died; *die Zeitung* newspaper; *die Kirche* church.

1. Einen Tag vor der Hochzeit machen Freunde viel Lärm.
2. Ein besonderer Tag im Mai für die Mutti.
3. Ein paar Tage oder Wochen nach der Geburt.
4. Fünfzig Jahre nach der Hochzeit.
5. Ein wichtiges Dokument für die Universität.
6. Renate wird dann sechzehn. Ein Jahr später wird sie siebzehn.
7. Ein besonderes Ereignis für Monika vor der Hochzeit. Rolf und Monika geben dem Partner einen Ring.
8. Annelieses Großmutter ist am Dienstag gestorben. Es steht heute in der Zeitung.
9. Am Hochzeitstag gehen sie vor der Kirche zu diesem Büro.
10. Sie bekommen das nach der Hauptschule.
11. Dieser Tag ist ungefähr sechs Wochen nach Ostern.

Persönliches

1. Wann hast du Geburtstag?
2. Wie alt wirst du?
3. Was für ein Geschenk möchtest du zum Geburtstag bekommen?
4. Wird dich jemand *(someone)* zum Geburtstag besuchen? Wer?
5. Wann haben drei Personen in deiner Familie Geburtstag? Wer sind sie?

Rollenspiel

You and a classmate decide how much money you want to spend for one of your classmates whose birthday is coming up. Each of you makes a list that includes at least three items and their prices in euro. Then you ask your partner the following: how much money do you have, how much do you want to spend, what is the cost for each selected item and, finally, what are your reasons for purchasing one of these items? If appropriate, you may decide to buy one gift together. Be as creative as possible.

Wörter und Ausdrücke

Discussing Birthdays and Gift Ideas

Wann hast du Geburtstag? When is your birthday?
Am ersten... On the first of...
Am dritten... On the third of...

Was für ein Geschenk bekommst du? What kind of present are you getting?
  Schmuck. Jewelry.
  Eine Kamera. A camera.
  Einen Fernseher. A TV set.
  Kleidung. Clothing.
  Ein Radio. A radio.
  Ohrringe. Earrings.

Hast du eine Idee, was du bekommst? Do you have an idea what you're getting?
Ich glaube schon. I think so.
Einen Radiowecker. A clock radio.
Du bist wirklich ein Genie! You're really a genius!

Am ersten Schultag (in der ersten Klasse) bekommen die meisten Kinder eine Schultüte. (On the first day of school [in first grade] most children get a cone-filled bag with sweets.)

Zungenbrecher

Am zehnten Zehnten um zehn Uhr zehn zogen zehn zahme Ziegen zehn Zentner Zucker zum Zoo.

On October 10 at 10:10 ten tame goats dragged one hundred pound bags of sugar to the zoo.

Lektion B

die Wohnung oder
das Haus

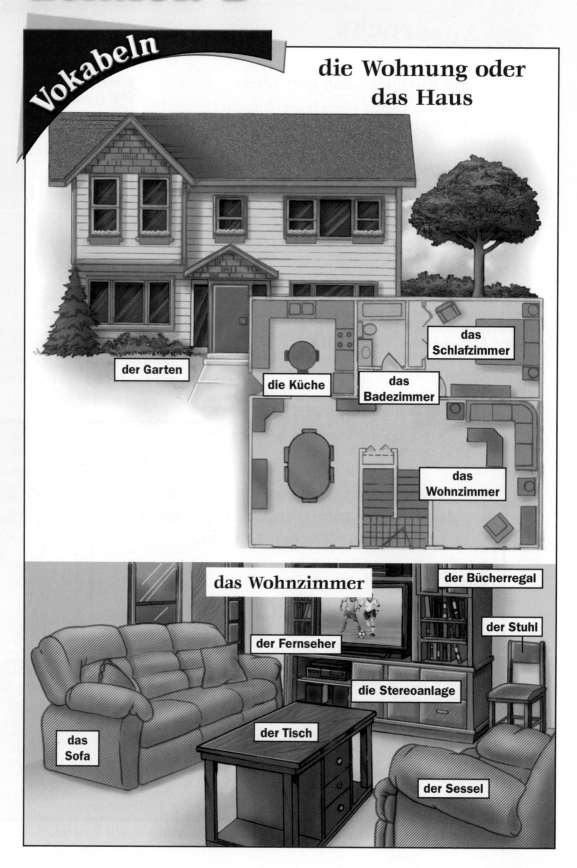

der Garten

die Küche

das
Badezimmer

das
Schlafzimmer

das
Wohnzimmer

das Wohnzimmer

der Bücherregal

der Stuhl

der Fernseher

die Stereoanlage

der Tisch

das
Sofa

der Sessel

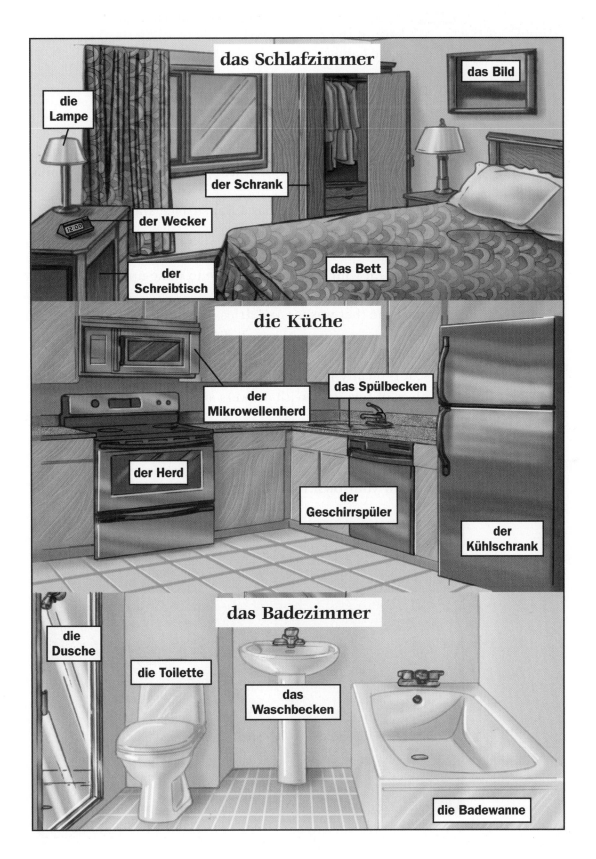

das Schlafzimmer

das Bild

die Lampe

der Schrank

der Wecker

der Schreibtisch

das Bett

die Küche

der Mikrowellenherd

das Spülbecken

der Herd

der Geschirrspüler

der Kühlschrank

das Badezimmer

die Dusche

die Toilette

das Waschbecken

die Badewanne

12 Was ist das?

Identify the German words that are described.

> **BEISPIEL** a device that enables you to read when the rest of the room is dark
> *eine Lampe*

1. piece of furniture that you'll use to rest on during the night
2. device consisting of shelves to hold books
3. oven in which liquid can be heated at accelerated speed
4. electronic system of transmitting images and sound over a wire or through space
5. piece of furniture that has a flat surface and four legs
6. tub in which you can bathe
7. appliance for keeping food and other items cool
8. device on which you set the time to wake up in the morning
9. machine that washes and dries dishes
10. place where you would wash dishes if you didn't have a dishwasher
11. seat typically having four legs and standing next to a table
12. piece of furniture with drawers at which you can study

13 Mein Zimmer

Describe at least five objects that you have in your living room or in your own room.

Was hat sie alles in ihrem Zimmer?

Wen laden wir ein?

Wen laden wir zur Party ein?

Wie viele kommen denn?

Zehn oder zwölf.

OLIVER: Wen laden wir zur Party ein?

FLORIAN: Ohne deine Freunde geht's nicht.

OLIVER: In unserer Wohnung haben wir keinen Platz. Dein Haus ist doch sehr groß. Können wir die Party nicht da machen?

FLORIAN: Klar. Wie viele kommen denn?

OLIVER: Zehn oder zwölf. So genau weiß ich das noch nicht.

FLORIAN Es geht im Wohnzimmer oder im Garten.

OLIVER: Für den Sonntag soll das Wetter schön sein.

FLORIAN: Dann sind wir lieber im Garten.

OLIVER: Also los! Rufen wir gleich alle an!

14 Was passt hier?

Complete the dialog using the appropriate forms of the verbs listed.

warten	**haben**	**sein**	**regnen**	**einladen**
werden	**kommen**	**machen**	**sprechen**	**wissen**
stimmen				

Wen wirst du zum Geburtstag (1)?

Ich (2) noch nicht.

Wann (3) du es wissen?

Morgen. Ich muss erst mit meinem Vater (4). Ich glaube, unser Wohnzimmer (5) zu klein.

Wir können die Party auch im Garten (6).

Das (7). Aber was machen wir, wenn es (8)?

Dann (9) ihr alle zu mir rüber. Wir (10) viel Platz im Haus. Warum machen wir die Party nicht gleich bei dir?

Da hast du wirklich Recht. Wir müssen nicht bis zum Wochenende (11).

15 Fragen

Beantworte diese Fragen!

1. Wen wird Oliver einladen?
2. Warum kann Oliver die Party nicht in seiner Wohnung haben?
3. Weiß Oliver genau, wie viele Jugendliche zur Party kommen?
4. Wann und wo wird die Party sein?
5. Wie wissen Oliver und Florian, wer kommen wird?

Wo und für wie viele Leute ist diese Party?

Für dich

When it comes to visiting each other, Germans tend to be somewhat more formal than Americans. Casual visits are not common. Therefore, if you have been invited to a German home, you may consider it a special gesture of friendship. You may well expect that your visit has been carefully prepared for: the house will be very clean, at least one cake will be served with coffee or soft drinks, a good dinner may have been prepared and usually the family will be dressed up for the occasion.

If you have been invited for coffee and cake *(Kaffee und Kuchen)* or a meal *(Mahlzeit)*, you are expected to be there right on time. Do not come earlier, or more than 10 or 15 minutes later. It is customary to bring a bouquet of cut flowers *(Blumen)* for the hostess, usually an uneven number of five or seven stems. When presenting the flowers, do not forget to take off the wrapping before handing them to the hostess. You may want to bring a small gift of candy *(Bonbons)* or other sweets *(Süßigkeiten)* for the children.

eine Tasse Kaffee und ein Stück Kuchen

Süßigkeiten

Kaffee + Kuchen

Was kann man hier bekommen?

Accusative Prepositions

The accusative case always follows these prepositions:

durch	through
für	for
gegen	against
ohne	without
um	around

*Wir fahren **durch die Stadt.***	We are driving through the city.
*Hast du ein Geschenk **für deine Freundin?***	Do you have a present for your girlfriend?
*Sie spielen **gegen die Jungen.***	They are playing against the boys.
*Ich komme **ohne das Buch.***	I'm coming without the book.
*Gehst du **um die Ecke?***	Are you going around the corner?

Contractions

These accusative prepositions and articles are contracted as long as there is no special emphasis on the article.

durch	**+**	**das**	**=**	**durchs**
für	**+**	**das**	**=**	**fürs**
um	**+**	**das**	**=**	**ums**

Wie viel bezahlst du fürs Rockkonzert?	How much are you paying for the rock concert?
Fahr doch nicht so schnell ums Haus!	Don't drive so fast around the house!

Viele Leute gehen durch die Stadt.

16 Immer ohne diese Sachen!

Herr Kowalski is annoyed with some of his students because they forget periodically to bring certain items to school.

BEISPIEL Renate
Renate, warum kommst du immer ohne ein Buch?

1. Uwe
2. Stefan und Susanne
3. Rainer

4. Natascha
5. Boris und Axel
6. Angelika

17 Wie viel bezahlst du für...?

Tell how much you are paying for the different items.

BEISPIEL Ich bezahle vierhundert Euro für die Gitarre.

€ 400,–

€ 50,–

€ 20,–

€ 200,–

1.
2.
3.

€ 130,–

€ 450,–

€ 30,–

4.
5.
6.

18 Ganze Sätze, bitte!

Form complete sentences using the information provided.

BEISPIEL   wir / fahren / durch / Stadt
Wir fahren durch die Stadt.

1. Peter / fahren / um / Bahnhof
2. ich / bezahlen / ein paar Euro / für / Buch
3. Frau Riehmann / kommen / ohne / Mantel
4. meine Freundin / haben / kein Geschenk / für / Onkel
5. Katja und ihre Freundin / gehen / durch / Schule

Herzlichen Glückwunsch zum Geburtstag![1]

Jürgen Sternkes Geburtstag ist am vierten April. An diesem Tag wird er[2] sechzehn Jahre alt. Was für Geschenke wird er bekommen? Er hofft, dass[3] er von seinen Eltern einen Motorroller[4] bekommt. Die anderen Geschenke sind für ihn nicht so wichtig[5].

Wünschst du dir etwas Besonderes?

Soll das ein
Witz sein, Vati?

Vater: In drei Tagen hast du Geburtstag. Wen willst du denn einladen?

Jürgen: Christian, Silke und Gabi. Die kommen bestimmt[6].

Mutter: Was für einen Kuchen[7] möchtest du gern?

Jürgen: Schwarzwälder Kirschtorte[8] natürlich[9]. Die esse ich doch besonders gern.

Vater: Wünschst du dir etwas Besonderes?[10]

Jürgen: Soll das ein Witz[11] sein, Vati?

Vater: Na ja, wir müssen ja auch eine Auswahl haben.

Jürgen: Ich hoffe, euer Geschenk hat zwei Räder[12] und einen Motor[13].

Jürgen spricht mit
seinem Vater über sein
Geburtstagsgeschenk.

Jürgen ruft seine Freunde an. Alle drei werden kommen. Endlich[14] ist Jürgens Geburtstag da. Christian, Silke und Gabi begrüßen[15] Jürgen mit „Herzlichen Glückwunsch zum Geburtstag". Frau Sternke bringt schon bald die Schwarzwälder Kirschtorte. Die schmeckt allen besonders gut. Dann macht Jürgen ein paar Geschenke auf[16]. Von Christian bekommt er eine CD. Gabi und Silke geben Jürgen zusammen

Schwarzwälder Kirschtorte

ein Geschenk — einen Helm. Jürgen will wissen, warum er einen Helm bekommt. Bevor[17] es eine Antwort[18] gibt, will Herr Sternke Jürgen das große Geschenk zeigen[19]. Deshalb gehen sie ums Haus. Da steht es: ein Motorroller für Jürgen.

Jürgen: Toll! Klasse! Super! Kann ich gleich fahren?

Vater: Moment mal! Nicht so schnell! Zuerst zeige ich dir, wie alles funktioniert[20].

Jürgen: Das brauchst du nicht. Ich weiß das schon.

Vater: So? Woher weißt du denn, wie man Motorroller fährt?

Jürgen wird ganz rot. Herr Sternke lächelt[21] und weiß natürlich die Antwort. Christian hat ein Moped[22] und bestimmt fährt er es manchmal. Jürgen sitzt schnell auf[23] dem Motorroller und fährt langsam ohne den Helm durch den Garten. Das gefällt Herrn Sternke nicht und er sagt seinem Sohn, er soll nur mit dem Helm auf der Straße fahren. Das macht er auch gleich und fährt ein paar Mal[24] um die Ecke. Natürlich darf Christian auch auf dem Motorroller fahren.

Später am Nachmittag sitzen die vier Freunde am Tisch im Wohnzimmer und spielen Karten.

Kann ich gleich fahren?

Herr Sternke sitzt auf dem Sofa und sieht fern. Frau Sternke bringt später am Abend noch eine Kalte Platte. Die schmeckt besonders gut. Jürgen will am nächsten Tag[25] seinen Schulfreunden den Motorroller zeigen. Die werden aber staunen[26]!

---

[1]*Herzlichen Glückwunsch zum Geburtstag!* Happy birthday!; [2]*er wird sechzehn* he will be sixteen; [3]*er hofft, dass...* he hopes that...; [4]*der Motorroller* motor scooter; [5]*wichtig* important; [6]*bestimmt* definitely, for sure; [7]*der Kuchen* cake; [8]*die Schwazwälder Kirschtorte* Black Forest Cherry Torte; [9]*natürlich* of course; [10]*Wünschst du dir etwas Besonderes?* Are you wishing for something special?; [11]*der Witz* joke; [12]*das Rad* wheel; [13]*der Motor* motor, engine; [14]*endlich* finally; [15]*begrüßen* to greet; [16]*aufmachen* to open; [17]*bevor* before; [18]*die Antwort* answer; [19]*zeigen* to show; [20]*funktionieren* to function, work; [21]*lächeln* to smile; [22]*das Moped* moped; [23]*sitzen auf* to sit on; [24]*ein paar Mal* a few times; [25]*am nächsten Tag* on the next day; [26]*staunen* to be surprised

Kalte Platte

Was bringt Jürgens Mutter?

Was macht Herr Sternke?

Kapitel 8

19 Die richtige Reihenfolge

Arrange the sentences in the proper sequence according to what happened in the *Lesestück*.

1. Jürgens Mutter bringt die Schwarzwälder Kirschtorte.
2. Jürgen ruft Christian, Gabi und Silke an.
3. Jürgen fährt auf dem Motorroller durch den Garten.
4. Jürgen will wissen, warum er von Gabi und Silke einen Helm bekommt.
5. Jürgen macht Geschenke auf.
6. Jürgen will seinen Schulfreunden den Motorroller zeigen.
7. Jürgen will drei Freunde zum Geburtstag einladen.
8. Jürgen und seine Freunde spielen Karten.
9. Die drei Freunde sagen: „Herzlichen Glückwunsch zum Geburtstag, Jürgen."
10. Jürgen hofft, dass seine Mutter eine Schwarzwälder Kirschtorte backen wird.
11. Die Torte schmeckt sehr gut.
12. Jürgen und sein Vater gehen ums Haus.
13. Silke, Gabi und Christian sagen Jürgen, dass sie zu seinem Geburtstag kommen werden.

20 Fragen

Beantworte diese Fragen!

1. Wie alt wird Jürgen am vierten April?
2. Was für ein Geschenk möchte er von seinen Eltern bekommen?
3. Wie viele Freunde wird Jürgen zum Geburtstag einladen?
4. Was für einen Kuchen isst Jürgen gern?
5. Wie weiß Jürgen, dass seine Freunde zum Geburtstag kommen?
6. Was für ein Geschenk bekommt Jürgen von Christian?
7. Warum gehen alle ums Haus?
8. Warum muss Herr Sternke Jürgen nicht sagen, wie der Motorroller funktioniert?
9. Was gefällt Herrn Sternke nicht?
10. Was machen Jürgen und seine Freunde später?

Persönliches

You would like to buy a gift for someone who has a special occasion coming up. Describe what and when this occasion is, how much money you want to spend, what you want to buy and why. Be as creative as possible.

Rollenspiel

You want to give your friend a surprise birthday party. You discuss this with one of your classmates. Your conversation should include such details as: the age of your friend, the place, day and time you would like to have the party, whom to invite, what to have to eat and drink, what to do at the party and so on.

Praktisches

Divide the class into groups of four to plan a surprise party for a friend. Working on their own, Student 1 prepares an invitation (*die Einladung*) that says for whom and why the party is being given, the time and date and the party's location. Student 2 decides whom to invite. Student 3 makes a list of appropriate gifts that guests might bring. Student 4 plans what food and beverages will be served.

Then have all group members meet. Each group member presents his or her ideas. After discussing all the suggestions that have been offered, the group decides on the final invitation, guest list, gift suggestions and refreshments. Groups may turn in the party plans to the teacher, or each group may compare their plan with the other groups to see which party will be the most fun.

Was kaufen sie alles für die Party?

Schreiben

Describe your apartment or your house. Your description may refer to these questions: *Wie viele Zimmer gibt es?, Gefällt dir ein Zimmer besonders? Warum? (Es ist neu, schön, groß.)* Here is a sample description:

Meine Wohnung ist groß. Wir haben ein Wohnzimmer, eine Küche, ein Esszimmer, ein Badezimmer und drei Schlafzimmer. Mein Zimmer gefällt mir sehr. Ich lese dort und höre oft Musik im Radio. Mir gefällt besonders die Musik von... Unsere Küche ist klein, aber wir haben dort einen Kühlschrank, einen Herd und einen Geschirrspüler. Wir essen immer im Esszimmer. Da stehen ein Tisch und sechs Stühle. Einen Fernseher gibt es auch da. Unsere Familie sieht dort oft fern, besonders am Abend.

Land und Leute

Österreich

Österreich ist eine Republik. Das Land liegt in der Mitte[1] von Europa. Österreich ist ungefähr so groß wie der Staat Maine. Es hat fast acht Millionen Einwohner. Ungefähr 98% (Prozent) sprechen deutsch. Österreichs Nationalfahne[2] ist rot-weiß-rot. Das Land liegt zum größten Teil[3] in den Alpen. Der höchste Berg[4] ist der Großglockner. Die Donau ist der längste Fluss[5]. Sie fließt[6] von Westen nach Osten.

Die Hauptstadt von Österreich ist Wien. Mehr als 20% der Österreicher wohnen in der Hauptstadt. Wien liegt im Osten Österreichs. Da ist das Land flach[7]. Die Donau fließt durch Wien. Im Süden liegt Graz, auch eine große Stadt. Linz liegt im Nordosten. Die Donau fließt auch durch Linz. Nach Wien, Graz, und Linz kommt Salzburg im Nordwesten.

Österreich liegt zum größten Teil in den Alpen.

Mit einer Seilbahn *(cable car)* kommt man schnell auf den Berg.

Auch im Winter kommen viele Touristen zu Besuch.

Salzburg ist eine beliebte[8] Stadt. Viele Touristen kommen im Sommer zum Musikfest[9] nach Salzburg. Innsbruck ist die fünftgrößte Stadt in Österreich. Diese Stadt liegt im Westen und ist während[10] jeder Jahreszeit beliebt. Besonders schön ist es da im Winter.

Welche Städte möchtest du in Österreich besuchen? Wien, Graz, Linz, Salzburg oder Innsbruck? Warum möchtest du sie gern sehen?

---

[1]*in der Mitte* in the center; [2]*die Nationalfahne* national flag; [3]*zum größten Teil* for the most part; [4]*der höchste Berg* the highest mountain; [5]*der längste Fluss* the longest river; [6]*fließen* to flow; [7]*flach* flat; [8]*beliebt* popular; [9]*das Musikfest* music festival; [10]*während* during

Wandern in den Bergen ist sehr beliebt.

Na, wer kommt denn hier?

21 Was passt hier?

1. Österreich liegt	A. im Süden
2. Der höchste Berg heißt	B. der längste Fluß
3. Die Donau fließt	C. nach Salzburg
4. Wien ist	D. in den Alpen
5. Graz liegt	E. die Hauptstadt
6. Österreich ist	F. im Osten
7. Die Hauptstadt liegt	G. Großglockner
8. Viele Touristen kommen zum Musikfest	H. durch Linz und Wien
9. Die Donau ist	I. eine Republik
10. Zum größten Teil liegt das Land	J. in der Mitte von Europa

Wörter und Ausdrücke

Describing a House or an Apartment

das Haus house
die Wohnung apartment

das Wohnzimmer living room
    das Sofa sofa
    der Sessel armchair, easy chair
    das Bücherregal bookshelf
    die Stereoanlage stereo system

das Schlafzimmer bedroom
    der Schrank cupboard, closet
    das Bett bed
    der Schreibtisch desk
    der Wecker alarm clock
    das Bild picture

die Küche kitchen
    der Mikrowellenherd microwave oven
    der Kühlschrank refrigerator
    der Herd stove
    der Geschirrspüler dishwasher
    das Spülbecken sink (kitchen)

das Badezimmer bathroom
    die Badewanne bathtub
    die Dusche shower
    die Toilette toilet
    das Waschbecken sink (bathroom)

Talking about an Invitation

Wen laden wir ein? Whom do we invite?
Habt ihr genug Platz? Do you have enough room?
Rufen wir gleich alle an! Let's call everyone right away!

Sie sitzen am Schreibtisch.

Häuser in Norddeutschland

moderne Wohnungen in Leipzig

Rückblick

22 **Was machst du am Samstag?**

You'll have plenty of time on Saturday. Your friend asks what you're planning to do. Create an appropriate dialog.

Freund(in): Was machst du am Samstag?

Du: (1)

Freund(in): Komm doch mit zu Tanja!

Du: (2)

Freund(in): Sie hat Geburtstag.

Du: (3)

Freund(in): Peter, Natalie und vielleicht auch Jürgen und Anne.

Du: (4)

Freund(in): So gegen sieben.

Du: (5)

23 **Bianca hat Geburtstag.**

Complete each sentence using an appropriate word.

1. Biancas ___ ist morgen. Sie wird vierzehn.
2. Sie wird ein paar ___ einladen.
3. Die ___ beginnt um halb fünf.
4. Alle bringen ___ mit.
5. Biancas Schulfreunde wünschen ihr „Herzlichen ___ zum Geburtstag!"
6. Bianca bekommt von Thomas ein ___.
7. Heidi gibt Bianca eine ___.
8. Die Mädchen hören ___; die Jungen sehen fern.
9. Um halb sieben bringt ihre Mutter eine Kalte ___ ins Wohnzimmer.
10. Um acht Uhr gehen alle nach ___.

24 Was passt hier?

Classify the following words as belonging to one of these categories: *Familie, Geschenk, Haus, Fach.*

1. Ohrringe
2. Bruder
3. Schlafzimmer
4. Geschichte
5. Bad
6. Rechner
7. Eltern
8. Küche
9. Computerspiel
10. Chemie

In welchem Zimmer ist er?

25 Sprich mit einem Schulkameraden!

Pretend that you are on the phone with your friend (classmate). Discuss the following details: Tell your partner that you have a present and would like to bring it. He or she wants to know why you have a present. Give a reason. Ask your classmate if he or she would like to see it. Your friend does. Finally, determine a time to get together.

26 Wo findet man das alles?

Im Wohnzimmer? Im Schlafzimmer? In der Küche? Im Bad? Indicate where you may find these items, some of which could be found in more than one room.

BEISPIEL Schreibtisch
Der Schreibtisch steht im Wohnzimmer.

1. das Bücherregal
2. die Badewanne
3. der Schrank
4. das Sofa
5. der Geschirrspüler
6. die Stereoanlage
7. das Bett
8. der Sessel
9. der Wecker
10. der Tisch

27 Gegenteile

Provide a word that means the opposite for each word listed.

1. klein
2. lang
3. langsam
4. plus
5. kalt

6. gut
7. leicht
8. billig
9. drinnen
10. neu

Was weißt du?

1. *Wer hat Geburtstag?* Indicate who among your friends or relatives has a birthday soon. In your description include when the birthday takes place, what gift you might buy and the cost for that item.

2. Describe two similarities and two differences of special occasions in this country versus Germany. *Auf Englisch!*

3. Ask at least five of your classmates when their birthdays are (including the day and the month). Then put the dates in chronological order, writing out the dates. (Example: *Robert hat am sechsten Mai Geburtstag.*)

4. *Zum Geburtstag möchte ich...* Imagine that you could get any birthday present you wish. Indicate the presents you would like to receive, and why. Name your top three choices.

5. *Was soll ich kaufen?* Pretend you just moved into a house or apartment. Your room is completely empty. List the five most important items that you would like to have in your room.

6. *Dort möchte ich wohnen.* Imagine the house or apartment of your dreams! On a separate sheet of paper, draw the floor plan of your ideal residence, labeling all the rooms in German. It may have one or two floors. Then choose any room in this house or apartment and make a larger drawing of it on another piece of paper, adding whatever you would buy to decorate and furnish the room. You may either draw the decorations and furniture or find pictures of them in magazines to cut out and attach to your drawing.

Vokabeln

also so; *Also, was ist dein Geschenk?* So, what is your present? *8A*

anrufen to call (on the phone) *8B*

die **Antwort,-en** answer *8B*

aufmachen to open *8B*

die **Badewanne,-n** bathtub *8B*

das **Badezimmer,-** bathroom *8B*

begrüßen to greet *8B*

bestimmt definitely, for sure *8B*

das **Bett,-en** bed *8B*

bevor before *8B*

das **Bild,-er** picture *8B*

das **Bücherregal,-e** bookshelf *8B*

dass that *8B*

dritt- third *8A*

durch through *8B*

die **Dusche,-n** shower *8B*

einladen to invite *8B*

endlich finally *8B*

euer your (familiar plural) *8A*

der **Fernseher,-** TV, television set *8A*

funktionieren to function, work *8B*

der **Garten,** ⸚ garden *8B*

der **Geburtstag,-e** birthday *8A*

gegen against *8B*

genau exact(ly) *8B*

das **Genie,-s** genius *8A*

das **Geschenk,-e** present, gift *8A*

der **Geschirrspüler,-** dishwasher *8B*

der **Herd,-e** stove *8B*

herzlich sincere, cordial; *Herzlichen Glückwunsch zum Geburtstag!* Happy birthday! *8B*

hoffen to hope *8B*

ihr her, their, your *8A*

Ihr your (formal singular and plural) *8A*

die **Kamera,-s** camera *8A*

die **Kleidung** clothes, clothing *8A*

die **Küche,-n** kitchen *8B*

der **Kuchen,-** cake *8B*

der **Kühlschrank,** ⸚**e** refrigerator *8B*

lächeln to smile *8B*

die **Lampe,-n** lamp *8B*

los: Also los! Let's go! *8A*

das **Mal,-e** time(s); *ein paar Mal* a few times *8B*

der **Mikrowellenherd,-e** microwave oven *8B*

das **Moped,-s** moped *8B*

der **Motor,-en** motor, engine *8B*

der **Motorroller,-** motor scooter *8B*

nächst- next *8B*

natürlich natural(ly), of course *8B*

der **Ohrring,-e** earring *8A*

die **Party,-s** party *8B*

der **Platz,** ⸚**e** place, seat *8B*

das **Rad,** ⸚**er** wheel *8B*

das **Radio,-s** radio *8A*

der **Radiowecker,-** clock radio *8A*

das **Schlafzimmer,-** bedroom *8B*

der **Schmuck** jewelry *8A*

der **Schrank,** ⸚**e** cupboard, closet *8B*

der **Schreibtisch,-e** desk *8B*

die **Schwarzwälder Kirschtorte** Black Forest Cherry Torte *8B*

sein his, its *8A*

der **Sessel,-** armchair *8B*

sitzen auf to sit on *8B*

das **Sofa,-s** sofa *8B*

das **Spülbecken,-** kitchen sink *8B*

staunen to be astonished, surprised *8B*

die **Stereoanlage,-n** stereo system *8B*

die **Toilette,-n** toilet *8B*

das **Waschbecken,-** bathroom sink *8B*

der **Wecker,-** alarm clock *8B*

werden to become, be; *Er wird sechzehn.* He'll be sixteen. *8B*

wichtig important *8B*

der **Witz,-e** joke *8B*

die **Wohnung,-en** apartment *8B*

das **Wohnzimmer,-** living room *8B*

wünschen to wish *8B*

zeigen to show *8B*

Auf dem Bücherregal sind viele Bücher.

Was ist im Kühlschrank?

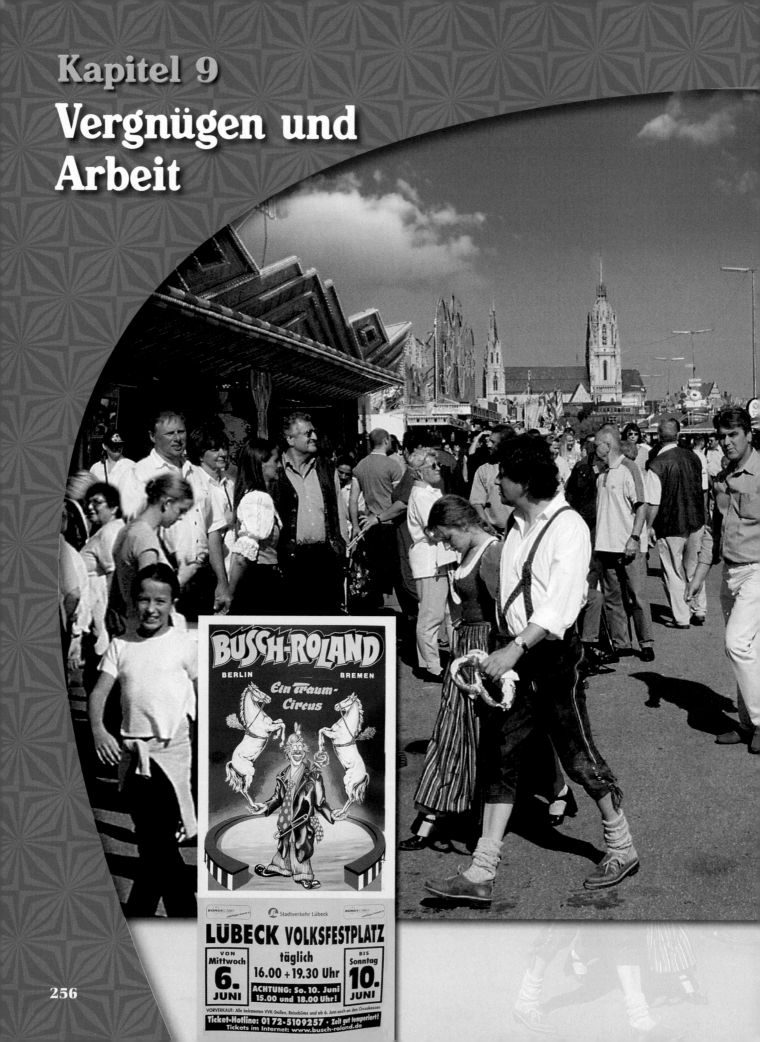

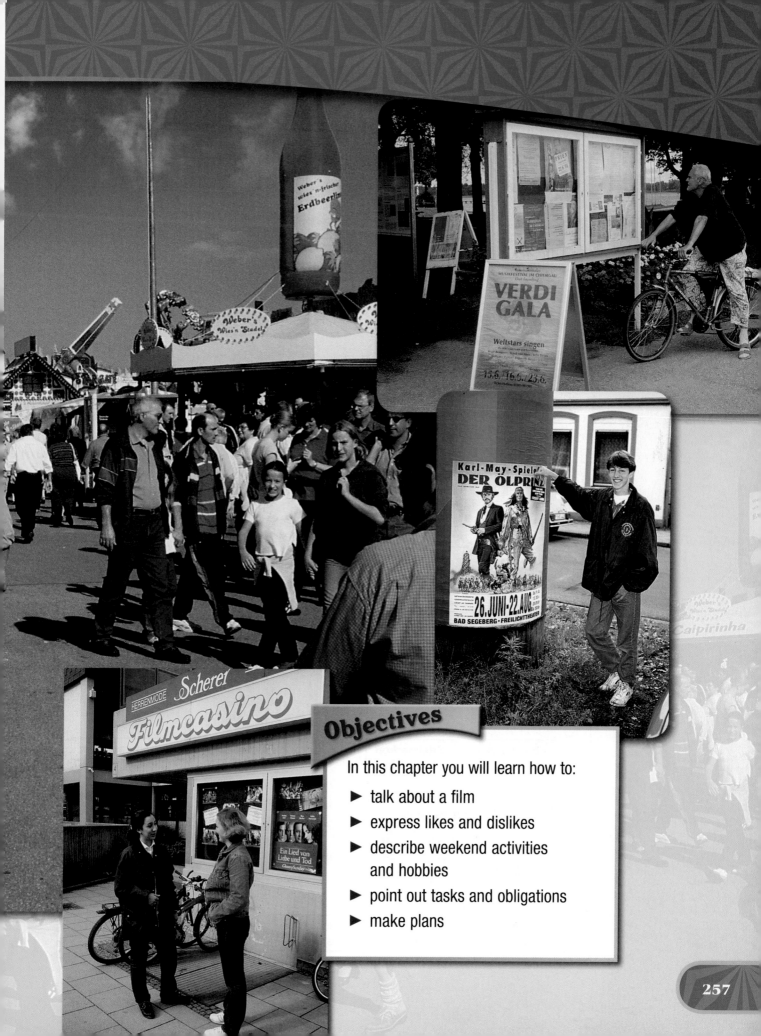

Objectives

In this chapter you will learn how to:

- ► talk about a film
- ► express likes and dislikes
- ► describe weekend activities and hobbies
- ► point out tasks and obligations
- ► make plans

Lektion A

Kino und Hobbys

Kino

Hobbys

Schach spielen **Briefmarken sammeln** **Poster sammeln** **Münzen sammeln**

Rockmusik hören **Zeitungen lesen** **Klarinette spielen** **Ski laufen** **fotografieren**

1 Was machen alle am Wochenende?

Tell what everyone is doing this weekend based on the illustrations.

BEISPIEL Renate
Renate sieht fern.

1. Holger und Axel   2. Dieters Freund   3. Petra

4. Annes Vater   5. Lisa und Tanja   6. Wir

2 Und was machst du gern?

Tell your classmates five activities that you would like to do.

Was machen sie gern?

Er liest gern.

Was gibt's im Kino?

Wen ruft Karin an?

Um wie viel Uhr fängt der Film denn an?

Um halb fünf.

KARIN: Ich muss jetzt noch schnell einkaufen. Hast du heute Nachmittag etwas vor?

GÜLTEN: Nein, noch nicht. Was schlägst du vor?

KARIN: Vielleicht kommt Sarah später rüber.

GÜLTEN: Was gibt's denn im Kino?

KARIN: Hier in der Zeitung steht es. Im Filmcasino läuft ein Liebesfilm aus Amerika. Er soll toll sein.

GÜLTEN: Um wie viel Uhr fängt der Film denn an?

KARIN: Um halb fünf.

GÜLTEN: Warum rufst du nicht Sarah an? Sie kommt vielleicht auch mit.

KARIN: Wo ist mein Handy? Ach ja, hier. Bestimmt bringt sie Tobias mit.

3 Was fehlt hier?

Complete the narrative using the appropriate forms of
the verbs listed.

schlagen	wissen	haben	mitbringen
sollen	sein	einkaufen	stehen
rufen	rüberkommen	mitkommen	

Karin (1) am Nachmittag nichts vor. Jetzt muss sie aber (2)
gehen. Gülten will (3), was Karin vorschlägt. Karin meint,
dass Sarah vielleicht (4). In der Zeitung (5), welcher Film
im Filmcasino läuft. Karin glaubt, dass er super (6). Der
Film aus Amerika (7) um 4 Uhr 30 anfangen. Gülten (8)
vor, dass Karin Sarah anruft. Vielleicht wird Sarah auch ins
Kino (9). Karin hat ein Handy und (10) Sarah auch gleich
an. Sie glaubt, dass Sarah Tobias zum Kino (11).

4 Fragen

Beantworte diese Fragen!

1. Was wird Karin gleich machen?
2. Wer kommt vielleicht später zu Karin rüber?
3. Wie wissen Karin und Gülten, was im Kino läuft?
4. Was für ein Film läuft im Filmcasino?
5. Wie soll er sein?
6. Wann beginnt der Film?
7. Was für ein Telefon hat Karin?
8. Wen wird Sarah bestimmt mitbringen?

Was läuft im Kino?

About half of all films in Germany come from the United States. Almost all American films are dubbed with a German soundtrack—there are no subtitles; the English has been carefully translated into German to match the lip movements. In many large cities there are movie theaters that play films in English without subtitles.

Movie theaters are required by law to indicate the age of admittance for each film (similar to our rating system). The standard phrase, for example, is *frei ab 14 Jahren* (admittance 14 years or older).

Wie alt müssen Kinder sein, um diesen Film zu sehen?

There are over 4,300 theaters in Germany today. Before the main feature starts, for about 30 minutes numerous commercials are shown advertising local, regional and national companies' products and services.

Sprache

Verbs with Separable Prefixes

You can combine verbs with prefixes and thus change their meaning. In most cases such prefixes are prepositions, just as in English (to take—to undertake).

> *(anrufen) Warum rufst du Monika nicht an?* Why don't you call Monika?

> *(einladen) Steffie lädt Rainer zur Party ein.* Steffie is inviting Rainer to the party.

The prefixes, which you can add or eliminate, are called *separable*. The prefixes are separated from their verbs and placed at the end of the sentence.

> *(vorhaben) Was **hast** du heute **vor**?* What are you planning (to do) today?

> *(fernsehen) Wir **sehen** am Abend **fern**.* We are watching TV at night.

These are the verbs with separable prefixes you have learned so far:

anfangen to begin, start	**herkommen** to come here
anhaben to have on, wear	**losgehen** to start
anrufen to call (on the phone)	**mitbringen** to bring along
aufmachen to open	**mitkommen** to come along`
einkaufen to shop	**rüberkommen** to come over
einladen to invite	**vorhaben** to plan
fernsehen to watch television	**vorschlagen** to suggest

The accent is always on the separable prefix (**an**fangen, **vor**haben).

5 Was ist denn alles bei Joachim los?

Today is Joachim's birthday. Summarize everything that is going on.

BEISPIEL seine Eltern / an Joachims Geburtstag / viel / vorhaben
Seine Eltern haben an Joachims Geburtstag viel vor.

1. sein Vater / für die Geburtstagsparty / einkaufen
2. seine Mutter / die Großeltern / einladen
3. seine Freundin / um vier Uhr / rüberkommen
4. sein Freund / am Abend / anrufen
5. Joachim / seine Geschenke / aufmachen

6 Fragen

Beantworte diese Fragen!

BEISPIEL Was macht Tina auf? (ein Geschenk)
Sie macht ein Geschenk auf.

1. Was hat Elisabeth heute an? (ein Pulli)
2. Wer kommt ins Kino mit? (alle)
3. Was haben Peter und Uwe am Abend vor? (nichts)
4. Um wie viel Uhr kauft Herr Sorge in der Stadt ein? (um drei Uhr)
5. Wie viele Jungen lädt Tanja zur Party ein? (fünf)
6. Wen bringt Heiko zum Kino mit? (seine Freundin)
7. Wo sieht Petra fern? (im Wohnzimmer)

7 Ergänze diesen Dialog!

Complete the conversation using the appropriate prefixes.

A: Zuerst rufe ich meinen Sohn Bernd (1). Hoffentlich hört er das Telefon.

B: Warum soll er es denn nicht hören?

A: Ach wissen Sie, er sieht jeden Tag um diese Zeit (2). Das Telefon ist in der Küche und der Fernseher ist im Wohnzimmer. Dann hört er das Telefon oft nicht.

B: Warum wollen Sie denn mit Bernd sprechen?

A: Ich habe viel in der Stadt (3). Später kommt noch meine Schwester (4). Bernd muss nicht warten, bis ich zu Hause bin.

B: Ich komme in die Stadt (5). Ich muss auch dorthin. Ist das OK?

A: Klar. Ich kaufe bei Schuhmanns in der Kantstraße (6). Die haben heute ein Sonderangebot.

B: Also, gehen wir gleich (7).

A: Einen Moment, bitte. Ich bringe noch genug Geld (8).

B: Haben Sie keine warme Kleidung (9)? Es ist doch heute sehr kalt.

A: Meine Jacke ist im Auto.

8 Kombiniere...

Was	kaufst	Dieter	in der Stadt	ein
Warum	bringt	Sabine	zu Hause	mit
Wann	macht	Herr Sauer	im Kaufhaus	auf
Wer	habt	ihr	heute	vor
Wo	ruft	du	für die Party	an
			die Geschenke	
			viel Geld	

Entertainment

Entertainment in Germany is a national pastime. Put simply—Germans love to be entertained. This is obvious to the visitor who sees numerous billboards *(Reklametafeln)* and round columns *(Litfaßsäulen)* covered with posters announcing the various events taking place in town. Local newspapers *(Zeitungen)* and brochures *(Broschüren)* distributed by the tourist office provide all the information on entertainment and attractions in the area.

Was gibt's hier alles zu tun?

Larger cities provide the most opportunities for different types of entertainment. Internationally known stars tour Germany throughout the year. American rock stars have made a long-lasting impact, particularly among the younger generation.

Neighborhood movie theaters *(Kinos)* feature both German and foreign films. American films are particularly popular. Admission is between performances only. Children are not allowed at adult showings, and certain age groups are excluded from other films under the German Youth Protection Law *(Jugendschutzgesetz)*.

Because of its long tradition of cultural diversity, Germany has always been extremely rich in theaters *(Theater)*, operas *(Opern)* and concert halls *(Konzertsäle)*, museums *(Museen)*, and libraries *(Bibliotheken or Büchereien)*, most of which are generously supported by state and local subsidies. In Germany there are 400 theaters, 140 professional orchestras and more than 3,000 museums. Most Germans buy their theater tickets *(Theaterkarten)* well in advance or they subscribe to season tickets *(Abonnement)*. If tickets are still available, they can be purchased shortly before the start of the performance at the theater ticket office *(Abendkasse)*.

Vorverkauf
jetzt
an den Kassen
unserer Theater

Öffnungszeiten:
Mo   10:00–18:00 Uhr
Di–Sa 10:00–20:00 Uhr
So   11:00 Uhr
bis Vorstellungsbeginn

KOMÖDIE
AM KURFÜRSTENDAMM
THEATER

Wo kann man die
Theaterkarten kaufen?

eine Litfaßsäule

When buying tickets, you need to know the differences in seating. *Parkett* in German means "orchestra," a *Loge* is a box, *1. Rang* means "first balcony," *Balkon* is usually the center part of the first balcony and *Gallerie* is the gallery. *Reihe 7, Platz 10* would mean "7th row, seat number 10." Germans usually dress up and check their coats at the checkroom *(die Garderobe)* when visiting a theater, opera or concert.

Outdoor theaters *(Freilichttheater)* present plays during the summer months for local audiences and tourists. Small-time entertainment is provided by various groups, especially university students. To the delight of shoppers, most shopping areas attract musicians who depend on the audience's generosity.

auf dem Jahrmarkt

Every large city has a zoo *(Zoo* or *Tiergarten)*, which caters to all ages. American and European circus troupes *(Zirkus)* tour the country every year. As in the United States, German cities hold fairs *(Jahrmarkt* or *Volksfest)* at least once or twice a year, offering carnival attractions of many types and the traditional rides for thrill-seekers.

There are numerous festivals in Germany throughout the year. Dressed in their folk costumes, various groups provide color and entertainment for the townspeople and visitors alike. The largest bands and crowds can be seen at the annual *Oktoberfest* in *München*, where several million people during the 16-day festival congregate in an atmosphere that the Germans call *Gemütlichkeit*. The *Oktoberfest* takes place from late September to early October, but the famous *Karneval* in *Köln* is usually held during the month of February. Hundreds of thousands of people line the streets to watch the parade with many floats and bands.

Wir machen Circus so wie Sie ihn lieben mit 50 Tieren und 25 Artisten

Der Große Circus
ATLANTIK
CLOPPENBURG
Parkplatz-Famila / Getränke-Markt
vom So. +17.00 Uhr
Fr. + Sa. - 15.00 + 18.00 Uhr
So. - 11.00 + 15.00 Uhr
14 JUNI
17 bis

ATLANTIK

Wann kommt der Zirkus hierher?

auf dem Oktoberfest

9 Was passt hier?

Match each item with its related description. You will not need all the words.

1. small pamphlet
2. arena often covered by a tent and used for entertainment shows
3. place where objects of lasting interest are displayed
4. specific place to sit at a sporting event
5. flat surface (panel or wall) designed to carry outdoor advertising
6. well-known event during the winter
7. building for dramatic stage performances
8. paper that contains news, editorials and advertising
9. cultural or entertainment event held in many cities every year
10. place where animals can be viewed
11. place that shows films
12. place where clothing items are checked

A. *das Volksfest*
B. *die Garderobe*
C. *die Litfaßsäule*
D. *der Platz*
E. *das Oktoberfest*
F. *der Zirkus*
G. *die Bibliothek*
H. *der Karneval*
I. *das Kino*
J. *die Broschüre*
K. *das Theater*
L. *das Museum*
M. *die Zeitung*
N. *das Parkett*
O. *der Tiergarten*
P. *die Reklametafel*

Sprache

Compound Nouns

The article of a compound noun is determined by the article of the last word in the compound.

der Nachbar, das Land = das Nachbarland

die Geburt, der Tag = der Geburtstag

Kannst du ein paar zusammengesetzte Hauptwörter *(compound nouns)* finden?

10 Was passt zusammen?

Can you do this word puzzle? Combine each numbered word with a word shown in the box to form a compound noun that you have already learned.

das Fach   der Plan   die Zeit   das Brot

das Essen   der Freund   der Tag   die Karte

der Schuh   das Café   der Spüler   das Stück

die Marke   das Konzert   das Spiel

1. die Hand
2. die Stunde
3. der Brief
4. der Liebling
5. der Abend
6. die Geburt
7. die Wurst
8. der Computer
9. die Schule
10. das Land
11. das Eis
12. das Jahr
13. das Geschirr
14. der Rock
15. die Kleidung

Persönliches

1. Wie oft gehst du ins Kino?
2. Welche Filme siehst du gern?
3. Was für ein Hobby hast du?
4. Was machst du am Wochenende?
5. Welche Rockband hast du gern? Warum?

Rollenspiel

You and your classmate would like to go to see a film. Both of you talk about at least six films that are presently showing in local theaters. You discuss why or why not you would like to see each film and agree on one which both of you would like to see first. In your conversation, include such items as likes and dislikes and any other reasons for seeing or not seeing a particular film.

Wörter und Ausdrücke

Talking about Weekend Activities and Hobbies

Was habt ihr am Wochenende vor? What are you doing on the weekend?
   Ich gehe ins Kino. I'm going to the movie theater.
   Ich gehe einkaufen. I'm going shopping.

Was schlägst du vor? What are you suggesting?
Was läuft im Kino? What are they showing at the movie theater?
   Ein Liebesfilm. A love story.
   Ein Horrorfilm. A horror film.
   Eine Komödie. A comedy.

Wann fängt der Film an? When does the film start?

Hobbys hobbies
   Schach spielen playing chess
   Briefmarken (Poster, Münzen) sammeln collecting stamps (posters, coins)
   Rockmusik hören listening to rock music
   Zeitungen lesen reading newspapers
   Klarinette spielen playing clarinet
   Ski laufen skiing
   fotografieren taking pictures

Zungenbrecher

Donaudampfschifffahrtsgesellschaftskapitänvertretergattin

Wife of deputy of the captain of the Danube Steamboat Company

Lektion B

Was musst do oft oder manchmal zu Hause machen?

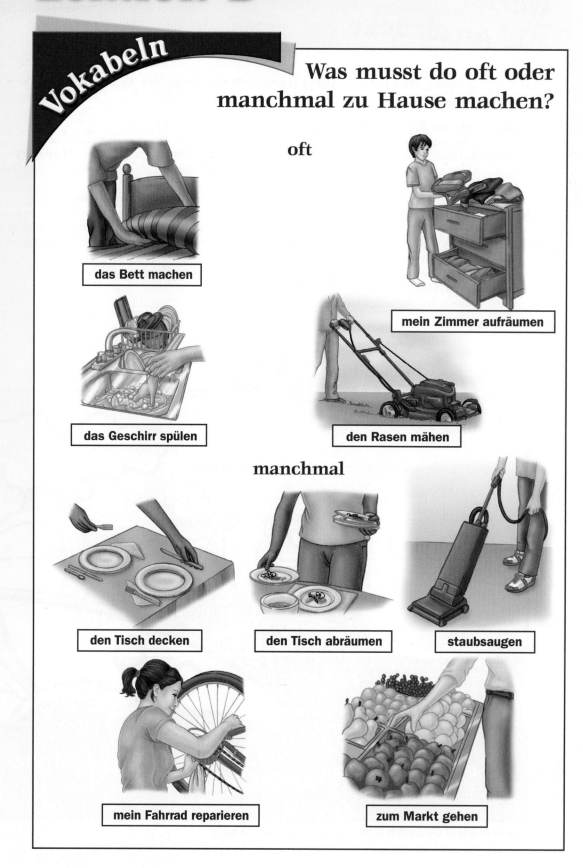

oft

das Bett machen

mein Zimmer aufräumen

das Geschirr spülen

den Rasen mähen

manchmal

den Tisch decken

den Tisch abräumen

staubsaugen

mein Fahrrad reparieren

zum Markt gehen

11 Was müssen sie machen?

Thomas and Heike have to take care of their own responsibilities and have to help their parents with the daily chores. Tell what each is doing.

1.

2.

3.

4.

5.

6.

7.

8.

12 Was musst du zu Hause machen?

Describe six tasks that you and other members of your family have to do during the week.

BEISPIEL Meine Mutter muss in der Stadt einkaufen.

Was müssen sie machen?

Alles geht in die Waschmaschine.

13 Was machst du gern oder nicht gern?

Look at the photos and decide which activities you like and which you don't like. Explain your answers.

BEISPIEL Ich spiele Fußball gern. Ich habe viel Spaß.
Ich spiele Fußball nicht gern. Es gefällt mir nicht.

1.

2.

3.

4.

5.

6.

Treffen wir uns vor dem Kino!

Warum kommen die beiden denn so spät?

Hallo!

Immer mit der Ruhe!

Soll das ein Witz sein?

Wir haben schon Karten.

GÜLTEN:	Warum kommen die beiden denn so spät? Der Film beginnt in ein paar Minuten.
KARIN:	Sarah muss noch ihr Zimmer aufräumen. Tobias soll im Garten den Rasen mähen.
GÜLTEN:	So lange dauert das doch nicht. Sie wissen ja, wann der Film läuft.
KARIN:	Da kommen sie schon.
GÜLTEN:	Macht schnell! Warum seid ihr so langsam?
TOBIAS:	Immer mit der Ruhe! Zuerst kommt die Arbeit und dann das Vergnügen.
KARIN:	Ein weiser Mann! Wir haben schon die Karten.
SARAH:	Danke! Das ist aber nett. Jetzt müssen wir kein Geld ausgeben.
GÜLTEN:	Soll das ein Witz sein?
TOBIAS:	Also, los! Gehen wir!

14 Falsch

The followng statements are incorrect. Provide the correct statements in German.

1. Der Film soll in ein paar Stunden anfangen.
2. Tobias räumt sein Zimmer auf.
3. Tobias und Sarah haben keine Idee, wann der Film beginnt.
4. Tobias meint: „Zuerst soll er Spaß haben und dann die Arbeit machen."
5. Tobias und Sarah kaufen schnell die Kinokarten.
6. Alle vier warten noch ein paar Minuten, bis sie ins Kino gehen.

15 Fragen

Beantworte diese Fragen!

1. Wo warten Gülten und Karin?
2. Was muss Sarah noch zu Hause machen?
3. Wo mäht Tobias den Rasen?
4. Warum sollen Tobias und Sarah schnell machen?
5. Wer hat schon Karten für den Film?

Für dich

Bavaria Film produziert viele deutsche Filme.

More resources are being invested in German cinema today than ever before—both in movie theaters and in feature film production. Since the early 1990s media corporations and international cinema groups have been investing more heavily in German cinema. Multiplex cinemas with up to 18 screens and more than 5,000 seats have been opened in many major cities.

New creative films by young directors have also emerged as a result of consumer demand as well as financial and cultural support from the federal and state government. During the past ten years German films have been internationally acclaimed with the release of such titles as *Good Bye, Lenin!* and *Das Leben der anderen* (The Life of Others) which received an Oscar for the best foreign film in 2007.

The Command Form

Familiar Command

To form commands in English, the speaker simply takes the infinitive without "to," for example, "go," "run" or "write." In German, the familiar command form in the singular of most verbs is constructed by eliminating the *en* from the infinitive, that is, by maintaining the stem. In German, commands (imperative sentences) are always followed by an exclamation point.

Geh! geh(en)	Go!
Schreib! schreib(en)	Write!

NOTE: Familiar commands of verbs with stem vowel changes *e* to i or *e* to *ie* (as introduced in *Kapitel* 7) are formed by eliminating the verb ending from the *du*-form *(essen - Iss!, geben - Gib!, lesen - Lies!, sehen - Sieh!, sprechen - Sprich!, helfen - Hilf!)*.

When you address more than one person, the familiar (plural) form is as follows:

Kommt zu Peter rüber!	Come over to Peter!
Spielt im Park!	Play in the park!

It is helpful to remember that the familiar plural command is the same as the *ihr*-form but without *ihr*.

Formal Command

The singular and the plural formal command are formed by inverting subject and verb.

Sprechen Sie deutsch, bitte!	Please speak German!
Hören Sie die Musik!	Listen to the music!

You will notice right away that this formation is identical to the construction of a question. There is, however, a distinct difference between the intonation of a question and a formal command.

The *wir*-Command Form (Let's...)

The *wir*-command form is used when asking for some action in the sense of **Let's** (do something)...!

Gehen wir!	Let's go!
Treffen wir uns vor dem Kino!	Let's meet in front of the movie theater!

Command Form Used in Public or Official Language

Besides the common command forms already discussed, you may encounter another command form used mostly in legal documents or on official signs at train stations, airports and so on.

(sign in front of a house or driveway)

Bitte hier nicht parken!   Please don't park here!

(sign inside a train or airport)

Nicht rauchen!   Don't smoke!

(announcement of train departure)

Türen schließen!   Close doors!

Notice that these commands use the infinitive verb form.

Ausfahrt freihalten!

16   Was sollen sie alles machen?

You have invited several of your friends to a birthday party. You tell each friend what to do before and during the party.

BEISPIEL   den Tisch decken
Deck bitte den Tisch!

1. einen Kuchen kaufen
2. mit Anke über die Party sprechen
3. das Wohnzimmer aufräumen
4. mit unseren Freunden Karten spielen
5. etwas früher kommen
6. bis neun Uhr bleiben

Hilf mir bitte in der Küche!

17 Herr Krügers Klasse

Herr Krüger, the German teacher, is instructing several of his students on what they are supposed to do.

BEISPIEL   Heidi und Renate / jetzt nach Hause gehen
                Heidi und Renate, geht jetzt nach Hause!

1. Dieter und Sonja / die Hausaufgaben machen
2. Tina und Anne / Klavier spielen
3. Angelika und Hans / das Deutschbuch lesen
4. Uwe und Lisa / einen Brief schreiben
5. Sascha und Rolf / nicht so laut sprechen
6. Holger und Maria / das Lesestück beginnen
7. Susi und Anja / zwanzig Karten kaufen

18 Sag ihnen das!

Select the appropriate verbs from the list to complete the sentences, using command forms.

essen	schenken	kommen	rufen	gehen
machen	trinken	lesen	besuchen	

1. ___ her, Helmut!
2. ___ schnell, Anne und Julia!
3. ___ Sie doch die schöne Stadt!
4. ___ dein Brot und ___ deine Milch!
5. ___ Tante Hilda eine Bluse, Bärbel und Boris!
6. ___ das Buch bis Freitag, Steffie!
7. ___ wir doch am Samstag Nachmittag ins Kino!
8. ___ Sie bitte Frau Ehrhard an!

Stell die Teller bitte auf den Tisch!

19 Was bedeutet das?

Can you figure out what these instructions mean?

1. Langsamer fahren!
2. Etwas lauter sprechen!
3. Parken verboten!
4. Bitte nicht rauchen!
5. Bitte das Wasser nicht trinken!

Lesestück

Lesestück Lesestück Lesestück Lesestück

Die Rockgruppe *Pastell*

Pastell ist eine Rockgruppe in Deutschland. Die Mitglieder[1] sind 16 bis 18 Jahre alt. Sie kommen nicht alle aus Deutschland. Drei Mitglieder kommen aus anderen Ländern.

Mitglieder der Rockgruppe *Pastell*

Die Rockgruppe ist in Europa sehr bekannt. Dort spielen und singen sie besonders in Frankreich und England bei vielen Konzerten — manchmal vor mehr als 10 000 Fans. Ihre CD „Alle Farben dieser Welt" ist ganz beliebt. Auch im Fernsehen — in der ARD und im ZDF — sieht man[2] sie manchmal.

Die *Pastell* Rockgruppe hat fünf Mitglieder: Mona Schulte (Sängerin[3]), Dennis Eisermann (beide aus Deutschland), Ugur Erdogan aus der Türkei, Daniel Genova aus Italien und Alina Toivanen aus Finnland. Hier sprechen die Stars über sich selbst[4]:

Mona

Mona

Ich heiße Mona Christiane Schulte. Ich komme aus Wuppertal in Deutschland. Ich spiele Cello, Klavier und ich singe. Mein Hobby ist Texte schreiben (Gedichte, Lieder, Geschichten[5]) und auch Briefe an Freunde. Ich habe Freunde auf der ganzen Welt[6]. Mit der Band *Pastell* habe ich schon mehr als 300 Konzerte in anderen Ländern gemacht. Ich spiele manchmal auch gern Fußball. Wirklich!

Ugur

Ich heiße Ugur Erdogan. Ich bin
Türke[7]. In der Gruppe *Pastell* spiele
ich Bass. Ich bin außerdem[8] in einer
Fußballmannschaft[9] und habe jede
Woche dreimal[10] Training. Sport
bedeutet mir viel[11]. Ich mache auch
Krafttraining[12]. Dann interessiere ich
mich noch[13] für schnelle Autos. Ich bin
16 Jahre alt.

Daniel

Ich heiße Daniel Genova. Ich bin
Italiener. Meine Hobbys sind
Schwimmen und Computer. Bei
Pastell bin ich Sänger, zusammen
mit Mona. Mir gefallen Konzerte
sehr. Das ist aufregend[14]. Mein
Vorbild[15] ist Michael Schumacher.
Ich bin 17 Jahre alt.

Alina

Ich heiße Alina Toivanen. Ich komme aus
Finnland. Meine Hobbys sind Schlagzeug[16],
Internet, Reisen[17], Kosmetik. Ich habe eine
Zwillingsschwester[18]. Die macht aber nicht Musik
mit mir. Ich bin froh, *Pastell* zu kennen und
mitzumachen[19].

Dennis

Mein Name ist Dennis Eisermann. Ich
bin Gitarrist von *Pastell*. Mein Vater
hat mir schon als Kind Gitarre spielen
beigebracht[20]. Ich habe Heavy Metall
gern, besonders Bon Jovi, Guns'n'Roses,
Aerosmith. Ich bin 18 Jahre alt.

[1]*das Mitglied* member; [2]*man* one, you, people;
[3]*die Sängerin* singer; [4]*über sich selbst sprechen* to
talk about themselves; [5]*Gedichte, Lieder, Geschichten* poems,
songs, stories; [6]*auf der ganzen Welt* in the whole world; [7]*der Türke* the Turk (Turkish);
[8]*außerdem* besides; [9]*die Fußballmannschaft* soccer team; [10]*dreimal* three times; [11]*Sport
bedeutet mir viel.* Sports means a lot to me.; [12]*Krafttraining machen* to do strength
training; [13]*Dann interesssiere ich mich noch...* Then I'm also interested in...; [14]*aufregend*
exciting; [15]*das Vorbild* model; [16]*das Schlagzeug* drums, percussions; [17]*Reisen* traveling;
[18]*die Zwillingsschwester* twin sister; [19]*ich bin froh...mitzumachen* I'm glad to participate;
[20]*hat mir schon als Kind beigebracht* already taught me as a child

Pastell ist auch bei vielen Kindern beliebt.

♪ Alle Farben dieser Welt

Rot wie die Liebe ist das Herz
blau wie die Treue ist der Schmerz.
Grün wie die Hoffnung, grenzenlos,
ist meine Freude riesengroß.

Alle Farben dieser Welt
habe ich mir vorgestellt.
Wie ein Maler sehne ich
mich nach Farben und nach Licht.

Golden wie der Sonnenstrahl
spiegelt sich der Wasserfall.
Lila ist der Ozean,
kein Taucher kommt dort unten an.

Alle Farben dieser Welt
habe ich mir vorgestellt.
Wie ein Maler sehne ich
mich nach Farben und nach Licht.

Ich schau nach oben,
wo der Regenbogen steht,
der nie zu Ende geht.

Alle Farben dieser Welt
habe ich mir vorgestellt.
Wie ein Maler sehne ich
mich nach Farben und nach Licht.

20 Etwas über die Rockstars

Match the names with the hobbies listed. There may be more than one person with the same hobby, and more than one hobby per person.

1. Mona Schulte
2. Ugur Erdogan
3. Daniel Genova
4. Alina Toivanen
5. Dennis Eisermann

A. singt bei *Pastell* und schwimmt gern
B. spielt schon Jahre lang Gitarre
C. interessiert sich für schnelle Autos
D. spielt Klavier und singt
E. hört gern Bon Jovi
F. hat jede Woche Fußballtraining
G. schreibt gern Texte
H. ist gern im Internet
I. kommt aus Italien
J. hat eine Schwester

21 Fragen

Beantworte diese Fragen!

1. Wie viele von den *Pastell* Mitgliedern kommen nicht aus Deutschland?
2. Wer spielt Cello?
3. Wo im Fernsehen kann man *Pastell* manchmal sehen?
4. Wer von den fünf Rockstars kommt aus einem Land nordöstlich von Deutschland? Wie heißt dieses Land?
5. Wer hört gern die Hits von Aerosmith?
6. In welchen beiden Ländern (nicht Deutschland) spielt die *Pastell* Rockgruppe oft?
7. Wen hat Daniel als Vorbild?
8. Welche beiden Mitglieder spielen Fußball?

Persönliches

Pretend you are going to a rock concert. Describe such details as preparing to buy tickets, how you will get there and who will be playing.

Rollenspiel

Discuss with one of your classmates which film he or she would like to see, the reason for making the suggestion, what time it starts and when you should leave to be on time. Reverse roles.

Praktisches

Was machst du am Wochenende? In groups of three, students will decide what two activities they would like to do together this weekend. First, each student lists five activities that he or she would like to participate in and gives reasons for each choice (for example, everyone likes this activity, the weather is going to be warm, this is an inexpensive activity, everyone can participate, etc.). Then students share their lists with their group. Student 1 reads his or her list while Students 2 and 3 record the information under the appropriate columns headed *Was ich gern mache* and *Was ich nicht gern mache.* After each student has finished, the group tallies the results to come up with two activities they would like to do, and the reasons for the choices. A spokesperson may present the results to the class.

Schreiben

Select one of the two topics and follow the instructions to complete the activity.

1. Describe two hobbies or activities you enjoy and give reasons why you like them. Example:

   Ich sammle Briefmarken. Meine Mutter bekommt fast jeden Monat einen Brief aus Deutschland. Die Briefmarken sind oft sehr bunt. Ich sammle schon ein paar Jahre Briefmarken und habe viele Briefmarken, auch von Ländern wie Frankreich, England und Österreich. Viele Briefmarken sind neu, aber ein paar sind schon sehr alt. Eine Briefmarke ist von 1949.

2. Describe at least two activities that you like to do. Your description may include: name of each activity, a short description, how often/how long you are involved in each activity and whether or not you do each activity by yourself or with others. The following is an example:

Am Sonnabend spiele ich Tennis. Wir spielen jede Woche nicht weit von der Schule. Manchmal spielen wir auch am Dienstag oder Donnerstag Tennis. Das Spiel dauert oft eine Stunde. Meine Schulfreunde sind sehr gut. Sie spielen schon ein paar Jahre. Bald werde ich bestimmt auch besser sein.

Wörter und Ausdrücke

Talking about Obligations and Chores

das Bett machen to make the bed
das Zimmer aufräumen to clean up the room
das Geschirr spülen to wash dishes
den Rasen mähen to mow the lawn
den Tisch decken (abräumen) to set (clear) the table
staubsaugen to vacuum
das Fahrrad reparieren to repair the bicycle
zum Markt gehen to go to the market

Talking about Movie-related Topics

Treffen wir uns vor dem Kino! Let's meet in front of the movie theater!
Was für ein Film läuft im Kino? What kind of film is running (showing) at the movie theater?
Wann beginnt der Film? When does the film start?
Zuerst kommt die Arbeit und dann das Vergnügen. First comes work and then pleasure. (Business before pleasure.)
Was gibst du für die Karten aus? What are you spending for the tickets?

Was für ein Film läuft im Kino?

Bücher lesen ist ein Vergnügen!

22 Was passt hier?

Select the words from the list to complete the dialog.

glaube	kosten	hat	gibt	läuft
gehen	bringe	möchte	kommt	weiß
beginnt	sind			

A: Möchtest du ins Kino (1) ?

B: Was für ein Film (2) denn heute?

A: Im Capitol (3) es einen Film aus Frankreich.

B: Wie viel (4) die Karten?

A: Alle Karten (5) heute preiswert...nur vier Euro.

B: Um wie viel Uhr (6) der Film?

A: Ich (7) es nicht. Ich (8) , so gegen halb sieben.

B: Wer (9) denn mit?

A: Renate (10) heute keine Zeit. Ihre Schwester (11) aber mitkommen.

B: Gut, ich (12) meinen Bruder mit.

A: Bis später!

Um wie viel Uhr beginnt das Theater?

23 Was fehlt hier?

Complete each sentence using the separable prefixes listed. You may be able to use a prefix more than once.

| mit | los | ein | dahin | aus | fern | rüber | an | vor |

Was hat Maria heute Nachmittag __(1)__? Vielleicht kauft sie im Kaufhaus etwas __(2)__. Zuerst ruft sie ihre Freundin Lisa __(3)__.

Maria: Was machst du denn?

Susanne: Ich sehe __(4)__. Im ARD gibt es einen tollen Film. Und du?

Maria: Ich schlage __(5)__, wir gehen in die Stadt. Komm doch __(6)__!

Susanne: Wann gehst du denn?

Maria: Um drei. Warum kommst du nicht zu mir __(7)__. Wir gehen dann von hier __(8)__.

Susanne: Ich habe nicht viel Geld. Deshalb gebe ich auch nichts __(9)__.

Maria: Das ist OK. Ich lade dich zu einem Eis __(10)__.

Susanne: Danke!

24 Was machen alle gern?

Complete each sentence using an appropriate word.

1. Herr Haller ___ am Morgen gern die Zeitung.

2. Meine Freundin ___ im Winter gern Ski.

3. Die Jugendlichen ___ in der Rockband Gitarre und Keyboard.

4. ___ Sarah gern? Nein, sie hat keine Kamera.

5. Svens Schulfreunde ___ gern Poster und Münzen.

6. Wir ___ gern Rockmusik.

7. Am Wochenende ___ Claudia und Tanja gern in die Disko.

8. Nach der Schule ___ ich oft fern. Um diese Zeit gibt es immer interessante Fernsehprogramme.

25 Was passt zusammen?

Euro	Klarinette	Bett	Geburtstag
Fußball	Anzug	Amerika	Milch
Moment	Juli	Klasse	Mittwoch

1. Land
2. Sport
3. Kleidungsstück
4. Musikinstrument
5. Geschenk
6. Schule
7. Kühlschrank
8. Geld
9. Tag
10. Minute
11. Monat
12. Schlafzimmer

Ist zehn Euro viel Geld?

26 Kommt Rainer mit?

Complete the conversation using the appropriate forms of the verbs given in parentheses.

Rainer: Was (laufen) __(1)__ denn im Kino?

Axel: Im Palast-Kino (geben) __(2)__ es einen tollen Film aus Amerika.

Rainer: Der soll nicht besonders gut sein. Ich glaube, der (gefallen) __(3)__ mir nicht.

Axel: Im Astoria gibt's ein Drama aus Frankreich. Den Film (sehen) __(4)__ du bestimmt nicht gern. Ich gehe lieber ins Palast-Kino.

Rainer: Um wie viel Uhr (fahren) __(5)__ du denn dorthin?

Axel: Nach dem Abendessen, so gegen halb sieben.

Rainer: Vielleicht komme ich schon jetzt rüber. Was (essen) __(6)__ du denn zum Abendessen?

Axel: Kalte Platte mit Wurst und Käse.

Rainer: Na, dann bin ich bald bei dir. Tschüs.

27 Was sollen sie machen?

Pretend you are your classmate's parent and that you are instructing him or her what to do.

BEISPIEL dein Buch lesen
Lies dein Buch!

Was macht er?

1. die Hausaufgaben machen
2. den Tisch decken
3. das Geschirr spülen
4. dein Fahrrad reparieren
5. den Rasen mähen
6. dein Bett machen
7. zum Markt gehen
8. deutsch sprechen

28 Neue Wörter, bitte!

Create compound nouns by adding appropriate nouns, including the new article. Then use each compound noun in a sentence.

BEISPIEL Computer___
das Computerspiel. Ich kaufe ein Computerspiel im Kaufhaus.

1. Geburts___
2. Käse___
3. Radio___
4. Kleidungs___
5. Lieblings___
6. Kauf___
7. Wochen___
8. Fernseh___
9. Eis___
10. Mittag___

Heute haben sie viel Computerarbeit.

Was weißt du?

1. *Sprich über einen Film!* Talk to your classmate about the following:
   - a film you would like to see
   - where the film is showing
   - what time it starts
   - how much a ticket costs
   - who will come along

2. *Was machen sie am Wochenende oder was für Hobbys haben sie?* Identify three people you know, and say what they usually do on weekends or what hobbies they have.

3. *Was musst du zu Hause oft machen?* Describe at least four activities or chores that you are required to do at home.

4. *Diese Rockband oder dieser Rockstar gefällt mir.* Identify a rock band or a rock star you like. In your description include such details as how many members are in the band, how old they are, what instruments the various band members play and anything else you know about them.

5. Complete each of the following sentences:
   1. *Am Wochenende lade ich...*
   2. *Gibst du viel Geld für...?*
   3. *Was schlägst du...?*
   4. *Wen bringt ihr...?*
   5. *Am Nachmittag sehe ich...*

6. Can you form four compound nouns from these words? What do these words mean?

der Fußball	*die Liebe*	*die Schule*	*die Freundin*
die Marke	*der Film*	*der Brief*	*die Mannschaft*

Vokabeln

abräumen to clear (table) 9B
anfangen to start, begin 9A
aufräumen to clean up (room) 9B
aufregend exciting 9B
außerdem besides 9B
ausgeben to spend (money) 9B
die **Band,-s** band 9B
bedeuten to mean; *es bedeutet mir viel* it means a lot to me 9B
beibringen to teach; *hat mir als Kind...beigebracht* taught me as a child 9B
die **Briefmarke,-n** stamp 9A
das **Cello,-s** cello 9B
decken to cover; *den Tisch decken* to set the table 9B
dreimal three times 9B
einkaufen to shop; *einkaufen gehen* to go shopping 9A
England England 9B
Europa Europe 9B
der **Fan,-s** fan 9B
Finnland Finland 9B
fotografieren to take pictures 9A
die **Fußballmannschaft,-en** soccer team 9B
das **Gedicht,-e** poem 9B
die **Geschichte,-n** story 9B
das **Geschirr** dishes 9B
das **Handy,-s** cell phone 9A
das **Hobby,-s** hobby 9A
der **Horrorfilm,-e** horror film 9A
sich **interessieren für** to be interested in 9B

das **Internet** Internet 9B
das **Kind,-er** child 9B
das **Kino,-s** movie theater 9A
die **Klarinette,-n** clarinet 9A
die **Komödie,-n** comedy 9A
das **Konzert,-e** concert 9B
die **Kosmetik** cosmetics 9B
das **Krafttraining** strength training; *Krafttraining machen* to do strength training 9B
laufen to run; *Ski laufen* to ski 9A
der **Liebesfilm,-e** love story 9A
das **Lied,-er** song 9B
mähen to mow 9B
man one, you, they, people 9B
der **Mann,-̈er** man 9B
der **Markt,-̈e** market 9B
mitbringen to bring along 9A
das **Mitglied,-er** member 9B
mitmachen to participate 9B
die **Münze,-n** coin 9A
der **Name,-n** name 9B
das **Poster,-** poster 9A
der **Rasen,-** lawn; *den Rasen mähen* to mow the lawn 9B
reisen to travel; *Reisen* traveling 9B
reparieren to repair 9B
die **Rockmusik** rock music 9A
sammeln to collect 9A

der **Sänger,-** singer (male) 9B
ie **Sängerin,-nen** singer (female) 9B
das **Schach** chess 9A
das **Schlagzeug** drums, percussion 9B
singen to sing 9B
Ski laufen to ski 9A
spülen to wash, rinse 9B
der **Star,-s** star (entertainment) 9B
staubsaugen to vacuum 9B
der **Text,-e** text 9B
das **Training** training 9B
der **Türke,-n** Turk (male) 9B
das **Vergnügen** pleasure; *Zuerst kommt die Arbeit und dann das Vergnügen.* Business before pleasure. 9B
das **Vorbild,-er** idol, model 9B
vorhaben to plan, intend (to do) 9A
vorschlagen to suggest 9A
weise wise; *ein weiser Mann* a wise man 9B
die **Welt,-en** world; *auf der ganzen Welt* in the whole world 9B
das **Wochenende,-n** weekend 9A
die **Zeitung,-en** newspaper 9A
das **Zimmer,-** room 9B
die **Zwillingsschwester,-n** twin sister 9B

Sein Hobby ist Comicbücher lesen.

Laufen sie Ski?

Kapitel 10
Sport

Objectives

In this chapter you will learn how to:

► talk about various sports and hobbies
► express likes and dislikes
► describe a sports event
► inquire about personal preferences
► identify parts of the body

Lektion A

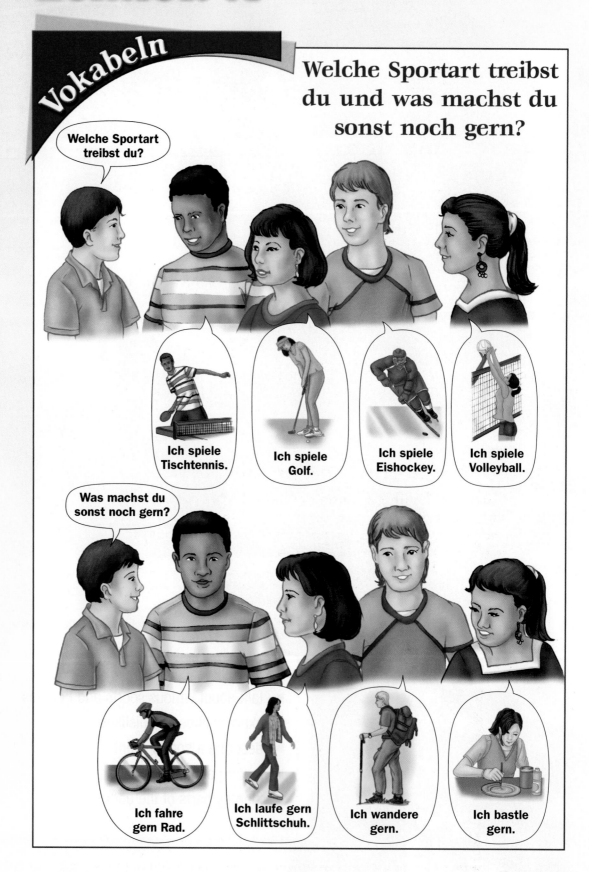

Vokabeln

Welche Sportart treibst du und was machst du sonst noch gern?

Welche Sportart treibst du?

Ich spiele Tischtennis.

Ich spiele Golf.

Ich spiele Eishockey.

Ich spiele Volleyball.

Was machst du sonst noch gern?

Ich fahre gern Rad.

Ich laufe gern Schlittschuh.

Ich wandere gern.

Ich bastle gern.

1 Was machen diese Leute gern?

Tell what these people are doing based on the illustrations.

1. Renate

2. wir

3. meine Freunde

4. Dieter und Bastian

5. Katrins Schwester

6. ich

2 Was macht Katrin alles im Juli?

Katrin is planning various activities during the month of July. Describe each one. Begin your description with all the Sunday activities for the month followed by all the activities for each of the other six days.

	Sonntag	Montag	Dienstag	Mittwoch	Donnerstag	Freitag	Sonnabend
J U L I	1. mit Peter zu Hause basteln	2.	3. Tennis spielen	4. mit Freundinnen Fußball spielen	5.	6.	7.
	8.	9.	10.	11.	12. schwimmen	13.	14.
	15.	16. mit den Eltern in den Bergen wandern	17. Tennis spielen	18. mit Freundinnen Fußball spielen	19.	20. mit dem Rad zu Tante Renate fahren	21.
	22.	23.	24.	25.	26. schwimmen	27.	28. mit Freundinnen Basketball spielen
	29.	30.	31.				

Spielen wir doch Fußball!

Von wem ist denn dieser Fußball?

Warum stehen wir hier und
sprechen über unsere Geschenke?

Du hast Recht.

ROBERT: Von wem ist denn dieser Fußball?

ACHIM: Von meiner Schwester. Zum Abitur möchte sie
einen Tennisschläger.

ROBERT: Zu meinem Geburtstag wünsche ich mir neue
Skier. Ich hoffe, ich bekomme die von meinen
Eltern.

ACHIM: Bestimmt. Sie schenken dir immer tolle Sachen.

ROBERT: Warum stehen wir hier und sprechen über unsere
Geschenke?

ACHIM: Du hast Recht. Spielen wir doch Fußball!

3 Was passt hier?

1. Von seiner Schwester hat
2. Achim meint,
3. Achims Schwester bekommt
4. Robert möchte
5. Die Eltern schenken
6. Beide Jungen werden

A. Fußball spielen
B. ihrem Sohn oft ganz tolle Geschenke
C. vielleicht einen Tennisschläger zum Abitur
D. Achim einen Fußball
E. ein Paar Skier zum Geburtstag
F. sie sollen Fußball spielen

4 Fragen

Beantworte diese Fragen!

1. Was hat Achim in seiner Hand?
2. Wer wird vielleicht einen Tennisschläger bekommen? Warum?
3. Was möchte Robert zum Geburtstag?
4. Von wem bekommt er vielleicht dieses Geschenk?
5. Wie sind die Geschenke von Roberts Eltern oft?
6. Was werden Achim und Robert jetzt machen?

Was hat Achim in seiner Hand?

Für dich

Soccer is the most popular and most widely played sport in Germany. It is not only a team sport, but also is much enjoyed by millions of spectators every week during the soccer season which runs from late August until May or early June. During television broadcasts of international matches the battle for control of the leather ball holds many millions of people spellbound in front of their TV screens; you get the impression that all other forms of social life are nonexistent. Germany's accomplishments in World Cup competition have added considerably to the popularity of the sport. Germany won the World Cup three times (1954, 1972, 1990) and came in third place during the World Cup in 2006, which took place in Germany.

Deutschland spielt oft gegen andere Länder.

Sprache

Dative (Indirect Object)

In the sentence *Ich kaufe ein Buch*, you know that *Ich* is the subject, *kaufe* is the verb and *ein Buch* is the direct object or accusative.

Now, consider this sentence: *Ich kaufe dem Freund eine Karte*. In this sentence *dem Freund* is called the indirect object or dative. Whereas *eine Karte* is directly connected with the action of the verb, *dem Freund* is indirectly connected with the verb and therefore called the indirect object. The easiest way to identify the indirect object is to determine if "to" or "for" can be put before the noun. In the above example, it would be "I am buying a ticket **for** the friend." (Or: I am buying the friend a ticket.)

Definite Article

SINGULAR			PLURAL
	masculine	feminine	neuter
nominative	der	die	das	die
accusative	den	die	das	die
dative	dem	der	dem	den

In the plural, the dative article is always *den*, regardless of the gender of the noun. To form the dative plural an *-n* or *-en* is added to the plural, unless the plural noun already ends in *-n* or *-s*.

You are already familiar with the question word *wer?* (who?), which refers to the subject (person), and the question word *wen?* (whom?), which refers to the direct object (person). The question word *wem?* (to whom? for whom?) refers to the indirect object or dative case (person).

*Ich schicke **dem** Lehrer eine E-Mail.*	I'm sending the teacher an e-mail.
***Wem** schickst du eine E-Mail?*	To whom are you sending an e-mail?

Indefinite Article

SINGULAR				PLURAL
	masculine	feminine	neuter	
nominative	ein	eine	ein	meine
accusative	einen	eine	ein	meine
dative	einem	einer	einem	meinen

Note: The possessive adjectives (*mein, dein,* etc.) take the same endings as those of the indefinite article. The plural forms for *kein* are the same as those listed for *mein* above.

Also note that the possessive adjectives in the dative have the same endings as those of the definite and indefinite articles. The following is a summary of the possessive adjectives in the dative case (masculine, feminine, neuter):

meinem (meiner, meinem)	**unserem, unserer, unserem***
deinem (deiner, deinem)	**euerem, euerer, euerem***
seinem (seiner, seinem)	**ihrem, ihrer, ihrem**
ihrem (ihrer, ihrem)	**Ihrem, Ihrer, Ihrem**

*Ich schicke **meinem** Lehrer eine E-Mail.*	I'm sending my teacher an e-mail.
*Tanja schenkt **ihrer** Freundin eine Bluse zum Geburtstag.*	Tanja is giving her girlfriend a blouse for her birthday.

*Similar to the accusative possessive adjectives, the *e* is often dropped, especially in conversation. Example: *Wir schreiben unsrem Onkel eine Karte.*

5 Wem soll ich das denn schicken?

You have several items that
you are supposed to send off.
Can you take care of it?

BEISPIEL Onkel
Schick doch dem
Onkel eine E-Mail!

1. Freund

2. Schwester

3. Lehrerin

4. Frau

5. Großeltern

6 Wem kaufst du diese Sachen?

Indicate for whom you are buying the various items.

BEISPIEL meine Freundin / einen Rechner
Ich kaufe meiner Freundin einen Rechner.

1. sein Bruder / einen Tennisschläger

2. mein Vater / eine Karte

3. ihre Schwester / einen Pulli

4. dein Freund / ein Paar Handschuhe

5. meine Tante / eine Bluse

6. sein Onkel / ein Geschenk

7 Kombiniere...

Klaus und Willi	geben	zum Geburtstag	zwei Karten
Herr Reuter	schenkt	seinem Sohn	ein Fahrrad
Katharina	brauchen	ihrer Lehrerin	kein Geld
Wir	möchte	meinem Onkel	ein Poster

Aktuelles

Sport für alle

Sports are an extremely popular form of leisure-time activity in Germany. This is reflected not only in the popularity of sports television broadcasts, but also in the fact that there are more than 90,000 clubs affiliated with the German Olympic Federation (*Deutscher Olympischer Sportbund*). At least 27 million people, almost one-third of the population, are members of sports clubs, and another 12 million "do their own thing." In Germany, sports clubs and activities are autonomous, the various organizations being self-governing. The state provides support only where sports organizations lack the necessary funds.

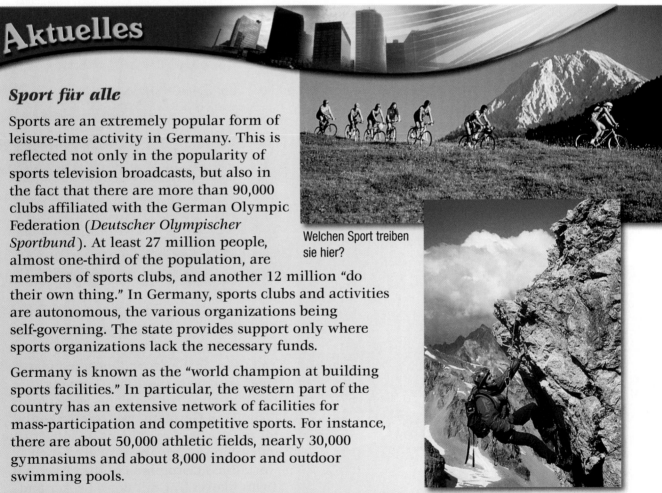

Welchen Sport treiben sie hier?

Germany is known as the "world champion at building sports facilities." In particular, the western part of the country has an extensive network of facilities for mass-participation and competitive sports. For instance, there are about 50,000 athletic fields, nearly 30,000 gymnasiums and about 8,000 indoor and outdoor swimming pools.

Germans are just as conscientious about physical fitness as Americans. There are numerous health and fitness clubs in Germany where members can work out and improve or maintain their physical condition. Running, jogging, hiking and walking are just some of the sports supported by the German Sports Federation. Throughout Germany, usually in a forest or park area, you can find designated exercise areas marked *Trimm-Dich-Pfad* (literally meaning "Slim Down Path"). Of course, the numerous hiking paths *(Wanderwege)*

Bergsteigen in den Alpen

found all over Germany further attest to the fact that Germans like to stay fit.

Soccer *(Fußball)* is by far the most popular sport, evidenced by Germany's biggest sports organization *(Deutscher Fußball-Bund)* which has over 6 million members. There are many leagues, ranging from the national league *(Bundesliga)* to district or regional leagues. The national league fields 18 teams that play a total of 34 games (17 at home and 17 away) during the soccer season. The team with the best record at the end of the season is the national champion or *Deutscher Fußballmeister*.

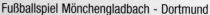
Fußballspiel Mönchengladbach - Dortmund

Tennis ist sehr beliebt.

The sport with the longest tradition in Germany is gymnastics *(Turnen)*, which became popular in the early 19th century and today is the second most popular sport with over 3 million Germans participating. For many decades, tennis *(Tennis)* in Germany was reserved only for the upper class. This is no longer true today. Since Germany produced such world-class champions in the 1980s and 1990s like Steffi Graf, Boris Becker and Michael Stich, tennis has skyrocketed in popularity more than any other sport in Germany and now ranks third on the list.

Over a million Germans belong to rifle and pistol clubs *(Schützenvereine)*. Many members enjoy the marksmanship training as well as hunting *(Jagen)* in areas that are leased to trained and licensed hunters. A less expensive sport is fishing *(Angeln)*. Germans fish not only in the lakes, but also in the various rivers.

Es gibt heute viele Golfplätze.

Table tennis *(Tischtennis)* is among the top 10 most popular sports. Besides numerous clubs, many people play this sport in schools, youth hostels or at home. Golf *(Golf)* was almost unknown in Germany 10 years ago. Now there are more than 600 golf courses in the country. Almost all of the German golfers have to belong to private golf clubs, which are quite expensive to join.

During the winter months, many Germans head for the mountains in southern Germany, Austria or Switzerland to go skiing *(Ski laufen)*. Those who master the skill after years of hard training can compete in local, national or even international competition.

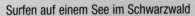
Ski laufen macht Spaß.

Water sports, such as sailing *(Segeln)*, enjoy a tremendous popularity among Germans. Sailing is popular particularly on the North Sea and Baltic Sea, as well as in the few sailing lakes that Germany has to offer. During the past 20 years, windsurfing *(Windsurfen)* has been enthusiastically received by Germans. There are well over a million people who participate in this sport.

Surfen auf einem See im Schwarzwald

Drachenfliegen

For those who enjoy participating in more challenging sports, Germany offers numerous opportunities. Gliding *(Segelfliegen)* is especially popular in central and southern Germany. There the hills and mountains provide favorable air currents needed to stay aloft for a long time. Recently, hot-air ballooning *(Ballonfahren)* has been received enthusiastically by many Germans. The challenge is not only to go up and stay in the air as long as possible, but also to come down in the original spot. Those who are most daring participate in a sport called hang-gliding *(Drachenfliegen)*, in which they jump off cliffs or hills strapped to a kite-like sail and glide high through the air. Finally, the sport of mountaineering *(Bergsteigen)* is practiced in the mountainous regions of Germany, Austria and Switzerland. Those who become experts eventually climb the many challenging peaks found in the Alps.

Hier fliegen sie viele Drachen *(kites).*

8 Was passt hier?

1. *Angeln*
2. *Ski laufen*
3. *Drachenfliegen*
4. *Tischtennis*
5. *Windsurfen*
6. *Fußball*
7. *Wandern*
8. *Jagen*
9. *Ballonfahren*
10. *Segelfliegen*
11. *Turnen*
12. *Bergsteigen*

A. hunting
B. hang-gliding
C. mountaineering
D. hiking
E. hot-air ballooning
F. windsurfing
G. soccer
H. fishing
I. skiing
J. gymnastics
K. gliding
L. table tennis

9 Welche Sportart?

Ergänze diese Sätze mit dem Namen einer Sportart. Auf Deutsch, bitte!

1. Many people play ___ in schools or at home.
2. The most popular sport in Germany is ___.
3. ___ is a sport where several people at a time go up and travel with the wind.
4. The ___ is Germany's biggest sports organization.
5. Germans who are interested in the sport of ___ have to obtain a license and find a land owner who lets them hunt.
6. A ___ is a designated exercise area, often located in a park or a forest.
7. The mountains and hills of central and southern Germany provide the right conditions for ___.
8. Most German sports clubs belong to the ___.
9. The mountain peaks of the Alps are popular for ___.
10. Germans who want to improve their marksmanship may want to join a ___.

Welcher Sport ist in Deutschland sehr beliebt?

Dative Prepositions

The dative case always follows these prepositions:

aus	out of, from
außer	besides, except
bei	with, near, at
mit	with
nach	after
seit	since
von	from, of
zu	to, at

*Tina kommt um halb zwei **aus der Schule.***
Tina is getting out of school at two o'clock.

***Außer einem Bruder** hat Holger noch eine Schwester.*
Besides a brother, Holger also has a sister.

*Herr Schulz wohnt **beim Bahnhof.***
Mr. Schulz lives near the train station.

*Kommst du **mit deiner Freundin zur Party?***
Are you coming to the party with your girlfriend?

*Wohin gehen wir **nach dem Film?***
Where are we going after the movie?

***Seit einem Jahr** wohne ich hier.*
I've been living here for one year.

*Ich komme **vom Kino.***
I'm coming from the movie theater.

*Barbara fährt **mit dem Fahrrad zur Schule.***
Barbara is riding her bicycle to school.

Contractions

These dative prepositions and articles are contracted as long as there is no special emphasis on the article.

bei	+	**dem**	=	**beim**
von	+	**dem**	=	**vom**
zu	+	**dem**	=	**zum**
zu	+	**der**	=	**zur**

10 Wo warten die Jugendlichen?

Indicate where these young people are waiting.

BEISPIEL Markt
Sie warten beim Markt.

1. Imbiss
2. Kino
3. Disko
4. Eiscafé
5. Schule
6. Bahnhof

11 Alle wollen zwei Kleidungsstücke kaufen.

Ask what else everyone wants to purchase besides what they have selected.

BEISPIEL Was kaufst du außer dem Paar Handschuhe?

12 Was wollen wir später machen?

Find out what your friends want to do after certain activities.

BEISPIEL Was wollen wir nach der Schule machen? (Kaufhaus)
Gehen wir doch zum Kaufhaus!

1. Was wollen wir nach dem Film machen? (Pizzeria)
2. Was wollen wir nach dem Konzert machen? (Disko)
3. Was wollen wir nach der Party machen? (Eiscafé)
4. Was wollen wir nach dem Mittagessen machen? (Bahnhof)
5. Was wollen wir nach der Arbeit machen? (Tante)

13 Was passt hier?

Provide the proper preposition for each sentence. Use these dative prepositions: *aus, außer, bei, mit, nach, seit, von, zu*. There may be more than one possible preposition in some sentences.

1. Treffen wir uns ___ deinem Haus!
2. Warum kommt ihr so spät ___ der Schule?
3. Ich lese eine E-Mail ___ meiner Cousine.
4. Monika geht ___ ihrer Freundin ins Kino.
5. Herr Schmidt ist ___ dem Monat Juni nicht mehr zu Hause.
6. Wohnst du weit ___ dem Bahnhof?
7. ___ seiner Mutter kommt auch sein Vater zum Fußballspiel.
8. Sie warten ___ dem Kaufhaus.
9. Was macht ihr ___ dem Geburtstag?
10. Fahren wir schon um acht ___ der Disko?

Persönliches

1. Welche Sportart treibst du?
2. Welche Sportart siehst du manchmal gern im Fernsehen?
3. Warum gefällt dir dieser Sport?
4. Was machst du außer Sport noch gern?
5. Welche Sportarten gibt es bei dir in der Schule?

Rollenspiel

Your classmate is trying to convince you to come along and participate in a certain sport. You really don't feel like it, and you give several reasons for not wanting to join. Although your classmate will try to be very persuasive, you seem to have an excuse for every possible question, request and enticement. Be as creative as possible.

Welchen Sport treiben diese Leute?

Wörter und Ausdrücke

Talking about Sports and Hobbies

Welche Sportart treibst du? In which sport do you participate?
Ich spiele... I play...
    Tischtennis table tennis
    Golf golf
    Eishockey ice hockey
    Volleyball volleyball

Was machst du sonst noch gern? What else do you like to do?
Ich laufe gern Schlittschuh. I like to (ice) skate.
Ich wandere gern. I like to hike.
Ich bastle gern. I like to do crafts.
Was möchtest du? What would you like?
Ich möchte einen Tennisschläger. I would like a tennis racquet.
Ich wünsche mir neue Skier. I would like to get new skis.
Sie schenken tolle Sachen. They are giving terrific things.

Zungenbrecher

Die Bürsten mit den schwarzen
Borsten bürsten besser als die Bürsten
mit den weißen Borsten bürsten.

The brushes with the black bristles brush better
than the brushes with the white bristles.

Lektion B

die Körperteile

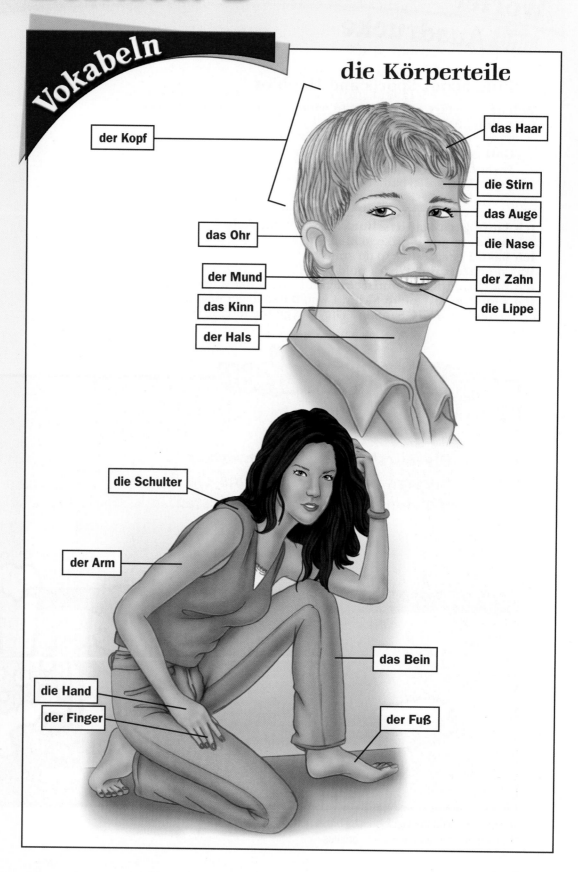

der Kopf

das Haar

die Stirn

das Auge

das Ohr

die Nase

der Mund

der Zahn

das Kinn

die Lippe

der Hals

die Schulter

der Arm

das Bein

die Hand

der Finger

der Fuß

14 Körperteile

Ergänze diese Sätze!

1. Ich spreche mit dem ___.
2. Ich schreibe mit der ___.
3. Ich denke *(think)* mit dem ___.
4. Ich zeige *(point...to)* mit dem ___ auf die Landkarte.
5. Ich höre mit dem ___.
6. Ich rieche *(smell)* mit der ___.
7. Ich habe ___ auf dem Kopf.
8. Ich kann mit den ___ sehen.

Ihre Uhr ist auf ihrem...

Sie hört mit dem...

Sie essen die Brezel mit dem...

Sie schreibt mit der...

Auf dem Fußballplatz

Pass auf, da kommt er!

Der braucht noch etwas Luft.

Au, mein Kopf!

Spielen wir weiter!

ACHIM: Wie gefällt dir dieser Fußball?

PETER: Der ist ja ganz neu! Spielen wir doch mit diesem Ball!

ACHIM: Moment mal! Der braucht noch etwas Luft...So, probieren wir ihn gleich aus!

ROBERT: Schieß ihn mal zu mir!

PETER: Pass auf, da kommt er!

ROBERT: Au, mein Kopf!

PETER: Das tut mir sehr Leid.

ACHIM: Tut es dir denn wirklich so weh?

ROBERT: Was meinst du? Es ist nicht nur mein Kopf, sondern auch meine Nase.

PETER: Komm! Ich helfe dir.

ACHIM: Kannst du noch spielen?

ROBERT: Na klar! Es geht mir schon viel besser. Spielen wir weiter!

15 Was fehlt hier?

Complete the paragraph using the appropriate words according to the dialog on page 310.

Achims (1) ist neu. Er und sein Freund wollen mit dem neuen Ball (2). Der Fußball hat nicht genug (3). Die Jungen (4) den neuen Ball gleich aus. Peter (5) ihn und er landet (lands) auf Roberts (6). Das (7) Peter natürlich sehr Leid. Nicht nur der Kopf, sondern auch die Nase tun Robert (8). Peter will Robert (9). Es geht Robert schon (10). Er wird jetzt auch (11).

16 Fragen

Beantworte diese Fragen!

1. Ist Achims Fußball alt?
2. Was braucht der Ball noch?
3. Was machen die Jungen gleich?
4. Was tut Robert weh?
5. Kann Robert weiterspielen?
6. Warum? Warum nicht?

Für dich

In Germany, unlike in the United States, schools do not offer organized sports, so local sports clubs are popular. Young people interested in playing soccer, for example, can try out for the local teams. Throughout the soccer season they are part of a league and may travel around the region to play against other teams. The boys in the dialogs of this chapter are members of the sports club of Gerlingen, a suburb of the city of Stuttgart. In this scenario, the Gerlingen players are being driven by their parents to Illingen, another Stuttgart suburb, to play against another team.

Bei welchem Sportklub spielen sie heute?

Verbs Followed by the Dative Case

There are a number of verbs in German that require the dative case. You have learned the following verbs so far that take the dative case:

gefallen to like, please

glauben to believe

helfen to help

Leid tun to be sorry

passen to fit, suit

schmecken to taste

stehen to suit

wehtun to hurt

Das Spiel gefällt den Zuschauern sehr gut.

Das Sweatshirt passt deiner Schwester sehr gut.   The sweatshirt fits your sister very well.

Kannst du deinem Vater helfen?   Can you help your father?

Remember that *gefallen (gefällst, gefällt)* and *helfen (hilfst, hilft)* have a vowel change with the personal pronouns *du, er, sie* and *es*.

17 Glaubst du ihnen?

Your classmate is asking whether or not you believe these people. Respond to your classmate accordingly.

BEISPIELE Glaubst du deiner Freundin? (Ja,...)
Ja, ich glaube meiner Freundin.

Glaubst du dem Fan. (Nein,...)
Nein, ich glaube dem Fan nicht.

1. Glaubst du der Lehrerin? Ja,...
2. Glaubst du meinem Onkel? Nein,...
3. Glaubst du seinem Vater? Ja,...
4. Glaubst du der Frau? Nein,...
5. Glaubst du dem Verkäufer? Ja,...
6. Glaubst du dem Mädchen? Nein,...

18 Wem soll Alexander bei der Arbeit helfen?

Indicate whom Alexander is supposed to help.

BEISPIEL sein Bruder
Er soll seinem Bruder helfen.

Die Dame soll ihren Kunden *(customers)* bei der Reise helfen.

1. seine Freundin
2. sein Lehrer
3. sein Vater
4. seine Schwester
5. seine Mutter
6. sein Cousin

19 Sätze, bitte!

Construct meaningful sentences using the cue words given.

BEISPIEL Kleid / Tante / stehen / nicht schlecht
Das Kleid steht meiner Tante nicht schlecht.

1. Hose / passen / Freund / sehr gut
2. Katrins Arbeit / gefallen / Lehrerin / gar nicht
3. Anzug / stehen / Großvater / ganz toll
4. Ich / können / Schulfreundin / nicht glauben
5. Wir / helfen / Eltern / zu Hause
6. Fuß / wehtun / Frau / sehr
7. Mittagessen / schmecken / Jugendlichen / nicht besonders

Wie gefällt der Freundin das Shirt?

Fußball — der Nationalsport

Jede Woche sehen Millionen Deutsche ihre beliebten Mannschaften[1] im Fernsehen. Andere sitzen nicht gern vor dem Fernsehen. Sie gehen lieber ins Stadion[2]. Dort können sie mit vielen anderen Zuschauern[3] ihre Lieblingsmannschaft 90 Minuten lang spielen sehen. Welcher Sport kann denn in Deutschland so beliebt sein? Fußball natürlich!

In der 1. Bundesliga[4] sind 18 Mannschaften. Jede Woche, meistens[5] am Wochenende, gibt es neun Spiele[6] in verschiedenen[7] deutschen Städten. Eine Mannschaft hat elf Spieler[8]. Das Spiel dauert 90 Minuten. Nach 45 Minuten gibt es eine Halbzeit[9] von zehn Minuten. Gehen wir doch einmal zu einem interessanten Spiel in der 1. Bundesliga zwischen Mönchengladbach und Dortmund. Schon eine Stunde vor dem Spiel kommen viele Fans zum Stadion. Die meisten[10] haben Karten, aber manche[11] wollen ihre Karten erst an der Kasse kaufen. Heute gibt es aber keine Karten mehr. Ein paar Leute[12] tragen bunte Hemden und Sweatshirts von ihrer Mannschaft. Viele Jugendliche bringen bunte Fahnen[13] mit.

An verschiedenen Imbissständen[14] kann man etwas zu essen und zu trinken bekommen, wie zum Beispiel[15] Bratwurst, Eis oder auch Cola. Viele stehen und essen, manche sitzen auf dem Rasen. Schon lange vor dem Spiel gehen die Zuschauer ins Stadion.

Endlich geht's los. Die Fußballfans jubeln[16] und schreien[17]. Sie wollen natürlich, dass ihre Mannschaft gewinnt[18]. Von den elf Spielern in einer Mannschaft darf nur der Torwart[19] den Ball in die Hand nehmen, aber nicht die anderen Spieler. Sie schießen den Ball mit dem Fuß oder köpfen[20] ihn. Im Spiel versuchen[21] die Spieler, den Ball ins Tor[22] zu schießen.

Viele Zuschauer sind schon lange vor dem Spiel da.

Gibt es heute noch Karten?

Die Fußballfans jubeln.

Wer wird den Ball bekommen?

Die Dortmunder schießen kurz vor der Halbzeit ein Tor. Die Fans schreien und schwenken[23] ihre Fahnen. Auf einer großen Tafel zeigt man die Statistik vom Spiel und natürlich auch, wie lange das Spiel noch dauert. Nach der Halbzeit wird das Tempo noch schneller. Die Mönchengladbacher spielen jetzt auch viel besser. Plötzlich[24] bekommt ein Dortmunder den Ball und schießt noch ein Tor. Jetzt steht es 2:0[25]. In den letzten Minuten passiert es[26] ganz plötzlich. Ein Mönchengladbacher Spieler hat den Ball und schießt ihn zu einem anderen Spieler. Dieser steht ganz frei[27] und versucht, den Ball ins Tor zu schießen, aber ein Dortmunder foult ihn. Jetzt gibt es einen Elfmeter[28]. Ein Mönchengladbacher schießt den Ball, aber der Torwart bekommt ihn nicht. Jetzt ist wirklich viel los. Die Zuschauer jubeln und die Spieler der Mönchengladbacher Mannschaft schreien und laufen in die Mitte vom Fußballplatz. Es steht jetzt 2:1. Leider kommt dieses Tor zu spät. Es dauert nicht mehr lange und das Spiel ist zu Ende[29]. Beide Mannschaften geben sich die Hand[30] und die Zuschauer verlassen[31] das Stadion.

Er schießt einen Elfmeter.

Wie steht es am Ende?

[1]*die Mannschaft* team; [2]*das Stadion* stadium; [3]*der Zuschauer* spectator; [4]*1. Bundesliga* First Federal League (top league in Germany); [5]*meistens* mostly; [6]*das Spiel* game; [7]*verschieden* different; [8]*der Spieler* player; [9]*die Halbzeit* halftime; [10]*die meisten* most of them; [11]*manche* a few; [12]*die Leute* people; [13]*die Fahne* flag; [14]*der Imbissstand* snack stand; [15]*wie zum Beispiel* as for example; [16]*jubeln* to cheer; [17]*schreien* to scream, yell; [18]*gewinnen* to win; [19]*der Torwart* goalkeeper; [20]*köpfen* to head (ball); [21]*versuchen* to try; [22]*das Tor* goal; [23]*schwenken* to swing; [24]*plötzlich* suddenly; [25]*es steht...* the score is...; [26]*In den letzten Minuten passiert es.* In the last minutes it happens.; [27]*steht frei* is open (position); [28]*der Elfmeter* penalty kick; [29]*ist zu Ende* is over; [30]*sich die Hand geben* to shake hands; [31]*verlassen* to leave

20 Was fehlt hier?

Complete each sentence using the correct verb form from the verbs listed below.

bringen	schießen	sitzen	kommen	verlassen
jubeln	kaufen	sein	stehen	geben
köpfen	sehen	spielen	essen	gewinnen

1. Viele Deutsche sitzen jede Woche vor dem Fernseher und ___ da Fußballspiele.
2. Fußball ___ in Deutschland ganz beliebt.
3. In der 1. Bundesliga ___ es 18 Mannschaften.
4. Elf Spieler ____ in einer Mannschaft.
5. Fans ___ schon lange vor dem Spiel zum Stadion.
6. Manche Leute wollen an der Kasse noch Karten ___.
7. Jugendliche ___ Fahnen mit.
8. An Imbissständen ___ manche Bratwurst.
9. Wer ___ auf dem Rasen? Ein paar Fans.
10. Die Fans wollen natürlich, dass ihre Mannschaft ___.
11. Die Spieler schießen den Ball mit dem Fuß oder sie ___ ihn.
12. Auf einer Tafel ___, wer ein Tor schießt.
13. Kurz vor dem Ende ___ ein Spieler einen Elfmeter.
14. Die Fans schreien und ___.
15. Nach dem Spiel ___ die Zuschauer das Stadion.

21 Fragen

Beantworte diese Fragen!

1. Was meinst du? Gehen mehr Deutsche ins Fußballstadion oder sehen sie die Spiele im Fernsehen?
2. Wie lange spielen die Mannschaften vor der Halbzeit?
3. Aus welchen beiden Städten kommen die Mannschaften?
4. Wo kann man meistens Karten bekommen?
5. Was haben manche Fans an?
6. Was essen und trinken manche Leute?
7. Wer darf den Fußball in die Hand nehmen?
8. Wie bekommen die Spieler ein Tor?
9. Was machen die Fans nach einem Tor?
10. Was passiert in diesem Spiel vor der Halbzeit?
11. Wie steht das Spiel am Ende und für wen?
12. Was machen die Spieler nach dem Spiel?

Dative

Personal Pronouns

As you have already learned, the direct object (accusative) is the result of the action (verb) of the sentence, whereas the indirect object receives the action indirectly through the direct object.

	direct object	
Ich kaufe	*eine Karte*	

	indirect object	**direct object**
Ich kaufe	*dem Freund*	*eine Karte*

Now let's substitute a personal pronoun for the indirect object in the last sentence.

	indirect object	**direct object**
Ich kaufe	*ihm*	*eine Karte*

Notice that there is no change in word order, but simply a substitution of an indirect object pronoun. For review, the pronouns you have already learned are included in the following table.

> *Schenkst du deiner Schwester ein Paar Tennisschuhe?*
> Are you giving your sister a pair of tennis shoes?

> *Schenkst du ihr ein Paar Tennisschuhe?*
> Are you giving her a pair of tennis shoes?

SINGULAR			PLURAL		
nominative	accusative	dative	nominative	accusative	dative
ich	mich	mir	wir	uns	uns
du	dich	dir	ihr	euch	euch
er	ihn	ihm	sie	sie	ihnen
sie	sie	ihr			
es	es	ihm	Sie	Sie	Ihnen
					(sg. & pl.)

22   Was bringen sie alles zur Party?

Everyone has agreed to bring a present to exchange.
Tell what everyone is bringing, using the correct
personal pronouns.

> **BEISPIEL**   Alexander bringt Günter eine CD. Was bringt
> Alexander Günter?
> Er bringt ihm eine CD.

1. Natascha bringt Katrin ein Buch. Was bringt Natascha
   Katrin?
2. Wolfgang bringt Anne ein T-Shirt. Was bringt Wolfgang
   Anne?
3. Dieter bringt Jürgen einen Fußball. Was bringt Dieter
   Jürgen?
4. Susanne bringt Hans eine Kamera. Was bringt Susanne
   Hans?
5. Erika bringt Jens einen Tennisschläger. Was bringt Erika
   Jens?

23   Wem kauft ihr ein Geschenk?

Indicate for whom you are buying a present.

> **BEISPIEL**   deiner Oma
> Wir kaufen ihr ein Geschenk.

1. Rainer
2. seiner Freundin
3. Katrin und Peter
4. meinem Freund
5. Gisela
6. Herr und Frau Krause

Er bekommt von seiner Oma ein Geschenk.

24 Wie geht es ihnen?

Ask how the various people are, using the information provided in your responses.

BEISPIEL Wie geht es dem Peter? (sehr gut)
Es geht ihm sehr gut.

1. Wie geht es der Regina? (nicht schlecht)
2. Wie geht es deiner Freundin? (ganz gut)
3. Wie geht es dem Alex? (super)
4. Wie geht es seinem Großvater? (besser)
5. Wie geht es Tina? (schlecht)

25 Neue Wörter, bitte!

Change into pronouns the italicized nouns with their corresponding articles.

BEISPIEL Die Zuschauer sprechen mit *den Spielern*.
Die Zuschauer sprechen mit ihnen.

1. Die Kleidungsstücke gefallen *den Mädchen*.
2. Monika kauft *ihrer Freundin* ein Geschenk.
3. Wir gehen mit *unserem Lehrer* zum Bahnhof.
4. Wie schmeckt *den Leuten* das Essen?
5. Kannst du *deiner Mutter* nicht helfen?
6. Gib *dem Ralf* doch den Fußball!
7. Wann fahren wir wieder zu *deinem Onkel*?
8. Außer *den Jungen* kommen noch viele Mädchen.
9. Angelika wohnt im Sommer bei *ihrer Tante*.

Persönliches

Was machst du gern? Describe what you and others would like to do this weekend. Here are some questions you may wish to use:

Was machst du dieses Wochenende?
Wo und wann machst du das?
Kommen noch andere? Wer?
Was ist da alles los?
Wie lange dauert es?
Wirst du etwas mitbringen? Was?

Rollenspiel

Was für Körperteile hat ein Mensch? Ein Mensch hat... Point to different parts of the body and have one of your classmates provide answers such as *Ein Mensch hat zwei Augen.* Then ask another question such as *Wozu braucht man Augen?* (Answer: *Zum Sehen.*) Reverse roles. Here are some additional useful words for your questions and answers: *denken* (to think), *riechen* (to smell). Others that you already know are: *hören, sprechen, essen, schwimmen, Schlittschuh laufen, wandern, schmecken,* etc.

Praktisches

Wir haben viel Spaß. Conduct a survey on sports and hobbies to see what your classmates are involved in. Begin by making a survey sheet with five columns where you will note the responses of five of your classmates. Ask your classmates the following questions:

1. *Welche Sportart treibst du? Was für ein Hobby hast du?*
2. *Warum hast du diese Sportart oder dieses Hobby gern?*
3. *Wo spielst du oder wo machst du dieses Hobby?*
4. *Wann treibst du diesen Sport oder wann machst du dieses Hobby?*
5. *Wie oft spielst du oder wie oft machst du dein Hobby?*
6. *Wie gut spielst du diesen Sport oder wie gut machst du dein Hobby?*
7. *Wer macht alles mit?*

As each classmate responds to your questions, record his or her responses in the appropriate column.

BEISPIEL	You:	*Welche Sportart treibst du gern?*
	Classmate 1:	*Volleyball.*
	You:	*Was machst du gern?*
	Classmate 2:	*Ich lese gern.*

After you have finished, turn in your survey sheet so that the results can be tallied. Your teacher may choose to conduct a survey orally. If so, be ready to respond.

Was machen sie gern?

Schreiben

Select a sport you're interested in. Imagine you are participating in a scheduled tournament or contest. Describe the tournament or contest, including some of these details: location, date, number of players or participants, length of game, how often the tournament or contest takes place and any other specific details. Here are some additional words that you may be able to use: *das Turnier* tournament; *die Schulmannschaft* school team; *der Trainer* coach. The following description may serve as an example:

Im Herbst spiele ich in unserer Schulmannschaft Fußball. Jeden Dienstag und Donnerstag spielen wir gegen eine andere Schulmannschaft. Dieses Jahr sind wir sehr gut. Es gibt achtzehn Spieler in unserer Mannschaft, aber nur elf spielen in einem Fußballspiel. Das Spiel dauert 80 Minuten. Nach 40 Minuten gibt es eine Halbzeit. Dann spricht immer unser Trainer und sagt, was wir gut machen und was wir besser machen sollen. Wir haben meistens zwölf Fußballspiele im Herbst. Viele Eltern und Schulfreunde kommen zum Spiel. Oft jubeln und schreien sie. Alle hoffen natürlich, dass wir gewinnen.

Wörter und Ausdrücke

Describing and Identifying Parts of the Body

die Körperteile parts of the body
der Kopf head
das Haar hair
das Ohr ear
der Mund mouth
das Kinn chin
der Hals neck
die Stirn forehead
das Auge eye
die Nase nose
der Zahn tooth
die Lippe lip
die Schulter shoulder
der Arm arm
die Hand hand
der Finger finger
das Bein leg
der Fuß foot

Talking about Soccer-related Topics

Der Ball braucht noch etwas Luft. The ball still needs some air.
Probieren wir ihn aus! Let's try it (the ball)!
Schieß ihn mal zu mir! Shoot it to me!
Pass auf! Watch out!
Spielen wir weiter! Let's play on!

Expressing Feelings

Au, mein Kopf! Ouch, my head!
Das tut mir Leid! I'm sorry.
Tut es dir weh? Does it hurt?
Es geht mir schon viel besser. I'm already feeling much better.

26 Was passt?

Welche Wörter gehören zu diesen vier Kategorien: Sport, Schule, Körper oder Kleidung?

BEISPIEL   Schwimmen
             Sport

1. Schulter
2. Mantel
3. Schlittschuh laufen
4. Stundenplan
5. Stirn
6. Rock
7. Hals
8. Tafel
9. Bein
10. Basketball
11. Landkarte
12. Tischtennis
13. Krawatte
14. Kopf
15. Hausaufgaben

27 Alexander spielt gern Basketball.

Complete the paragraph using appropriate forms of the verbs listed.

haben	machen	werden	liegen	spielen
gehen	beginnen	müssen	sein	fahren

Alexander (1) auf ein Gymnasium in Göttingen. Diese Stadt (2) in Norddeutschland. Alexander (3) ein sehr guter Tennisspieler. Er (4) drei Tage die Woche mit seinem Rad zum Tennisklub.

Im Herbst (5) er in einer Jugendmannschaft Basketball. Im Frühling (6) er bei einer Tischtennismannschaft mit. Seine Mannschaft (7) die besten Spieler in der Stadt Göttingen. Alexander und seine Klubspieler (8) am Donnerstag noch ein Spiel gegen Lüneburg spielen. Er hofft, seine Mannschaft (9) dann gewinnen. Das Tischtennisspiel (10) am Sonnabend um zwei Uhr. Die beste Mannschaft wird Tischtennismeister von Norddeutschland.

28 Was ist dein Lieblingssport?

Describe your favorite sport in one or two paragraphs. Your description might answer questions such as: When do you participate (time of year)? Where and how often do you practice? With whom do you play? How often does your team participate?

29 Ergänze die folgenden Sätze!

Complete each sentence using an appropriate dative form.

1. Susanne kauft ___ ein Geschenk.
2. Hilfst du ___ bei der Arbeit?
3. Nach ___ muss ich nach Hause.
4. Sprich doch mit ___!
5. Um wie viel Uhr kommst du aus ___?
6. Wir kommen mit ___ zur Disko.
7. Das Kleid steht ___ sehr gut.
8. Wann schickst du ___ einen Brief?

Er kommt aus dem Haus.

Die Lehrerin hilft den Jungen bei den Hausaufgaben.

30 Wie sagt man das?

From the list below, select appropriate words to complete the conversational exchanges.

muss	fahren	mähen	gewinnt	glaube
gehe	treibst	wirst	kaufe	machst
brauchst	ist	bleibt	spielen	

1. A: Was ___ du im Sommer?

   B: Wir fahren mit den Rädern nach Österreich.

   A: Wie lange ___ ihr denn dort?

   B: Bestimmt zwei Wochen.

2. A: Welche Sportart ___ du denn?

   B: Ich spiele gern Golf.

   A: Ist der Sport nicht teuer?

   B: Nicht für mich. Ich ___ oft mit meinem Vater zum Golfplatz. Der bezahlt für mich.

3. A: Wie weit ___ der Fußballplatz denn von hier?

   B: Bestimmt noch fünf Kilometer.

   A: Dann ___ wir lieber mit unseren Rädern.

4. A: Am Sonntag ___ wir gegen die beste Mannschaft.

   B: Ich hoffe, ihr ___.

   A: Das ___ ich nicht. Wir sind nicht so gut.

5. A: Um wie viel Uhr ___ du auf dem Fußballplatz sein?

   B: Wie immer, um vier. Kommst du auch?

   A: Nein, ich ___ meinem Vater helfen.

   B: Was musst du denn machen?

   A: Ich soll den Rasen ___.

6. A: Ist Rainer denn so gut?

   B: Ja, er spielt schon seit vier Jahren Tennis.

   A: Ich ___ aber heute einen tollen Tennisschläger.

   B: Du ___ mehr als einen guten Tennisschläger.

31 Ergänze diesen Dialog!

Complete the dialog between Karsten and Uwe. You may use only one specific word in each space indicated. The last letter for each possible answer has been provided. The first letters of the completed words, when read in sequence, will tell you that you have correctly completed this dialog.

Karsten: Am Freitag gehen wir alle in die (1) o.

Uwe: Um wie viel Uhr geht's denn los?

Karsten: Die Band spielt um (2) t.

Uwe Ist das nicht zu (3) t?

Karsten: Die Musik beginnt (4) r um diese Zeit. Wir werden (5) n um halb acht da sein.

Uwe: Ist es denn sehr (6) r?

Karsten: Nein, ganz preiswert, nur drei Euro für eine Karte.

Uwe: Gut. Ich komme auch. Wo ist das Telefon?

Karsten: Wen (7) t du denn an?

Uwe: Zuerst möchte (8) h mit Katrin sprechen. Sie ist so (9) t.

Karsten: Ich glaube, (10) e Nachmittag ist sie zu Hause.

Uwe: Ich (11) e gern mit ihr, besonders wenn die Band langsame Musik spielt.

Karsten: Und mit wem soll (12) h zur Disko kommen?

Uwe: Es (13) t doch viele nette Schulfreundinnen. Bestimmt kennst du eine.

Zuerst möchte ich mit Katrin sprechen.

Katrin ist heute Nachmittag zu Hause.

Was weißt du?

1. Describe a sport you are participating in or that you like to follow on TV or in the newspaper. Your description should include the name of the sport, how many players are required, two or three observations on how the sport is played and when (during the year) the sport is played.

2. *Sport in Deutschland und in den USA.* List at least four differences or similarities between sports in Germany and those commonly played in the United States. *Auf Englisch!*

3. *Was machst du gern?* Write a paragraph on this topic. Your description should include one or two activities that you like. List the activity/activities and give reasons why you like it/them.

4. *Körperteile.* Describe the following parts of the body: *der Mund, der Fuß, das Auge, das Ohr, die Hand.*

5. *Welcher Sport ist an deiner Schule sehr beliebt?* Explain which sport is popular at your school. Give as much information and insight as possible.

Der Schiedsrichter *(referee)* spricht mit den Spielern.

Was macht hier Spaß?

Ist dieser Sport auch in Amerika beliebt?

Vokabeln

das **Abitur** final examination (*Gymnasium*) *10A*
der **Arm,-e** arm *10B*
Au! Ouch! *10B*
aufpassen to pay attention, watch out *10B*
das **Auge,-n** eye *10B*
ausprobieren to try out, test *10B*
der **Ball,-̈e** ball *10B*
basteln to do crafts *10A*
das **Bein,-e** leg *10B*
das **Beispiel,-e** example; *wie zum Beispiel* as for example *10B*
die **Bundesliga** Federal League; *1. Bundesliga* top Federal League *10B*
der **Deutsche,-n** German (male) *10B*
direkt direct(ly) *10B*
das **Eishockey** ice hockey *10A*
der **Elfmeter,-** penalty kick *10B*
das **Ende** end; *zu Ende sein* to be over *10B*
die **Fahne,-n** flag *10B*
der **Finger,-** finger *10B*
foulen to foul *10B*
der **Fuß,-̈e** foot *10B*
der **Fußballplatz,-̈e** soccer field *10B*
gewinnen to win *10B*
das **Golf** golf *10A*
das **Haar,-e** hair *10B*
die **Halbzeit,-en** halftime *10B*
der **Hals,-̈e** neck *10B*

die **Hand,-̈e** hand; *sich die Hand geben* to shake hands *10B*
der **Imbissstand,-̈e** snack stand *10B*
jubeln to cheer *10B*
das **Kinn,-e** chin *10B*
köpfen to head (ball) *10B*
der **Körperteil,-e** part of the body *10B*
Leid tun to be sorry; *Es tut mir Leid.* I'm sorry. *10B*
letzt- last *10B*
die **Leute** (pl.) people *10B*
die **Lieblingsmannschaft,-en** favorite team *10B*
die **Lippe,-n** lip *10B*
die **Luft** air *10B*
manche some, a few *10B*
die **Mannschaft,-en** team *10B*
meist- most; *die meisten* most of them; *meistens* mostly *10B*
der **Mund,-̈er** mouth *10B*
die **Nase,-n** nose *10B*
der **Nationalsport** national sport *10B*
die **Nummer,-n** number *10B*
das **Ohr,-en** ear *10B*
passieren to happen *10B*
plötzlich suddenly *10B*
Rad fahren to bike *10A*
schenken to give (a gift) *10A*
schießen to shoot *10B*
Schlittschuh laufen to ice skate *10A*
schreien to scream, yell *10B*

die **Schulter,-n** shoulder *10B*
schwenken to swing *10B*
der **Ski,-er** ski *10A*
sondern but; *nicht nur...sondern auch...* not only...but also... *10B*
das **Spiel,-e** game *10B*
der **Spieler,-** player *10B*
die **Sportart,-en** kind of sport *10A*
das **Stadion,-dien** stadium *10B*
die **Statistik,-en** statistics *10B*
die **Stirn,-en** forehead *10B*
das **Tempo** tempo, speed *10B*
der **Tennisschläger,-** tennis racquet *10A*
das **Tischtennis** table tennis *10A*
das **Tor,-e** goal *10B*
der **Torwart,-̈er** goalkeeper *10B*
treiben to do; *Sport treiben* to participate in sports *10A*
verlassen to leave *10B*
verschieden different *10B*
versuchen to try, attempt *10B*
der **Volleyball** *10A*
wandern to hike *10A*
wehtun to hurt; *Tut es dir weh?* Does it hurt you? *10B*
weiterspielen to continue playing *10B*
sich **wünschen** to want (for birthday) *10A*
der **Zahn,-̈e** tooth *10B*
der **Zuschauer,-** spectator *10B*

Viele fahren gern Rad.

Im Stadion sind heute viele Zuschauer.

Kapitel 11
Reisen

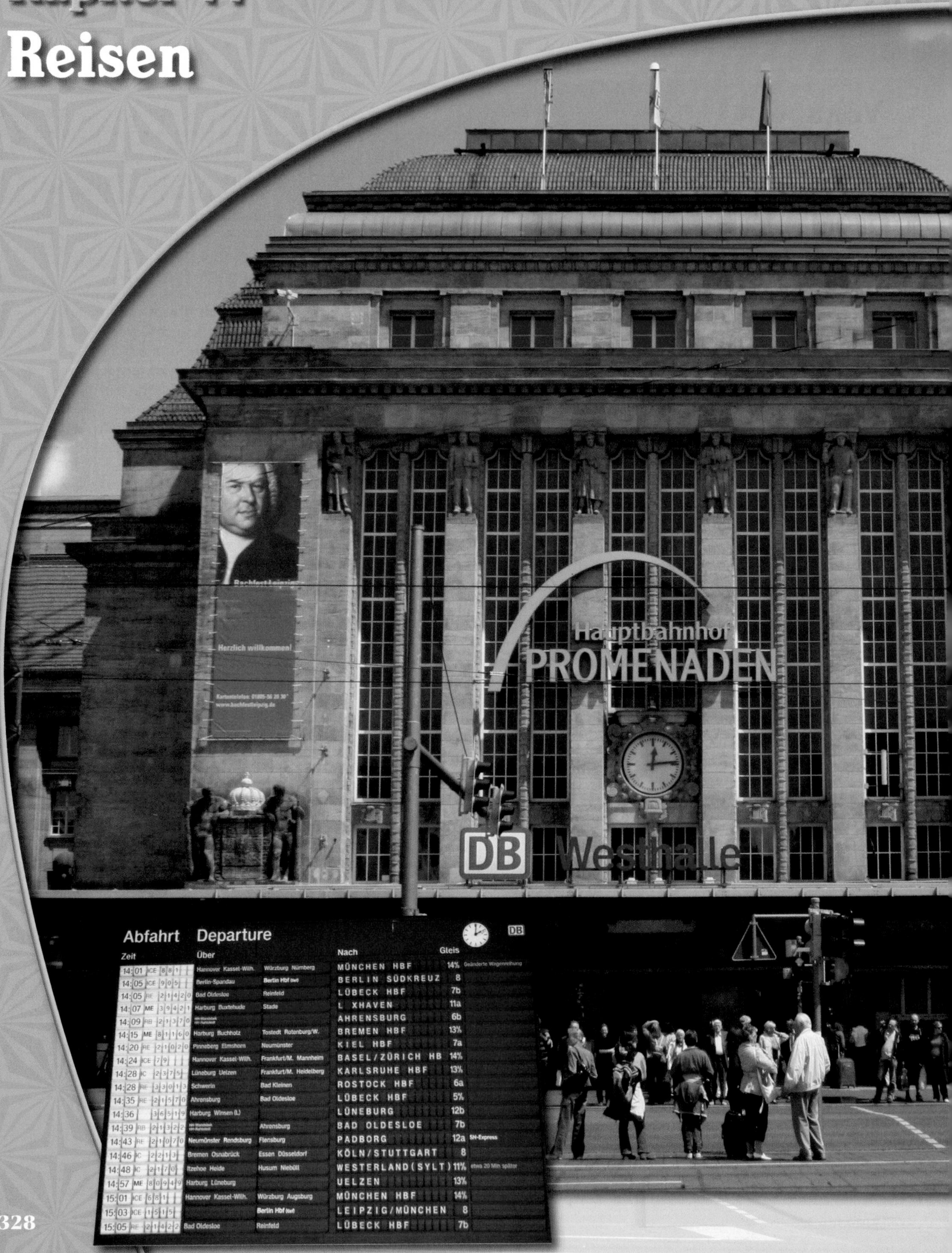

Objectives

In this chapter you will learn how to:

► talk about traveling
► ask for and give directions
► identify important places in a city
► describe a trip
► ask for information

Lektion A

1 Wie kommt Klaus nach Bremen?

Tell how Klaus gets to Bremen.

BEISPIEL Mit dem Fahrrad.

1.

2.

3.

4.

5.

6.

2 Wie kommt man am besten dorthin?

Select one of the following phrases for each situation:
zu Fuß, mit dem Schiff, mit dem Auto, mit dem Flugzeug.

1. Lisa wohnt in Washington und will im Sommer nach München reisen.

2. Herr Schmidt geht gern zum Eiscafé Milano. Es ist nur eine Ecke von seiner Wohnung.

3. Heiko und Günter wollen von New York nach England reisen. Die Reise dauert sechs Tage.

4. Tina bekommt zu ihrem Geburtstag nächste Woche bestimmt ein Fahrrad. Jeden Tag geht sie jetzt noch mit ihrer Freundin um halb acht in die Schule.

5. Krämers wollen im Winter mit der ganzen Familie Ski laufen. Von Augsburg nach Garmisch-Partenkirchen sind es 130 Kilometer.

6. Die meisten Touristen fliegen nach Europa, aber manche wollen lieber eine längere Reise machen.

Hast du die
Fahrkarten schon gekauft?

Das haben wir ja
schnell geschafft.

Hier steht's.

Frau Hoffmann: Das haben wir ja schnell geschafft.

Herr Hoffmann: Ja, mit der U-Bahn hat es nicht lange gedauert.

Frau Hoffmann: Genau wann fährt denn der Zug ab?

Herr Hoffmann: Sehen wir einmal auf dem Fahrplan nach!

Frau Hoffmann: Hier steht's. Abfahrt Frankfurt, 12 Uhr 5 auf Gleis 6, Ankunft Zürich, 15 Uhr 58.

Herr Hoffmann: Wir müssen aber in Basel noch umsteigen.

Frau Hoffmann: Hast du die Fahrkarten schon gekauft?

Herr Hoffmann: Ja, das habe ich direkt im Internet gemacht.

3 Die richtige Antwort

Select the appropriate response for each question.

1. Warum müssen sie umsteigen?
2. Was hast du im Internet gemacht?
3. Was steht denn auf dem Fahrplan?
4. Warum fährst du nicht mit der U-Bahn?
5. Wo steht der Zug?
6. Warum hast du das nicht geschafft?
7. Um wie viel Uhr fährt die U-Bahn?
8. Warum siehst du da nach?

A. Ich habe nicht genug Zeit gehabt.
B. Hier steht's. Sie kommt bald.
C. Zum Bahnhof kann ich zu Fuß gehen.
D. Ich will wissen, wie viel die Fahrkarten kosten.
E. Auf Gleis acht.
F. Ich habe da die Karten gekauft.
G. Wann, wohin und um wie viel Uhr die Züge fahren.
H. Der Zug fährt nicht direkt dorthin.

4 Was fehlt hier?

Complete each sentence using an appropriate word.

1. Wir sehen schnell auf diesem Fahrplan___. Dann wissen wir die Ankunftszeit.
2. Auf dem Fahrplan ___, wann der Bus abfährt. Ja, er zeigt die Abfahrtszeit.
3. Ich habe die Karten im Internet ___. Ist das preiswerter?
4. Wie lange ___ es mit dem Zug? Ungefähr drei Stunden.
5. Steigt ihr in Basel ___? Ja, von dort geht's nach Zürich weiter.
6. Habt ihr den Zug ___? Nein, leider nicht.
7. Unsere Abfahrt ist um halb vier, unsere ___ zwei Stunden später.
8. Von wo fährt der Zug ab? Von ___ drei.

Für dich

Ein Beamter *(official)* hilft dieser Dame.

Upon entering a train station *(Bahnhof),* you should become familiar with the facilities. If you need information about a specific train, look for the schedules usually posted in a prominent location. There are normally two such schedules. One is marked *Abfahrt* (departure), the other *Ankunft* (arrival). The first schedule gives destinations, times of departure and other valuable information. In case you want to learn about these details in more privacy and at your leisure, you should look for the information office, marked either *Reiseauskunft* or *Information.*

The major stations have installed large overhead departure schedules that indicate the departure time, type of train, destination and other information such as possible transfers. If you are in a hurry or need speedy personal attention, look for an official wearing a uniform. The official usually has a detailed train schedule and will have an answer to your questions at his or her fingertips.

Ankunft

Was steht auf diesem Fahrplan?

Sprache

Present Perfect Tense (Regular Verbs)

The present perfect is used more frequently in German conversation than in English. It is often called the "conversational past."

> *haben* + (*ge* + *er/sie/es* verb form)
>
> *Er hat es gesagt.* He has said it.

In English, three forms (*He has said, He was saying* or *He said*) may be used. To simplify, only the present perfect form is used throughout.

The form *gesagt* (asked) is called the past participle, which in German is placed at the end of the sentence.

> *Ich habe ein Rad gekauft.* I bought a bike.

The regular verbs you have learned so far are:

basteln to do crafts
brauchen to need
dauern to last, take
decken to set (table)
glauben to believe
hoffen to hope
holen to get, fetch
hören to hear
jubeln to cheer
kaufen to buy
kosten to cost
lächeln to smile
lernen to learn
machen to do, make
mähen to mow
meinen to mean
passen to fit
regnen to rain
reisen to travel*

sagen to say
sammeln to collect
schaffen to manage, make (it)
schenken to give (a gift)
schicken to send
schmecken to taste
schneien to snow
schwenken to swing
spielen to play
spülen to wash, rinse
staunen to be astonished, surprised
stimmen to be correct
üben to practice
wandern to hike*
warten to wait
wohnen to live
wünschen to wish

*Note that the present perfect tense of *reisen (gereist)* and *wandern (gewandert)* takes the forms of *sein (ich bin gereist, du bist gewandert...)*. See *Lektion B* of this chapter for more details about verbs dealing with motion.

The past participle of verbs with inseparable prefixes (like *be-*) is simply the *er, sie, es* form of the present tense. This is also true of verbs ending in *-ieren*.

Ich habe meine Freundin besucht.   I visited my girlfriend.

Was hast du denn fotografiert?   What did you take pictures of?

Ich habe Ihre Reservierung gemacht.

5 Andreas Wochenende

Was hat Andrea am Wochenende gemacht?

> **BEISPIEL** viel Rockmusik hören
> Sie hat viel Rockmusik gehört.

1. drei E-Mails schicken
2. ihren Freund besuchen
3. Karten für ein Konzert kaufen
4. den Rasen mähen
5. beim Fußballspiel fotografieren
6. ihrem Vater eine CD schenken
7. Hausaufgaben für Montag machen
8. mit Anna Tennis spielen

6 Was ist alles los?

Kannst du beschreiben, was die Jugendlichen gemacht haben?

> **BEISPIEL** Katharina / Laura / besuchen
> Katharina hat Laura besucht.

1. Uli / Rockmusik hören
2. Susanne und Claudia / zu Hause basteln
3. Ralf / mit seiner Mannschaft Fußball spielen
4. Maria / viele Briefmarken sammeln
5. Toni / manchmal Geschirr spülen
6. Dieters Freunde / den Tisch zum Geburtstag decken

Sie haben zwei Fahrkarten gekauft.

7 Was passt hier?

Complete the sentences using the proper past participles of the verbs listed.

kaufen	wohnen	schwenken	schmecken
regnen	dauern	warten	passen

1. Habt ihr lange in der Schule ___?
2. Heute scheint die Sonne, aber am Wochenende hat es ___.
3. Haben Sie die Jeans ___?
4. Die Arbeit hat drei Stunden ___.
5. Das Kleid hat Monika nicht ___.
6. Die Fans haben ihre Fahnen ___.
7. Wie hat das Eis ___?
8. Frau Taukes Wohnung ist in der Schillerstraße. Früher hat sie in der Brandstraße ___.

Aktuelles

Mit dem Zug fahren

The German railway system is a quick and reliable means of transportation. Over 30,000 trains crisscross Germany every day. Many trains are comfortably equipped and fully air-conditioned. If you have a reserved seat, you can look at a chart located at your designated track or platform (*Gleis* or *Bahnsteig*) to determine exactly where your train car or coach will stop. This assures you that you won't have to walk much farther once the train arrives and you're ready to get on.

Der Zug steht schon am Gleis.

```
DB          Reservierung
CIV 80
            InterCityExpress                    1 Sitzplatz

     VON                ->NACH
13.10  8:45 FRANKFURT M  ->KOELN HBF   13.10 11:00  2

ZUG   922 ICE   Wagen  6  Sitzplatz   55

Großraumwagen                      1 Fenster

                                    PREIS EURO ****5,00
          4534
29612114  •          809530031999
29612111-43          BARZAHLUNG     110700037 Frankfurt
                                              (Main)Hbf   10:27
```

Sie fahren Zweiter Klasse.

Standard train tickets are valid for one day for distances up to 100 kilometers. For longer distances, a single ticket is valid for four days and a return ticket for one month. Tickets for single and return trips for distances of 51 kilometers or more are valid on any train, without a surcharge. International tickets are valid for two months and a trip may be broken up as often and as long as is desired within that period.

Most Germans travel second class *(Zweite Klasse)*. A second-class compartment *(Abteil)* usually has vinyl seats; they're not luxurious, but fairly comfortable. First-class seats *(Erste Klasse)* are more plush and rather expensive. These accommodations are recommended only if you want to assure yourself of a seat during rush hour and you did not reserve a seat in advance. If you're not sure, you can purchase a second-class ticket and pay the difference after you have boarded the train. The German Rail *(Deutsche Bahn* or abbreviated *DB)* offers a discount card called *BahnCard* that entitles the traveler to a discount of 25% to 50% depending which *BahnCard* is purchased.

Shortly before departure there will be the final call over the loudspeaker and a warning that the train is ready to depart. Once the train has left the station, you can

Sie steigen ein.

Der Zug fährt gleich ab.

DB bedeutet *Deutsche Bahn.*

relax and examine your surroundings. You will find the compartment and the other facilities quite comfortable. Remember, most Germans travel by train and not by plane as in the United States. Therefore, special care is taken to ensure a pleasant environment on trains. If you don't want to bring your own sandwiches, you can have a warm or cold meal in the train car labeled *Restaurant* or *Speisewagen*. Don't be surprised if someone else sits down at your table after asking you *Ist hier noch frei?* This is quite common here and in most German restaurants.

If you want to take a nap, even second-class seats are usually adjustable. They are always adjustable in first class. On a longer trip, you can reserve sleeping quarters in the *Schlafwagen* (sleeper) or in a *Liegewagen* (couchette) for an additional fee.

Some of the long-distance trains have very modern facilities such as a conference room, a playroom for small children and even a party car called *Gesellschaftswagen* where social functions can be arranged.

The most frequently used train in Germany is the *Intercity (IC)*, which links more than 100 German cities and runs at one-hour intervals between 7 A.M. and 11 P.M. *Intercity* trains that travel beyond the German border are called *Eurocity (EC)*. The various stops are usually posted outside on some of the cars. These *Intercity* trains never stop in small towns. A surcharge is required for travel in the fast and luxurious *Eurocity* and *Intercity* trains. This fee includes a seat reservation (*Platzkarte*).

Faced with unrelenting competition from other means of transportation—cars, ships, airplanes—the *Deutsche Bahn* has streamlined and modernized its operations. A negative consequence of this streamlining is the fact that in rural areas service has been eliminated on the basis that it was no longer profitable.

The fastest and most modern train in Germany today is the *Intercity Express (ICE)* which is 1,300 feet long. The *ICE* can cover the distance from Munich to Frankfurt in about three hours, with a speed of 150 miles an hour on some sections of its route.

Hier findet man alle Ankunfts- und Abfahrtszeiten der Züge.

This supermodern train has an aerodynamic design and provides travelers with every imaginable comfort. The high-tech *ICE* offers travelers Internet connection, telephones, fax machines, fully equipped offices, videos, audio connections for three radio stations and three preprogrammed audio programs, as well as a 40-seat restaurant.

Travelers on the *ICE* have a choice between a standard compartment and open-seating coaches with seats in rows or facing each other. Large tables are fitted between the seats—to work on or, perhaps, play games to pass the time. For passengers who are physically disabled, there is a second-class coach providing wheelchair access.

Ist dieses Abteil voll?

For business people traveling relatively short distances, the *ICE* and the *IC* trains are very practical and convenient. From downtown locations it is always quicker to get to the main railway station (traditionally in the center of the city) than to the nearest airport.

Um wie viel Uhr fährt der Zug ab?

8 Wovon spricht man hier?

Identify what is being described. You may not know all the words, but you should be able to identify the descriptive item.

1. Dieser Zug fährt nicht nur durch Deutschland sondern auch in andere Länder.
2. Hier kann man im Zug etwas zu essen bekommen.
3. In deutschen Zügen gibt es zwei Klassen. Die meisten Deutschen reisen in dieser Klasse.
4. Man braucht sie, wenn man garantiert auf einem bestimmten Platz sitzen will.
5. Das ist ein anderes Wort für *Gleis*.
6. Die meisten Deutschen fahren mit diesem Zug.
7. Wenn man billiger mit dem Zug fahren möchte, dann kann man diese Karte kaufen.
8. In manchen Zügen können Gruppen Partys haben. Dann sind sie dort.
9. Wenn Leute von einem Tag zum anderen reisen, dann wollen sie nicht sitzen. Sie sind lieber in diesem Wagen.

9 Warum oder warum nicht?

Give five reasons why train travel would or would not be beneficial to you.

Wohin gehen diese Leute?

In welcher Klasse reisen die beiden Mädchen?

Persönliches

1. Bist du im letzten Sommer, Herbst, Winter oder Frühling gereist? Wohin?
2. Wohin fährst du gern in die Ferien? Warum?
3. Wie kommst du jeden Tag zur Schule?
4. Wie kommst du von deinem Haus oder deiner Wohnung zum nächsten Kaufhaus?
5. Wie weit ist die Stadtmitte von deinem Haus oder deiner Wohnung? Wie kommst du dorthin?

Rollenspiel

Create your own dialog by using the following information as a guideline. Be as creative as possible.

You are at the railroad station and have plenty of time. You are at the ticket window to buy your ticket, but have several questions that you direct at the official *(der Beamte/die Beamtin)*. Use the following details as a guideline in your conversation with that official (your classmate):

- tell where you are going
- ask what time the train leaves and when it arrives
- inquire from which track (platform) it leaves
- ask availability of first- or second-class seating
- find out the cost
- ask if it's a direct connection or if you have to transfer and where

Reverse roles after you have discussed the above and any related topics.

Um wie viel Uhr fährt der Zug nach Bremen ab?

Wörter und Ausdrücke

Means of Transportation

das Verkehrsmittel means of transportation
das Flugzeug airplane
der Zug train
das Motorrad motorcycle
das Boot boat
die U-Bahn subway
die Straßenbahn streetcar
das Schiff ship

Talking about Traveling

Wohin fliegst du? Where are you flying?
Hast du Fahrkarten gekauft? Did you buy tickets?
Wann fährt der Zug ab? When is the train departing?
Hast du es geschafft? Did you make it?
Sehen wir einmal auf dem Fahrplan nach! Let's just look at the schedule.
Hier steht's...Abfahrt...Ankunft. Here it is... departure...arrival.
Wir müssen umsteigen. We'll have to transfer.

Was kaufen sie an den Automaten?

Glücklich ist der Tourist,
wenn er auf einer Tour ist
und in einer Tour isst.

The tourist is happy when he is on a tour and is constantly eating.

Lektion B

10 Wie komme ich dorthin?

Imagine you are a tour guide in Germany and you need to give directions to various people.

BEISPIEL Wie komme ich zum Kaufhaus? (hier nach links)
Gehen Sie hier nach links.

1. Wie komme ich zur Post? (geradeaus)
2. Wie komme ich zum Museum? (zwei Ecken, dann nach rechts)
3. Wie komme ich zum Kaufhaus? (auf dieser Straße bis zum Bahnhof)
4. Wie komme ich zum Kino? (eine Ecke, dann links)
5. Wie komme ich zum Café? (immer geradeaus bis zur Bahnhofstraße)

11 Stadtplan von Berlin

Look at the Berlin map in the front of this book and give instructions on how to get from one place to another. Your directions may suggest walking, riding some public transportation or driving a car.

BEISPIELE Lützowplatz - Siegessäule
Gehen Sie geradeaus, dann kommen Sie direkt zur Siegessäule.

Funkturm - Theater des Westens
Fahren Sie bis Neue Kantstraße, biegen Sie rechts ab und fahren Sie geradeaus. Sie sehen dann das Theater des Westens auf der linken Seite.

1. Gedenkstätte Berliner Mauer – Alexanderplatz
2. Rathaus Schöneberg – Europa-Center
3. Philharmonie – Neue Nationalgalerie
4. Berliner Dom – Prenzlauer Berg
5. Flughafen Berlin-Tempelhof – Friedrichshain
6. Friedrich-Ludwig Jahn Sportpark – Fischerinsel

Wie kommt man zum Brandenburger Tor?

Dialog

Warum haben wir so viel Gepäck mitgenommen?

Ich weiß nicht, warum wir so viel Gepäck mitgenommen haben.

Die stehen hier gleich um die Ecke auf der linken Seite.

Oh, der Zug ist schon angekommen.

HERR HOFFMANN:	Entschuldigen Sie! Können Sie mir sagen, wo die Kofferkulis sind?
DAME:	Die stehen hier gleich um die Ecke auf der linken Seite.
HERR HOFFMANN:	Danke!
FRAU HOFFMANN:	Ich weiß nicht, warum wir so viel Gepäck mitgenommen haben.
HERR HOFFMANN:	Na, deine Schwester hat uns für zwei Wochen eingeladen. Da brauchen wir schon große Koffer.
FRAU HOFFMANN:	Du hast Recht. Vor drei Jahren sind wir nur ein paar Tage da gewesen.
HERR HOFFMANN:	Es hat uns aber dort so gut gefallen.
FRAU HOFFMANN:	Wie kommen wir jetzt zum Gleis sechs?
HERR HOFFMANN:	Das ist direkt da drüben rechts.
FRAU HOFFMANN:	Oh, der Zug ist schon angekommen.
HERR HOFFMANN:	Gut. Steigen wir gleich ein!

12 Falsch

The following statements are incorrect. Provide the correct answers using complete sentences.

1. Herr und Frau Hoffmann fahren vom Gleis acht ab.
2. Sie warten ein paar Minuten, bis der Zug ankommt.
3. Hoffmanns finden einen Kofferkuli gleich rechts um die Ecke.
4. Sie fahren zu Herrn Hoffmanns Schwester.
5. Dieses Mal haben Hoffmanns nicht so viel Gepäck wie das letzte Mal mitgenommen.
6. Hoffmanns steigen nach ein paar Minuten in den Zug ein.

13 Fragen

Beantworte diese Fragen!

1. Mit wem spricht Herr Hoffmann außer seiner Frau?
2. Was brauchen Hoffmanns für ihr Gepäck?
3. Wie viele Tage werden sie in Zürich bleiben?
4. Wo steht der Zug?
5. Warum steigen sie gleich ein?

Für dich

If you have little luggage to carry, you won't have any problems taking it directly to the train. However, if you have more luggage than you can carry easily, look for a luggage cart marked *Kofferkuli*. You can place your luggage on the cart and wheel it right to the train. In most cities, there is no charge for the use of these carts but you need to deposit a 1 or 2 euro coin into a device on the handlebar which is refunded upon returning the cart. Be sure to give yourself plenty of time to get to the train. The trains of the German Rail *(Deutsche Bahn)*—often marked with the initials *DB*—are usually on time and won't wait for you.

The destination and departure times, particularly in major cities like Frankfurt, are also indicated on an electronic overhead sign posted near the platform *(Bahnsteig)* or train track *(Gleis)*. The information on these signs changes as soon as a train has departed.

Die Leute warten auf den nächsten Zug.

Present Perfect Tense (Irregular Verbs)

The irregular verbs, as the term suggests, do not follow the same pattern when forming the past participle as the regular verbs. Some of these verbs use *sein* instead of *haben*. Therefore, you must learn each past participle individually.

Hast du mit Tanja gesprochen? Have you spoken with Tanja?

Sie ist nach Hause gefahren. She has driven home.

Verbs that use a form of *sein* must both (a) indicate motion or change of condition and (b) be intransitive, that is, verbs that cannot have a direct object. This is true in cases like *gehen, laufen, kommen, fahren* and *schwimmen*.

Hast du schon mit Andrea gesprochen? Have you spoken already with Andrea?

Wir sind acht Stunden nach Europa geflogen. We have flown for eight hours to Europe.

Here are the irregular forms for most of the verbs you have learned so far:

INFINITIVE	PAST PARTICIPLE
anrufen (to call on the phone)	angerufen
beginnen (to begin)	begonnen
bekommen (to receive, get)	bekommen
bleiben (to stay)	ist geblieben
bringen (to bring)	gebracht
einladen (to invite)	eingeladen
einsteigen (to get in, board)	ist eingestiegen
essen (to eat)	gegessen
fahren (to drive)	ist gefahren
finden (to find)	gefunden
fliegen (to fly)	ist geflogen
geben (to give)	gegeben
gefallen (to like)	gefallen
gehen (to go)	ist gegangen
haben (to have)	gehabt
helfen (to help)	geholfen
kennen (to know)	gekannt
kommen (to come)	ist gekommen
laufen (to run)	ist gelaufen

lesen (to read)	**gelesen**
liegen (to lie, be located)	**gelegen**
nehmen (to take)	**genommen**
scheinen (to shine)	**geschienen**
schießen (to shoot)	**geschossen**
schreiben (to write)	**geschrieben**
schreien (to scream, yell)	**geschrien**
schwimmen (to swim)	**ist geschwommen**
sehen (to see)	**gesehen**
sein (to be)	**ist gewesen**
singen (to sing)	**gesungen**
sitzen (to sit)	**gesessen**
sprechen (to speak)	**gesprochen**
stehen (to stand)	**gestanden**
tragen (to carry)	**getragen**
treffen (to meet)	**getroffen**
trinken (to drink)	**getrunken**
verlassen (to leave)	**verlassen**
vorschlagen (to suggest)	**vorgeschlagen**
wissen (to know)	**gewusst**

Verbs with inseparable prefixes *(bekommen)* do not have the *ge-* in the past participle.

Dieter hat meinen Brief bekommen.   Dieter has received my letter.

Verbs with separable prefixes have the *ge-* as part of the participle.

Susi hat mich angerufen.   Susi has called me.

Wen habt ihr zur Party eingeladen?   Whom have you invited to the party?

The accent or emphasis is always on the separable prefix *(**an**gerufen, **ein**geladen)*.

Ein paar Jugendliche sind schon eingestiegen.

14 Jeder Tag

Was hat Boris an jedem Tag gemacht?

BEISPIEL Was hat Boris am Montag gemacht? (ein paar E-Mails schreiben)
Am Montag hat er ein paar E-Mails geschrieben.

1. Was hat Boris am Sonntag gemacht? (einen Film sehen)
2. Was hat Boris am Freitag gemacht? (seinem Onkel helfen)
3. Was hat Boris am Mittwoch gemacht? (ein Buch lesen)
4. Was hat Boris am Samstag gemacht? (Heidi ein Geschenk bringen)
5. Was hat Boris am Donnerstag gemacht? (in seiner Band singen)
6. Was hat Boris am Dienstag gemacht? (mit seiner Oma sprechen)

15 Habe ich dir das schon gesagt?

Imagine you are at a party and your friend is filling you in on several events that took place while you were gone. Play your friend's part.

BEISPIEL meine Arbeit im Kaufhaus beginnen
Ich habe meine Arbeit im Kaufhaus begonnen.

1. wenig Zeit für Hausaufgaben haben
2. zwei CDs aus Deutschland bekommen
3. zehn Kilometer laufen
4. einen Nachmittag bei meiner Oma bleiben
5. am Montag bei meiner Cousine sein
6. in Mathe eine Eins bekommen
7. eine Stunde im See schwimmen
8. am Wochenende Freunde einladen

Heute hat sie viel Zeit für Hausaufgaben gehabt.

16 In der Disko

Was ist in der Disko los gewesen?

BEISPIEL die Jugendlichen / zur Disko gehen
Die Jugendlichen sind zur Disko gegangen.

1. Gisela / ihren Freund vor der Disko treffen
2. Die Musik / schon um halb acht beginnen
3. Viele / in der Disko stehen
4. Ein paar Jungen und Mädchen / Cola trinken
5. Andere / etwas essen
6. Viele Jugendliche / bis zehn Uhr bleiben
7. Viktor / erst um halb neun kommen

17 *sein* oder *haben?*

Complete the sentences using forms of *sein* or *haben*.

1. Wann ___ ihr nach Hause gekommen?
2. Die Jugendlichen ___ Tischtennis gespielt.
3. Es ___ gestern viel geschneit.
4. Angelika ___ mir die Schultasche gebracht.
5. Meine Freunde ___ im Wohnzimmer gewesen.
6. Viele Zuschauer ___ lange vor dem Stadion gewartet.
7. Um wie viel Uhr ___ ihr Frühstück gegessen?
8. ___ Sie mit dem Zug gefahren?
9. Was ___ du am Abend getrunken?
10. Wir ___ zur Post gelaufen.

18 Kombiniere...

Haben	deine Lehrerin	mit dir zu Hause	zu Hause	gewesen
Hat	Svens Schulfreund	mit den Eltern	in die Ferien	gefahren
Sind	Herr und Frau Stock	gestern	nach Hause	gelaufen
Ist	die Jugendlichen	in der Schule	am Telefon	gesprochen

Viele sind mit dem
Bus gefahren.

Wie ist die Reise gewesen?

Cornelia hat schon seit Wochen geplant[1], ihren Vater in Mainz zu besuchen. Im Mai ist sie mit ihrer Freundin Nina nach Mainz gefahren. Dort wohnt ihr Vater. Beide Mädchen sind eine Woche in Mainz geblieben. Sie sind heute Abend wieder in Koblenz angekommen. Cornelias Mutter will natürlich hören, wie die Reise gewesen ist und was alles passiert ist. Cornelia erzählt[2] ihr jetzt von ihrer Reise und ihrem Besuch[3] bei ihrem Vater in Mainz:

Cornelias Vater wohnt in Mainz.

Wie du ja weißt, sind wir von Koblenz mit einem Schiff auf dem Rhein bis Boppard gefahren. Leider hat es geregnet und wir haben am Rhein nicht viel gesehen. In Boppard sind Nina und ich ausgestiegen[4] und haben gleich am Rhein ein paar Postkarten gekauft. Dann sind wir zum Bahnhof gegangen. Vom Rhein ist der Bahnhof nur fünf Minuten zu Fuß.

Wir haben noch zwei Stunden Zeit gehabt. Deshalb habe ich am Schalter gefragt[5], was man noch in kurzer Zeit in Boppard sehen kann. Eine Dame hat uns vorgeschlagen, das Museum zu besuchen. Das haben wir auch gemacht. Das kleine[6] Museum ist sehr interessant gewesen. Es hat die Geschichte der Stadt und der Gegend[7] in Bildern gezeigt.

Sie sind mit einem Schiff nach Boppard gefahren.

Bei einem Imbiss am Bahnhof haben wir etwas gegessen und getrunken. Die Karten nach Mainz haben wir an einem Automaten gekauft. Es hat nicht lange gedauert, bis der Zug angekommen ist. Die Reise nach Mainz hat ungefähr eine Stunde gedauert. Vati hat schon auf dem Bahnsteig gewartet. Er hat uns beide mit einem Geschenk begrüßt. Dann sind wir mit dem Auto zu seiner Wohnung gefahren.

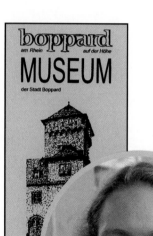

Cornelia ist mit ihrer Freundin Nina gefahren.

Nina ist Cornelias Freundin.

Während der Woche haben wir viel gesehen: die Stadtmitte, das Gutenberg Museum und ein paar kleine Städte am Rhein. Das Wetter ist auch besser gewesen und wir haben alle drei viel Spaß gehabt.

Was hat Cornelia am Schalter gefragt?

¹*planen* to plan; ²*erzählen* to tell; ³*der Besuch* visit; ⁴*aussteigen* to get off; ⁵*am Schalter fragen* to ask at the (ticket) counter; ⁶*klein* little; ⁷*die Gegend* area

Hat es lange gedauert, bis der Zug angekommen ist?

19   Was passt hier?

1. Cornelia hat ihren Vater

2. Ihre Freundin ist auf ihrer Reise

3. Cornelia hat ihrer Mutter von ihrer Reise

4. Zuerst sind Nina und Cornelia mit einem Schiff

5. In Boppard haben beide Postkarten

6. In einem kleinen Museum haben sie etwas über die Geschichte von Boppard

7. Sie haben auch noch an einem Imbiss etwas

8. Die Reise von Boppard nach Mainz hat ungefähr eine Stunde

9. Cornelias Vater hat schon in Mainz auf Nina und Cornelia

10. Das Wetter ist während dieser Woche nicht schlecht

A. gewartet

B. mitgekommen

C. gelernt

D. gewesen

E. gefahren

F. gekauft

G. gedauert

H. besucht

I. gegessen

J. erzählt

20 Fragen

Beantworte diese Fragen!

1. Warum ist Cornelia nach Mainz gefahren?
2. Wer ist mitgekommen?
3. Was will Cornelias Mutter wissen?
4. Wie sind Cornelia und Nina nach Boppard gekommen?
5. Ist der Bahnhof in Boppard weit vom Rhein?
6. Was haben Nina und Cornelia in Boppard gemacht?
7. Wo haben sie Karten nach Mainz bekommen?
8. Wo hat Cornelias Vater gewartet?
9. Was hat er für beide Mädchen mitgebracht?
10. Haben sie während der Woche nur Mainz gesehen?

Persönliches

1. Wohin bist du in den letzten zwei oder drei Jahren gereist?
2. Mit wem bist du gefahren?
3. Wie bist du dorthin gekommen?
4. Was hast du dort gemacht?
5. Wie hat es dir dort gefallen? Warum?
6. Möchtest du noch einmal dorthin fahren? Wann?

Rollenspiel

Imagine yourself in the center of a German city giving directions to travelers (your classmates) who need your assistance. Can you come up with different directions for these questions?

1. Können Sie mir bitte sagen, wie ich zum Bahnhof komme?
2. Wo gibt es hier ein Café?
3. Wie komme ich von hier zum Museum?
4. Ist die Post hier in der Nähe?
5. Wie weit ist das Kaufhaus von hier und wie komme ich dorthin?

Praktisches

Imagine that you and three other family members (your classmates) are going on a short vacation together by car this summer. Each family member (you, your father, mother, sister, brother, grandmother, etc.) lists 15 essential items to bring along. However, you are all traveling together in a very small car and space is at a premium. Each of you needs to cut your list to 5 items, and write one important reason why you should be permitted to take along that item. Then get together with the other three family members, each reading your list and giving your reasons. The group must reach a consensus on what 5 items each person is allowed to bring along. Once your final list has been completed, your group leader may want to read your group's list to other classmates to compare it with theirs.

Schreiben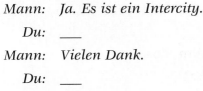

Select one of the two topics and follow the instructions to complete the activity.

1. Imagine that while studying the train schedule, an older gentleman comes up to you and asks for your help; he has difficulty reading the small print on the *Ankunft* (arrival) schedule. Can you help him out? Here are some of the questions you may have to respond to. Write the responses, being as creative as possible.

   Mann: Können Sie das lesen?

   Du: ___

   Mann: Meine Enkelin kommt heute aus Münster hier an.

   Du: ___

   Mann: Nein, sie muss in Düsseldorf umsteigen.

   Du: ___

   Mann: Ich glaube, der Zug kommt etwas später. Es ist vielleicht der nächste.

   Du: ___

   Mann: Ja. Es ist ein Intercity.

   Du: ___

   Mann: Vielen Dank.

   Du: ___

Kann der Herr alles klar lesen?

2. Write a short narrative or dialog or a combination of the two, including the following details: Your friend returned from a trip. Find out if your friend went by car or train...with whom he or she went...when he or she left...where your friend went... how far it was...what your friend saw there...when he or she returned. The following description serves as a sample for such a narrative or dialog:

Mein Freund hat im Sommer eine Reise gemacht. Er ist drei Wochen in den Ferien gewesen und ist am Wochenende wieder zu Hause angekommen.

Du:	*Bist du mit dem Zug gefahren?*
Freund:	*Nein, wir sind mit dem Auto gefahren.*
Du:	*Wer ist mitgekommen?*
Freund:	*Meine Schwester und meine Mutter.*
Du:	*Wann seid ihr denn abgefahren?*
Freund:	*Schon vor drei Wochen.*
Du:	*Wohin seid ihr denn gereist?*
Freund:	*Wir haben unsere Tante und unseren Onkel in der Schweiz besucht.*
Du:	*Habt ihr viel gesehen?*
Freund:	*Oh ja, Berge, Seen und natürlich viele Touristen.*

Wir haben noch viel über die Reise gesprochen. Dann hat mein Freund mich gefragt, wann und wohin ich denn in die Ferien fahren werde.

Wir haben viele Berge und Seen gesehen.

Wörter und Ausdrücke

Asking For and Giving Directions

Entschuldigen Sie, bitte! Excuse me, please!

Wie komme ich zur Stadtmitte? How do I get downtown (to the center of the city)?

Gehen Sie geradeaus. Go straight ahead.

Biegen Sie rechts (links) ab. Turn right (left).

Die Post ist auf der linken (rechten) Seite. The post office is on the left (right) side.

Können Sie mir sagen...? Can you tell me...?

Vielleicht kann der Herr (die Dame) Ihnen Auskunft geben? Perhaps the gentleman (the lady) can you give you information.

Es ist ganz in der Nähe. It's nearby.

Gehen Sie am Café und am Museum vorbei. Go past the café and the museum.

Es ist neben dem Kaufhaus. It's next to the department store.

Talking More about Traveling

Warum hast du so viel Gepäck mitgenommen? Why did you take so much luggage along?

Wo sind the Kofferkulis? Where are the luggage carts?

Du hast so viel Gepäck (so viele Koffer). You have so much luggage (so many suitcases).

Der Zug ist schon angekommen. The train has already arrived.

Steigen wir ein! Let's get in! (Let's get on!)

Entschuldigen Sie! Um wie viel Uhr fährt ein Zug nach Bremen?

Ist sie eingestiegen?

21 Bitte schön?

Pretend to be an official at a railroad station answering questions for tourists who are not familiar with the station or the German train system.

1. Wo ist der Zug nach Bonn, bitte?
2. Haben Sie einen Fahrplan?
3. Wie lange dauert die Reise nach Bremen?
4. Um wie viel Uhr kommt der Zug aus Wien an?
5. Wo ist Gleis acht, bitte?
6. Wie weit ist es von hier nach Stuttgart?
7. Wann fährt der Zug nach Berlin ab?
8. Wissen Sie, wie viel Uhr es ist?

22 Wie sagt man's?

From the list below, select the appropriate words to complete the various conversational exchanges.

dauert	Spaß	teuer	Euro	schwimmen
zwanzig	dorthin	Fahrkarte	stimmt	geradeaus
habe	weit	Stadtmitte	los	fahrt

1. A: Wann kommt der Zug?

   B: In ___ Minuten.

   A: Gut, dann ___ ich noch Zeit.

   B: Ja, das ___.

2. A: Ja, bitte?

   B: Eine ___ nach München, bitte.

   A: Die kostet 35 ___.

   B: Das ist aber sehr ___.

Was wollen sie wissen?

3. A: Warum ___ ihr wieder zur Ostsee?

   B: Wir haben letztes Jahr eine tolle Reise ___ gemacht.

   A: Ist es da im Mai nicht etwas kühl?

   B: Ja, aber wir werden nicht in der Ostsee ___. Es ist natürlich viel zu kalt.

4. A: Wie kommt man von hier zur ___?

   B: Fahren Sie immer ___.

   A: Wie ___ ist das denn noch?

   B: Ungefähr zehn Minuten.

5. A: Morgen geht's schon früh ___.

   B: Warum fahrt ihr nicht etwas später?

   A: Unsere Reise ___ acht Stunden und wir wollen nicht erst am Abend ankommen.

   B: Na, dann viel ___!

23 Beende diese Sätze!

Complete each sentence using an appropriate past participle.

BEISPIEL Wem hast du das Buch ___? Meiner Schwester.
Wem hast du das Buch geschenkt? Meiner Schwester.

1. Was habt ihr im Fernsehen ___? Eine Komödie.

2. Hat es am Wochenende ___? Nein, es hat geschneit.

3. Wie hat dir Katrins Pulli ___? Er ist wirklich toll.

4. Wie lange hat eure Reise denn ___? Sechs Stunden.

5. Ich habe Bernd letztes Jahr einen Brief ___. Wo wohnt er denn jetzt?

6. Warum hast du deinen Kaffee nicht ___? Ich habe keinen Durst.

7. Wie viele Stunden seid ihr von Boston nach Frankfurt ___? Ungefähr sieben Stunden.

8. Haben Sie schon lange auf den Bus ___? Nein, nur ein paar Minuten.

9. Hast du Peter zum Geburtstag ___? Ja, und auch seine Freundin.

10. Wann seid ihr mit dem Zug in Hamburg ___? Um 16 Uhr 20.

24 Neue Wörter, bitte!

Provide the proper personal pronouns for the italicized words.

BEISPIEL Ich habe *meiner Freundin* ein Buch geschenkt.
Ich habe ihr ein Buch geschenkt.

1. Seine Freunde bringen *Birgit* ein Geschenk mit.
2. Wir haben *Peters Eltern* eine Karte geschickt.
3. Was hast du *deinem Vater* gesagt?
4. Ich kaufe *seiner Schwester* ein Computerspiel.
5. Warum schenken wir *unserem Lehrer* nicht die CD?
6. Wie geht es *ihrem Großvater?*

25 Beschreibe jedes Wort!

Describe each word in a complete sentence. *Auf Deutsch, bitte!*

1. Bahnhof
2. Fahrplan
3. Kaufhaus
4. Post

5. Café
6. Schalter
7. Fahrrad
8. Flugzeug

Was weißt du?

1. *Was machst du vor einer Reise?* Describe some of the steps you need to take before going on a trip.

2. *Was gibt's alles auf einem Bahnhof?* Select three items or facilities found at a German railroad station and say at least two sentences about each one.

3. *Wer gebraucht diese?* Select four means of transportation and indicate who among your friends or relatives uses each one and why.

4. *Ich weiß, wie man dorthin kommt.* Pick a place (café, school, post office, etc.) and describe how you get there from your home.

5. *Wen besuchst du?* Imagine that you are planning to visit someone during the summer. Write a short description including such details as whom you are visiting, when you are going, how you will get there, how long you will stay and what you will do there.

Vokabeln

abbiegen to turn (to) *11B*
abfahren to depart, leave *11A*
die **Abfahrt,-en** departure *11A*
ankommen to arrive *11B*
die **Ankunft,-̈e** arrival *11A*
die **Auskunft,-̈e** information *11B*
aussteigen to get off *11B*
der **Automat,-en** automat, (vending) machine *11B*
der **Besuch,-e** visit *11B*
das **Boot,-e** boat *11A*
das **Café,-s** café *11B*
einsteigen to get in/on, board *11B*
entschuldigen:
Entschuldigen Sie! Excuse me! *11B*
erzählen to tell *11B*
die **Fahrkarte,-n** ticket *11A*
fliegen to fly *11A*
das **Flugzeug,-e** airplane *11A*
fragen to ask *11B*
fremd foreign; *Ich bin fremd hier.* I'm a stranger here. *11B*
Fuß: zu Fuß gehen to walk *11A*

die **Gegend,-en** area *11B*
das **Gepäck** luggage, baggage *11B*
geradeaus straight ahead *11B*
das **Gleis,-e** track, platform *11A*
das **Jahr,-e** year; *vor drei Jahren* three years ago *11B*
klein little, small *11B*
der **Koffer,-** suitcase *11B*
der **Kofferkuli,-s** luggage cart *11B*
links left; *auf der linken Seite* on the left side *11B*
mitnehmen to take along *11B*
das **Motorrad,-̈er** motorcycle *11A*
das **Museum, Museen** museum *11B*
nachsehen to check *11A*
die **Nähe** nearness, proximity; *in der Nähe* nearby *11B*
neben next to *11B*
planen to plan *11B*
die **Post** post office *11B*
die **Postkarte,-n** postcard *11B*
rechts right *11B*
schaffen to manage (it), make (it); *Das haben wir geschafft.* We made it. *11A*
der **Schalter,-** (ticket) counter *11B*

das **Schiff,-e** ship *11A*
der **See,-n** lake *11A*
die **Seite,-n** side *11B*
die **Stadtmitte** center of city, downtown *11B*
die **Straßenbahn,-en** streetcar *11A*
die **U-Bahn,-en** subway *11A*
umsteigen to transfer *11A*
das **Verkehrsmittel,-** means of transportation *11A*
vorbeigehen to go past *11B*
der **Zug,-̈e** train *11A*

Für sein Gepäck braucht er einen Kofferkuli.

Die Auskunft ist im Reisezentrum.

Auf welchem Gleis fährt der Zug ab?

Lektion A

Musikinstrumente

1 Frag deine Schulfreunde!

1. Was für ein Musikinstrument spielst du?
2. Wie viel kostet dieses Musikinstrument neu?
3. Wo spielst du es?
4. Wie lange spielst du es schon?
5. Wer spielt in deiner Familie ein Musikinstrument?
6. Gibt es in deiner Schule eine Band? Was für Musikinstrumente gibt es da?
7. Wie heißt deine Lieblingsband? Wie heißen die Rockstars und welche Musikinstrumente spielen sie?

Welche Musikinstrumente spielen sie?

Nadine bringt ihre Flöte mit.

Was bringt Katja mit?

Simone ruft ihre Freundinnen an.

Simone sitzt im Wohnzimmer und sieht fern. Heute gibt's wirklich kein interessantes Fernsehprogramm. Deshalb will sie lieber CDs hören. Aber auch das macht heute keinen Spaß. Endlich ruft sie ihre Freundinnen Nadine und Katja an. Sie sollen mit ihren Musikinstrumenten rüberkommen. Es dauert auch nicht lange, bis Simones Freundinnen da sind. Katja bringt ihre Geige und Nadine ihre Flöte mit. Simone spielt auch schon ein paar Jahre Geige. Alle drei wollen Mozarts „Eine kleine Nachtmusik" in der Schule spielen. Bis dann müssen sie noch ein paar Mal üben. Später am Abend kommen noch ein paar andere Schulfreunde. Alle sitzen am Tisch und spielen Karten. Das macht besonders viel Spaß!

2 Die richtige Reihenfolge

Put these sentences in the correct order according to what happened in the narrative.

1. Heute üben sie für die Schule.
2. Nadine und Katja werden zu Simone rüberkommen.
3. Simone hört CDs.
4. Die drei Mädchen spielen mit ihren Schulfreunden Karten.
5. Beide Freundinnen tragen ihre Musikinstrumente ins Haus.
6. Simone sieht fern.
7. Sie spielen „Eine kleine Nachtmusik".
8. Simone ruft Nadine und Katja an.

3 Fragen

1. Warum will Simone kein Fernsehprogramm sehen?
2. Hört sie heute gern CDs?
3. Wen ruft sie an?
4. Was sollen beide Freundinnen mitbringen?
5. Muss Simone lange warten, bis Katja und Nadine zu ihr kommen?
6. Was für Musikinstrumente spielen Nadine und Katja?
7. Hat Simone erst vor kurzer Zeit angefangen, Geige zu spielen?
8. Was werden sie in der Schule spielen?
9. Was macht später am Abend besonders viel Spaß?

Was macht besonders viel Spaß?

Für dich

Amadeus Mozart (1756–1791) was an Austrian composer whose works combine luminous beauty of sound with classical grace and technical perfection. Mozart was taught to play the harpsicord, violin and organ by his father and began composing before he was 5. At the age of 6, he and his older sister played in concerts at the royal court in Vienna.

By the age of 13, Mozart had written concertos, sonatas and symphonies as well as a German operetta and an Italian opera. He wrote *Eine kleine Nachtmusik,* a serenade for strings, in the space of three months. It exemplifies elegant pieces written for social occasions.

4 Nächste Woche gibt's viel zu tun

Herr und Frau Kästner haben drei Kinder — Achim, Willi und Erika. Nächste Woche wollen sie eine Woche Frau Kästners Schwester in Berlin besuchen. Sie sagen ihren Kindern, was es während der Zeit alles zu tun gibt. Ergänze die folgenden Sätze! Folge dem Beispiel!

BEISPIEL Willi / müssen / Rasen mähen
Willi muss den Rasen mähen.

1. Erika / sollen / Geschirr spülen
2. Achim / werden / Sachen einkaufen
3. Willi / dürfen / Film im Kino sehen
4. Achim / können / Freund besuchen
5. Erika und Willi / wollen / Wohnung staubsaugen
6. Achim / müssen / Buch lesen
7. Willi / werden / Vater E-Mails schicken
8. Achim und Erika / sollen / Mutter anrufen

5 Was fehlt hier?

Complete each sentence using the appropriate form of the modal auxiliary.

BEISPIEL (können) ___ du mir bei der Arbeit helfen?
Kannst du mir bei der Arbeit helfen?

1. Ich (möchten) ___ gern ins Eiscafé gehen.
2. (wollen) ___ ihr nicht zur Party mitkommen?
3. Das (dürfen) ___ wir leider nicht machen.
4. (können) ___ er seinem Freund nicht helfen?
5. Warum (mögen) ___ die Jugendlichen das nicht essen?
6. Ich weiß auch nicht, warum Gisela schon so früh nach Hause gehen (sollen) ___.
7. Dieter (wollen) ___ im Sommer seinen Onkel in Liechtenstein besuchen.
8. (möchten) ___ du mit uns in die Stadt fahren?

Aktuelles

Music: Classical to Pop

Few art forms are as universally known as music. The Beatles and the Rolling Stones, Beethoven and Mozart, to name but a few examples, probably eclipse Michelangelo and Goethe in terms of worldwide fame; their language is more abstract and more universal than the conceptual forms of the fine arts or of literature. The subordinate role of spoken or written language is apparent here from the predominance of English-language pop music. German was long regarded as too stiff and hard a language for the rebellious, critical or even emotional pop sound. Consequently, German groups produced songs with English lyrics; not until the late 1970s did some groups invent a German sound that could be molded to the international pop style such as BAP, Herbert Grönemeyer, Marius Müller-Westerhagen, Nena, Xavier Naidoo and Tokio Hotel. Thus, a growing number of young musicians followed the trend of the

Viele deutsche Rockgruppen spielen amerikanische Hits.

"new German wave," in which irony, another hallmark of postmodernist culture, frequently played a decisive role. Not that the Germans have turned their back on the international scene: almost all international stars make regular appearances in Germany.

Little needs to be said about the standing of classical music in Germany. The country, with its numerous orchestras and opera houses, is extremely well endowed, and has long attracted worldwide interest. This preeminence attracts a wealth of musical talent to Germany and, as a result, the majority of members of large orchestras as well as conductors and singers come from abroad.

Between the classical and pop worlds lie the highly successful musicals of the last two decades, in particular, those produced by Andrew Lloyd Webber. These productions demand the utmost in technical skill on the part of the performers, and commercial marketing skills on the part of the promoters. High-profile advertising for individual productions whips up interest over several years, drawing huge audiences reluctant to miss the spectacle.

Am Schlagzeug ist er ein Experte.

Die Gitarre ist immer ein wichtiges Musikinstrument in einer Band.

Singen macht besonders viel Spaß.

6 Wer sind diese Leute?

In one or two sentences, identify each famous person or group and say why they are famous. You may have to go to the library or use the Internet to find out more information.

Johann Wolfgang von Goethe

1. the Beatles
2. the Rolling Stones
3. Ludwig van Beethoven
4. Wolfgang Amadeus Mozart
5. Michelangelo
6. Johann Wolfgang von Goethe
7. Andrew Lloyd Webber

7 Ein Interview

Robert, an exchange student from the United States, is enrolled at a German Gymnasium for a year. The school newspaper wants to find out various details about him. Complete the questions using the verbs indicated in parentheses.

1. Wie (gefallen) ___ dir Deutschland?
2. Wie lange (sprechen) ___ du schon deutsch?
3. Wann (fahren) ___ du wieder zurück?
4. Welche Bücher (lesen) ___ du gern?
5. Welche Fächer (nehmen) ___ du hier?
6. Was (essen) ___ du gern?
7. Welche Städte (sehen) ___ du noch außer unserer Stadt?
8. Was (geben) ___ es alles in deiner Gegend zu sehen?

Sie interviewt Robert.

Robert geht ein Jahr auf ein Gymnasium.

8 Was fehlt hier?

Complete each sentence using the appropriate separable prefix from the list.

ab	an	auf	aus	ein
fern	los	mit	rüber	vorbei

1. Räum bitte den Tisch ___!
2. Was kaufst du in der Stadt ___?
3. Um wie viel Uhr sehen wir denn ___?
4. Pass ___! Der Zug kommt.
5. Bring doch deine Freundin ___!
6. Warum gibst du so viel Geld ___?
7. Kommst du später zu uns ___?
8. Ich rufe Gabi gleich mit meinem Handy ___.
9. Wann geht das Konzert denn ___?
10. Gehen Sie an der Post ___! Dann sehen Sie schon gleich das Kaufhaus.

Persönliches

Beschreibe, was du am Wochenende alles machst. Du kannst über eins der folgenden Themen sprechen oder schreiben. Du brauchst nicht nur die Fragen unten (below) zu beantworten. Schreib oder diskutiere so viel wie möglich! Sei kreativ!

1. *ins Kino gehen:* Wie heißt der Film? Mit wem gehst du? Wann fängt der Film an? Wie ist der Film gewesen?

2. *Sport treiben:* Welchen Sport treibst du? Wer und wie viele Jugendliche machen mit? Was machst du bei diesem Sport? Wo spielst du?

3. *zu einer Party gehen:* Wer kommt alles? Was ist da los? An welchem Tag und um wie viel Uhr ist die Party? Bringst du etwas mit? Was?

4. *ein Musikinstrument spielen:* Was für ein Musikinstrument spielst du? Wie oft musst du üben? Spielst du nur zu Hause oder auch in einer Band?

Was für ein Musikinstrument spielt sie?

Rollenspiel

With one or two of your classmates, talk about an upcoming event such as a dance, sports activity, party, and so forth. Give them reasons why they should come along. Your reasons could include such things as having lots of fun, meeting others, good food, great music or other entertainment. Respond to their questions, being as creative as possible. Then reverse roles.

Was machen die Jungen gern?

Vielleicht geht ihr zu einem Rockkonzert?

Wörter und Ausdrücke

Was spielt sie?

Inquiring about Musical Instruments

Was für ein Musikinstrument spielst du?
  What kind of musical instrument do you play?
  Trompete. Trumpet.
  Blockflöte. Recorder.
  Geige. Violin.
  Flöte. Flute.
  Saxophon. Saxophone.
  Keyboard. Keyboard.

Was für ein Musikinstrument spielt er?

Sie spielen Geige.

Zungenbrecher

Er sang leider lauter laute
Lieder zur Laute.

Unfortunately he sang lots of loud songs to the lute.

Lektion B

Machen wir Musik!

Nadine hat eine neue Flöte.

Sie fangen gleich an.

Simone begrüßt ihre Freundinnen.

Katja und Nadine wohnen nicht weit von Simones Haus entfernt. Deshalb sind sie schnell bei Simone. Sie klingeln. Simone macht auch gleich die Tür auf.

Nadine: Hast du schon meine neue Flöte gesehen?

Simone: Die ist ja toll! Bestimmt kannst du jetzt besser spielen.

Katja: Meine Geige ist auch ganz neu, nicht wie deine, Simone.

Simone: Wir haben ja schon den ersten Teil geübt. Fangen wir doch hier an!

Nadine: Also, los! Machen wir Musik!

Katja: Spielen wir nicht zu laut? Das stört doch bestimmt deinen Vater.

Simone: Nein, der sitzt in der Küche und macht da seine Arbeit fürs Büro. Er hat unsere Musik immer sehr gern.

Alle drei üben „Eine kleine Nachtmusik", bis sie es gut spielen können. Nach ungefähr einer Stunde hören sie auf. Simones Vater hat ihnen Kuchen angeboten. Der schmeckt ihnen auch sehr gut. Bald kommen ein paar andere Schulfreunde. Sie kommen alle oft zusammen, sprechen über die Schule, über Sport oder sie spielen Karten.

9 Von wem spricht man hier?

Diese Person oder Personen...

1. wohnen ganz in der Nähe von Simone.
2. ist in der Küche.
3. hat eine neue Geige.
4. kommen später zu Simone.
5. üben einen Teil von Mozarts Serenade.
6. macht die Haustür auf.
7. gibt ihnen Kuchen.
8. hören auf Musik zu spielen.
9. klingeln an der Tür.
10. sprechen über Sport.

10 Was fehlt hier?

Complete each sentence using at least one appropriate word.

1. Das Essen schmeckt ___.
2. Warum fängst du ___?
3. Stör bitte ___!
4. Übst du ___?
5. Sie klingeln ___.
6. Sprechen wir ___!
7. Kannst du nicht ___?
8. Er sitzt oft ___.
9. Hast du die Musik ___?
10. Ihre Flöte ___.

Wo klingeln sie?

Wo sitzt Simones Vater?

Für dich

Most Germans live in a rather small, close network of social relationships that are determined by tradition and custom as well as by education and job status. Home life is of greatest significance, both as a shelter from the turmoils and stresses of the outside world and as an expression

Sie sitzen gern im Wohnzimmer.

of one's own private standing. Most German homemakers take great pride in the way their home is furnished and maintained, sometimes even at the cost of cultivating social contacts.

All of this means, of course, that not only foreigners but also Germans who have to move to another location may find it difficult to make new friends. Generally, Germans do not like to move as often as Americans. However, higher unemployment in certain areas has forced many Germans to relocate in recent years.

11 Welche Wörter passen hier zusammen?

Classify each word as belonging to one of these five categories: *Sportart, Körperteil, Verkehrsmittel, Musikinstrument, Fach.*

1. Bein
2. Schwimmen
3. Kopf
4. Straßenbahn
5. Geige
6. Geschichte
7. Fußball
8. Erdkunde
9. Schulter
10. Klavier
11. Motorrad
12. Stirn
13. Flugzeug
14. Schlagzeug
15. Naturwissenschaften

Zwei Jungen spielen Schlagzeug.

das Flugzeug

12 Was fehlt?

Supply the German equivalent for the words given in parentheses.

1. Wo wohnt *(your brother)* ___, Herr Weise?
2. *(Their father)* ___ besucht *(my aunt)* ___.
3. Hast du *(your sister)* ___ bei der Arbeit geholfen, Tina?
4. *(Our school)* ___ ist nicht weit.
5. *(My girlfriend)* ___ holt *(her video)* ___.
6. Warum kaufst du *(his tickets)* ___?
7. Ich bin ohne *(my books)* ___ in die Schule gegangen.
8. Fährst du mit *(your moped)* ___ in die Stadt, Bernd?
9. Bringt doch *(your ball)* ___, Dieter und Heike!

13 Ergänze die Sätze!

Complete the narrative by adding the proper word endings where necessary.

Fünf Tage die Woche gehen wir schon um halb acht zu unser (1) Schule. Mein (2) Freundin Karin kommt immer pünktlich. Manchmal kommt sie auch mit ihr (3) Schwester. Unser (4) Mathelehrer, Herr Dietrich, bringt jeden Montag unser (5) Hausaufgaben. Mein (6) Note in Mathe ist ganz gut. Karin hat Mathe nicht gern. Deshalb sind ihr (7) Noten nicht besonders gut. In der zweiten Stunde haben wir unser (8) Englischlehrerin, Frau Braun. Ihr (9) Klasse ist immer interessant. Am letzten Freitag im Monat fahre ich mit mein (10) Fahrrad zur Schule. An diesem Tag kommt immer mein (11) Vater zu Besuch. Dann fahren wir oft mit sein (12) Auto zu sein (13) Haus. Er wohnt in einer anderen Stadt.

Frau Braun, die Englischlehrerin

14 Beende diese Sätze!

1. Nach ___ können wir zum Eiscafé gehen.
2. Wohnt er nicht bei ___?
3. Um wie viel Uhr kommt ihr aus ___?
4. Das Auto steht nicht weit von ___.
5. Sie fahren zu ___.
6. Außer ___ spielt auch der Vater Tennis.
7. Ich fahre mit ___ in die Stadt.
8. Die Touristen fahren von ___ zu ___.

Lesestück

Tanzen macht Spaß!

Daniela und Gabriella haben schon ein paar Jahre modernen Tanz gelernt. Einmal[1] die Woche, am Dienstag, fahren sie mit der Straßenbahn in die Stadtmitte von Luzern. Gleich in der Nähe vom Bahnhof gehen sie in ein Tanzstudio. Dort sehen sie sich die neusten Fotos auf einer Tafel an[2]. Jede Woche gibt es da Fotos von den Schülern dieses Tanzstudios. Manche sind Anfänger[3], andere sind Fortgeschrittene[4] wie Daniela und Gabriella. Beide haben schon bei verschiedenen Aufführungen[5] mitgemacht.

Daniela und Gabriella gehen jede Woche zum Tanzstudio.

Daniela und Gabriella sehen sich noch kurz vor der Tanzstunde ein Fotoalbum an.

Daniela: Sieh mal! Das ist vor zwei Jahren gewesen. Zu der Zeit haben wir noch nicht so gut getanzt.

Gabriella: Da hast du Recht. Siehst du, wie steif[6] wir da stehen?

Daniela: Es ist wirklich toll, wie viel wir in den letzten beiden Jahren gelernt haben.

Was macht Gabriella?

Gabriella: Na ja. Übung macht den Meister![7]

Daniela: Die Anfänger kommen aus dem Studio. Jetzt sind wir dran.[8]

Übung macht den Meister!

Frau Kundmüller ist die Lehrerin im Tanzstudio. Zuerst müssen alle Jugendlichen zehn Minuten Leibesübungen machen[9]. Dann spielt die Lehrerin eine CD mit moderner Musik. Während[10] alle tanzen, sagt sie ihnen genau, was sie machen sollen. Das Tanzen geht im Takt und mit Rhythmus[11]. Ein großer Spiegel[12] zeigt den Jugendlichen, wie gut sie tanzen. Frau Kundmüller findet, dass alle Tänzer die Schritte[13] schon gut gelernt haben. Sie sollen aber besser als eine Gruppe zusammen arbeiten[14] und ihre Bewegungen[15] mehr mit der Musik koordinieren.

Jetzt sind wir dran.

In zwei Wochen werden sie und auch die Anfänger zeigen müssen, was sie können. In Zug, einer kleinen Stadt ungefähr 30 Kilometer von Luzern entfernt[16], gibt es dann eine musikalische Aufführung. Die fortgeschrittenen Schüler[17] haben bei dieser Aufführung einen großen Teil. Frau Kundmüller und ihre Schüler hoffen, dass ein paar hundert Leute aus der Gegend zur Stadthalle kommen werden.

[1]*einmal* once; [2]*sich ansehen* to look at; [3]*der Anfänger* beginner; [4]*der Fortgeschrittene* advanced (student); [5]*die Aufführung* performance; [6]*steif* stiff; [7]*Übung macht den Meister!* Practice makes perfect!; [8]*dran sein* to be one's turn; [9]*Leibesübungen machen* to do physical exercises; [10]*während* while; [11]*im Takt und mit Rhythmus gehen* to go with the beat and rhythm; [12]*der Spiegel* mirror; [13]*der Schritt* step; [14]*arbeiten* to work; [15]*die Bewegung* movement; [16]*entfernt* away; [17]*der Schüler* student

In einem Spiegel können sie sehen, wie gut sie tanzen.

Alle koordinieren ihre Bewegungen mit der Musik.

Was machen sie?

15 Welche Wörter passen?

Complete the paragraphs using the appropriate forms of the verbs listed.

koordinieren	hören	sein	zeigen
geben	sehen	werden	fahren
müssen	mitmachen	glauben	machen
sagen			

In Luzern (1) es ein Tanzstudio. Dorthin (2) Gabriella und Daniela jede Woche. Auf einer Tafel im Tanzstudio (3) Fotos von den Jugendlichen. Bei den Tanzaufführungen haben die beiden Mädchen schon oft (4). In einem Fotoalbum (5) Daniela und Gabriella noch andere Fotos.

Die Tänzer (6) zuerst ihre Leibesübungen. Während sie tanzen, (7) sie Musik. Ein Spiegel (8) allen, wie sie tanzen. Die Lehrerin (9), dass ihre Tanzklasse ganz gut ist. Sie (10) ihnen noch, dass die Jugendlichen ihre Bewegungen etwas besser (11) sollen. In zwei Wochen (12) sie in Zug zeigen, was sie gelernt haben. Bestimmt (13) viele Leute zur Aufführung kommen.

16 Was haben alle am Wochenende gemacht?

BEISPIEL Rainer / seine Tante besuchen
Rainer hat seine Tante besucht.

1. Angelikas Vater / nach Süddeutschland fahren
2. meine Freunde / in die Disko gehen
3. Thomas / ein paar Fernsehprogramme sehen
4. die Jugendlichen / im Tanzstudio tanzen
5. ihre Freundin / Tennis spielen
6. seine Schwester / ihre Freundinnen einladen
7. Herr Schreiber / seinen Wagen waschen
8. unser Lehrer / viel arbeiten

Was haben sie am Wochenende gemacht?

17 Was fehlt hier?

Complete the dialog using the present perfect tense of
the verbs listed.

warten	**sein**	**helfen**	**sehen**	**haben**
sagen	**lesen**	**schreiben**	**machen**	**dauern**

A: Warum hast du gestern keine Zeit (1) ?

B: Ich habe Katrina eine lange E-Mail (2) .

A: Warum hast du mir das nicht (3) ? Ich habe lange auf dich
(4) .

B: Ich habe auch meiner Mutter bei der Arbeit (5) . Das hat
noch eine Stunde (6) .

A: Was hast du denn am Abend (7) ?

B: Gegen sieben habe ich einen tollen Film im Fernsehen
(8) .

A: Fernsehen? Ich habe ein Buch (9) .

B: Hoffentlich ist er so gut wie der Film (10) .

Persönliches

1. Tanzt du gern? Warum oder warum nicht?

2. Welche Musik gefällt dir?

3. Hast du ein Fotoalbum? Welche Fotos sind in diesem
Fotoalbum?

4. Gibt es in deiner Klasse eine Tafel? Was kann man da lesen?

5. Hast du schon einmal bei einer Aufführung mitgemacht?
Wann ist das gewesen und welche Rolle hast du gespielt?

6. Welches Hobby hast du sehr gern? Bist du ein Anfänger/eine
Anfängerin oder ein Fortgeschrittener/eine
Fortgeschrittene?

Sie tanzen sehr gern.

Rollenspiel

A well-known rock band is in town and your friend wants you to come along to the concert. Tickets are hard to come by, therefore, your friend needs your decision immediately. Unfortunately, you don't have enough money, but your friend has several solutions. Develop a conversation with one of your classmates in which you discuss the financial situation and figure out how you can manage to buy a ticket. Reverse roles.

Praktisches

Was für ein Musikinstrument hast du gespielt? You want to find out what musical instruments your classmates played when they were younger. Draw a grid and insert in German five common musical instruments. Then poll 10 of your classmates to determine which instrument(s) they used to play. In your survey:

1. Name each instrument and ask your classmates, one by one, if they played it.

2. As each classmate answers your question, put a check mark by the appropriate response.

3. After you have finished asking questions, count the number of students who played each instrument. Figure out the percentage of those asked. Be ready to share your findings with the rest of the class.

Schreiben

Select one of the two topics and follow the instructions to complete the activity.

1. Write a dialog or a narrative using the following details: Call your friend...ask him or her to go to a dance...provide information about where and when the dance takes place... decide where to meet...your friend asks who is playing. Be as creative as possible. Here is a sample dialog:

Du:	Willst du mit mir zum Tanz gehen?
Freundin:	Wo und wann gibt es denn einen Tanz?
Du:	Um halb acht in der Disko.
Freundin:	Gut, ich komme mit. Wo sollen wir uns treffen?
Du:	Bei mir, so gegen sieben Uhr.
Freundin	Welche Band spielt denn?
Du:	Die Rockband aus... Du kennst sie doch.
Freundin:	Toll! Bis später!

2. Imagine your committee has been put in charge of making the necessary preparations for the next school dance. Make a list of questions that need to be addressed and then ask others in your class. Some of your questions might be:

> *Welche Band soll spielen?*
> *Wann soll der Tanz beginnen?*
> *Wen sollen wir einladen?*
> *Was brauchen wir alles?*
> *Wie viel soll eine Karte kosten?*

Land und Leute

Die Schweiz

Die Schweiz ist zu jeder Jahreszeit beliebt.

Die Schweiz ist ein sehr beliebtes Land. Jedes Jahr kommen viele Besucher[1] in die Schweiz. Dieses kleine Land ist halb so groß wie[2] der Staat South Carolina.

Die Schweiz hat fünf Nachbarländer: Frankreich, Italien, Österreich, Liechtenstein und Deutschland. Mehr als sieben Millionen Einwohner wohnen in diesem Land. 65% sprechen deutsch, 18% französisch, 10% italienisch und 7% andere Sprachen[3]. Die Nationalfahne ist rot und hat ein weißes Kreuz[4] in der Mitte.

Winter in Graubünden

Basel, die zweitgrößte Stadt

Der größte Teil der Schweiz liegt in den Bergen. Der Monte Rosa (4 600 m) ist der höchste Berg. Der Rhein ist der längste Fluss. Er fließt 376 Kilometer durch das Land und dann durch Deutschland und die Niederlande zur Nordsee[5].

Die größte Stadt der Schweiz ist Zürich. Diese Stadt liegt am Zürichsee. Die zweitgrößte Stadt ist Basel. Wie Zürich liegt auch Basel im Norden der Schweiz. Der Rhein fließt durch Basel.

Zürich ist die größte Stadt.

Genf ist eine andere große Stadt. Diese Stadt liegt im Süden am Genfer See, an der Grenze zu[6] Frankreich. Bern, die Hauptstadt der Schweiz, ist die viertgrößte Stadt und liegt im Westen. Dann kommt Luzern. Diese Stadt liegt in der Mitte der Schweiz.

Während der Sommermonate besuchen die Touristen die Schweiz sehr gern. Hier können sie viel in den Bergen wandern. Warum kommen auch viele Besucher im Winter in die Schweiz? Während dieser Jahreszeit ist die Schweiz ein Paradies. Tausende fahren in die Schweiz und laufen dort Ski.

---

[1]*der Besucher* visitor; [2]*so...wie* as...as; [3]*die Sprache* language; [4]*das Kreuz* cross; [5]*die Nordsee* North Sea; [6]*an der Grenze zu* at the border with

Welche Farben hat die Nationalfahne?

18 Was passt hier?

1. Der längste Fluss ist
2. Die Nationalfahne hat
3. Die zweitgrößte Stadt ist
4. Der höchste Berg ist
5. Mehr als vier Millionen sprechen
6. Genf liegt
7. Im Winter kann man in der Schweiz
8. Der Rhein fließt
9. Die Schweiz ist
10. Bern ist

A. halb so groß wie der Staat South Carolina.
B. Basel.
C. zur Nordsee.
D. deutsch.
E. Ski laufen.
F. die Hauptstadt.
G. ein Kreuz in der Mitte.
H. an der Grenze zu Frankreich.
I. der Monta Rosa.
J. der Rhein.

19 Fragen

1. Besuchen viele Touristen die Schweiz?
2. Wie groß ist die Schweiz?
3. Wie viele Nachbarländer hat die Schweiz?
4. Welche sind das?
5. Sprechen alle deutsch?
6. Ist das Land flach?
7. Von wo bis wo fließt der Rhein?
8. Wie heißt die Hauptstadt der Schweiz?
9. Wo liegt Luzern?
10. Kommen Besucher nur im Sommer in die Schweiz?

Wörter und Ausdrücke

Practicing Music

Wir haben den ersten Teil geübt. We practiced the first part.
Fangen wir doch hier an! Let's start here!
Machen wir Musik! Let's make music!
Das stört. That's disturbing.
Sie hören auf. They are stopping.

Vokabeln

anbieten to offer *12B*
arbeiten to work *12B*
der **Anfänger,-** beginner *12B*
sich **ansehen** to look at *12B*
die **Aufführung,-en** performance *12B*
aufhören to stop, quit *12B*
die **Bewegung,-en** movement *12B*
die **Blockflöte,-n** recorder *12A*
das **Büro,-s** office *12B*
dran sein to be one's turn; *Sie ist dran.* It's her turn. *12B*
einmal once *12B*
entfernt away *12B*
die **Flöte,-n** flute *12A*
der **Fortgeschrittene,-n** advanced (student) *12B*
das **Foto,-s** photo *12B*
das **Fotoalbum,-alben** photo album *12B*

die **Geige,-n** violin *12A*
das **Keyboard,-s** keyboard *12A*
koordinieren to coordinate *12B*
die **Leibesübung,-en** physical exercise *12B*
modern modern *12B*
musikalisch musical *12B*
das **Musikinstrument,-e** musical instrument *12A*
der **Rhythmus** rhythm *12B*
das **Saxophon,-e** saxophone *12A*
der **Schritt,-e** step *12B*
der **Schüler,-** student (elementary through secondary school) *12B*
der **Spaß** fun; *Es macht Spaß.* It's fun. *12A*
der **Spiegel,-** mirror *12B*

die **Stadthalle,-n** city hall *12B*
steif stiff *12B*
stören to disturb, bother, annoy *12B*
das **Studio,-s** studio *12B*
der **Takt,-e** beat *12B*
die **Tanzstunde,-n** dance lesson *12B*
der **Tanz,-̈e** dance *12B*
das **Tanzstudio,-s** dance studio *12B*
die **Trompete,-n** trumpet *12A*
die **Tür,-en** door *12B*
üben to practice *12B*
die **Übung,-en** exercise, practice; *Übung macht den Meister!* Practice makes perfect! *12B*
während while *12B*

Sie arbeitet im Büro.

Das Kartenspiel macht Spaß.

Sie klingelt an der Tür.

Sie sehen sich das Fotoalbum an.

Grammar Summary

Personal Pronouns

SINGULAR	nominative	accusative	dative
1st person	ich	mich	mir
2nd person	du	dich	dir
3rd person	er sie es	ihn sie es	ihm ihr ihm
PLURAL			
1st person	wir	uns	uns
2nd person	ihr	euch	euch
3rd person	sie	sie	ihnen
formal form (singular or plural)	Sie	Sie	Ihnen

Definite Article

	SINGULAR			PLURAL
	masculine	feminine	neuter	
nominative	der	die	das	die
accusative	den	die	das	die
dative	dem	der	dem	den

Question Words: *Wer? Was?*

nominative	wer	was
accusative	wen	was
dative	wem	

Indefinite Article

	SINGULAR			PLURAL
	masculine	feminine	neuter	
nominative	ein	eine	ein	keine
accusative	einen	eine	ein	keine
dative	einem	einer	einem	keinen

Regular Verb Forms — Present Tense

	gehen	finden	heißen
ich	gehe	finde	heiße
du	gehst	findest	heißt
er, sie, es	geht	findet	heißt
wir	gehen	finden	heißen
ihr	geht	findet	heißt
sie, Sie	gehen	finden	heißen

Irregular Verb Forms — Present Tense

	haben	sein	wissen
ich	habe	bin	weiß
du	hast	bist	weißt
er, sie, es	hat	ist	weiß
wir	haben	sind	wissen
ihr	habt	seid	wisst
sie, Sie	haben	sind	wissen

Command Forms

familiar (singular)	Geh!	Warte!	Sei!	Hab!
familiar (plural)	Geht!	Wartet!	Seid!	Habt!
formal (singular/plural)	Gehen Sie!	Warten Sie!	Seien Sie!	Haben Sie!
wir-form (Let's...)	Gehen wir!	Warten wir!	Seien wir!	Haben wir!

Plural of Nouns

	SINGULAR	PLURAL
no change or add umlaut	das Zimmer die Mutter	die Zimmer die Mütter
add -n, -en or -nen	die Ecke der Herr die Freundin	die Ecken die Herren die Freundinnen
add -e or ⸚e	der Tag die Stadt	die Tage die Städte
add ⸚er	das Buch das Fach	die Bücher die Fächer
add -s	das Auto das Büro	die Autos die Büros

Inverted Word Order

1. Formation of questions beginning with the verb: *Spielst du heute Fußball?*
2. Formation of questions beginning with a question word: *Wohin gehen Sie heute Nachmittag?*
3. Command forms: *Komm zu uns rüber! Lauft schnell! Besuchen Sie doch das Museum! Gehen wir ins Kino!*

Negation

Verbs (*nicht*) *Kommen sie nicht zu uns?*
Nouns (*kein*) *Ich habe keine Karte.*

Modal Auxiliaries

	dürfen	können	mögen	müssen	möchten	sollen	wollen
ich	darf	kann	mag	muss	möchte	soll	will
du	darfst	kannst	magst	musst	möchtest	sollst	willst
er, sie, es	darf	kann	mag	muss	möchte	soll	will
wir	dürfen	können	mögen	müssen	möchten	sollen	wollen
ihr	dürft	könnt	mögt	müsst	möchtet	sollt	wollt
sie, Sie	dürfen	können	mögen	müssen	möchten	sollen	wollen

Future Tense (*werden* + infinitive)

ich	werde
du	wirst
er, sie, es	wird
wir	werden
ihr	werdet
sie, Sie	werden

Sie werden dieses Jahr nach Deutschland fahren. Wirst du ins Kino gehen?

Verbs with Stem Vowel Change (2nd & 3rd person singular only)

	a to *ä*	*e* to *i*	*e* to *ie*
ich	fahre	spreche	sehe
du	fährst	sprichst	siehst
er, sie, es	fährt	spricht	sieht
wir	fahren	sprechen	sehen
ihr	fahrt	sprecht	seht
sie, Sie	fahren	sprechen	sehen

Prepositions

dative	accusative	contraction
aus	durch	durch das = durchs
außer	für	für das = fürs
bei	gegen	bei dem = beim
mit	ohne	—
nach	um	um das = ums
seit		—
von		von dem = vom
zu		zu dem = zum/zu der = zur

Verbs Followed by Dative Case

antworten   gefallen   glauben   helfen   Leid tun   passen   schmecken   wehtun

Gabi hilft ihrer Mutter. Der Anzug gefällt mir.

The verb *glauben* may take either the dative or accusative. If used with a person, the dative follows *(Ich glaube ihm)*. If used with an object, the accusative is used *(Ich glaube das nicht)*.

Possessive Adjectives

	SINGULAR			PLURAL
	masculine	feminine	neuter	
nominative	mein	meine	mein	meine
accusative	meinen	meine	mein	meine
dative	meinem	meiner	meinem	meinen

The endings of possessive adjectives are the same as those of the indefinite article (*ein*-words). Possessive adjectives are *mein, dein, sein, ihr, sein, unser, euer, ihr, Ihr.*

Numbers

0 = null	11 = elf	22 = zweiundzwanzig
1 = eins	12 = zwölf	30 = dreißig
2 = zwei	13 = dreizehn	40 = vierzig
3 = drei	14 = vierzehn	50 = fünfzig
4 = vier	15 = fünfzehn	60 = sechzig
5 = fünf	16 = sechzehn	70 = siebzig
6 = sechs	17 = siebzehn	80 = achtzig
7 = sieben	18 = achtzehn	90 = neunzig
8 = acht	19 = neunzehn	100 = einhundert
9 = neun	20 = zwanzig	101 = hunderteins
10 = zehn	21 = einundzwanzig	

Time

1:00	Es ist ein Uhr.	11:45	Es ist Viertel vor zwölf.
2:00	Es ist zwei Uhr.	5:10	Es ist zehn Minuten nach fünf.
3:30	Es ist halb vier.	7:58	Es ist zwei Minuten vor acht.
10:15	Es ist Viertel nach zehn.		

Irregular Verbs—Present Perfect Tense (Past Participle)

The following list contains all the irregular verbs used in *Deutsch Aktuell 1*. Verbs with separable or inseparable prefixes are not included when the basic verb form has been introduced (example: *kommen*, *ankommen*). If the basic verb has not been introduced, then the verb with its prefix is included. Verbs with stem vowel changes, as well as those constructed with a form of *sein*, have also been indicated.

INFINITIVE	STEM VOWEL CHANGE	PAST PARTICIPLE	MEANING
abbiegen		ist abgebogen	to turn (to)
anbieten		angeboten	to offer
anrufen		angerufen	to call up
aussteigen		ist ausgestiegen	to get off
beginnen		begonnen	to begin
bekommen		bekommen	to get, receive
bleiben		ist geblieben	to stay, remain
bringen		gebracht	to bring
einladen	lädt ein	eingeladen	to invite
essen	isst	gegessen	to eat
fahren	fährt	ist gefahren	to drive
finden		gefunden	to find
fliegen		ist geflogen	to fly
fließen		ist geflossen	to flow
geben	gibt	gegeben	to give
gefallen	gefällt	gefallen	to like
gewinnen		gewonnen	to win
haben	hat	gehabt	to have
heißen		geheißen	to be called
helfen	hilft	geholfen	to help
kennen		gekannt	to know (person)
kommen		ist gekommen	to come
laufen	läuft	ist gelaufen	to run, walk
lesen	liest	gelesen	to read
liegen		gelegen	to lie, be located
nehmen	nimmt	genommen	to take
scheinen		geschienen	to shine
schießen		geschossen	to shoot
schreiben		geschrieben	to write
schreien		geschrien	to scream
schwimmen		ist geschwommen	to swim
sehen	sieht	gesehen	to see
sein	ist	ist gewesen	to be
singen		gesungen	to be
sprechen	spricht	gesprochen	to speak, talk
stehen		gestanden	to stand
treffen	trifft	getroffen	to meet
treiben		getrieben	to do (sports)
trinken		getrunken	to drink
tun	tut	getan	to do
verlassen	verlässt	verlassen	to leave
wissen	weiß	gewusst	to know (fact)

German-English Vocabulary

All the words introduced in *Deutsch Aktuell 1* have been summarized in this section. The numbers following the meaning of individual words or phrases indicate the chapter in which they appear for the first time. When there is more than one meaning for a word or a phrase and it appears in different chapters, both chapter numbers are listed. (Example: *das* that 1; the 2) Nouns have been listed with their respective articles and plural forms. Words preceded by an asterisk (*) are passive and appear following the *Land und Leute* reading selection in Chapters 4, 8 and 12. All other words are active and appear throughout the text.

A

abbiegen to turn (to) *11*

der **Abend,-e** evening; *heute Abend* this evening; *am Abend* in the evening *3*

das **Abendessen** supper, dinner *6*

aber but *3*

abfahren to depart, leave *11*

die **Abfahrt,-en** departure *11*

das **Abitur** final examination *(Gymnasium) 10*

abräumen to clear (table) *9*

ach ja oh yes *3*

acht eight *1*

achtzehn eighteen *1*

achtzig eighty *2*

alle all; *alle zwölf Minuten* every twelve minutes *5*

alles everything; *Das ist alles.* That's all. *5*

also so; *Also, was ist dein Geschenk?* So, what is your present? *8*

alt old *1*

Amerika America *5*

an (am) at, on, to; *am Telefon* on the telephone *2*

anbieten to offer *12*

**andere other *4*

anfangen to start, begin *9*

der **Anfänger,-** beginner *12*

anhaben to have on, wear *7*

ankommen to arrive *11*

die **Ankunft,-e** arrival *11*

anrufen to call (on the phone) *8*

sich **ansehen** to look at *12*

die **Antwort,-en** answer *8*

der **Anzug,-e** suit *7*

der **Apfelsaft** apple juice *6*

Appetit appetite; *Guten Appetit!* Enjoy your meal! *6*

der **April** April *5*

die **Arbeit,-en** work *4*

arbeiten to work *12*

der **Arm,-e** arm *10*

Au! Ouch! *10*

auch also, too *2*

auf on, on top of *4*

die **Aufführung,-en** performance *12*

aufhören to stop, quit *12*

aufmachen to open *8*

aufpassen to pay attention, watch out *10*

aufräumen to clean up (room) *9*

aufregend exciting *9*

das **Auge,-n** eye *10*

der **August** August *5*

aus from, out of *1*

außer besides, except *10*

außerdem besides *9*

ausgeben to spend (money) *9*

die **Auskunft,-e** information *11*

der **Ausländer,-** foreigner *4*

ausprobieren to try out, test *10*

aussteigen to get off *11*

die **Auswahl** selection, choice *2; eine Auswahl an* a selection in *3*

das **Auto,-s** car *5*

der **Automat,-en** automat, (vending) machine *11*

B

die **Badewanne,-n** bathtub *8*

das **Badezimmer,-** bathroom *8*

der **Bahnhof,-e** train station *3*

bald soon *5*

der **Ball,-e** ball *10*

die **Band,-s** band *9*

der **Basketball,-e** basketball *3*

basteln to do crafts *10*

Bayern Bavaria *4*

bedeuten to mean; *es bedeutet mir viel* it means a lot to me *9*

bedienen to wait on *7*

beginnen to begin *3*

begrüßen to greet *8*

bei at, near, with; *bei uns bleiben* to stay with us *3*

beibringen to teach; *hat mir als Kind...beigebracht* taught me as a child *9*

beide both *3*

beige beige *7*

das **Bein,-e** leg *10*

das **Beispiel,-e** example; *wie zum Beispiel* as for example *10*

bekannt well known *3*

bekommen to get, receive *4*

Belgien Belgium *5*

beliebt popular *8*

der **Berg,-e** mountain *8*

besonders especially *5; etwas Besonderes* something special *8*

besser better *7*

bestimmt definitely, for sure, certain(ly) *8*

der **Besuch,-e** visit *11*

besuchen to visit *5*

der **Besucher,-** visitor *12*

das **Bett,-en** bed *8*

bevor before *8*

die **Bewegung,-en** movement *12*

bezahlen to pay *5*

das **Bild,-er** picture *8*

billig cheap *7*

die **Biologie** biology *4*

bis until; *Bis später!* See you later! *2*

bitte please *5; Bitte schön?* May I help you? *6*

blau blue 7

bleiben to stay 3

der **Bleistift,-e** pencil 4

die **Blockflöte,-n** recorder 12

die **Bluse,-n** blouse 7

das **Boot,-e** boat 11

die **Boutique,-n** boutique 7

die **Bratwurst,-̈e** bratwurst 6

brauchen to need 4

braun brown 7

der **Brief,-e** letter 6

die **Briefmarke,-n** stamp 9

bringen to bring 6

das **Brot,-e** bread 6

das **Brötchen,-** hard roll 6

der **Bruder,-̈** brother 2

das **Buch,-̈er** book 3

das **Bücherregal,-e** bookshelf 8

das **Bundesland,-̈er** federal state (Germany) 4

die **Bundesliga** Federal League; *1. Bundesliga* top Federal League 10

bunt colorful 7

das **Büro,-s** office 12

der **Bus,-se** bus 4

die **Butter** butter 6

C

die **Campingreise,-n** camping trip 7

die **CD,-s** CD 2

das **Cello,-s** cello 9

charmant charming 3

die **Chemie** chemistry 4

die **Cola,-s** cola 6

der **Computer,-** computer 3

das **Computerspiel,-e** computer game 3

der **Cousin,-s** cousin (male) 2

die **Cousine,-n** cousin (female) 2

D

da there; *da drüben* over there 1

Dänemark Denmark 5

Danke! Thank you! 5; *Danke schön.* Thank you very much. 6

dann then 3

das that 1; the 2

dass that 8

dauern to take, last 3

decken to cover; *den Tisch decken* to set the table 9

dein your (familiar singular) 1

denn (used for emphasis) 2

der the 2

deshalb therefore, that's why 5

deutsch German; *Er spricht deutsch.* He speaks German. 5

Deutsch German (subject) 3

der **Deutsche,-n** German 10

Deutschland Germany 2

der **Dezember** December 5

die the 2

der **Dienstag,-e** Tuesday 2

dies- this 2

dir: von dir about you 3

direkt direct(ly) 10

die **Disko,-s** disco 3

doch (used for emphasis) *Komm doch mit!* Why don't you come along! 3

der **Donnerstag,-e** Thursday 2

dort there 3

dorthin (to) there 7

dran sein to be one's turn; *Sie ist dran.* It's her turn. 12

draußen outside 6

drei three 1

dreimal three times 9

dreißig thirty 2

dreizehn thirteen 1

drinnen inside 7

dritt- third 8

du you (familiar singular) 1; *Du, ich komme mit.* Hey, I'll come along. 8

dunkel dark 4

durch through 8

dürfen may, to be permitted to 6

der **Durst** thirst; *Durst haben* to be thirsty 6

die **Dusche,-n** shower 8

E

die **E-Mail,-s** e-mail; *eine E-Mail schicken* to send an e-mail 6

echt real(ly) 2

die **Ecke,-n** corner 1

ein(e) a, an 1

einkaufen to shop; *einkaufen gehen* to go shopping 9

einladen to invite 8

einmal once 12

eins one 1

einsteigen to get in, board 11

der ***Einwohner,-** inhabitant 4

das **Eis** ice cream 6

das **Eiscafé,-s** ice cream parlor, café 6

das **Eishockey** ice hockey 10

die **Eisschokolade** chocolate sundae 6

der **Eistee** iced tea 6

elf eleven 1

der **Elfmeter,-** penalty kick 10

die **Eltern** (pl.) parents 2

das **Ende** end; *zu Ende sein* to be over 10

endlich finally 8

eng tight 7

England England 9

englisch English; *Er spricht englisch.* He speaks English. 5

das **Englisch** English (subject) 4

entfernt away 12

die ***Entfernung,-en** distance 4

entschuldigen: Entschuldigen Sie! Excuse me! 11

er he 1

das **Erdbeereis** strawberry ice cream 6

der **Erdbeershake,-s** strawberry shake 6

die **Erdkunde** geography 4

erst- first 4

erzählen to tell 11

es it 1

essen to eat 6

etwas some, something, a little 3

euer your (familiar plural) 8

der **Euro,-s** euro 5

Europa Europe 9

F

das **Fach,-̈er** (school) subject *4*

die **Fahne,-n** flag *10*

fahren to drive, go, ride *5*

die **Fahrkarte,-n** ticket *11*

der **Fahrplan,-̈e** schedule *5*

das **Fahrrad,-̈er** bicycle *5*

die **Familie,-n** family *2*

der **Fan,-s** fan *9*

die **Farbe,-n** color; *Welche Farbe hat...?* What color is...? *7*

fast almost *4*

der **Februar** February *5*

die **Ferien** (pl.) vacation; *in den Ferien* on vacation; *in die Ferien fahren* to go on vacation *5*

fernsehen to watch television; *im Fernsehen* on television *3*

der **Fernseher,-** TV, television set *8*

das **Fernsehprogramm,-e** television program *3*

der **Film,-e** film, movie *3*

finden to find; *Ich finde es langweilig.* I think it's boring. *4*

der **Finger,-** finger *10*

Finnland Finland *9*

der **Fisch,-e** fish *6*

*_**flach** flat *8*

fliegen to fly *11*

*_**fließen** to flow *8*

die **Flöte,-n** flute *12*

das **Flugzeug,-e** airplane *11*

der *_**Fluss,-̈e** river *8*

der **Fortgeschrittene,-n** advanced (student) *12*

das **Foto,-s** photo *12*

das **Fotoalbum,-alben** photo album *12*

fotografieren to take pictures *9*

foulen to foul *10*

fragen to ask *11*

Frankreich France *5*

französisch French; *Er spricht französisch.* He speaks French. *5*

das **Französisch** French *4*

die **Frau,-en** Mrs., woman *1*

der **Freitag,-e** Friday *2*

fremd foreign; *Ich bin fremd hier.* I'm a stranger here. *11*

der **Freund,-e** boyfriend *1*

die **Freundin,-nen** girlfriend *1*

froh glad, happy *4*

früh early *4*

der **Frühling,-e** spring *5*

das **Frühstück** breakfast *4*

fünf five *1*

fünfzehn fifteen *1*

fünfzig fifty *2*

funktionieren to function, work *8*

für for *3*; *für dich* for you *1*

der **Fuß,-̈e** foot *10*; *zu Fuß gehen* to walk *11*

der **Fußball,-̈e** soccer, soccer ball *3*

die **Fußballmannschaft,-en** soccer team *9*

der **Fußballplatz,-̈e** soccer field *10*

G

ganz quite, *ganz gut* quite well, pretty good *1*; *noch nicht ganz* not quite yet *4*

der **Garten,-̈e** garden *8*

geben to give; *es gibt* there is (are) *7*; *Was gibt's im Fernsehen?* What is there on TV? *3*; *sich die Hand geben* to shake hands *10*

der **Geburtstag,-e** birthday *8*

das **Gedicht,-e** poem *9*

gefallen to like; *Wie gefällt dir...?* How do you like...? *3*

gegen about, around; *so gegen sieben* around seven (o'clock) *2*; against *8*

die **Gegend,-en** area *11*

gehen to go; *Wie geht's?, Wie geht es Ihnen?* How are you? *1*; *Das geht nicht.* That's not possible. *3*; *Gehen wir!* Let's go! *9*; *Es geht mir schon besser.* I'm feeling better already. *10*

die **Geige,-n** violin *12*

gelb yellow *7*

das **Geld** money *5*

das **Gemüse** vegetable(s) *6*

genau exact(ly) *8*

das **Genie,-s** genius *8*

genug enough *4*

das **Gepäck** luggage, baggage *11*

geradeaus straight ahead *11*

gern gladly, with pleasure; *gern spielen* like to play *3*; *gern haben* to like; *Das hast du ja sehr gern.* You like it very well. *4*

das **Geschäft,-e** store, shop *7*

das **Geschenk,-e** present, gift *8*

die **Geschichte** history *4*

die **Geschichte,-n** story *9*

das **Geschirr** dishes *9*

der **Geschirrspüler,-** dishwasher *8*

gewinnen to win *10*

die **Gitarre,-n** guitar *3*

das **Glas,-̈er** glass *6*

glauben to believe *7*; *Ich glaube schon.* I believe so. *8*

gleich immediately, right away; *gleich um die Ecke* right around the corner *1*

das **Gleis,-e** track *11*

das **Golf** golf *10*

grau gray *7*

die *_**Grenze,-n** border; *an der Grenze zu* at the border with *12*

groß large, big *2*; *größt-* biggest *4*

die **Größe,-n** size *7*

die **Großeltern** (pl.) grandparents *2*

die **Großmutter,-̈** grandmother *2*

der **Großvater,-̈** grandfather *2*

grün green *7*

Grüß dich! Hi! Hello! *1*

gut good, *ganz gut* quite well *1*

H

das **Haar,-e** hair *10*

haben to have *3*

halb half; *um halb fünf* at 4:30 *2*

die **Halbzeit,-en** halftime *10*

Hallo! Hi! Hello! *1*

der **Hals,-̈e** neck *10*

der **Hamburger,-** hamburger *6*

die **Hand,-̈e** hand; *sich die Hand geben* to shake hands *10*

der **Handschuh,-e** glove *7*

das **Handy,-s** cell phone *9*

die *Hauptstadt,-̈e capital (city) 4

das Haus,-̈er house 4; *zu Hause* at home 2; *nach Hause gehen* to go home 3

die Hausaufgabe,-n homework; *Hausaufgaben machen* to do homework 3

das Heft,-e notebook 4

heiß hot 5

heißen to be called; *Wie heißt du?, Wie heißen Sie?* What's your name? 1

helfen to help 3

hell light 7

der Helm,-e helmet 5

das Hemd,-en shirt 7

der Herbst,-e fall, autumn 4

der Herd,-e stove, 8

herkommen to come here; *Komm her!* Come here! 4

der Herr,-en Mr., gentleman 1

herzlich sincere, cordial; *Herzlichen Glückwunsch zum Geburtstag!* Happy birthday! 8

heute today 2

hier here 1

der Hit,-s hit (song) 3

das Hobby,-s hobby 9

*höchst- highest 8

hoffen to hope 8

holen to get, fetch 3

Holland Holland 5

hören to hear, listen to 2

der Horrorfilm,-e horror film 9

die Hose,-n pants, slacks 7

hundert hundred 2

der Hunger hunger; *Hunger haben* to be hungry 6

I

ich I 1

die Idee,-n idea 3

ihr you (familiar plural) 1; her 2; their, your 8

Ihr your (formal singular and plural) 8

der Imbiss,-e snack bar (stand) 6

der Imbissstand,-̈e snack stand 10

immer always 3

in in; *im Norden* in the north 2

die Informatik computer science 4B

die Informatikaufgabe,-n computer science assignment 4

die Insel,-n island; *Insel Rügen* name of island in the *Ostsee* (Baltic Sea) 6

interessant interesting 1

sich interessieren für to be interested in 9

das Internet Internet 9

Italien Italy 5

italienisch Italian; *Er spricht italienisch.* He speaks Italian. 5

J

ja yes 1; *Da ist er ja schon.* There he is. 5

die Jacke,-n jacket 7

das Jahr,-e year; *vor drei Jahren* three years ago 11

die Jahreszeit,-en season 5

der Januar January 5

die Jeans (pl.) jeans 7

jed- every, each 4

jetzt now 3

jubeln to cheer 10

der Jugendliche,-n teenager, young person 7

der Juli July 5

der Junge,-n boy 1

der Juni June 5

K

der Kaffee coffee 6

der Kakao hot chocolate, cocoa 6

kalt cold 5

die Kalte Platte cold-cut platter 6

die Kamera,-s camera 8

kaputt broken 5

die Karte,-n ticket, card 3

die Kartoffel,-n potato 6

der Käse cheese 6

das Käsebrot,-e cheese sandwich 6

die Kasse,-n cash register 5; ticket counter 10

kaufen to buy 4

das Kaufhaus,-̈er department store 2

kein(e) no 3

der Kellner,- waiter, food server 6

kennen to know (person, place) 1

das Keyboard,-s keyboard 12

der *Kilometer,- kilometer 4

das Kind,-er child 9

das Kinn,-e chin 10

das Kino,-s movie theater 9

klar clear; *na klar* of course 7

die Klarinette,-n clarinet 9

Klasse! Great! Terrific! 5

die Klasse,-n class 4

das Klavier,-e piano 3

das Kleid,-er dress 7

die Kleidung clothes, clothing 8

das Kleidungsstück,-e clothing item 7

klein little, small 11

klingeln to ring (bell); *Es klingelt.* The bell is ringing. 4

klug smart, intelligent 4

der Koffer,- suitcase 11

der Kofferkuli,-s luggage cart 11

kommen to come 1

die Komödie,-n comedy 9

können can, to be able to 6

das Konzert,-e concert 9

koordinieren to coordinate 12

der Kopf,-̈e head 5

köpfen to head (ball) 10

der Körperteil,-e part of the body 10

die Kosmetik cosmetics 9

kosten to cost 6

das Krafttraining strength training; *Krafttraining machen* to do strength training 9

die Krawatte,-n tie 7

die Kreide chalk 4

das *Kreuz,-e cross 12

der Krimi,-s detective story, thriller 3

die Küche,-n kitchen 8

der Kuchen,- cake 8

kühl cool 5

der Kuli,-s (ballpoint) pen 4

der Kühlschrank,-̈e refrigerator 8

kurz short 7

L

    lächeln to smile *8*

die **Lampe,-n** lamp *8*

das **Land,-̈er** country *5*

die **Landkarte,-n** map *4*

    lang(e) long time *4;* long *7;* *längst-* longest *8*

    langsam slow *4*

    langweilig boring *4*

das **Latein** Latin *4*

    laufen to run; *Ski laufen* to ski *9*

    lecker delicious *6*

der **Leckerbissen** (pl.) treat *6*

der **Lehrer,-** teacher (male) *4*

die **Lehrerin,-nen** teacher (female) *4*

die **Leibesübung,-en** physical exercise *12*

    leicht easy *4*

    Leid tun to be sorry; *Es tut mir Leid.* I'm sorry. *10*

    leider unfortunately *6*

    lernen to learn *4*

    lesen to read *3*

    letzt- last *10*

die **Leute** (pl.) people *10*

    lieber rather; *Ich möchte lieber...essen.* I would rather eat... *6*

der **Liebesfilm,-e** love story *9*

das **Lieblingseis** favorite ice cream *6*

das **Lieblingsfach,-̈er** favorite (school) subject *4*

die **Lieblingsmannschaft,-en** favorite team *10*

    *Liechtenstein Liechtenstein *12*

das **Lied,-er** song *9*

    *liegen to be located, lie *4*

das **Lineal,-e** ruler *4*

die **Linie,-n** line *5*

    links left; *auf der linken Seite* on the left side *11*

die **Lippe,-n** lip *10*

    los: Da ist viel los. There is a lot going on. *7; Also los!* Let's go! *8*

    losgehen to start; *Wann geht's denn los?* When will it start? *7*

die **Luft** air *10*

    Luxemburg Luxembourg *5*

M

    machen to do, make; *Was machst du?* What are you doing? *2; Macht schnell!* Hurry! *9; Musik machen* to make music *12*

das **Mädchen,-** girl *1*

    mähen to mow *9*

der **Mai** May *5*

    *mal times *4*

das **Mal,-e** time(s); *ein paar Mal* a few times *8*

    man one, you, they, people *9*

    manche some, a few *10*

    manchmal sometimes *4*

der **Mann,-̈er** man *9*

die **Mannschaft,-en** team *10*

der **Mantel,-̈** coat *7*

der **Markt,-̈e** market *9*

die **Marmelade,-n** jam, marmalade *6*

der **März** March *5*

die **Mathematik (Mathe)** mathematics (math); *die Mathestunde/Matheklasse* math class *4*

    mehr more; *es gibt keine Karten mehr* there are no more tickets available *3; mehr als* more than *4*

    mein my *1*

    meinen to mean, think; *Meinst du?* Do you think so? *4*

    meist- most; *die meisten* most of them; *meistens* mostly *10*

der **Mikrowellenherd,-e** microwave oven *8*

die **Milch** milk *6*

die ***Million,-en** million *4*

    minus minus *1*

die **Minute,-n** minute *1*

    mir: mit mir with me *3*

    mit with *2*

    mitbringen to bring along *9*

das **Mitglied,-er** member *9*

    mitkommen to come along; *Komm mit!* Come along! *2*

    mitmachen to participate *9*

    mitnehmen to take along *11*

der **Mittag,-e** noon; *heute Mittag* today at noon *3*

das **Mittagessen** lunch *6*

die ***Mitte** center, middle *8*

der **Mittwoch,-e** Wednesday *2*

    möchten would like to *3*

    modern modern *12*

    mögen to like *6*

der **Moment,-e** moment; *Moment mal!* Just a moment! *3*

der **Monat,-e** month *5*

der **Montag,-e** Monday *2*

das **Moped,-s** moped *8*

    morgen tomorrow *2*

der **Morgen,-** morning; *heute Morgen* this morning *3*

der **Motor,-en** motor, engine *8*

das **Motorrad,-̈er** motorcycle *11*

der **Motorroller,-** motor scooter *8*

der **Mund,-̈er** mouth *10*

die **Münze,-n** coin *9*

das **Museum, Museen** museum *11*

die **Musik** music *2*

    musikalisch musical *12*

das ***Musikfest,-e** music festival *8*

das **Musikgeschäft,-e** music store *7*

das **Musikinstrument,-e** musical instrument *12*

    müssen to have to, must *6*

die **Mutter,-̈** mother *2*

die **Mutti,-s** mom *2*

N

    na well; *na gut, na ja* oh well *2; na und* so what *3; na klar* of course *7*

    nach after, to; *nach Hause gehen* to go home *3*

das **Nachbarland,-̈er** neighboring country *5*

der **Nachmittag,-e** afternoon; *heute Nachmittag* this afternoon *3*

die **Nachricht,-en** news *3*

    nachsehen to check *11*

    nächst- next *8*

die **Nähe** nearness, proximity; *in der Nähe* nearby *11*

der **Name,-n** name *9*

die **Nase,-n** nose 10

die ***Nationalfahne,-n** national flag 8

der **Nationalsport** national sport 10

natürlich natural(ly), of course 8

die **Naturwissenschaften** (pl.) natural sciences 4

neben next to 11

nehmen to take 7

nein no 1

nervös nervous 4

nett nice 1

neu new 1

neun nine 1

neunzehn nineteen 1

neunzig ninety 2

nicht not 1

nichts nothing 6

nie never 4

die **Niederlande** Netherlands 5

noch still, yet; *noch nicht ganz* not quite yet 4

der **Norden** north; *im Norden* in the north 2

die ***Nordsee** North Sea 12

die **Note,-n** grade 4

der **November** November 5

null zero 1

die **Nummer,-n** number 10

nur only 1; *nicht nur... sondern auch* not only... but also 10

das **Nusseis** nut-flavored ice cream 6

O

ob if, whether 7

oft often 6

ohne without 4

das **Ohr,-en** ear 10

der **Ohrring,-e** earring 8

der **Oktober** October 5

die **Oma,-s** grandma 2

der **Onkel,-** uncle 2

der **Opa,-s** grandpa 2

orange orange 7

der ***Osten** east 4

Österreich Austria 5

P

paar: ein paar a few 5

das **Paar,-e** pair 7

das **Papier** paper 4

das ***Paradies** paradise 12

die **Party,-s** party 8

passen to fit 7

passieren to happen 10

die **Pause,-n** recess, break; *Große Pause* long recess 4

die **Physik** physics 4

die **Pizza,-s** pizza 6

die **Pizzeria,-s** pizza restaurant 6

planen to plan 11

die **Platte,-n** plate; *Kalte Platte* cold-cut platter 6

der **Platz,¨e** place, seat 8

plötzlich suddenly 10

plus plus 1

Polen Poland 5

die **Pommes frites** (pl.) french fries; *die Pommes* colloquial for "french fries" 6

die **Post** post office 11

das **Poster,-** poster 9

die **Postkarte,-n** postcard 11

praktisch practical 7

der **Preis,-e** price 5

preiswert reasonable 5

das **Problem,-e** problem 3

der **Pulli,-s** sweater, pullover 7

der **Pullover,-** sweater, pullover 7

Q

die **Qualität,-en** quality 7

die **Quittung,-en** receipt 7

R

das **Rad,¨er** bike 5; wheel 8; *Rad fahren* to bike 10

der **Radiergummi,-s** eraser 4

das **Radio,-s** radio 8

der **Radiowecker,-** clock radio 8

die **Radtour,-en** bike tour; *eine Radtour machen* to go on a bike tour 5

der **Rasen,-** lawn; *den Rasen mähen* to mow the lawn 9

der **Rechner,-** calculator 4

das **Recht** right; *Recht haben* to be right 4

rechts right 11

reduziert reduced 7

regnen to rain 5

der **Reifen,-** tire 5

die **Reise,-n** trip 5

reisen to travel; *Reisen* traveling 9

die **Religion,-en** religion 4

reparieren to repair 9

der **Rhein** Rhine River 5

der **Rhythmus** rhythm 12

richtig right, correct 7

der **Rock,¨e** skirt 7

die **Rockgruppe,-n** rock group 2

das **Rockkonzert,-e** rock concert 3

die **Rockmusik** rock music 9

rosa pink 7

rot red 7

rüberkommen to come over 2

die **Ruhe** peace, quiet; *Immer mit der Ruhe!* Take it easy! 5

S

die **Sache,-n** thing, item 5

sagen to say, tell 3

der **Salat,-e** salad 6

sammeln to collect 9

der **Samstag,-e** Saturday 2

der **Sänger,-** singer (male) 9

die **Sängerin,-nen** singer (female) 9

der **Sauerbraten** sauerbraten (marinated beef roast) 6

das **Saxophon,-e** saxophone 12

das **Schach** chess 9

schaffen to manage (it), make (it); *Das haben wir geschafft.* We made it. 11

der **Schalter,-** (ticket) counter 11

die **Scheibe,-n** slice; *eine Scheibe Brot* a slice of bread 6

scheinen to shine 5

schenken to give (a gift) 10

schick chic, smart (looking) 7

schicken to send 6

schießen to shoot 10

das **Schiff,-e** ship 11

das **Schlafzimmer,-** bedroom 8

die **Schlagsahne** whipped cream 6

das **Schlagzeug** drums, percussion 9

der **Schlauberger** smartie 3
schlecht bad 1
Schlittschuh laufen to ice skate 10
der **Schluchsee** name of lake (located in the Black Forest) 7
schmecken to taste; *Schmeckt dir...?* Do you like (to eat)...? 6
der **Schmuck** jewelry 8
schneien to snow 5
schnell fast 3
das **Schokoeis** chocolate ice cream 6
die **Schokolade** chocolate 6
der **Schokoshake,-s** chocolate shake 6
schon already 2
schön beautiful 5
der **Schrank,¨e** cupboard, closet 8
schreiben to write; *schreiben an* to write to 6
der **Schreibtisch,-e** desk 8
schreien to scream, yell 10
der **Schuh,-e** shoe 7
die **Schule,-n** school 3
der **Schüler,-** student (elementary through high school) 12
der **Schulfreund,-e** schoolmate 4
die **Schultasche,-n** schoolbag 4
die **Schulter,-n** shoulder 10
schwarz black 7
der **Schwarzwald** Black Forest 7
die **Schwarzwälder Kirschtorte** Black Forest Cherry Torte 8
die **Schweiz** Switzerland 5
schwenken to swing 10
schwer hard, difficult 4
die **Schwester,-n** sister 2
schwimmen to swim 3
sechs six 1
sechzehn sixteen 1
sechzig sixty 2
der **See,-n** lake 11
sehen to see; *ein Fernsehprogramm sehen* to watch a television program 3; *Sieh mal!* Just look! 7
sehr very 1

sein to be 1
sein his 7, its 8
seit since 10
die **Seite,-n** side 11
der **September** September 5
der **Sessel,-** armchair 8
das **Shirt,-s** shirt 7
sie she, they 1
Sie you (formal) 1
sieben seven 1
siebzehn seventeen 1
siebzig seventy 2
singen to sing 9
sitzen to sit 6; *sitzen auf* to sit on 8
der **Ski,-er** ski 10; *Ski laufen* to ski 9
so so; *so spät* so late 2
****so...wie** as...as 12
die **Socke,-n** sock 7
das **Sofa,-s** sofa 8
der **Sohn,¨e** son 2
sollen should, to be supposed to 6
der **Sommer,-** summer 3
die **Sommerferien** (pl.) summer vacation 7
das **Sonderangebot,-e** special (sale) 7
sondern but; *nicht nur... sondern auch* not only... but also 10
der **Sonnabend,-e** Saturday 2
die **Sonne** sun 5
der **Sonntag,-e** Sunday 2
sonst besides, otherwise; *Sonst noch etwas?* Anything else? 5
das **Spaghetti Eis** strawberry sundae 6
Spanien Spain 5
spanisch Spanish; *Er spricht spanisch.* He speaks Spanish. 5
der **Spaß** fun; *Viel Spaß!* Have fun! 3; *Es macht Spaß.* It's fun. 12
spät late; *Bis später!* See you later! 2
die **Spätzle** spaetzle (kind of homemade pasta) 6
der **Spiegel,-** mirror 12
das **Spiel,-e** game 10
spielen to play 3
der **Spieler,-** player 10

der **Sport** sport(s) 4; *Sport treiben* to participate in sports 10
die **Sportart,-en** kind of sport 10
die **Sportschau** sports show (news) 3
die ****Sprache,-n** language 12
sprechen to speak, talk; *er/sie spricht* he/she speaks 5; *sprechen über* to talk about 6; *über sich selbst sprechen* to speak about oneself 9
das **Spülbecken,-** kitchen sink 8
spülen to wash, rinse 9
der ****Staat,-en** state 4
stabil solid, sturdy 5
das **Stadion,-dien** stadium 10
die **Stadt,¨e** city; *in die Stadt gehen* to go downtown 2
die **Stadthalle,-n** city hall 12
die **Stadtmitte** center of city, downtown 11
der **Star,-s** star (entertainment) 9
stark strong; *stark reduziert* greatly reduced 7
die **Statistik,-en** statistics 10
staubsaugen to vacuum 9
staunen to be astonished, surprised 8
stehen to stand, be; *Da steht es.* There it is. 5; *Das steht dir gut.* It looks good on you. 7; *es steht...* the score is... 10; *frei stehen* to be open 10
steif stiff 12
die **Stereoanlage,-n** stereo system 8
der **Stiefbruder,¨** stepbrother 2
stimmen to be correct; *Das stimmt.* That's right. 4
die **Stirn,-en** forehead 10
stören to disturb 12
die **Straßenbahn,-en** streetcar 11
der **Strumpf,¨e** stocking 7
das **Studio,-s** studio 12
der **Stuhl,¨e** chair 4
die **Stunde,-n** hour 3
der **Stundenplan,¨e** class schedule 4
der ****Süden** south 4

super super, great *2*

das **Sweatshirt,-s** sweatshirt *7*

T

das **T-Shirt,-s** T-shirt *7*

die **Tafel,-n** (chalk) board *4*

der **Tafellappen,-** rag (to wipe off [chalk] board) *4*

der **Tag,-e** day; *Tag!* Hello! *Guten Tag!* Hello! *1*

der **Takt,-e** beat *12*

die **Tanzstunde,-n** dance lesson *12*

die **Tante,-n** aunt *2*

der **Tanz,-̈e** dance *12*

tanzen to dance *3*

das **Tanzstudio,-s** dance studio *12*

die **Tasse,-n** cup *6*

tausend thousand *2*

der ***Teil,-e** part, section; *zum größten Teil* for the most part *8*

das **Telefon,-e** telephone *2*

das **Tempo** tempo, speed *10*

das **Tennis** tennis *3*

der **Tennisschläger,-** tennis racquet *10*

teuer expensive *5*

der **Text,-e** text *9*

der **Tisch,-e** table *4*

das **Tischtennis** table tennis *10*

die **Tochter,-̈** daughter *2*

die **Toilette,-n** toilet *8*

toll great, terrific *2*

das **Tor,-e** goal *10*

der **Torwart,-̈er** goalkeeper *10*

der ***Tourist,-en** tourist *12*

tragen to wear *7*

das **Training** training *9*

sich **treffen** to meet *4*; *Treffen wir uns!* Let's meet! *9*

treiben to do; *Sport treiben* to participate in sports *10*

trinken to drink *6*

die **Trompete,-n** trumpet *12*

Tschau! See you! Bye! *1*

die **Tschechische Republik** Czech Republic *5*

Tschüs! See you! Bye! *1*

die **Tür,-en** door *12*

der **Türke,-n** Turk (male) *9*

die **Türkei** Turkey *6*

U

die **U-Bahn,-en** subway *11*

üben to practice *10*

die **Übung,-en** exercise, practice; *Übung macht den Meister!* Practice makes perfect. *12*

die **Uhr,-en** clock, watch; *Um wie viel Uhr?* At what time?; *Es ist zwei Uhr.* It's two o'clock. *2*

um around, at; *um die Ecke* around the corner *1*; *Um wie viel Uhr?* At what time? *2*

umsteigen to transfer *11*

und and *1*

***ungefähr** approximately *4*

unser our *5*

V

das **Vanilleeis** vanilla ice cream *6*

der **Vater,-̈** father *2*

der **Vati,-s** dad *2*

die ***Vereinigten Staaten von Amerika** United States of America *4*

das **Vergnügen** pleasure; *Zuerst kommt die Arbeit und dann das Vergnügen.* Business before pleasure. *9*

verkaufen to sell *5*

der **Verkäufer,-** salesperson (male) *5*

die **Verkäuferin,-nen** salesperson (female) *7*

das **Verkehrsmittel,-** means of transportation *11*

verlassen to leave *10*

verschieden different *10*

versuchen to try, attempt *10*

das **Video,-s** video *3*

Videothek name of video rental store *3*

viel much *1*

vielleicht perhaps *2*

vier four *1*

das **Viertel,-** quarter *3*

vierzehn fourteen *1*

vierzig forty *2*

der **Volleyball** volleyball *10*

von from *1*

vor before, in front of *3*

vorbeigehen to go past *11*

das **Vorbild,-er** model *9*

vorhaben to plan, intend (to do) *9*

vorschlagen to suggest *9*

W

die **Wahl** choice; *Wer die Wahl hat, hat die Qual!* The more choices, the more problems. *7*

während during *8*; while *12*

wandern to hike *10*

wann when *3*

warm warm *5*

warten to wait *4*

warum why *3*

was what *2*; *Was für ein...?* What kind of a...? *3*

das **Waschbecken,-** bathroom sink *8*

der **Wecker,-** alarm clock *8*

wehtun to hurt; *Tut es dir weh?* Does it hurt you? *10*

weiß white *7*

weise wise; *ein weiser Mann* a wise man *9*

weit far *1*

weiterspielen to continue playing *10*

welch- which *2*

die **Welt,-en** world; *auf der ganzen Welt* in the whole world *9*

wem (to) whom *10*

wen whom *4*

wer who *1*

werden will, shall *6*; to become, be; *Er wird sechzehn.* He'll be sixteen. *8*

der ***Westen** west *4*

das **Wetter** weather *5*

wichtig important *8*

wie how, what; *Wie heißt du?, Wie heißen Sie?* What's your name? *Wie geht's?, Wie geht es Ihnen?* How are you?; *wie viel* how much *1*; *wie viele* how many *4*; *so groß wie* as big as *4*

German-English Vocabulary

wieder again 7

Wiedersehen! Bye! *Auf Wiedersehen!* Good-bye! 1

das **Wiener Schnitzel** breaded veal cutlet 6

der **Winter,-** winter 5

wir we 1

wirklich really 1

wissen to know 7

der **Witz,-e** joke 8

wo where 1

die **Woche,-n** week 3

das **Wochenende,-n** weekend 9

woher where from 1

wohin where (to) 2

wohnen to live 1

die **Wohnung,-en** apartment 8

das **Wohnzimmer,-** living room 8

wollen to want to 6

die **Wolljacke,-n** cardigan 7

wünschen to wish 8; *sich wünschen* to want (for birthday) 10

die **Wurst,-̈e** sausage 6

das **Wurstbrot,-e** sausage sandwich 6

Z

der **Zahn,-̈e** tooth 10

zehn ten 1

zeigen to show 8

die **Zeit,-en** time 2

die **Zeitung,-en** newspaper 9

das **Zimmer,-** room 9

das **Zitroneneis** lemon ice cream 6

zu at, to; *zu Hause* at home; *zum Kaufhaus gehen* to go to the department store 2; too 3

zuerst first 3

der **Zug,-̈e** train 11

zusammen together 3

der **Zuschauer,-** spectator 10

zwanzig twenty 1

zwei two 1

die **Zwillingsschwester,-n** twin sister 9

zwölf twelve 1

English-German Vocabulary

A

a ein(e) *1*
about gegen *2*
after nach *3*
  afternoon der Nachmittag,-e; *this afternoon* heute Nachmittag *3*
again wieder *7*
against gegen *8*
air die Luft *10*
  airplane das Flugzeug,-e *11*
alarm clock der Wecker,- *8*
all alle *5; That's all.* Das ist alles. *5*
almost fast *4*
already schon *2*
also auch *2*
always immer *3*
America Amerika *5*
an ein(e) *1*
and und *1*
answer die Antwort,-en *8*
apartment die Wohnung,-en *8*
appetite der Appetit *6*
apple juice der Apfelsaft *6*
approximately ungefähr *4*
April der April *5*
area die Gegend,-en *11*
arm der Arm,-e *10*
armchair der Sessel,- *8*
around um *1; around the corner* um die Ecke *1; around seven (o'clock)* so gegen sieben *2*
arrival die Ankunft,⸚e *11*
to **arrive** ankommen *11*
as...as so...wie *12*
to **ask** fragen *11*
to **astonished: be astonished** staunen *8*
at an, bei, um, zu *2; At what time?* Um wie viel Uhr? *at 4:30* um halb fünf *2*
attempt versuchen *10*
August der August *5*
aunt die Tante,-n *2*

Austria Österreich *5*
automat der Automat,-en *11*
autumn Herbst,-e *4*
away entfernt *12*

B

bad schlecht *1*
baggage das Gepäck *11*
ball der Ball,⸚e *10*
band die Band,-s *9*
basketball der Basketball,⸚e *3*
bathroom das Badezimmer,- *8; bathroom sink* das Waschbecken,- *8*
bathtub die Badewanne,-n *8*
Bavaria Bayern *4*
to **be** sein *1; to be located* liegen *3; to be correct* stimmen *4; to be permitted to* dürfen *6; to be able to* können *6; He'll be sixteen.* Er wird sechzehn. *8; to be interested in* sich interessieren für *9; There it is.* Da steht es. *5; to be open (in a game)* frei stehen *10; to be sorry* Leid tun *10; to be over* zu Ende sein *10*
beat der Takt,-e *12*
beautiful schön *5*
bed das Bett,-en *8*
bedroom das Schlafzimmer,- *8*
before vor *3;* bevor *8*
to **begin** beginnen *3;* anfangen *9*
beginner der Anfänger,- *12*
beige beige *7*
Belgium Belgien *5*
to **believe** glauben *7; I believe so.* Ich glaube schon. *8*
besides
besides sonst *5;* außerdem *9;* außer *10*
better besser *7*
bicycle das Fahrrad,⸚er *5*
big groß *2; biggest* größt- *4*

bike das Rad,⸚er *5; bike tour* die Radtour,-en *5; to go on a bike tour* eine to Radtour machen *5*
to **bike** Rad fahren *10*
biology die Biologie *4*
birthday der Geburtstag,-e *8; Happy birthday!* Herzlichen Glückwunsch zum Geburtstag! *8*
black schwarz *7*
Black Forest der Schwarzwald *7; Black Forest Cherry Torte* die Schwarzwälder Kirschtorte *8*
blouse die Bluse,-n *7*
blue blau *7*
board: (chalk) board die Tafel,-n *4*
to **board** einsteigen *11*
boat das Boot,-e *11*
body: part of the body der Körperteil,-e *10*
book das Buch,⸚er *3*
bookshelf das Bücherregal,-e *8*
border die Grenze,-n; *at the border with* an der Grenze zu *12*
boring langweilig *4*
both beide *3*
boutique die Boutique,-n *7*
boy der Junge,-n *1*
boyfriend der Freund,-e *1*
bratwurst die Bratwurst,⸚e *6*
bread das Brot,-e *6*
breaded veal cutlet das Wiener Schnitzel *6*
break Pause,-n *4; long recess* Große Pause *4*
breakfast das Frühstück *4*
to **bring** bringen *6; to bring along* mitbringen *9*
broken kaputt *5*
brother der Bruder,⸚ *2*
brown braun *7*
bus der Bus,-se *4*

but aber *3;* sondern *10; not only...but also* nicht nur... sondern auch *10*
butter die Butter *6*
to **buy** kaufen *4*
Bye! Tschau!, Tschüs!, Wiedersehen! *Good-bye! Auf Wiedersehen! 1*

C

café Eiscafé,-s, *6*
cake der Kuchen,- *8*
calculator der Rechner,- *4*
to **call** *(on the phone)* anrufen *8*
camera die Kamera,-s *8*
camping trip die Campingreise,-n *7*
can können *6*
capital (city) die Hauptstadt,¨e *4*
car das Auto,-s *5*
card die Karte,-n *3*
cardigan die Wolljacke,-n *7*
cash register die Kasse,-n *5*
CD die CD,-s *2*
cell phone das Handy,-s *9*
cello das Cello,-s *9*
center die Mitte *8; center of city* die Stadtmitte *11*
certain(ly) bestimmt *8*
chair der Stuhl,¨e *4*
chalk die Kreide *4*
charming charmant *3*
cheap billig *7*
to **check** nachsehen *11*
to **cheer** jubeln *10*
cheese der Käse *6; cheese sandwich* das Käsebrot,-e *6*
chemistry die Chemie *4*
chess das Schach *9*
child das Kind,-er *9*
chin das Kinn,-e *10*
chocolate die Schokolade *6; chocolate sundae* die Eisschokolade *6; chocolate ice cream* das Schokoeis *6; chocolate shake* der Schokoshake,-s *6*
choice die Auswahl
choice die Wahl; *The more choices, the more problems.* Wer die Wahl hat, hat die Qual! *7*

city die Stadt,¨e *2; city hall* die Stadthalle,-n *12*
clarinet die Klarinette,-n *9*
class die Klasse,-n *4; class schedule* der Stundenplan,¨e *4*
to **clean up** *(room)* aufräumen *9*
to **clear** *(table)* abräumen *9*
clear klar *7*
clock die Uhr,-en *2; clock radio* der Radiowecker,- *8*
closet der Schrank,¨e *8*
clothes die Kleidung *8*
clothing Kleidung *8; clothing item* das Kleidungsstück,-e *7*
coat der Mantel,¨ *7*
cocoa der Kakao *6*
coffee der Kaffee *6*
coin die Münze,-n *9*
cola die Cola,-s *6*
cold kalt *5*
cold-cut platter Kalte Platte *6*
to **collect** sammeln *9*
color die Farbe,-n *7; What color is...?* Welche Farbe hat...? *7*
colorful bunt *7*
to **come** kommen *1; to come along* mitkommen *2; Come along!* Komm mit! *2; to come over* rüberkommen *2; to come here* herkommen; *Come here!* Komm her! *4*
comedy die Komödie,-n *9*
computer der Computer,- *3; computer science* die Informatik *4 computer game* das Computerspiel,-e *3; computer science assignment* die Informatikaufgabe,-n *4*
concert das Konzert,-e *9*
cool kühl *5*
to **coordinate** koordinieren *12*
cordial herzlich *8*
corner die Ecke,-n *1*
correct richtig *7*
cosmetics die Kosmetik *9*
to **cost** kosten *6*
counter *(ticket)* der Schalter,- *11*

country das Land,¨er *5*
cousin (male) der Cousin,-s *2; (female)* die Cousine,-n *2*
to **cover** decken *9*
cross das Kreuz,-e *12*
cup die Tasse,-n *6*
cupboard der Schrank,¨e *8*
Czech Republic die Tschechische Republik *5*

D

dad der Vati,-s *2*
dance der Tanz,¨e *12; dance studio* das Tanzstudio,-s *12; dance lesson* die to Tanzstunde,-n *12*
to **dance** tanzen *3*
dark dunkel *4*
daughter die Tochter,¨ *2*
day der Tag,-e *1*
December der Dezember *5*
definitely bestimmt *8*
delicious lecker *6*
Denmark Dänemark *5*
to **depart** abfahren *11*
department store das Kaufhaus,¨er *2*
departure die Abfahrt,-en *11*
desk der Schreibtisch,-e *8*
detective story der Krimi,-s *3*
different verschieden *10*
difficult schwer *4*
dinner das Abendessen *6*
direct(ly) direkt *10*
disco die Disko,-s *3*
dishes das Geschirr *9*
dishwasher der Geschirrspüler,- *8*
to **disturb** stören *12*
to **do** machen *2; What are you doing?* Was machst du? *2; to do (crafts)* basteln *10*
door die Tür,-en *12*
downtown die Stadtmitte *11*
dress das Kleid,-er *7*
to **drink** trinken *6*
to **drive** fahren *5*
drums das Schlagzeug *9*
during während *8*

E

e-mail die E-Mail,-s 6; *to
send an e-mail* eine
E-Mail schicken 6
each jeder 4
ear das Ohr,-en 10
early früh 4
earring der Ohrring,-e 8
east der Osten 4
easy leicht 4
to **eat** essen 6
eight acht 1
eighteen achtzehn 1
eighty achtzig 2
eleven elf 1
end das Ende 10
engine der Motor,-en 8
England England 9
English *(subject)* das
Englisch 4; *He speaks
English.* Er spricht
englisch. 5
enough genug 4
eraser der Radiergummi,-s 4
especially besonders 5
euro der Euro,-s 5
Europe Europa 9
evening der Abend,-e; *this
evening* heute Abend 3; *in
the evening* am Abend 3
every jeder 4
everything alles
exact(ly) genau 8
example das Beispiel,-e 10;
as for example wie zum
Beispiel 10
except außer 10
exciting aufregend 9
Excuse me! Entschuldigen
Sie! 11
exercise die Übung,-en 12;
physical exercise die
Leibesübung,-en 12
expensive teuer 5
eye das Auge,-n 10

F

fall der Herbst,-e 4
family die Familie,-n 2
fan der Fan,-s 9
far weit 1
fast schnell 3
father der Vater,⸚ 2

favorite subject das
Lieblingsfach,⸚er 4;
favorite team die
Lieblingsmannschaft,-en 10
February der Februar 5
to **fetch** holen 3
few: a few ein paar 5;
manche 10
fifteen fünfzehn 1
fifty fünfzig 2
film der Film,-e, 3
finally endlich 8
to **find** finden 4
finger der Finger,- 10
Finland Finnland 9
first zuerst 3; erst- 4
fish der Fisch,-e 6
to **fit** passen 7
five fünf 1
flag die Fahne,-n 10
flat flach 8
to **flow** fließen 8
flute die Flöte,-n 12
to **fly** fliegen 11
food server Kellner,- 6
for für 3; *for you* für dich 1
forehead die Stirn,-en 10
foreign fremd 11
foreigner der
Ausländer- 4
forty vierzig 2
to **foul** foulen 10
four vier 1
fourteen vierzehn 1
France Frankreich 5
French *(subject)* das
Französisch 4; *He speaks
French.* Er spricht
französisch. 5
french fries die Pommes
frites (pl.) 6
Friday der Freitag,-e 2
from aus, von 1
front: in front of vor 3
fun der Spaß; *Have fun!* Viel
Spaß! 3; *It's fun.* Es macht
Spaß. 12
to **function** funktionieren 8

G

game das Spiel,-e 10
garden der Garten,⸚ 8
genius das Genie,-s 8
gentleman der Herr,-en 1

geography die
Erdkunde 4
German deutsch 5; *German
(subject)* Deutsch 3; *He
speaks German.* Er spricht
deutsch. 5; *German
(person)* der
Deutsche,-n 10
Germany Deutschland 2
to **get** holen 3; bekommen 4; *to
get in* einsteigen 11; *to get
off* aussteigen 11
gift das Geschenk,-e 8
girl das Mädchen,- 1
girlfriend die
Freundin,-nen 1
to **give (a gift)** schenken 10
to **give** geben 7; *to give (a gift)*
schenken 10
glad froh 4; *gladly* gern 3
glass das Glas,⸚er 6
glove der Handschuh,-e 7
to **go** gehen 1; *to go (by
vehicle)* fahren 5; *Let's go!*
Gehen wir! 9; *to go past*
vorbeigehen 11
goal das Tor,-e 10
goalkeeper der
Torwart,⸚er 10
golf das Golf 10
good gut 1
grade die Note,-n 4
grandfather der
Großvater,⸚ 2
grandma die Oma,-s 2
grandmother die
Großmutter,⸚ 2
grandpa der Opa,-s 2
grandparents die
Großeltern (pl.) 2
gray grau 7
great toll, super 2; *Great!*
Klasse! 5
green grün 7
to **greet** begrüßen 8
guitar die Gitarre,-n 3

H

hair das Haar,-e 10
half halb 2
halftime die
Halbzeit,-en 10
hamburger der
Hamburger,- 6

hand die Hand,⸚e *10; to shake hands* sich die Hand geben *10*

to **happen** passieren *10*

happy froh *4*

hard schwer *4*

to **have** haben *3; to have to* müssen *6; to have on* anhaben *7*

he er *1*

to **head** *(ball)* köpfen *10*

head der Kopf,⸚e *5*

to **hear** hören *2*

Hello! Hallo!, Grüß dich!, Guten Tag! *1*

helmet der Helm-e *5*

to **help** helfen *3; May I help you?* Bitte schön? *2*

her ihr *2*

here hier *1*

Hi! Hallo!, Grüß dich! *1*

highest höchst- *8*

to **hike** wandern *10*

his sein *7*

history die Geschichte *4*

hit *(song)* der Hit,-s *3*

hobby das Hobby,-s *9*

Holland Holland *5*

home: at home zu Hause *2; to go home* nach Hause gehen *3*

homework die Hausaufgabe,-n; *to do homework* Hausaufgaben machen *3*

to **hope** hoffen *8*

horror film der Horrorfilm,-e *9*

hot heiß *5*

hot chocolate der Kakao, *6*

hour die Stunde,-n *3*

house das Haus,⸚er *4*

how wie *1; How are you?* Wie geht's? *1; how much* wie viel *1; how many* wie viele *4*

hundred hundert *2*

hunger der Hunger; *to be hungry* Hunger haben *6*

to **hurry** schnell machen *9*

to **hurt** wehtun; *Does it hurt you?* Tut es dir weh? *10*

I

I ich *1*

ice cream das Eis *6; favorite ice cream* das Lieblingseis *6; ice cream parlor* das Eiscafé,-s, *6*

ice hockey das Eishockey *10*

to **ice skate** Schlittschuh laufen *10*

idea die Idee,-n *3*

if ob *7*

immediately gleich *1*

important wichtig *8*

in in *2; in the north* im Norden *2*

information die Auskunft,⸚e *11*

inhabitant der Einwohner,- *4*

inside drinnen *7*

intelligent klug *4*

to **intend** *(to do)* vorhaben *9*

interesting interessant *1*

Internet das Internet *9*

to **invite** einladen *8*

island die Insel,-n *6*

it es *1*

Italian italienisch; *He speaks Italian. Er spricht italienisch. 5*

Italy Italien *5*

item die Sache,-n *5*

its sein *8*

J

jacket die Jacke,-n *7*

jam die Marmelade,-n *6*

January der Januar *5*

jeans die Jeans (pl.) *7*

jewelry der Schmuck *8*

joke der Witz,-e *8*

July der Juli *5*

June der Juni *5*

K

keyboard das Keyboard,-s *12*

kilometer der Kilometer,- *4*

kitchen die Küche,-n *8*

kitchen sink das Spülbecken,- *8*

to **know** *(person, place)* kennen *1; to know (fact)* wissen *7*

L

lake der See,-n *11*

lamp die Lampe,-n *8*

language die Sprache,-n *12*

large groß *2*

last letzt- *10*

to **last** dauern *3*

late spät *2; See you later! Bis später! 2*

Latin das Latein *4*

lawn der Rasen,- *5*

league die Liga *10*

to **learn** lernen *4*

to **leave** verlassen *10;* abfahren *11*

left links; *on the left side* auf der linken Seite *11*

leg das Bein,-e *10*

lemon ice cream das Zitroneneis *6*

letter der Brief,-e *6*

to **lie** liegen

Liechtenstein Liechtenstein *12*

light hell *7*

to **like** gefallen *3;* gern haben *4; How do you like...?* Wie gefällt dir...? *3;* mögen *6*

line die Linie,-n *5*

lip die Lippe,-n *10*

to **listen to** hören *2*

little klein *11; a little* etwas *3*

to **live** wohnen *1*

living room das Wohnzimmer,- *8*

long lang(e) *7; long time* lang(e) *4; longest* längst- *8*

to **look at** sich ansehen *12*

love story der Liebesfilm,-e *9*

luggage das Gepäck *11; luggage cart* der Kofferkuli,-s *11*

lunch das Mittagessen *6*

Luxembourg Luxemburg *5*

M

to **make** machen; *to make music* Musik machen *12; We made it.* Das haben wir geschafft. *11*

man der Mann,-er *9*

to **manage (it)** schaffen *9*

map die Landkarte,-n *4*

March der März *5*

market der Markt,-e *9*

marmalade die Marmelade,-n

mathematics (math) die Mathematik (Mathe); *math class* die Mathestunde/ Matheklasse *4*

may dürfen *6*

May der Mai *5*

to **mean** meinen *4*; bedeuten *9*; *it means a lot to me* es bedeutet mir viel *9*

means of transportation das Verkehrsmittel,- *11*

to **meet** treffen *4*; *Let's meet!* Treffen wir uns! *9*

member das Mitglied,-er *9*

microwave oven der Mikrowellenherd,-e *8*

middle die Mitte *8*

milk die Milch *6*

million die Million,-en *4*

minus minus *1*

minute die Minute,-n *1*

mirror der Spiegel,- *12*

model das Vorbild,-er *9*

modern modern *12*

mom die Mutti,-s *2*

moment der Moment,-e; *Just a moment!* Moment mal! *3*

Monday der Montag,-e *2*

money das Geld *5*

month der Monat,-e *5*

moped das Moped,-s *8*

more mehr *3*; *there are no more tickets available* es gibt keine Karten mehr *3*; *more than* mehr als *4*

morning der Morgen,-; *this morning* heute Morgen *3*

most meist-; *most of them* die meisten *10*; *mostly* meistens *10*

mother die Mutter,- *2*

motor der Motor,-en *8*

motor scooter der Motorroller,- *8*

motorcycle das Motorrad,-er *11*

mountain der Berg,-e *8*

mouth der Mund,-er *10*

movement die Bewegung,-en *12*

movie der Film,-e, *3*; *movie theater* das Kino,-s *9*

to **mow** mähen *9*; *to mow the lawn* den Rasen mähen *9*

Mr. der Herr,-en *1*

Mrs. die Frau,-en *1*

much viel *1*

museum das Museum, Museen *11*

music die Musik *2*; *music festival* das Musikfest,-e *8*; *music store* das Musikgeschäft,-e *7*

musical musikalisch *12*

musical instrument das Musikinstrument,-e *12*

must müssen *6*

my mein *1*

N

name der Name,-n *9*; *What's your name?* Wie heißt du?, Wie heißen Sie? *1*

national flag die Nationalfahne,-n *8*

national sport der Nationalsport *10*

natural(ly) natürlich *8*

natural sciences die Naturwissenschaften (pl.) *4*

near bei

nearby in der Nähe *11*

nearness die Nähe, *11*

neck der Hals,-e *10*

to **need** brauchen *4*

neighboring country das Nachbarland,-er *5*

nervous nervös *4*

Netherlands die Niederlande *5*

never nie *4*

new neu *1*

news die Nachricht,-en *3*

newspaper die Zeitung,-en *9*

next nächst- *8*; *next to* neben *11*

nice nett *1*

nine neun *1*

nineteen neunzehn *1*

ninety neunzig *2*

no nein *1*; kein(e) *3*

noon der Mittag,-e; *today at noon* heute Mittag *3*

north der Norden *2*; *in the north* im Norden *2*

North Sea die Nordsee *12*

nose die Nase,-n *10*

not nicht *1*

notebook das Heft,-e *4*

nothing nichts *6*

November der November *5*

now jetzt *3*

number die Nummer,-n *10*

nut-flavored ice cream das Nusseis *6*

O

October der Oktober *5*

of course natürlich *8*

to **offer** anbieten *12*

office das Büro,-s *12*

often oft *6*

old alt *1*

on an *2*; auf *4*

once einmal *12*

one eins *1*; man *9*

only nur *1*; *not only...but also* nicht nur...sondern auch *10*

to **open** aufmachen *8*

orange orange *7*

other ander- *4*

otherwise sonst *5*

Ouch! Au! *10*

our unser *5*

outside draußen *6*

P

pair das Paar,-e *7*

pants die Hose,-n *7*

paper das Papier *4*

paradise das Paradies *12*

parents die Eltern (pl.) *2*

part der Teil,-e *8*; *for the most part* zum größten Teil *8*

to **participate** mitmachen *9*; *to participate in sports* Sport treiben *10*

party die Party,-s *8*

to **pay** bezahlen *5*; *to pay attention* aufpassen *10*

peace die Ruhe *5*

pen (*ballpoint*) der Kuli,-s *4*

penalty kick der Elfmeter,- *10*

pencil der Bleistift,-e *4*

people die Leute (*pl.*) *10*

percussion das Schlagzeug *9*

performance die Aufführung,-en *12*

perhaps vielleicht *2*

photo das Foto,-s *12*; *photo album* das Fotoalbum,-alben *12*

physics die Physik *4*

piano das Klavier,-e *3*

picture das Bild,-er *8*

pink rosa *7*

pizza die Pizza,-s *6*

pizza restaurant die Pizzeria,-s *6*

place der Platz,¨e *8*

to **plan** vorhaben *9*; planen *11*

plate die Platte,-n *6*

to **play** spielen *3*; *to continue playing* weiterspielen *10*

player der Spieler,- *10*

please bitte *5*

pleasure das Vergnügen; *Business before pleasure.* Zuerst kommt die Arbeit und dann das Vergnügen. *9*

plus plus *1*

poem das Gedicht,-e *9*

Poland Polen *5*

popular beliebt *8*

post office die Post *11*

postcard die Postkarte,-n *11*

poster das Poster,- *9*

potato die Kartoffel,-n *6*

practical praktisch *7*

practice die Übung,-en; *Practice makes perfect!* Übung macht den Meister! *12*

to **practice** üben *10*

present das Geschenk,-e *8*

price der Preis,-e *5*

problem das Problem,-e *3*

proximity Nähe *11*

pullover der Pullover,- *7*; der Pulli,-s *7*

Q

quality die Qualität,-en *7*

quarter das Viertel,- *3*

quiet die Ruhe *5*

to **quit** aufhören *12*

quite ganz *1*; *quite well* ganz gut *1*; *not quite yet* noch nicht ganz *4*

R

radio das Radio,-s *8*; *clock radio* der Radiowecker,- *8*

rag (*to wipe off chalkboard*) der Tafellappen,- *4*

to **rain** regnen *5*

rather lieber *6*; *I would rather eat...* Ich möchte lieber...essen. *6*

to **read** lesen *3*

really wirklich *1*; each *2*

reasonable preiswert *5*

receipt die Quittung,-en *7*

to **receive** bekommen *4*

recess die Pause,-n *4*

recorder die Blockflöte,-n *12*

red rot *7*

reduced reduziert *7*

refrigerator der Kühlschrank,¨e *8*

religion die Religion,-en *4*

to **repair** reparieren *9*

rhythm der Rhythmus *12*

to **ride** fahren *5*

right richtig *7*; *right around the corner* gleich um die Ecke *1*; *to be right* Recht haben *4*; rechts (*direction*); *That's right.* Das stimmt. *4*

to **ring** (*bell*) klingeln *4*; *The bell is ringing.* Es klingelt. *4*

to **rinse** spülen *9*

river der Fluss,¨e *8*

rock concert das Rockkonzert,-e *3*

rock group die Rockgruppe,-n *2*

rock music die Rockmusik *9*

roll das Brötchen,- *6*

room das Zimmer,- *9*

ruler das Lineal,-e *4*

to **run** laufen *9*

S

salad der Salat,-e *6*

sale: special (sale) das Sonderangebot,-e *7*

salesperson (male) der Verkäufer,- *5*

salesperson (female) die Verkäuferin,-nen *7*

Saturday der Samstag,-e *2*; der Sonnabend,-e *2*

sauerbraten (marinated beef roast) der Sauerbraten *6*

sausage die Wurst,¨e *6*; *sausage sandwich* das Wurstbrot,-e *6*

saxophone das Saxophon,-e *12*

to **say** sagen *3*

schedule der Fahrplan,¨e *5*

schick chic *9*

school die Schule,-n *3*

schoolbag die Schultasche,-n *4*

schoolmate der Schulfreund,-e *4*

to **scream** schreien *10*

season die Jahreszeit,-en *5*

seat der Platz,¨e *8*

section der Teil,-e *8*

to **see** sehen *3*; *See you!*; Tschau!, Tschüs! *1*

selection die Auswahl *2*; *a selection in* eine Auswahl an *3*

to **sell** verkaufen *5*

to **send** schicken *6*

September der September *5*

to **set** (*the table*) den Tisch decken *9*

seven sieben *1*

seventeen siebzehn *1*

seventy siebzig *2*

shall werden *6*

she sie *1*

to **shine** scheinen *5*

ship das Schiff,-e *11*

shirt das Hemd,-en *7*; das Shirt,-s *7*

shoe der Schuh,-e *7*

to **shoot** schießen *10*
shop das Geschäft,-e *7*
to **shop** einkaufen *9; to go shopping* einkaufen gehen *9*
short kurz *7*
should sollen *6*
shoulder die Schulter,-n *10*
to **show** zeigen *8*
shower die Dusche,-n *8*
side die Seite,-n *11*
since seit *10*
sincere herzlich *8*
to **sing** singen *9*
singer *(male)* der Sänger,- *singer (female)* die Sängerin,-nen *9*
sister die Schwester,-n *2; twin sister* die Zwillingsschwester,-n *9*
to **sit** sitzen *6; to sit on* sitzen auf *8*
six sechs *1*
sixteen sechzehn *1*
sixty sechzig *2*
size die Größe,-n *7*
ski der Ski,-er *10; to ski* Ski laufen *9*
skirt der Rock,-e *7*
slacks die Hose,-n *7*
slice die Scheibe,-n *6; a slice of bread* eine Scheibe Brot *6*
slow langsam *4*
small klein *11*
smart klug *4; smart (looking)* schick *7*
smartie der Schlauberger *3*
to **smile** lächeln *8*
snack bar der Imbiss,-e *6;* der Imbissstand,-e *10*
to **snow** schneien *5*
so also; *So, what is your present? Also, was ist dein Geschenk? 8*
soccer der Fußball,-e *3*
soccer ball der Fußball,-e, *3*
soccer field der Fußballplatz,-e *10*
soccer team die Fußballmannschaft,-en *9*
sock die Socke,-n *7*
sofa das Sofa,-s *8*

solid stabil *5*
some etwas *3;* manche *10*
something etwas *3*
sometimes manchmal *4*
son der Sohn,-e *2*
song das Lied,-er *9*
soon bald *5*
south der Süden *4*
spaetzle *(kind of homemade pasta)* die Spätzle *6*
Spain Spanien *5*
Spanish spanisch; *He speaks Spanish.* Er spricht spanisch. *5*
to **speak** sprechen *5; to speak about oneself* über sich selbst sprechen *9*
special besonders *5; something special* etwas Besonderes *8*
spectator der Zuschauer,- *10*
speed das Tempo *10*
to **spend** *(money)* ausgeben *9*
sport(s) der Sport *4; to participate in sports* Sport treiben *10; sports show (news)* die Sportschau *3*
spring der Frühling,-e *5*
stadium das Stadion, -dien *10*
stamp die Briefmarke,-n *9*
to **stand** stehen *5*
star *(entertainment)* der Star,-s *9*
to **start** anfangen *9; to start* losgehen *7; When will it start? Wann geht's denn los? 7*
state der Staat,-en *4*
statistics die Statistik,-en *10*
to **stay** bleiben *3*
stepbrother der Stiefbruder,- *2*
stereo system die Stereoanlage,-n *8*
stiff steif *12*
still noch *4*
stocking der Strumpf,-e *7*
to **stop** aufhören *12*
store das Geschäft,-e *7*
story die Geschichte,-n *9; detective story* der Krimi,-s *3*

stove der Herd,-e *8*
straight ahead geradeaus *11*
strawberry ice cream das Erdbeereis *6*
strawberry shake der Erdbeershake,-s *6*
strawberry sundae das Spaghetti Eis *6*
streetcar die Straßenbahn,-en *11*
strength training das Krafttraining; *to do strength training* Krafttraining machen *9*
strong stark *7*
student *(elementary through high school)* der Schüler,- *12; (advanced)* der Fortgeschrittene,-n *12*
studio das Studio,-s *12*
sturdy stabil *5*
subject *(school)* das Fach,-er *4*
subway die U-Bahn,-en *11*
suddenly plötzlich *10*
to **suggest** vorschlagen *9*
suit der Anzug,-e *7*
suitcase der Koffer,- *11*
summer der Sommer,- *3; summer vacation* die Sommerferien (pl.) *7*
sun die Sonne *5*
Sunday der Sonntag,-e *2*
super super *2*
supper das Abendessen *6*
supposed: to be supposed to sollen *6*
surprised: to be surprised staunen *8*
sweater der Pullover,- *7; der* Pulli,-s *7*
sweatshirt das Sweatshirt,-s *7*
to **swim** schwimmen *3*
to **swing** schwenken *10*
Switzerland die Schweiz *5*

T

T-shirt das T-Shirt,-s *7*
table der Tisch,-e *4*
table tennis das Tischtennis *10*

to **take** nehmen 7; *to take (time)* dauern 3; *to take pictures* fotografieren 9; *to take along* mitnehmen 11

talk sprechen; *he/she speaks* er/sie spricht 5; *to talk about* sprechen über 6

to **taste** schmecken 6

tea tea 6; *iced tea* der Eistee 6

to **teach** beibringen 9; *taught me as a child* hat mir als Kind...beigebracht 9

teacher *(male)* der Lehrer,- 4; *(female)* die Lehrerin,-nen 4

team die Mannschaft,-en 10

teenager der Jugendliche,-n, 7

telephone das Telefon,-e 2; *cell phone* das Handy,-s 9

television (set) der Fernseher,- 8; *on television* im Fernsehen 3; *television program* die Fernsehprogramm,-e 3

to **tell** sagen 3; erzählen 11

tempo das Tempo 10

ten zehn 1

tennis das Tennis 3; *tennis racquet* der Tennisschläger,- 10

terrific toll 2; *Terrific!* Klasse! 5

to **test** ausprobieren 10

text der Text,-e 9

Thank you! Danke! 5; *Thank you very much.* Danke schön. 6

that das 1; dass 8

the der, die, das 2

their ihr 8

then dann 3

there da 1; dort 3; *over there* da drüben 1; *there (to)* dorthin 7

therefore deshalb 5

they sie 1; man 9

thing die Sache,-n 5

to **think** meinen 4; *Do you think so?* Meinst du? 4

third dritt- 8

thirst der Durst 6; *to be thirsty* Durst haben 6

thirteen dreizehn 1

thirty dreißig 2

this dieser 2

thousand tausend 2

three drei 1; *three times* dreimal 9

thriller der Krimi,-s 3

through durch 8

Thursday der Donnerstag,-e 2

ticket Karte,-n 3; die Fahrkarte,-n 11

ticket counter die Kasse,-n 10

tie die Krawatte,-n 7

tight eng 7

time die Zeit,-en 2; *At what time?* Um wie viel Uhr? 2

times mal 4; *a few times* ein paar Mal 8

tire der Reifen,- 5

to an, zu 2; *to go to the department store* zum Kaufhaus gehen 2

today heute 2

together zusammen 3

toilet die Toilette,-n 8

tomorrow morgen 2

too auch 2; zu 3

tooth der Zahn,-̈e 10

tourist der Tourist,-en 12

track das Gleis,-e 11

train der Zug,-̈e 11; *train station* der Bahnhof,-̈e 3

training das Training 9

to **transfer** umsteigen 11

to **travel** reisen 9; *traveling* Reisen 9

treats (pl.) der Leckerbissen 6

trip die Reise,-n 5

trumpet die Trompete,-n 12

to **try** versuchen 10; *to try out* ausprobieren 10

Tuesday der Dienstag,-e 2

Turk *(male)* der Türke,-n 9

Turkey die Türkei 6

to **turn (to)** abbiegen 11

TV der Fernseher,- 8

twelve zwölf 1

twenty zwanzig 1

twin sister die Zwillingsschwester,-n 9

two zwei 1

uncle der Onkel,- 2

unfortunately leider 6

United States of America die Vereinigten Staaten von Amerika 4

until bis 2

vacation die Ferien (pl.); *on vacation* in den Ferien; *to go on vacation* in die Ferien fahren 5

to **vacuum** staubsaugen 9

vanilla ice cream das Vanilleeis 6

vegetable(s) das Gemüse 6

vending machine der Automat,-en 6

very sehr 1

video das Video,-s 3; *video rental store* die Videothek 3

violin die Geige,-n 12

to **visit** der Besuch,-e 11

visit besuchen 5

visitor der Besucher,- 12

volleyball der Volleyball 10

to **wait** warten 4; *to wait on* bedienen 7

waiter der Kellner,-

to **walk** zu Fuß gehen 11

to **want to** wollen 6; *to want (for birthday)* sich wünschen 10

warm warm 5

to **wash** spülen 9

watch die Uhr,-en 2

to **watch out** aufpassen 10

to **watch television** fernsehen 3

we wir 1

to **wear** tragen, anhaben 7

weather das Wetter 5

Wednesday der Mittwoch,-e 2

week die Woche,-n 3

weekend das Wochenende,-n 9

well-known bekannt 3

west der Westen 4

what was 2; *What kind of a...?* Was für ein...? 3; *What's your name?* Wie heißt du?, Wie heißen Sie? 1

wheel das Rad,-̈er 8

when wann 3

where wo 1; *where from* woher 1; *where (to)* wohin 2

whether ob 7

which welcher 2

while während 12

whipped cream die Schlagsahne 6

white weiß 7

who wer 1; *to whom* wen 4; *whom* wem 10

why warum 3

will werden 6

to **win** gewinnen 10

winter der Winter,- 5

wise weise; *a wise man* ein weiser Mann 9

to **wish** wünschen 8;

with mit 2; bei 3; *to stay with us* bei uns bleiben 3

without ohne 4

woman die Frau,-en 1

to **work** funtionieren *(gadget)* 8; arbeiten 12

work die Arbeit,-en 4

world die Welt,-en; *in the whole world* auf der ganzen Welt 9

would like to möchten 3

to **write** schreiben 6; *to write to* schreiben an 6

Y

year das Jahr,-e; *three years ago* vor drei Jahren 11

to **yell** schreien 10

yellow gelb 7

yes ja 1

yet noch 4; *not quite yet* noch nicht ganz 4

you *(familiar singular)* du 1; *(familiar plural)* ihr 1; *(formal)* Sie 1; man 9

your *(familiar singular)* dein 1; *(familiar plural)* euer 8; *(formal singular and plural)* Ihr

Z

zero null 1

Index

Acknowledgments

The author wishes to express his gratitude to the following people who assisted in the photography scenes in Germany, Austria and Switzerland:

Hans-Joachim Bubke and Family
(Wilhelmshaven, Germany)
Dr. Reinhold Frigge (Witten, Germany)
Dr. Wieland Held and Family (Leipzig, Germany)
Julius Haag (Sigmaringen, Germany)
Daniel Herzl (Salzburg Panorama Tours,
Salzburg, Austria)
Guido Kauls (Minneapolis, Minnesota)
Derya Kaya (Bergkamen, Germany)
Gerd Kraft and Family (Gerlingen, Germany)
Werner Kundmüller (Ingolstadt, Germany)

Daniela Küng and Family (Lucerne, Switzerland)
Günter Müller and Family (Boppard, Germany)
Antje Radtke (Berlin, Germany)
Uwe Schlaugk and Family (Krailling, Germany)
Sandra Schlünder and Family
(Bergkamen, Germany)
Peter Sternke and Family (Berlin, Germany)
Helmut Strunk and Family (Essen, Germany)
Dr. Hartmut Voigt (Leverkusen, Germany)
Heike Zinke (Bad Homburg, Germany)

The following organizations also assisted in the photography sessions:
Camping-Oase Thiessow (Thiessow, Germany)
Deutsche Lufthansa AG, Frankfurt am Main, Germany
Jugendherberge Bacharach (Bacharach, Germany)
Jugendherberge Bingen (Bingen, Germany)
Jugendherberge Rüdesheim (Rüdesheim, Germany)
Jugendherberge St. Goar (St. Goar, Germany)
Karstadt AG (Essen, Germany)
Ostsee-Campingplatz Göhren (Göhren, Germany)
TS Reisebüro (Salzburg, Austria)

The author appreciates the input of the following Minnesota German teachers during a focus group session: Jutta Crowder (St. Paul Academy), Chandra Hanke (Fridley High School), Dan Murray (Eden Prairie High School), Sarah Magnuson (Buffalo High School), Jean Neitzel (West Lutheran High School), Gretchen Ortenzio (Minnetonka High School, David Rutledge (Tartan High School), Sally Sailer (Fridley Middle School), Gloria Speiker (Prior Lake High School), Ruth Stark (Chisago Lakes High School).

The author also would like to thank his wife, Rosie, for showing such tremendous patience and understanding during the development of this series and for her valuable contribution before, during and after the various trips throughout German-speaking countries.

The following German instructors provided valuable comments for *Deutsch Aktuell:*

Sandra Achenbach, Webb School of Knoxville, Knoxville, Tennessee; *Dirk Ahlers*, Marquette Senior High School, Marquette, Michigan; *Anna L. Alexander*, Edmond Memorial High School, Edmond, Oklahoma; *Connie Allison*, MacArthur High School, Lawton, Oklahoma; *Constance L. Anderson*, Red Bank High School, Chattanooga, Tennessee; *Laura Anderson*, Yuma High School, Yuma, Arizona; *Thomas F. Andris*, Marietta Senior High School, Marietta, Georgia; *Virginia Apel*, Northside College Prep, Chicago, Illinois; *Susan Armitage*, Prairie High School, Cedar Rapids, Iowa; *Jennifer Baker*, North Brunswick Township High School, North Brunswick, New Jersey; *Lynn A. Baldus*, St. Ansgar High School, St. Ansgar, Iowa; *Sandra Banks*, Galesburg High School, Galesburg, Illinois; *Gregg Barnett*, Oak Grove High School,

San Jose, California; *David Beal*, Lee's Summit North High School, Lee's Summit, Missouri; *James J. Becker*, Dickinson High School, Dickinson, North Dakota; *Michele Bents*, Millard North High School, Omaha, Nebraska; *Tammy L. Berlin*, Waggener Traditional High School, Louisville, Kentucky; *Michael W. Beshiri*, Heritage High School, Conyers, Georgia; *Jayne E. Bingham*, Woodland High School, Catersville, Georgia; *Tery Binkerd*, Viewmont High School, Bountiful, Utah; *Judy Birkel*, Heritage Christian School, Indianapolis, Indiana; *Krista Boerman*, Western High School, Auburn, Michigan; *Paul Boling*, Patton Junior High School, Ft. Leavenworth, Kansas; *Seth H. Boyle*, Elk Grove High School, Elk Grove, California; *Barbara Boys*, Methacton High School, Norristown, Pennsylvania; *Susan Scott Brafford*, Prince George High School,

Prince George, Virginia; *Rick Brairton*, Chatham High School, Chatham, New Jersey; *Ursula Brannon*, Jarman Jr. High & Carl Albert High School, Midwest City, Oklahoma; *Carol Bruinsma*, Brookings High School, Brookings, South Dakota; *Carol H. Buller*, Midland High School, Midland, Michigan; *Sandra Burkhard*, Highland High School, Gilbert, Arizona; *Delores T. Buth*, Blaine High School, Blaine, Minnesota; *Friederike Butler*, Paradise Valley High School, Phoenix, Arizona; *Jacqueline A. Cady*, Bridgewater-Raritan Regional High School, Bridgewater, New Jersey; *Judith M. Cale*, Bennett High School, Bennett, Colorado; *Patrick Carr*, Blanchet High School, Seattle, Washington; *Carah Casler*, Reynoldsburg High School, Reynoldsburg, Ohio; *Ron Cates*, Ooltewah High School, Ooltewah, Tennessee; *Vance Chadaz*, Ogden High School, Ogden, Utah; *Stephanie Christensen*, Flathead High School, Kalispell, Montana; *Diane Christiansen*, Brisco Middle School, Beverly, Massachusetts; *Maria Monica Colceriu*, South High School, Pueblo, Colorado; *Brian Colucci*, Burgettstown Junior/Senior High School, Burgettstown, Pennsylvania; *Nancy Cowchok*, Wilmington Christian School, Hockessin, Delaware; *Jutta Crowder*, St. Paul Academy and Summit School, St. Paul, Minnesota; *Marilyn Davidheiser*, Franklin Co. High School, Winchester, Tennessee; *Cathy DeEsch*, Bangor Area Middle School, Bangor, Pennsylvania; *Frau Delacroix*, Massaponax High School, Fredericksburg, Virginia; *Corinne de Mattos*, Shaw High School, Columbus, Georgia; *Susan W. DeNyse*, Fairfield Senior High School, Fairfield, Ohio; *Daniel Desmond*, Centennial High School, Ellicott City, Maryland; *D. Dietrich-Lemon*, Carlson High School, Rockwood, Michigan; *Brigitte Dobbins*, Hampton High School, Hampton, Virginia; *Mariea Dobbs*, Central High School, Harrison, Tennessee; *Diane L. Dunk*, Eisenhower High School, New Berlin, Wisconsin; *Eugene Endicott*, Central Middle School, Ogden, Utah; *Paul Engberson*, West Jefferson High School, Terreton, Idaho; *Connie Evenson*, Pelican Rapids High School, Pelican Rapids, Minnesota; *Renee Fait*, Lakeland Union High School, Minocqua, Wisconsin; *Kathy Falatovich*, York Suburban High School, York, Pennsylvania; *Mary B. Farquhar*, Lowell High School, San Francisco, California; *Jay Feist*, Archbishop Alter High School, Kettering, Ohio; *Margaret M. Fellerath*, York Suburban Middle School, York, Pennsylvania; *Bro. Charles Filbert*, *F.S.C.*, Calvert Hall College High School, Baltimore, Maryland; *Fredrick Fischer*, Marquette Catholic High School, Alton, Illinois; *Marjorie A. Fischer*, Rocky Point High School, Rocky Point, New York; *Thomas Fischer*, Overbrook Regional Senior High School, Pine Hill, New Jersey; *Jan Fisher*, Harlem High School, Machesney Park, Illinois; *Lou Flanagan*, Crosby-Ironton Junior/Senior High School, Crosby, Minnesota; *Tessie A. Flynn*, East Detroit High School, Eastpointe, Michigan; *Antje Fortier*, Shelton High School, Shelton, Washington; *John Foster*, Duchesne High School, Duchesne, Utah; *Regine Fougeres*, Chenley High School, Pittsburgh, Pennsylvania; *Janet Fox*, Revere Middle School, Bath, Ohio; *S. Michelle France*, Lewis-Palmer High School, Monument, Colorado; *Jason Frank*, Waterford Kettering High School, Waterford, Michigan; *Joan H. Franklin*, North Catholic High School, Pittsburgh, Pennsylvania; *Wendy L. Freeman*, Hillcrest High School, Idaho Falls, Idaho; *Paula G. Freshwater*, Solon Middle School, Solon, Ohio; *Donah Gehlert*, Stow-Monroe Falls High School, Stow, Ohio; *Linda Gevaert*, Martin Luther High School, Greendale, Wisconsin; *Michealle Gibson*, Sauk Centre High School, Sauk Centre, Minnesota; *Christine Gildner*, University High School, Orlando, Florida; *James V. Goddard*, Howard A. Doolin Middle School, Miami, Florida; *John D. Goetz*, Mayer Lutheran High School, Mayer, Minnesota; *Joe Golding*, Pennsauken High School, Pennsauken, New Jersey; *Sally Goodhart*, Gloucester High School, Gloucester, Virginia; *Candie Graham*, Canton High School, Canton, Illinois; *Sandra Gullo*, Tri-City Christian Academy, Somersworth, New Hampshire; *Aaron Gwin*, Hazelwood East High School, St. Louis, Missouri; *John F. Györy*, G.A.R. Memorial Junior/Senior High School, Wilkes-Barre, Pennsylvania; *Amy Hallberg*, Chaska High School, Chaska, Minnesota; *Gerald E. Halliday*, Clearfield High School, Clearfield, Utah; *Byron Halling*, Escondido Charter High School, Escondido, California; *Laura Halvorson*, Willmar Senior High School, Willmar, Minnesota; *Mary P. Hansen*, St. Agnes High School, St. Paul, Minnesota; *Rena W. Harris*, Lutheran High School, Springfield, Illinois; *Jennifer L. Harrison*, Roy School District 74, Roy, Michigan; *Peri V. Hartzell*, Field Kindley High School, Coffeyville, Kansas; *Janet Harvis*, Harrison High School, Farmington Hills, Michigan; *Barbara Hassell*, Lord Botetourt High School, Daleville, Virginia; *Nellie Hastings*, Alan B. Shepard High School, Palos Heights, Illinois; *Rebecca Hauptmann*, Clifford Smart Middle School, Commerce, Michigan; *Chrystal Heimberger-Hallam*, Chaparral High School, Las Vegas, Nevada; *Thomas Hengstenberg*, Owensville High School, Owensville, Missouri; *Hege Herfindahl*, BBE High School, Belgrade, Minnesota; *Arthur P. Herrmann*, White Station High School, Memphis, Tennessee; *Helga Hilson*, Edmonds-Woodway High School, Edmonds, Washington; *Stephen C. Hintz*, Shoreland Lutheran High School, Somers, Wisconsin; *Shirley S. Hipsher*, Trenton High School, Trenton, Michigan;

Acknowledgments

Nicholas R. Hoffmann, Walnut High School, Walnut, Iowa; *Arthur D. Holder,* Judge Memorial Catholic High School, Salt Lake City, Utah; *T. Marshall Hopkins,* Central Mountain High School, Mill Hall, Pennsylvania; *Jolene Huddleston,* Kaysville Junior High School, Kaysville, Utah; *Tracy Hughes,* Atlee High School, Mechanicsville, Virginia; *Amy L. Hull,* Jones Academic Magnet High School, Chicago, Illinois; *Daniel Hunter,* Jersey Shore Area High School, Jersey Shore, Pennsylvania; *Nicole B. Ingram,* Preble-Shawnee High School, Camden, Ohio; *Patricia S. Iversen,* Lee's Summit High School - Div. I, Lee's Summit, Missouri; *Camille Jensen,* Preston High School, Preston, Idaho; *Joan Jensen,* Chatham Middle School, Chatham, New Jersey; *Jane Jerauld,* Montrose Area Jr./Sr. High School, Montrose, Pennsylvania; *Walter J. Johnson,* Northeast Catholic High School, Philadelphia, Pennsylvania; *Richard B. Jones,* Ritenour High School, St. Louis, Missouri; *Rohnda Jones,* Lane Technical High School, Chicago, Illinois; *W. Clark Jones,* Vernal Junior High School, Vernal, Utah; *William Jones,* Howland High School, Warren, Ohio; *Sarah Juntune,* Okemos High School, Okemos, Michigan; *Linda Kaelin,* Lourdes High School, Oshkosh,Wisconsin; *Mary S. Katzenmayer,* Jacobs High School, Algonquin, Illinois; *Guido Kauls,* Minnehaha Academy, Minneapolis, Minnesota; *Kara Keller,* Perryville Senior High School, Perryville, Missouri; *Steve R. Kennedy,* Lenawee Christian School, Adrian, Michigan; *Wilfred Kittner,* United Faith Christian Academy, Charlotte, North Carolina; *Steven Knecht,* Layton High School, Layton, Utah; *Hans Koenig,* The Blake School, Hopkins, Minnesota; *Michael J. Korom,* Ninth Grade Center, Downingtown, Pennsylvania; *Barbara Kyle,* Rock Spring High School, Rock Spring, Wyoming; *Cynthia Lavalle-Lake,* Kearsley High School, Flint, Michigan; *Michael E. Leach,* Pandora-Sellor High School, Pandora, Ohio; *John Lenders,* Dearborn High School, Dearborn, Michigan; *Warren R. Love,* Gilbert High School, Gilbert, Arizona; *W. R. Lutz,* Seneca High School, Louisville, Kentucky; *Christopher Lynch,* St. John's Preparatory School, Danvers, Massachusetts; *Michael Marple,* Butler Traditional High School, Louisville, Kentucky; *Bert C. Marley,* Marsh Valley High School, Arimo, Idaho; *Amy Mason,* Lake Fenton High School, Fenton, Michigan; *Ingrid May,* Harding High School, Marion, Ohio; *Kaye Lynn Mazurek,* Walled Lake Central High School, Walled Lake, Michigan; *Anne B. McCahill,* Chancellor High School, Fredericksburg, Virginia; *E. McCarthy-Allen,* Champaign Central High School, Champaign, Illinois; *Linda R. McCrae,* Muhlenberg High School, Laureldale, Pennsylvania; *Bernie A. McKichan,* Sheboygan Falls High School, Sheboygan Falls, Wisconsin; *Mike McKinney,* Roxana High School, Roxana, Illinois; *Karlyn McPike,* Hicksville High School, Hicksville, Ohio; *Zig Meyer,* Blue Hill Community Schools, Blue Hill, Nebraska; *Zaiga Mion,* Hardanway High School, Columbus, Georgia; *Lisa Morrill,* Mansfield Middle School, Storrs Mansfield, Connecticut; *Peter Mudrinich,* Hudson High School, Hudson, Wisconsin; *Ursula Mudrinich,* River Falls High School, River Falls, Wisconsin; *Eleanor Munze,* Jefferson Twp. High School, Oak Ridge, New Jersey; *Kathleen S. Nardozzi,* Penn Hills High School, Pittsburgh, Pennsylvania; *Jean K. Neitzel,* NELHS, York, Nebraska; *JoAnn Nelson,* Jacksonville High School, Jacksonville, Illinois; *Jane Nicholson,* Logan High School, Logan, Utah; *Susanne Niebuhr,* North Pole High School, North Pole, Arkansas; *Nancy Oakes,* Mt. Zion High School, Mt. Zion, Illinois; *Adeline O'Brien,* Nazareth High School, Nazareth, Pennsylvania; *Rita M. Olson,* South Milwaukee High School, South Milwaukee, Wisconsin; *Barbara S. Oncay,* Dover High School, Dover, Delaware; *Damon Osipik,* Susan B. Anthony Middle School, Manhattan, Kansas; *Sr. Mary Perpetua, SCC,* Central Catholic High School, Reading, Pennsylvania; *Linda K. Perri,* Shakopee Junior High School, Shakopee, Minnesota; *Judith Pete,* Andrean High School, Merrillville, Indiana; *Siegmund Pfeifer,* Litchfield Senior High School, Litchfield, Minnesota; *Judith Potter,* John Carroll School, Bel Air, Maryland; *Lois Purrington,* Renville County West High School, Renville, Minnesota; *Christa Rains,* Peoria Heights High School, Peoria Heights, Illinois; *Jens Rehoer,* Orion High School, Orion, Illinois; *Edith A. W. Rentz,* Freeport High School, Freeport, Maine; *Julia S. Riggs,* Mesquite High School, Gilbert, Arizona; *Jerry L. Roach,* Baraga Area Schools, Baraga, Michigan; *Esther Rodabaugh,* Beaverton High School, Beaverton, Michigan; *Patti L. Roepke,* Chaska Middle School West, Chaska, Minnesota; *Linda Roller,* Bolivar High School, Bolivar, Missouri; *Brigitte Rose,* U.S. Grant High School, Van Nuys, California; *Cynthia H. Rovai,* Middletown High School, Middletown, Ohio; *Ralph Rowley,* Weber High School, Ogden, Utah; *Catherine Rubeski,* Framingham High School, Framingham, Massachusetts; *Jay T. Ruch,* Notre Dame High School, Easton, Pennsylvania; *Betsy Saurdiff,* Goodridge School, Goodridge, Minnesota; *Monica E. Schaffer,* Arcola Intermediate School, Norristown, Pennsylvania; *Cynthia K. Schauer,* Downingtown High School, Downingtown, Pennsylvania; *Ann S. Schemm,* South Park High School, Library, Pennsylvania; *Wesley A. Schmandt,* Kettle Moraine Lutheran, Jackson, Wisconsin; *Kurt Schneider,* Oconomowoc High School, Oconomowoc,

Wisconsin; *Peter Schroeck*, Watchung Hills Regional High School, Warren, New Jersey; *Tom Schwartz*, Huron Valley Lutheran High School, Westland, Michigan; *Tim Seeger*, Millard South High School, Omaha, Nebraska; *Mary Selberg*, Brookings High School, Brookings, South Dakota; *Yana Shinkarer*, St. Cecilia Academy, Nashville, Tennessee; *Kathy Shuster-Jory*, Bangor Area High School, Bangor, Pennsylvania; *John R. Siegel*, Lithia Springs High School, Lithia Springs, Georgia; *Sandra Siess*, SFBRHS, Washington, Missouri; *Sara Simpson*, Fyffe High School, Fyffe, Alabama; *Mellissa D. Sims*, Jackson High School, Jacksonville, Alabama; *Marsha Sirman*, Seaford Senior High School, Seaford, Delaware; *Vija S. Skudra*, Masconomet Reg. High School, Topsfield, Massachusetts; *Richard M. Slattery*, Hillcrest High School, Tuscaloosa, Alabama; *Helen Small*, Poquoson High School, Poquoson, Virginia; *Brian G. Smith*, H. H. Dow High School, Midland, Michigan; *Trevor J. Smith*, Sunset Junior High School, Sunset, Utah; *Pia Snyder*, Gladstone High School, Gladstone, Oregon; *Amy Sobeck*, Prince Edward High School, Farmville, Virginia; *Gisela Sommer*, Edwardsville High School, Edwardsville, Illinois; *Rebecca Stanton*, Sarta Margarita Catholic High School, Rancho Santa Margarita, California; *Ruth E. Stark*, Chisago Lakes High School, Lindstrom, Minnesota; *Brenda Stewart*, Millard North High School, Omaha, Nebraska; *Susan Stober*, Grandview High School, Aurora, Colorado; *Elaine Swartz*, Peabody Veterans Memorial High School, Peabody, Massachusetts; *Christina Thomas*, Perry High School, Pittsburgh, Pennsylvania; *Rich Thomas*, Watertown High School, Watertown, South Dakota; *William Thomas*, Limestone High School, Bartonville, Illinois; *Frank C. Thomsen*, Holmes Junior High School, Davis, California; *Rebecca A. Todd*, Lebanon High School, Lebanon, Missouri; *Michael Tollefson*, West High School, Madison, Wisconsin; *Tatjana Trout*, Sheldon High School, Sacramento, California;

Ronald Tullius, Robert G. Cole High School, San Antonio, Texas; *Teresa Underhill*, Lone Oak High School, Paducah, Kentucky; *Geraldine Van Doren*, Spotsylvania High School, Spotsylvania, Virginia; *Annelies Venus*, East Ridge Middle School, Ridgefield, Connecticut; *Madalyn Vieselmeyer*, Axtell High School, Axtell, Kansas; *Marianne Vornhagen*, Glen Oak High School, Canton, Ohio; *Amy C. Wagner*, Carlisle High School-Swartz Building, Carlisle, Pennsylvania; *Tonya Wagoner*, Harverson County High School, Cynthiana, Kentucky; *Janet Ward*, The Walker School, Marietta, Georgia; *Jon Ward*, Rigby High School, Rigby, Idaho; *Kimberly A. Warner*, Tipton High School, Tipton, Indiana; *Tom Watson*, Baltimore Lutheran School, Towson, Maryland; *Monty Weathers*, Dondero High School, Royal Oak, Michigan; *Jeanne Weiner*, Russell Middle School, Omaha, Nebraska; *Heide Westergard*, Shaker High School, Latham, New York; *Oksana Wheeler*, Trinton High School, Dodge Center, Minnesota; *Delos P. Wiberg*, Box Elder High School, Brigham City, Utah; *Diane Widmer*, North Forsyth High School, Cumming, Georgia; *Louise Wieland*, Rockland District High School, Union, Maine; *Birgitta Wiklund*, Pearland High School, Pearland, Texas; *Joan M. Wilson*, Sainte Genevieve High School, Sainte Genevieve, Missouri; *John Wilson*, Southeast Whitfield High School, Dalton, Georgia; *Ruth Wimp*, Alton High School, Alton, Illinois; *Diane Wippler*, Proctor High School, Proctor, Minnesota; *Kathy Witto*, Lutheran High School, Indianapolis, Indiana; *Lynne Woodward*, Langley High School, Pittsburgh, Pennsylvania; *Kristen M. Worm*, Fairbury High School, Fairbury, Nebraska; *Ava Wyatt*, Dalton High School, Dalton, Georgia; *E. Yancey*, Woodrow Wilson High School, Los Angeles, California; *Anne Yokers*, New Berlin West High School, New Berlin, Wisconsin; *Jennifer Zimmerman*, Morris Hills High School, Rockaway, New Jersey

Photo Credits

All the photos in the *Deutsch Aktuell 1* textbook not taken by the author have been provided by the following:

Achensee Tourismus: 290
Anderson, Leslie: 84 (upper left), 89 (lower right), 130, (upper right map), 171, 193 (top), 205 (top), 225 (lower left), 305
Andresr: TE37
Ammerland-Tourist-Information: 125 (center left)
Austrian National Tourist Office: 245 (all three), 250 (both)
Basel Tourism: xxv (top left and center)
Bavaria Film GmbH, Geiselgasteig: 274
Berchtesgadener Land Tourismus GmbH: vi (bottom left, 142 (bottom left and right)
Berlin Tourismus Marketing GmbH: xxi (top right)
Bern Tourismus: xxiv-xxv (background), xxiv (center left)
Bregenzer Tourismus: xxiii (center left and bottom)
Bronwyn Photo: 309 (top left)
Congress- und Tourismus Zentrale Nürnberg: xx (bottom and right)
Deutsche Bahn: ix (top), xviii (bottom left), 335, 338 (top), 340 (all three)
Dewald, Claudia: 32 (bottom left)
Fremdenverkehrsamt Landeshauptstadt München: 141 (bottom)
French Tourist Office: 139 (bottom)
Großglockner Tourismus GmbH: xxii-xxiii (background), xxii (bottom left)
Innsbruck Tourismus: xxiii (top right)
Inter Nationes: 296
iofoto: 37 (bottom right)
iStockphoto: TE18, 96 (1), 177 (model), 266 (top left), 370 (left)
Jim Lopes Photography: 357 (right)
Kämpf, Michael: 287 (top), 323 (bottom left), 370 (bottom right), 372 (top right)
Karlsruhe Tourismus: xix (top left)
Klein, Dieter: 37 bottom left), 228 (top), 240, 253, 283 (center right), 318, 323 (bottom right), 363 (bottom right), 368, 369 (all four), 372 (bottom)
Kurverwaltung Garmisch-Partenkirchen: 125 (bottom right), 291 (bottom left)
Lötschberg Tourismus: xxiv (center right), xxv (bottom right)

Mansi, René: TE21
Musik und Show: 372 (top left)
Neudert, Kati: 234
Nordseeheilbad Cuxhaven: 50, 302 (bottom)
Oberammergau Tourismus: xxi (center right)
Regionalverband Lavanttal: 302 (top left), 306
Shironsov, Dmitriy: TE37
Simson, David: 3 (bottom left and center), 6 (all three), 13, 23 (top right), 33 (bottom left), 35 (bottom left), 37 (bottom right), 38, 48, 54, 134 (top and bottom right), 136 (top left and right and bottom right), 151, 157 (left and center right), 164, 167 (top), 168, 241 (center and bottom right), 257 (top), 259 (both), 261, 262 (top), 266 (center left), 271 (both), 276, 277, 283 (both), 284, 289 (both), 309 (all four), 325 (bottom right), 338 (bottom), 352 (top right), 357 (left), 361 (center left and bottom right)
Stuttgart-Marketing GmbH: xix (center right)
Swiss-Image GmbH: 356, 383 (both), 384 (top and center)
Switzerland Tourism: viii (center),
Thüringer Tourismus GmbH: xxi (bottom left and right), 125 (top left), 326 (bottom left)
Tourism-Marketing GmbH Baden-Württemberg: vi (left), 32 (top), 142 (bottom), 301 (bottom)
Tourismus Linz: xxiii (bottom right)
Tourismus- und Congress GmbH Frankfurt am Main: xviii (center left)
Tourismusverband Lieser-Maltatal: 327 (bottom left)
Tourismusverband Saalbach Hinterglemm: xxii (bottom right)
Tourismusverband Schwaz-Pill: 300 (bottom)
Velusceac, Serg: 37 (bottom left)
Verkehrsamt Lech: 299 (bottom), 326 (bottom right)
Villach - Warmbad Tourismus GmbH: viii, 299 (top)
Vorarlberg Tourismus GmbH: xxii (center left)
Wackerhausen, Jacob: TE20
Waldinger, Karl-Georg: ix (top left), 278 (top right and bottom left), 279 (all four), 280
Werbegemeinschaft Seefeld: 301 (top)
Zürich Tourism: xxiv (bottom left)

Realia Credits

The publisher would like to thank the following sources for granting permission to reproduce certain material on the pages indicated:

Deutsche Bahn: 337
Deutscher Wetterdienst: 126
Dance Academy Luzern: 362
German Information Center: 142
Hohenzollern-Gymnasium Sigmaringen: 106
Karstadt AG: 231, 232
Sächsische Zeitung: 73
Salzburger Land Tourismus: 367
Tourist-Information Boppard: 352